Last Call for Liberty

JOE MARSHALL

ISBN 978-1-63525-189-0 (Paperback)
ISBN 978-1-63525-190-6 (Digital)

Copyright © 2017 by Joe Marshall

All rights reserved. No part of this publication may be reproduced, distributed, or transmitted in any form or by any means, including photocopying, recording, or other electronic or mechanical methods without the prior written permission of the publisher. For permission requests, solicit the publisher via the address below.

Christian Faith Publishing, Inc.
296 Chestnut Street
Meadville, PA 16335
www.christianfaithpublishing.com

Printed in the United States of America

To all of my family and relations, my loving and most patient wife, and both of my sons, whose own families I hope may one day get to enjoy the same Liberty "secured" for them by our founders in the Constitution of the United States of America

To all my countrymen, whose Liberty is the same, that you may recognize and take measure against that which has pledged to destroy it

And to God, for mankind alone *cannot* undo what mankind didn't do alone

Introduction

This project is not so much a "book" as it is a presentation—a guided or semiguided tour, if you will, where you can read for yourself, as I did, those who espouse *the Philosophy*, as I have come to call it, say who they are in their own words, in the context of the Liberty (as best as I can articulate) that they seek to destroy. Quotes are presented as taken from copies or transcripts of original documents. As such, some of the original phrasing and spellings used may be confusing. Adding to that, the Philosophy, over time, has developed its own verbage or lingo, which is, in some cases, designed to "throw off" readers not steeped in "their" philosophy. Odds are, you will have to look up some words in the dictionary. Expect to have to read and reread some passages two, or even three, times to comprehend some of the old phrasings and words used. You will come across made-up Philosophy-specific words and phrasings neither heard nor seen anywhere else, including words designed to have no meaning at all "relative to how you perceive them."

Don't be deterred. Consider it all a normal experience for one trying to pay attention. Adding to the mix is the fact that before the 1960s or so, liberals were called liberals because of their libertarian, profree enterprise, proproperty, pro–Individual-Liberty stand. These are now known as conservatives or "classic liberals." Today liberals are called liberals because they changed their title first from socialists to progressives, then from progressives to liberals taking the name already given to those who truly stood for Liberty as to deceivingly feign the same. Many, including Hillary Clinton, have even changed back to referring to themselves as "early-twentieth-century progressives." Only time will tell if and when they'll ever revert to calling themselves by what they've always been: socialists! And Bernie Sanders may have already proved that point. The term *conservative* has also been going through that same progressive "transformation."

The Liberty I champion, your Liberty, is not a Liberty that I have read about in a book, not a liberty I have heard about, been told about, or taught in a classroom. It's one of my own experience that I have lived and, as best I can against the sweeping tides against it, I continue to live. The degree I have successfully lived it is, of course, debatable; however, I have lived it nonetheless.

As you are probably aware, America was founded on certain "self-evident" truths as is spelled out in the Declaration of Independence. Such confirm our Founding Principles that "all men are created equal, that they are endowed by their Creator with certain unalienable Rights, that among these are Life, Liberty & the pursuit of Happiness.—That to secure these rights, Governments are instituted among Men, deriving their just powers from the consent of the governed." *The* revelation here, other than that our Rights and Liberty are natural and/or God-given, is that "Governments" are but a product of them, *not* the source or "positive provider" of them! Yet the Philosophy and/or collectivism hold that they are. How is it even possible that there is more to be gained by the surrender of "the whole of our everything" to the "power" of a mere product of our Liberty than we stand to gain from whole of it? It's *not*! It's impossible! Yet such is *the* earthly premise upon which the whole of collectivism is predicated, the spiritual premise being only the nonexistence, "annulment," or "annihilation" of God Himself.

But sadly, the positively redistributed collective and "conditional" human/civil rights of that collectivism are being both sold and accepted as some new and improved form of the Liberty they are *not*! After over a decade of research, I have come to know collectivism as *the* great deception that has long been seducing mankind into seeing tyranny as Liberty and Liberty as tyranny; or, as it were, slavery as freedom and freedom as slavery. That collectivism has *progressively* infiltrated every pillar of our once free society including our governments, schools, and churches as it has compromised truth itself. After over a decade of searching for truth (or if it even existed) in what pertains to our founding, our Liberty and the revolutionary progressive collectivism that stands against it in the doctrines of both individualism and collectivism, *Last Call for Liberty* is the result. Understand that I wrote this for my children that they would have a trusted source to help them decipher truth and Liberty from the convoluted "relative" anti-God, antitruth of that which has pledged to "abolish" them. However, we have been moved to share this timely and much-needed information not only with them but with all lovers of Liberty—all those who might yearn to be free and, once free, wish to remain so—and with "all Americans in the world"[1] in the hope that, in some small way, the sacred cause of Liberty may be furthered by it.

As I have had the honor of invoking true Individual Liberty for myself in my lifetime, I have put together what follows as a warning, but more importantly, as an effort to *mark* that which has emerged to stand against it—that it may be recognized for what it is before it's too late, that we have arrived *not*, at least yet, at Liberty's last gleaming.

May the reasonings of Liberty never be silenced.

For Liberty,
Joe Marshall

---

1   Lt. Col. Comdt. William Barrett Travis, letter from the Alamo, 1836.

CHAPTER 1

To the Center of the Web

On Friday July 13, 2012, in Roanoke, Virginia, President Obama yet again revealed his contempt for free America: America as founded. Even more importantly, what was also exposed in this coded speech was a sinister age-old anticapitalist, anti-individual, antiproperty, antifamily, and anti-God philosophy that is the fountain from which the coerced "fundamental transformation" of the United States of America flows! Though this philosophy is nothing new. Sadly for most, the direct threat this philosophy poses to our everyday life as we have known it may go unrecognized. First, as a sidenote, a fundamental understanding of our founding principles would be a prerequisite to recognizing any threat to them. They can be found in the Declaration of Independence and throughout the writings of our founders. That being said, next, what we as free Americans who do invoke, understand, and cherish our sacred Individual Liberty need to learn and understand is not only what this political philosophy is but from where it emanates; for just as we have our founders, they most assuredly have theirs. With this knowledge, it is this writer's hope that we, as a nation, can begin to comprehend what it is that truly awaits us if we were to allow this philosophy to gain the upper hand over our republic. Devastation by design! It will shake the very foundation, reducing to rubble every pillar of our uniquely American society to its complete and total annihilation! And upon the rubble will the "new normal" be built! *Not in my words—but theirs!*

Let us listen closely to what it is exactly our president is professing in this transcript:

> There are a lot of wealthy, successful Americans who agree with me—because they want to give something back. They know they didn't—look, *if you've been successful, you didn't get there on your own. You didn't get there on your own.* I'm always struck by people who think, well, it must be because I was just so smart. There are a lot of smart people out there. It must be because I worked harder than everybody else. Let me tell you something—there are a whole bunch of hardworking people out there. (Applause)
>
> If you were successful, somebody along the line gave you some help.
>
> There was a great teacher somewhere in your life. *Somebody helped to create this unbelievable American system that we have that allowed you to thrive. Somebody invested in roads and bridges. If you've got a business—you didn't build that. Somebody else made that happen.* The Internet didn't get invented on its own. Government research created the Internet so that all the companies could make money off the Internet.
>
> The point is, is that when we succeed, we succeed because of our individual initiative, but

also because we do things together[1] (emphasis added).

Again, for those who didn't get it—"if you've got a business—you didn't build that. Somebody else made that happen." And just so you know, this wasn't the first time we've heard this sentiment from any of our contemporary politicians. Another example came in September of 2011 in Andover, Massachusetts, when Elizabeth Warren, speaking on the terms as she sees them of what she referred to as America's underlying "social contract," stated the following:

> There is nobody in this country who got rich on his own. Nobody! You built a factory out there? Good for you! But I want to be clear: You moved your goods to market on the roads the rest of us paid for. You hired workers the rest of us paid to educate. You, uh, were safe in your factory because of police forces and fire forces that the rest of us paid for. You didn't have to worry that marauding bands would come and seize everything at your factory and hire someone to protect against this because of the work the rest of us did.[2]

This philosophy, as I said before, as foreign as it is, is anything but new. But what does it all mean? Is there more to this philosophy they're *not* telling us? Getting to the answer of such questions is what we endeavor to accomplish here in these few pages.

First, what we need to do here is both ask ourselves and answer for ourselves, what is it that came first: property, enterprise, and our Liberty to prosper, or government? Do we owe all who we are, have, and hope to be to "society," or is our society the product of a free and enterprising people? Was our Right to pursue Happiness endowed by government, or do "We hold these truths to be self-evident, that all men are created equal, that they are endowed by their Creator with certain unalienable Rights, that among these are Life, Liberty and the pursuit of Happiness—That to secure these rights, Governments are instituted among Men, deriving their just powers from the consent of the governed"? Buckle in and hold fast to your convictions as we submerge into an age-old underverse that we may examine it closer. Only there will we find where this has all been said and done before.

In 1886, Russian Pierre Kropotkin—a.k.a. the anarchist prince, who, per the Anarchist Black Cross, "advocated a communist society free of central government"—authored his infamous "anarchist essay," *Law and Authority*. In chapter 4, he explains:

> Socialists know what is meant by protection of property. Laws on property are not made to guarantee either to the individual or to society the enjoyment of the produce of their own labour. On the contrary, they are made to rob the producer of a part of what he has created, and to secure to certain other people that portion of the produce which they have stolen either from the producer or from society as a whole. When, for example, the law establishes Mr. So-and-So's right to a house, it is not establishing his right to a cottage he has built for himself, or to a house he has erected with the help of some of his friends. *In that case no one would have disputed his right* (emphasis added). On the contrary, the law is establishing his right to a house which is *not* the product of his labour; first of all, because he has had it built

for him by others to whom he has not paid the full value of their work; and next because that house represents a social value, which he could not have produced for himself. The law is establishing his right to what belongs to everybody in general to nobody in particular. The same house built in the midst of Siberia would not have the value it possesses in a large town, and, as we know, that value arises from the labour of something like fifty generations of men who have built the town, beautified it, supplied it with water and gas, fine promenades, colleges, theatres, shops, railways and roads leading in all directions. Thus, by recognising to the right of Mr. So-and-So to a particular house in Paris, London or Rouen, the law is unjustly appropriating to him a certain portion of the produce of the labour of mankind in general. And it is precisely because this appropriation and all other forms of property, bearing the same character, are a crying injustice, that a whole arsenal of laws, and a whole army of soldiers, policemen and judges are needed to maintain it against the good sense and just feeling inherent in humanity.

With the acknowledgment that Kropotkin is referring to his time, to this day, capital remains capital. Priests are still priests. Laws protecting property still protect property. Sworn law enforcement officers, both on the street and in our prisons, still stand their guard, enforcing those laws. To the anarchist, statist, communist, national socialist, and international socialist, capitalism remains "a system of exploitation" and suppression today. Occupy Wall Street's 99 percent vs. the 1 percent is proof enough of that. Marx and Engels's *Communist Manifesto*, published almost forty years prior to Kropotkin's *Law and Authority*, is still relevant today not only in the United States but throughout the globe. Not only is this philosophy relevant, it is prevalent in today's progressive politics! Both Democrat and Republican! Are not President Obama's speeches, including Roanoke, relevant? Even if Kropotkin, along with all the others we will meet, were all completely irrelevant to today's politics, which they are not, it would change nothing. The philosophy behind our president's words remains the same. And our journey here is not only to come to a fuller understanding of that philosophy but to trace it back to its source!

The open hostility to capital, the individual, property rights, free enterprise, the proprietor, and the laws that protect them, being a flowing single philosophy, Kropotkin exposes to us here in this one paragraph a much fuller context of the philosophy from which both Warren and Obama are speaking to us. But there's more. Kropotkin continues:

> As all the laws about property, which make up thick volumes of codes, and are the delight of our lawyers, have no other object than to protect the unjust appropriating of human labour by certain monopolists, there is no reason for their existence, and, on the day of the Revolution, social revolutionists are thoroughly determined to put an end to them. Indeed, a bonfire might be made with perfect justice of all laws bearing upon the so-called "rights of property," all title-deeds, all registers, in a word, of all that is in any way connected with an institution

which will soon be looked upon as a blot in the history of humanity, as humiliating as the slavery and serfdom of past ages.

So what is it that might constitute "all that is in any way connected" to the "laws about property"?

In chapter 1, Kropotkin tells us:

> Rebels are everywhere to be found, who no longer wish to obey the law without knowing whence it comes, what are its uses, and whither arises the obligation to submit to it, and the reverence with which it is encompassed.
>
> The rebels of our day are criticizing the very foundations of Society, which have hitherto been held sacred, and first and foremost amongst them that fetish, law. Just for this reason the upheaval which is at hand is no meet insurrection, it is a *Revolution*.
>
> The critics analyse the sources of law, and find there either a god, product of the terrors of the savages, and stupid, paltry and malicious as the priests who vouch for its supernatural origin, or else, bloodshed, conquest by fire and sword...Finally, they see the jailer on the way to lose all human feeling, the detective trained as a blood-hound, the police spy despising himself; "informing," metamorphosed into a virtue; corruption, erected into a system; all the vices, all the evil qualities of mankind countenanced and cultivated to insure the triumph of law.

> All this we see, and, therefore, instead of inanely repeating the old formula, "Respect the law," we say, "Despite law and all its attributes!" In place of the cowardly phrase, "Obey the law," our cry is "Revolt against all laws!"

If history has proven anything, it has proven that it most assuredly repeats itself. Is history repeating itself once again? Are we of this generation to once again be forced to bear witness to yet another *revolution* of such rebels? Only time and a broader sense of not only what we might stand to gain but of what we stand to lose from such a revolution can tell. So it is in *this* context we continue.

In chapter 2, he tells us:

> Like individual capital, which was born of fraud and violence, and developed under the auspices of authority, law has no title to the respect of men. Born of violence and superstition, and established in the interests of consumer, priest and rich exploiter, it must be utterly destroyed on the day when the people desire to break their chains.

In chapter 3, he tells us:

> The history of the genesis of capital has already been told by Socialists many times. They have described how it was born of war and pillage, of slavery and serfdom, of modern fraud and exploitation. They have shown how it is nourished by the blood of the worker, and how little by little it has conquered the whole

world. The same story, concerning the genesis and development of law has yet to be told....

Law, in its quality of guarantee...exist to keep up the machinery of government, which serves to secure to capital the exploitation and monopoly of the wealth produced. Magistrature, police, army, public instruction, finance, all serve one God- capital; all have but one object- to facilitate the exploitation of the worker by the capitalist...Thus the protection of exploitation directly by laws on property, and indirectly by the maintenance of the State of the results of pillage, slavery and exploitation, has followed the same phrases of development as capital; twin brother and sister, they have advanced hand in hand, sustaining one another with the suffering of mankind....

The major portion have but one object— to protect private property, i.e., wealth acquired by the exploitation of man by man. Their aim is to open out to capital fresh fields for exploitation, and to sanction the new forms which that exploitation continually assumes, as capital swallows up another branch of human activity, railways, telegraphs, electric light, chemical industries, the expression of man's thought in literature and science, etc. is both the spirit and the substance of our modern codes, and the one function of our costly legislative machinery.

And in chapter 4, he continues:

> It again is a complete arsenal of laws, decrees, ordinances, orders in council, and what not, all serving to protect the diverse forms of representative government, delegated or usurped, beneath which humanity is writhing. We know very well—Anarchists have often enough pointed out in their perpetual criticism of the various forms of government- that the mission of all governments, monarchical, constitutional, or republican, is to protect and maintain by force the privileges of the classes in possession, the aristocracy, clergy and traders. A good third of our laws- and each century possesses some tens of thousands of them the fundamental laws on taxes, excise duties, the organisation of ministerial departments and their offices, of the army, the police, the Church, etc., have no other end than to maintain, patch up, and develop the administrative machine. And this machine in its turn serves almost entirely to protect the privileges of the possessing classes....
>
> The third category of law still remains to be considered, that relating to the protection of the person and detection and prevention of "crime....
>
> First of all, as to so-called "crimes"—*assaults upon persons—it is well-known that two-thirds, and often as many as three-fourths, of such "crimes" are instigated by the desire to obtain possession of someone's wealth. This immense class*

> *of so-called "crimes and misdemeanours" will disappear on the day on which private property ceases to exist....*
>
> *In the next revolution we hope that this cry will go forth: "Burn the guillotine; demolish the prisons; drive away the judges, policemen and informers—the impurest race upon the face of the earth; treat as a brother the man who has been led by passion to do ill to his fellow; above all take from the ignoble products of middle-class idleness the possibility of displaying their vices in attractive colours; and be sure that but few crimes will mar our society"*[3] (emphasis added).

One should make special note here of what "above all" according to this philosophy, such a *revolution* must "take" from the middle class: "the ignoble products of middle-class idleness the possibility of displaying their vices in attractive colours; and be sure that but few crimes will mar our society." It is, in and of itself, very telling of what is to come.

And so you have it from the esteemed Kropotkin himself. It is our Individual Liberty, our freedom to provide for ourselves and our families, capitalism, our property rights, and even God Himself that represent the true crime in our society. As such they—along with every other aspect of our society, from our Constitution and representative republic that it ordains, on down to every law and law enforcement officer, every prison, and any business for profit—must all be taken down! We will revisit this again later. If the Obama administration and current government officials at large are going to be espousing this philosophy, there must be a lot more to "social justice" and the "fundamental transformation" of America than just the "redistribution of wealth."

Going back to Obama's Roanoke speech, he references some 23 times his alleged concerns for the security of, or the strengthening of, or the restoration of, the rebuilding of, and/or the importance of the middle class. He has done so again and again in speech after speech. However as Kropotkin has revealed, it isn't wholly consistent with this philosophy. Obama continually makes mention of the poor's ability to access the lower middle class; and the lower middle class, the middle, middle class; and the middle, the upper. But when it comes to the economy in general, his measure for us, not just in his speeches but in all puts forth, is nothing more than a promise of jobs, jobs, jobs. However, not once has he or his political philosophy shown any concern for procuring an environment necessary for more. *Why?* Well, if all we ever wanted was a job, then a job is all we'll ever have! But what of our aspirations to reach for greater heights than just clocking in and clocking out? Of following our own dreams and our own inspirations? Of owning our own businesses or, otherwise, becoming successful in our own right—where the sky, if not beyond, is the limit? Please allow me to introduce to you Mr. Saul Alinsky.

Saul Alinksy, a.k.a. the father of "community organizing," is much praised by those on the progressive left. Fresh out of college, Obama worked as a "community organizer" activist for the Developing Communities Project (DCP) of the Calumet Community Religious Conference (CCRC) in Chicago. Both were founded on the Alinsky model of community "agitation" to, in the words of Alinsky, "rub raw the sores of discontent." In his 1971 *Rules for Radicals*, Alinsky elaborates as to the conundrum and to who his activists truly are. In the final chapter, "The Way Ahead," he clarifies:

> "ORGANIZATION FOR ACTION will now and in the decades ahead center upon America's middle class. That is where the power is. When

more than three fourths of from both points of view of economics and their self-identification are middle class, it is obvious that their action or inaction will determine the direction of change... even if all the low-income parts of our population were organized—all blacks, Mexican American, Puerto-Ricans, Appalachian poor whites...it would not be powerful enough to get significant, basic, needed changes....

With rare exception, our activists and radicals are products of and rebels against our middle class society (emphasis added). All rebels must attack the power states in their society. Our rebels have contemptuously rejected the values and way of life of the middle class. They have stigmatized it as materialistic, decadent, bourgeos (capitalists), degenerate, imperialistic, war mongering, brutalizing, and corrupt. They are right; but *we must begin from where we are if we are to build power for change* (emphasis added), and the power and the people are in the big middle-class majority....

His middle-class identity, his familiarity with the values and problems, are invaluable for organization of his "own people". He has the background to go back and, examine, and try to understand the middle-class way;...He must know so he can be effective in communication, tactics, creating issues, and organization. He will look very differently upon his parents, their friends, and their way of life...He learns what their definition of Police is, and their language—he discards the rhetoric that always says "pig". Instead of hostile rejection he is seeking bridges of communication...He will view with strategic sensitivity the nature of middle-class behavior with its hangups over rudeness or aggressive, insulting, profane actions. All this and more must be grasped and used to radicalize parts of the middle-class....

With few exceptions, such as teachers, they have never gone beyond high school...Their lives have been 90% unfulfilled dreams. To escape their frustration they grasp at a last hope that their children will get a college education and realize those unfulfilled dreams. They are a fearful people,...they dread the possibility of property devaluation from non-whites moving into their neighborhood....They are beset by taxes on income, food, real estate, and automobiles...Their pleasures are simple: gardening a tiny back yard behind a small house, bungalow, or ticky tacky, in a monotonous subdivision,... going on a Sunday drive to the country, having a once-a-week dinner...at a Howard Johnsons....

They look at the unemployed poor as parasitical dependents, recipients of a vast variety of massive public programs all paid for by them, "the public"...The middle-classes are numb, bewildered, scared into silence. They don't know what if anything they can do. This is the job of today's radical—to fan the embers of hopelessness into a flame to fight....

> The revolution must manifest itself in the corporate sector... *The corporations must forget their nonsense about the "private sectors"... every American individual or corporation is public as well as private* (emphasis added);...We have a double commitment and corporations had better recognize this for the sake of their own survival...If the same predatory drives for profits can be partially transmutted for progress, then we will have opened a whole new ball game.

You are now reading for yourself, in their own words, how patronizing the despised, "materialistic, decadent, bourgeois, degenerate, imperialistic, war mongering, brutalizing, and corrupt," petty and pitiful racist middle class fits into their philosophy. Also, don't forget what Kropotkin called for in his *revolution*. Is not Alinsky calling for the same? Is he not also calling for middle class to be stripped of all their braggadocios excesses indicative of a bourgeoisie or capitalist society? And don't let it slip by that Kropotkin's cry also includes "and be sure that but few crimes will mar our society." Is he not also implying that the mere existence of a middle class, as well as the laws that protect their "property," are the cause of crime in society? This is *the* essence of "democratic socialism" revolutionary progressive collectivists aren't telling us! Once *used* by the revolution, the whole of the "middle class" is itself to be destroyed—the booster, if you will, to be ejected after liftoff. There is *no* way they are to ever reach the destination they've signed on to. Has the American middle class taken the bait to their own peril?

As to what Alinsky is telling us here, that in such a *revolution* "we must begin from where we are," back in the prologue of his book, Alinsky explains:

> "As an organizer I start from where the world is, as it is, not as I would like it to be. That we accept the world as it is does not in any sense weaken our desire to change it into what we believe it should be—it is necessary to begin where the world is if we are going to change it to what we think it should be. That means working in the system.[4]"

Coincidentally, Michelle Obama spoke of Obama's commitment to the very *exact same* mantra in her speech at the Democratic National Convention on August 28, 2008:

> "Barack stood up that day, and spoke words that have stayed with me ever since. He talked about "The world as it is" and "The world as it should be." And he said that all too often, we accept the distance between the two, and we settle for the world as it is—even when it doesn't reflect our values and aspirations. But he reminded us that we also know what our world should look like. He said we know what fairness and justice and opportunity look like. And he urged us to believe in ourselves—to find the strength within ourselves to strive for the world as it should be. And isn't that the great American story?
>
> People like Hillary Clinton…like Joe Biden…All of us driven by a simple belief that the world as it is just won't do—that we have an obligation to fight for the world as it should be.[5]

There is no questioning the effectiveness of Alinsky, and his "radicals"— "working in the system"—has undeniably paid them big, Big, BIG dividends in their "revolution." But what if it hadn't? Invoking both Mao and Lenin, Alinsky contemplates his options in the prologue of *Rules for Radicals*:

> What is the alternative to working "inside" the system? A mess of rhetorical garbage about "Burn the system down!" What else? Bombs? Sniping? Silence when the police are killed, and screams of "murdering fascist pigs" when others are killed? Attacking and baiting the police? Public suicide? "Power comes out of the barrel of a gun!" is an obsurd rallying cry when the other side has all the guns. Lenin was a pragmatist; ...he said the Bolsheviks stood for getting power through the ballot but would reconsider after they got the guns!
>
> Remember: once you organize people around something as commonly agreed upon as pollution, then an organized people is on the move.[4]

The "pollution" reference brings us to a whole other aspect of the Philosophy that ties in with progressivism's environmentalism and "global warming," which we'll be getting to a little later. But for now, we continue with how we in the middle class fit into that philosophy. For further clarification, we go to Vladimir Lenin. In his 1905 piece on *Petty-Bourgeois and Proletarian Socialism*, he ponders the same confusion regarding the prominence of the middle class in the "transformation" of a capitalist/bourgeoisie society, which you and I are questioning here in America today. The difference being, he considers it from his perspective as a Marxist/socialist revolutionary against the whole of the bourgeois that, by Marxist definition, includes the middle class. His deliberation is extensive but is revealing as to the existence of the two distinct "social wars" occurring in a "democratic-bourgeois movement"; the role of the middle class or petty bourgeoisie in that revolution; and, in the end, what fate awaits them/us and society as soon as their final objective is reached. Weighing all this, Lenin considers the subject:

> "What is the present-day peasant movement in Russia striving for? For land and liberty. What significance will the complete victory of this movement have? After winning liberty, it will abolish the rule of the landlords and bureaucrats in the administration of the state. After securing the land, it will give the landlords' estates to the peasants. Will the fullest liberty and expropriation of the landlords do away with commodity production? No, it will not. Will the fullest liberty and expropriation of the landlords abolish individual farming by peasant households on communal, or "socialised", land? No, it will not. Will the fullest liberty and expropriation of the landlords bridge the deep gulf that separates the rich peasant, with his numerous horses and cows, from the farm-hand, the day-labourer, i.e., the gulf that separates the peasant bourgeoisie from the rural proletariat? No, it will not. On the contrary, the more completely the highest *social-estate* (the landlords) is routed and annihilated, the more profound will the *class* distinction between the

bourgeoisie and the proletariat be. What will be the objective significance of the complete victory of the peasant uprising? This victory will do away with all survivals of serfdom, but it will by no means destroy the bourgeois economic system, or destroy capitalism or the division of society into classes—into rich and poor, the bourgeoisie and the proletariat."

As we now see, the victory of a democratic peasant /petty bourgeoisie (middle class) movement, though an improvement on society, would nonetheless be incomplete. There would still be "capitalism" and "classes" that would have to be "destroyed." Lenin continues:

Why is the present-day peasant movement a democratic-bourgeois movement? Because, after destroying the power of the bureaucracy and the landlords, it will set up a democratic system of society, without, however, altering the bourgeois foundation of that democratic society, without abolishing the rule of capital.

Are we then to understand that the "fundamental change" of our society is just the beginning?

How should the class-conscious worker, the socialist, regard the present-day peasant movement? He must support this movement, help the peasants in the most energetic fashion, help them throw off completely both the rule of the bureaucracy and that of the landlords. At the same time, however, lie should

> explain to the peasants that it is not enough to overthrow the rule of the bureaucracy and the landlords. When they overthrow that rule, they must at the same time prepare for the abolition of the rule of capital, the rule of the bourgeoisie, and for that purpose a doctrine that is fully socialist, i.e., Marxist, should be immediately disseminated.

And in that, you have the answer: it *is* just the beginning. Lenin's inquiry continues:

> Can a class-conscious worker forget the democratic struggle for the sake of the socialist struggle, or forget the latter for the sake of the former? No, a class-conscious worker calls himself a Social-Democrat for the reason that he understands the relation between the two struggles. *He knows that there is no other road to socialism save the road through democracy* (emphasis added), through political liberty. He therefore strives to achieve democratism completely and consistently in order to attain the ultimate goal—socialism.

Socialism is then, per Lenin, the "ultimate goal" of "organizing" the middle class! Take Lenin at his words:

> The democratic struggle is waged by the workers together with a section of the bourgeoisie, especially the petty bourgeoisie. On the other hand, the socialist struggle is waged

by the workers against the whole of the bourgeoisie. The struggle against the bureaucrat and the landlord can and must be waged together with all the peasants, even the well-to-do and the middle peasants. On the other hand, it is only together with the rural proletariat that the struggle against the bourgeoisie, and therefore against the well-to-do peasants too, can be properly waged.

And their fate will be their own destruction! For them to believe otherwise is only their ignorant, fanciful "petty-bourgeois utopia":

> Outside the class struggle, socialism is either a hollow phrase or a naïve dream…As a stratum of small landowners, of petty bourgeois, the peasantry, is fighting against all survivals of serfdom, against the bureaucrats and the landlords. Only those who are completely ignorant of political economy and of the history of revolutions throughout the world can fail to see that these are two distinct and different social wars.…
>
> We cannot calculate what portion of the price of provisions bought from a petty shopkeeper represents labour-value and what part of it represents swindling, etc.…
>
> Thus, we must combine the purely proletarian struggle with the general peasant struggle, but not confuse the two. We must support the general democratic and general peasant struggle, but not become submerged in this

non-class struggle; we must never idealise it with false catchwords such as "socialisation", or ever forget the necessity of organising both the urban *and the rural* proletariat in an entirely independent class party of Social-Democracy. While giving the utmost support to the most determined democratism, that party will not allow itself to be diverted from the revolutionary path by reactionary dreams and experiments in "equalisation" under the system of commodity production. The peasants' struggle against the landlords is now a revolutionary struggle; the confiscation of the landlords' estates at the present stage of economic and political evolution is revolutionary in every respect, and we back this revolutionary-democratic measure. However, to call this measure "socialisation", and *to deceive oneself and the people concerning the possibility of "equality" in land tenure under the system of commodity production, is a reactionary petty-bourgeois utopia* (emphasis added), which we leave to the socialist-reactionaries.[6]

Both Alinsky and Lenin would then agree that when it comes down to working "inside the system," it's necessary because "it is necessary to begin where the world is" if they "are going to change it to what we think it should be"! Later, in 1920, Lenin said so himself:

> Whilst you lack the strength to do away with bourgeois parliaments and every other type of reactionary institution, you *must* work within them because *it is there* (emphasis added)

that you will still find workers who are duped by the priests and stultified by the conditions of rural life; otherwise you risk turning into nothing but windbags.[7]

The middle class is in for a rude awakening from their utopian fantasy if they think they will somehow benefit from such a "democratic" transformation. As a class of capitalist bourgeoisie themselves, they must also be destroyed in order for such a classless society of "equality" to be realized. In fact, by being seduced into "class warfare," they only enable their own destruction! For without them and their vote, the revolutionaries would be nothing but windbags within our existing "democratic" system!

The preceding revelation is one that is necessary to comprehend the scope of deceit that defines this philosophy. It helps brings to light not only what these revolutionaries had in mind for us all those years ago; it helps to clarify why President Obama, referring to the *unsustainability* of middle-class decadence, might say the following to a gathering of young Africans at the closing of his Young African Leaders Initiative held in poverty-stricken Johannesburg, South Africa, in June of 2013:

> Countries that are still developing, obviously they shouldn't be resigned to poverty simply because the West and Europe and America got there first. That wouldn't be fair. But everybody is going to have to do something....
>
> Ultimately, if you think about all the youth that everybody has mentioned here in Africa, *if everybody is raising living standards to the point where everybody has got a car and everybody has got air conditioning, and everybody has got a big*

house, well, the planet will boil over[8] (emphasis added).

Unless, of course, as he then eludes, such an unsustainable prosperity is arrived at via an approved sustainable energy source within *his* proposed progressive/redistributive system. However, that overruling global system in all practicality does *not* yet exist. What does this mean? What are we to take from it? That until such a progressive globalism is finally implemented, these poor Africans cannot be allowed to prosper and enjoy such a middle-class prosperity? That we in middle-class America must first be forced to give up what we now have, worked so hard for, and enjoy before the poor of Africa are ever *allowed* to obtain it? And this from the same Obama who, time and again, has presented himself to us as "a warrior *for* the middle class," whose policies promote a "growing" middle class. Consider all the conflicting principles in just these few words. Then consider that our understanding and journey to the source of such a philosophy has only just begun.

In his 1871 *Man, Society, Freedom*, Michael Bakunin further expands on our understanding of the subject:

> The doctrinaire liberals (what today would be considered conservatives), reasoning from the premises of individual freedom, pose as the adversaries of the State. Those among them who maintain that the government, i.e., the body of functionaries organized and designated to perform the functions of the State is a *necessary evil*....
>
> They consider themselves liberals because their theory on the origin of society is based on the principle of individual freedom....

According to them individual freedom is not a creation, a historic product of society. They maintain, on the contrary, that individual freedom is anterior to all society and that all men are endowed by God with an immortal soul. Man is accordingly a complete being, absolutely independent, apart from and outside society. As a free agent, anterior to and apart from society, he necessarily forms his society by a voluntary act, a sort of contract, be it instinctive or conscious, tacit or formal. In short, according to this theory, individuals are not the product of society but, on the contrary, are led to create society....

Emerging from the state of the gorilla, man has only with great difficulty attained the consciousness of his humanity and his liberty...He was born a ferocious beast and a slave, and has gradually humanized and emancipated himself only in society, which is necessarily anterior to the birth of his thought, his speech, and his will. *He can achieve this emancipation only through the collective effort of all the members, past and present, of society, which is the source, the natural beginning of his human existence...Man completely realizes his individual freedom as well as his personality only through the individuals who surround him, and thanks only to the labor and the collective power of society. Without society he would surely remain the most stupid and the most miserable among all the other ferocious beasts...* Society, far from decreasing his freedom, on the contrary creates the individual freedom of all human beings. Society is the root, the tree, and liberty is its fruit. Hence, in every epoch, man must seek his freedom not at the beginning but at the end of history....

The first revolt is against the supreme tyranny of theology, of the phantom of God. As long as we have a master in heaven, we will be slaves on earth. Our reason and our will will be equally annulled. As long as we believe that we must unconditionally obey—and vis-a-vis—God, no other obedience is possible—we must of necessity passively submit, without the least reservation, to the holy authority of his consecrated and unconsecrated agents, messiahs, prophets, divinely inspired law-makers, emperors, kings, and all their functionaries and ministers, representatives and consecrated servitors of the two greatest institutions which impose themselves upon us, and which are established by God himself to rule over men; namely, the Church and the State. *All temporal or human authority stems directly from spiritual and/or divine authority. But authority is the negation of freedom. God, or rather the fiction of God, is the consecration and the intellectual and moral source of all slavery on earth, and the freedom of mankind will never be complete until the disastrous and insidious fiction of a heavenly master is annihilated* (emphasis added).

And so it is—that this philosophy holds that it is society and its government that "creates the individual freedom of all human beings" and "the freedom of mankind will never be complete until the disastrous and insidious fiction of a heavenly master is annihilated." Think about it. If the sovereign, or state, is to have complete control of both defining and enforcing a "general will' of its subjects, there can be no place in such a society for any religious doctrine espousing a higher entity than the state. As "God's will" incites *individual* "free will" subversive to the *collective* "general will"—lest they (the believers) perish in an everlasting lake of fire!—how can government have complete rule over its subjects if they hold to a higher authority?

It is important to note here that per this philosophy, it is only in the context of the collective (a Godless) society that "man completely realizes his individual freedom as well as his personality." Collective "individual freedom" is *not* the Individual Liberty of our founders. It is *not* the Individual Liberty protected in the Constitution. They are, by definition, 180-degree diabolical opposites! Such is the reality and difference, as we will see, between the Individual Liberty of Individual Rights and the "individual freedom" of such "rights" as human rights and civil rights.

Also, remember Bakunin's "personality" as it is the same *personality* that will be showing up again and again throughout this work.

Before continuing on to the core of this philosophy, let us venture into a more thorough, fuller context of some of Bakunin's assertions of government, God, the collective, the individual, the source of our Liberty, and to their proper places in "society." As historically, we have seen them before.

Thomas Hobbes wrote his *Leviathan* in 1651. It is a most extensive work going into greater detail regarding the "state of nature" or, as Bakunin says, "state of the gorilla" from which a bestial mankind "emerged" in order to obtain liberty in civil "society":

Introduction
> NATURE (the Art whereby God hath made and governes the World) is by the Art of man, as in many other things, so in this also imitated, that it can make an Artificial Anima. For seeing life is but a motion of Limbs, the begining whereoff is in some principall part within why may we not say, that all Automata (Engines that move themselves by springs and wheeles as doth a watch) have an artificiall life? For what is the Heart, but a Spring; and the Nerves, but so many Strings; and the Joynts, but so many Wheeles, giving motion to the whole Body, such as was intended by the Artificer? goes yet further, imitating that Ration all and most excellent worke of Nature, Man. For by Art is created that great LEVIATHAN called a COMMON-WEALTH, or STATE.
>
> The Wealth and Riches of all the particular members, are the Strength…Equity and Lawes, an artificiall Reason and Will. Lastly, the acts and Covenants, by which the parts of this Body Politique were at first made…, and united, resemble that Fiat, or the Let us make man, pronounced by God in the Creation.

Hobbes first refers to nature as "art whereby God hath made," then enlightens us as to His origin:

> Part 1 Of Man
> By the visible things of this world, and their admirable order, a man may conceive there

is a cause of them, which men call God; and yet not have an Idea, or Image of him in his mind.

And they that make little, or no enquiry into the naturall causes of things, yet from the feare that proceeds from the ignorance it selfe, of what it is that hath the power to do them much good or harm, are enclined to suppose, and feign unto themselves, severall kinds of Powers Invisible ; and to stand in awe of their own imaginations ; and in time of distresse to invoke them; as also in the time of an expected good successe, to give them thanks; making the creatures of their own fancy, their Gods. By which means it hath come to passe, that from the innumerable variety of Fancy, men have created in the world innumerable sorts of Gods. And this Feare of things invisible, is the naturall Seed of that, which every one in himself calleth Religion; and in them that worship, or feare that Power otherwise than they do, Superstition."

If and when you give thanks to God for any blessings, you give thanks to your "own imagination" to "Superstition". This is key for us to remember if we are to understand this philosophy. For if there is no God, no Creator, then from whom or what, do we receive our "rights", our "personality" and our "liberty"? And what is this condition, this State of Nature?

> CHAP. XIII. Of the NATURALL CONDITION of Mankind
>
> NATURE hath made men so equall, in the faculties of body, and mind; as that though

there bee found one man sometimes manifestly stronger in body, or of quicker mind then another ; yet when all is reckoned together, the difference between man, and man, is not so considerable, as that one man can thereupon claim to himselfe any benefit, to which another may not pretend, as well as he. For as to the strength of body, the weakest has strength enough to kill the strongest, either by secret machination, or by confederacy with others, that are in the same danger with himselfe. (p. 92)

So that in the nature of man...without a common Power to keep them all in awe, *they are at condition which is called Warre ; and such a warre; as is of every man, against every man.* (p. 96) (emphasis added)

It may peradventure be thought, there was never such a time, nor condition of warre as this; and I believe it was never generally so, over all the world : but there are many places, where they live so now. For the savage people in many places of America, except the govern ment of small Families, the concord whereof dependeth pn naturall lust, have no government at all; and live this day in that brutish manner, as I said before. (p. 99)

To this warre of every man against every man, this Warre,...nothing can be Unjust. The nothing is notions of Right and wrong, Justice and Injustice have there no place. Where there is no common Power, there Is no Law: where no Law, no Injustice...Justice, and Injustice are

> none of the Faculties neither of the Body, nor Mind. If they were, they might be in a man that were alone in the world, as well as his Senses, and Passions. They are Qualities, that relate to men in Society, not in Solitude. It is consequent also to the same condition, that there be no Propriety, no Dominion, no Mine and Thine distinct; but onely that to be every mans, that he can get ; and for so long, as he can keep it.

As Hobbes says in our "condition" or "state of nature," we are lawless in a constant state of war, "every man against every man." We can have nothing—no property, no wife, no husband, no child to call our own. If somebody can take them, they are theirs only till they are taken from them by another. Not even the food in your mouth would be yours if it could be taken from you. Remember this as this is a critical, fundamental aspect of the Philosophy we will be coming back to.

On another note, "without common power to keep them all in awe," there can be no "Justice. Nor can there be any Injustice" He continues:

> That a man be willing, when others are so too, as farre-forth, as for Peace, and defence of himselfe he shall think it necessary, to lay down this right to all things; and be contented with so much liberty against other men, as he would allow other men against himselfe…This is that Law of the Gospell; Whatsoever you require that others should do to you, that do ye to them. (p. 100)

But if we are willing to agree to collectively "lay down our right to all things," there would be peace, but

> *before the names of Just, and Unjust can have place, there must be some coercive Power*, to compell men equally to the performance of their Covenants, by the terrour of some punishment, greater than the benefit they expect by the breach of their Covenant; and to make good that Propriety, which by…Contract men acquire, in recompence of the universall Right they abandon: and such power there is none before the erection of a Common-wealth. *And this is also to be gathered out of the ordinary definition of Justice in the Schooles*: For they say, that Justice is the constant Will of giving to every man his own. And therefore where there is no Own, that is, no Propriety, there is no Injustice; and where there is no coerceive Power erected, that is, where there is no Common-wealth, there is no Propriety; all men having Right to all things: Therefore where there is no Common-wealth, there nothing is Unjust. So that the nature of Justice, consisteth in keeping of valid Covenants: but the Validity of Covenants begins not but with the Constitution of a Civill Power, sufficient to compell men to keep them: And then it is also that Propriety begins. (p. 109, emphasis added)

There *must* be a "coercive power" to compel and maintain the peace we collectively contract to achieve. Once that force is instituted, propriety or enterprise can begin. But we must immediately surrender any fruit from it to the collective, for justice is "the constant Will of giving to every man his own" and because "where there is no Common Wealth, there is no propriety." As a commonwealth is "all men having right to all things," or rather simply: it's better to have property you are forced to give away than to have a right to property you can never keep!

We must briefly touch on what Hobbes is pointing out here as to where and when we have "justice." The concept of when and where we have justice, or what is just or unjust, goes back to Plato's *Republic*. Fundamentally, where there is no "coercive power" *forcing* our compliance, there can be no justice! This *forced* compliance is only half of *the* fundamental principles of what will come to be known as *social justice*. The "laying down" of our right to "all things" is the other half! Put them together, and we have a *civil* coercive power forcibly taking from us all our everything we no longer have any claim to and forcing us to be content in whatever ration of life and liberty the coercive power keeping us all in awe sees fit to allow us. In so insinuating, does not such a philosophy then negate the relevance of, if not the very existence of, what Hobbes himself just referred to as the "Law of the Gospell"? Social justice is *not* freedom! It is *not* Liberty! It is, however, a strand of the web that will be coming back around again, again, and again throughout this work.

> If (in) Nature...men that think them selves equall, will not enter into conditions of Peace, but upon Equall termes, such equalitie must be admitted. And therefore for the ninth law of Nature, I put this, That every man acknowledge other for his Equall by Nature. The breach of this Precept is Pride...at the entrance against into conditions of Peace, no man require to

reserve to him-selfe any Right, which he is not content should be reserved to every one of the rest. As it is necessary for all men that seek peace, to lay down certaine Rights of Nature; that is to say, not to have libertie to do all they list: so is it necessarie for mans life, to retaine some; as right to governe their owne bodies; enjoy aire, water, motion, waies to go from place to place; and all things else without which a man cannot live, or not live well. If in this case, at the making of Peace, men require for them selves, that which they would not have to be granted to others, they do contrary to the precedent law, that commandeth the acknowledgment of naturall equalitie, and therefore also against the law of Nature. The observers of this law, are those we call Modest, and the breakers Arrogant men. The Greeks call the violation of this law…a desire of more than their share. (p. 118)

These are the Lawes of Nature, dictating Peace, for a means of the conservation of men in multitudes; and which onely concern the doctrine of Civill Society. (p. 120)

Part 2 Chapter 17 - OF COMMON-WEALTH

For if we could suppose a great Multitude of men to consent in the observation of Justice, and other Lawes of Nature, without a common Power to keep them all in awe; we might as well suppose all Man-kind to do the same ; and then there neither would be, nor need to be any Civill Government, or Common-wealth at all;

because there would be Peace without subjection." (130)

Without a "common power" enforcing laws to keep us "in awe," there is no peace. No peace, no liberty. By this common power, as we will see, we will be "forced to be free"!

> The only way to erect such a Common Power, as may be able to defend them from the invasion of Forraigners, and the injuries of one another...that by their owne Industrie... they may nourish themselves and live contentedly; is, to conferre all their power and, strength upon one Man, or upon one Assembly of men, that may reduce all their Wills, by plurality of voices, unto one Will....and therein to submit their Wills, every one to his Will, and their Judgements, to his Judgment. This is more than Consent, or Concord; it is a reall United of them all, in one and the same Person, made by Covenant of every man with every man... in such manner, as if every man should say to every man, I Authorise and give up my Right of Governing my selfe, to this Man, or to this Assembly of men, on this condition, that thou give up thy Right to him, and Authorise all his Actions in like manner. This done, the Multitude so united in one Person, is called a COMMON-WEALTH, in latine CIVITAS. This is the Generation of that great LEVIATHAN, or rather (to speak more reverently) of that Mortall

God, to which wee owe under the Immorlall God, our peace and defence.

The "common power" that keeps us "in awe" is now our "mortal God," to whom we must now slavishly surrender all our everything to!

> For by this Authoritie, given him by every particular man in the Common-Wealth, he hath the use of so much Power and Strength conferred on him, that by terror thereof, he is inabled to forme the wills of them all, to Peace at home, and mutuall ayd against their enemies abroad. And in him consisteth the Essence of the The De- Common- wealth; which (to define it,) is One Person, finition Of whose Acts a great Multitude, by mutuall Covenants of a one with another, have made themselves every one the wealth. Author, to the end he may use the strength and means of them all, as he shall think expedient, for their Peace and Common Defence. And he that carryeth this Person, is called SOVE-RAIGNE, and said to have Soveraigne Power; and every one besides his SUBJECT.... (pp. 131–132)
> And because it is injustice for a man to do any thing, for which he may be punished by his own authority, he is also upon that title, unjust. And whereas some men have pre tended for their disobedience to their Soveraign, a new Covenant, made, not with men, but with God; this also is unjust: for there is no Covenant with

God, but by mediation of some body that representeth Gods Person; which none doth but Gods Lieutenant, who hath the Soveraignty under God. But this pretence of Covenant with God, is so evident a lye, even in the pretenders own consciences, that it is not onely an act of an unjust, but also of a vile, and unmanly disposition. Because the Right of bearing the Person raigne of them all, is given to him they make Soveraigne, by Power of Covenant onely of one to another, and…cannot be forfeited. there can happen no breach of Covenant on the part of the Soveraigne; and consequently none of his Subjects, by any pretence of forfeiture, can be freed from his Subjection." (p. 135)

If the state or government, which alone has the "coercive power" to "keeps us in awe," is not your "God's Lieutenant who hath the Sovereignty" of standing between you and your God as *the* one and only official interpreter of His word, then having any faith or covenant with Him is "unjust." So if we are to have a religion, we can only have a "state religion," such as those declared by the likes of the Muslim Brotherhood, Hitler, ISIS, or the "Church of England" under King George, from which we have once already declared our Liberty and Independence from back in 1776! Hobbes continues:

Because every Subject is by this Institution Author of all the Actions, and Judgments of the Soveraigne Instituted; it followes, that whatsoever he doth,it can be no injury to any of his Subjects. (p. 136)

> But by this Institution of a Commonwealth, every particular man is Author of all the Soveraigne doth; and consequently he that complaineth of injury from his Soveraigne, complaineth of that whereof he himself is Author... And therefore it is annexed to the Soveraignty, to be Judge of what Of what Opinions and Doctrines are averse, and what are fit to be conducmg to Peace; and consequently, on what occasions, how farre, and what, men are to be trusted with all, them. In speaking to Multitudes of people; and who shall examine the Doctrines of all bookes before they be published. For the Actions of men proceed from their Opinions; and in the wel governing of Opinions. (p. 137)

As each individual in the collective is the author of their own surrender to the sovereign instituted, each is thereby the author of all that the sovereign does—whatsoever its judgments, whatsoever its wills, whatsoever its opinions. The sovereign can do no wrong. The government's opinions, judgments, and wills are yours as you are, by the covenant, the author of them yourself! Not only that, by the power keeping us all "in awe," you will be allowed no other will or opinion! Or, as Mayor Rahm Emanuel says regarding the controversy over Chick-fill-A's public support of traditional marriage, "If you're going to be part of the Chicago community, you should reflect the Chicago values." Hobbes goes on:

> In Monarchy there is this inconvenience; that any Subject, by the power of one man, for the enriching of a favourite or flatterer, may be deprived of all he possesseth; which I confesse

> is a great and inevitable inconvenience. But the same may as well happen, where the Soveraigne Power is in an Assembly: For their power is the same. (p. 146)

King, president, congress, or senate—their powers should all be the same and absolute!

> Part IV Of the Kingdom
> But to what purpose (may some man say) is such subtilty in a work of this nature, where I pretend to nothing but what is necessary to the doctrine of Government and Obedience? It is to this purpose, that men [373] may no longer suffer themselves to be abused, by them, that by this doctrine of Separated Essences,...For it is upon this ground, that when a Man is dead and buried, they say his Soule (that is his Life) can walk separated from his Body, arid is seen by night amongst the graves...And upon the same ground they say, that Faith, and Wisdome, and other Vertues are some times powred into a man, sometimes blown into him from Heaven ; as if the Vertuous, and their Vertues could be asunder ; and a great many other things that serve to lessen the dependance of Subjects on the Soveraign Power of their Countrey.

Now that you have surrendered all to the state, your forced obedience to it will protect you from such heresy as "people have souls," as well as a "great many other things that would serve to lesson the dependence of Subjects on the Sovereign Power of their Country"!

> For who will endeavour to obey the Laws, if he expect Obedience to be Powred or Blown into him? Or who will not obey a Priest, that can make God, rather than his Soveraign; nay than God himselfe? Or who, that is in fear of Ghosts, will not bear great respect to those that can make the Holy Water, that drives them from him? (pp. 526–527)
>
> Being once fallen into this Error of Separated Essences, they are thereby necessarily involved in many other absurdities that follow it. And in particular, of the Essence of a Man, which (they say) is his Soule, they affirm it, to be All of it in his little Finger, and All of it in every other Part (how small soever) of his Body; and yet no more Soule in the Whole Body, than in any one of those Parts. Can any man think that God is served with such absurdities? And yet all this is necessary to beleeve, to those that will beleeve the Existence of an Incorporeall Soule, Separated from the Body. (p. 527)
>
> They are troubled to make it seem possible, how a Soule can goe hence, without the Body to Heaven, Hell, or Purgatory…as this distinction was made to maintain the Doctrine of Free-Will, that is, of a Will of man, not subject to the Will of God. (p. 531)

Again, the notion of having "separate essence" or a soul is an "error." No God "is served with such absurdities." Such a notion only proliferates individual "free will," subverting the power that is supposed to "keeps us in awe" with God's law!

> As long as we consider them governed every one by his own Law: For in the condition of men that have no other Law but their own Appetites, there can be no generall Rule of Good, and Evill Actions. But in a Commonwealth this measure is false : Not the Appetite of Private men, but the Law, which is the Will and Appetite of the State is the measure. And yet is this Doctrine still practiced…no man calleth Good or Evill, but that which is so in his own eyes, without any regard at all to the Publique Laws…to which every Subject ought to think himself bound by the Law of Nature to the Civill Soveraign. And this private measure of Good, is a Doc trine, not onely Vain, but also Pernicious to the Publique State.

Individual Liberty, or the "having your own appetite," the calling of things good or evil from a doctrine other than that decreed by the sovereign or state, is "pernicious [causing insidious harm or ruin] to the publique state." One must live according to the "central plan" of the sovereign only! Or as Governor Andrew Cuomo (in his January 17, 2014, radio address, referring to *all* those living in New York, whose beliefs may hold to an Individual "Right to life," upholding the Second Amendment and/or believing in God and His Holy Commandments) said when—by *decreeing* them all "extreme," "absolutist," "proassault weapons," and/or "antigay"—he issued the executive determination that "they have no place in the State of NY because that's not who New Yorkers are."

> Lastly, for the Errors brought in from false, or uncertain Errors in History, what is

> all the Legend of fictitious Miracles, from in the lives of the Saints; and all the Histories of Tradition—Apparitions, and Ghosts, alledged by the Doctors of the Romane Church, to make good their Doctrines of Hell, and Purgatory, the power of Exorcisme, and other Doctrines which have no warrant, neither in Reason, nor Scripture; as also all those Traditions which they call the unwritten Word of God; but old Wives Fables? (p. 535)

God, along with "God's law," which is subversive to the "civil sovereign," are nothing more than "legend(s) of fictitious miracles" and "old wives' fables"!

> Whereof, though they find dispersed somewhat in the Writings of the ancient Fathers; yet those Fathers were men, that might too easily beleeve false reports....Let them be silenced by the Laws of those, to whom the Teachers of them are subject; that is, by the Laws Civill: For disobedience may law fully be punished in them, that against the Laws teach even true Philosophy. Is it because they tend to disorder in Government, as countenancing Rebellion, or Sedition? Then let them be silenced, and the Teachers punished by vertue of his Power to whom the care of the Publique quiet is committed; which is the Authority Civill. For whatsoever Power Ecclesiastiques take upon themselves (in any place where they are subject to the

State) in their own Right, though they call it Gods Right, is but Usurpation. (p. 537)

As the "Word of God" was written by men, it is "usurpation"! As for the "teachers" of this "rebellious" doctrine, "let them be silenced" and "punished" for "sedition" by the laws of the "civil sovereign"! However, Hobbes then concludes:

> There is nothing in this whole Discourse, nor in that I writ before of the same Subject in Latine, as far as I can perceive, contrary either to the Word of God, or to good Manners; or to the disturbance of the Publique Tranquillity.

To which he then adds:

> Therefore I think it may be profitably printed, and more profitably taught in the Universities, in case they also think so, to whom the judgment of the same belongeth. For seeing the Universities are the Fountains of Civill, and Morall Doctrine, from whence the Preachers, and the Gentry, drawing such water as they find, use to sprinkle the same (on) People.[10] (p. 556)

Later, the Fabian Socialists, among others, would successfully work, under their coat of arms of a "wolf in sheep's clothing," to do just that all across the globe.

In 1762, Jean Jacques Rousseau spelled out it out a little clearer for us in his *The Social Contract or Principles of Political Right*. Some of which should, by now, start to sound familiar:

Book I

1- MAN is born free; and everywhere he is in chains…the social order is a sacred right which is the *basis* of all other rights. Nevertheless, this right does not come from nature, and must therefore be founded on conventions….

6 –The problem is to find a form of association which will defend and protect with the whole common force the person and goods of each associate, and in which each, while uniting himself with all, may still obey himself alone, and remain as free as before. This is the fundamental problem of which the Social Contract provides the solution.

These clauses, properly understood, may be reduced to one—the total alienation of each associate, together with all his rights, to the whole community; for, in the first place, as each gives himself absolutely, the conditions are the same for all; and, this being so, no one has any interest in making them burdensome to others.

Each man, in giving himself to all, gives himself to nobody; and as there is no associate over whom he does not acquire the same right as he yields others over himself, he gains an equivalent for everything he loses, and an increase of force for the preservation of what he has.

"Each of us puts his person and all his power in common under the supreme direction of [the general will], and, in our corporate capacity, we receive each member as an indivisible part of the whole."

At once, in place of the individual personality of each contracting party, this act of association creates a moral and collective body, composed of as many members as the assembly contains votes, and receiving from this act its unity, its common identity, its life and its will. This public person, so formed by the union of all other persons formerly took the name of *city*, and now takes that of *Republic* or *body politic*; it is called by its members *State* when passive. *Sovereign* when active, and *Power* when compared with others like itself. Those who are associated in it take collectively the name of *people*, and severally are called *citizens*, as sharing in the sovereign power, and *subjects*, as being under the laws of the State....

7 - In fact, each individual, as a man, may have a particular will contrary or dissimilar to the general will which he has as a citizen. His particular interest may speak to him quite differently from the common interest: his absolute and naturally independent existence may make him look upon what he owes to the common cause as a gratuitous contribution, the loss of which will do less harm to others than the payment of it is burdensome to himself; and, regarding the moral person which constitutes the State as a *persona ficta*, because not a man, he may wish to enjoy the rights of citizenship without being ready to fulfil the duties of a subject. The continuance of such an injustice

> could not but prove the undoing of the body politic....
>
> In order then that the social compact may not be an empty formula, it tacitly includes the undertaking, which alone can give force to the rest, [*that whoever refuses to obey the general will shall be compelled to do so by the whole body. This means nothing less than that he will be forced to be free*]; for this is the condition which, by giving each citizen to his country, secures him against all personal dependence. In this lies the key to the working of the political machine; *this alone legitimises civil undertakings.* (emphasis added).

So it is not until we as people leave the state of nature, which according to both Rousseau and Hobbes is nothing but a lawless free-for-all, and enter into a collective covenant or society and surrender ourselves and all we have to it that we obtain any liberty or freedom. And again, if your individual interests happen to run different from the "common interest" or "general will," "in order that the social compact may not be an empty formula," "whoever refuses to obey will be forced to be free":

> 8 – THE passage from the state of nature to the civil state produces a very remarkable change in man, by substituting justice for instinct in his conduct, and giving his actions the morality they had formerly lacked...Although, in this state, he deprives himself of some advantages which he got from nature, he gains in return others so great, his faculties are so stimulated and developed, his ideas so extended, his feel-

ings so ennobled, and his whole soul so uplifted, that, did not the abuses of this new condition often degrade him below that which he left, he would be bound to bless continually the happy moment which took him from it for ever, and, instead of a stupid and unimaginative animal, made him an intelligent being and a man.

Let us draw up the whole account in terms easily commensurable. *What man loses by the social contract is his natural liberty and an unlimited right to everything he tries to get and succeeds in getting; what he gains is civil liberty* (emphasis added) and the proprietorship of all he possesses. If we are to avoid mistake in weighing one against the other, we must clearly distinguish natural liberty, which is bounded only by the strength of the individual, from civil liberty, which is limited by the general will; and possession; and possession, which is merely the effect of force or the right of the first occupier, from property, which can be founded only on a positive title.

Any and all possessions, property, or wealth gained by proprietorship is not yours to keep. By right of the first occupier, or sovereign, which is the state, it all belongs to the state as you would have nothing if not for the state. "If you've got a business—you didn't build that. Somebody else made that happen." It's also the only context in which Nancy Pelosi's "unemployment creates jobs" can possibly make any sense! As when on unemployment, welfare, SSI, or other state-rationed income, that income is no more than is necessary for a measured menial existence. Therefore, no money or property can be saved or "horded" by any individual. All such monies must therefore be spent just to survive. By social design, it inevitably flows through their hands back to the collective from whence it came.

Don't let it slide that "what man loses by the social contract is his natural liberty and an unlimited right to everything he tries to get and succeeds in getting; what he gains is civil liberty." What we see here from Hobbes and Rousseau is the origin of where the Philosophy says we surrendered our "Natural Liberty" to the collective or the government, as it is *the* origin of the "social contract" of which Elizabeth Warren speaks. The "civil liberty" or "moral liberty" we obtain in surrendering our Natural Liberty is also referred to as positive "rights" or civil "rights" of civil origin. We will be coming back to this again in the coming chapters.

> *We might, over and above all this, add, to what man acquires in the civil state, moral liberty, which alone makes him truly master of himself; for the mere impulse of appetite is slavery, while obedience to a law which we prescribe to ourselves is liberty* (emphasis added).
>
> 9 - EACH member of the community gives himself to it, at the moment of its foundation, just as he is, with all the resources at his command, including the goods he possesses. This act does not make possession, in changing hands, change its nature, and become property in the hands of the Sovereign; but, as the forces of the city are incomparably greater than those of an individual, public possession is also, in fact, stronger and more irrevocable, without being any more legitimate, at any rate from the point of view of foreigners. For the State,

> in relation to its members, is master of all their goods by the social contract, which, within the State, is the basis of all rights....
>
> *The right of the first occupier, though more real than the right of the strongest, becomes a real right only when the right of property has already been established. Every man has naturally a right to everything he needs; but the positive act which makes him proprietor of one thing excludes him from everything else. Having his share, he ought to keep to it, and can have no further right against the community. This is why the right of the first occupier, which in the state of nature is so weak, claims the respect of every man in civil society. In this right we are respecting not so much what belongs to another as what does not belong to ourselves* (emphasis added).

"[M]oral liberty which alone makes him truly master of himself" doesn't really make him "master of himself" in the sense that you might understand it as that would *truly* be individualism! Nope, "moral liberty" is the *surrender* of himself, along with a simultaneous surrender of all others in that society to the state; a mutual surrender by social contract. That surrender is *the* social contract that forms the "general will," whereby "whoever refuses to obey the general will shall be compelled to do so by the whole body. This means nothing less than that he will be forced to be free; for this is the condition which, by giving each citizen to his country, secures him against all personal dependence."

In Rousseau's Social Contract, you become master of nothing. However, all others are "forced" by the "general will" to no longer be your master as you all have the same master now! Moreover, as "moral liberty," or our mutual surrender is now justice (Socrates) forcing us to be free, any and all individuality, Individual Liberty, Individual Rights, entrepreneurial spirit, independence, self-sufficiency, self-accomplishments, Judeo-Christian spirituality and morality, property rights, and freedom in general—all are now immoral and unjust! This is something to keep in mind as it will come into play over and over and over throughout the whole of not only this work but throughout the whole of the Philosophy and the whole of the ongoing assault against our Individual Liberty, which alone is True Freedom.

To bring the point of one "having his share, he ought to keep to it and can have no further right against the community" home in the same context, read these two short clips from two contemporary politicians:

> I do think at a certain point you've made enough money. But, you know, part of the American way is, you know, you can just keep on making it. (President Obama, April 28, 2010, Quincy, Illinois)
>
> It's time for a new beginning, for an end to government of the few, by the few and for the few, time to reject the idea of an "on your own" society and to replace it with shared responsibility for shared prosperity. I prefer a "we're all in it together" society. (Hillary Clinton, May 29 2007, Manchester School of Technology, Manchester, New Hampshire)

This is today's progressivism—not in my words but theirs—in the fuller context of its own collective, "shared responsibility for a shared prosperity" philosophy!

Book II

1 - THE first and most important deduction from the principles we have so far laid down is that the general will alone can direct the State according to the object for which it was instituted, i.e., the common good: for if the clashing of particular interests made the establishment of societies necessary, the agreement of these very interests made it possible. The common element in these different interests is what forms the social tie; and, were there no point of agreement between them all, no society could exist. It is solely on the basis of this common interest that every society should be governed....

4 - *Each man alienates, I admit, by the social compact, only such part of his powers, goods and liberty as it is important for the community to control; but it must also be granted that the Sovereign is sole judge of what is important* (emphasis added)....

So long as the subjects have to submit only to conventions of this sort, they obey no-one but their own will; and to ask how far the respective rights of the Sovereign and the citizens extend, is to ask up to what point the latter can enter into undertakings with themselves, each with all, and all with each.

5 - The social treaty has for its end the preservation of the contracting parties. He who wills the end wills the means also, and the means must involve some risks, and even some losses. He who wishes to preserve his life at oth-

> ers' expense should also, when it is necessary, be ready to give it up for their sake. Furthermore, *the citizen is no longer the judge of the dangers to which the law-desires him to expose himself; and when the prince says to him: "It is expedient for the State that you should die," he ought to die, because it is only on that condition that he has been living in security up to the present, and because his life is no longer a mere bounty of nature, but a gift made conditionally by the State* (emphasis added).

Not only do you owe to the state in this philosophy all your wealth and all your holdings for the security of them, *you owe your very life* as it is "but a gift made conditionally by the state." Not quite the philosophy most of us have grown up with where we owe our life to no one but God. Rousseau continues:

> 8 - Religion, considered in relation to society, which is either general or particular, may also be divided into two kinds: the religion of man, and that of the citizen…religion…gives men two codes of legislation, two rulers, and two countries, renders them subject to contradictory duties, and makes it impossible for them to be faithful both to religion and to citizenship. Such are the religions of the Lamas and of the Japanese, and such is Roman Christianity, which may be called the religion of the priest. It leads to a sort of mixed and anti-social code which has no name….
>
> In their political aspect, all…of religion have their defects. The third is so clearly bad,

that it is waste of time to stop to prove it such. All that destroys social unity is worthless; all institutions that set man in contradiction to himself are worthless.

The second is good in that it unites the divine cult with love of the laws, and, making country the object of the citizens' adoration, teaches them that service done to the State is service done to its tutelary god. It is a form of theocracy, in which there can be no pontiff save the prince, and no priests save the magistrates. To die for one's country then becomes martyrdom; violation of its laws, impiety; and to subject one who is guilty to public execration is to condemn him to the anger of the gods: *Sacer estod.*" There remains therefore the religion of man or Christianity—not the Christianity of to-day, but that of the Gospel, which is entirely different. By means of this holy, sublime, and real religion all men, being children of one God, recognise one another as brothers, and the society that unites them is not dissolved even at death.

But this religion, having no particular relation to the body politic, leaves the laws in possession of the force they have in themselves without making any addition to it; and thus one of the great bonds that unite society considered in severally fails to operate. Nay, more, so far from binding the hearts of the citizens to the State, it has the effect of taking them away from all earthly things. I know of nothing more contrary to the social spirit.

Christianity as a religion is entirely spiritual, occupied solely with heavenly things; the country of the Christian is not of this world. He does his duty, indeed, but does it with profound indifference to the good or ill success of his cares. Provided he has nothing to reproach himself with, it matters little to him whether things go well or ill here on earth....

Christianity preaches only servitude and dependence. Its spirit is so favourable to tyranny that it always profits by such a *régime*. True Christians are made to be slaves, and they know it and do not much mind: this short life counts for too little in their eyes....

Now, it matters very much to the community that each citizen should have a religion. That will make him love his duty; but the dogmas of that religion concern the State and its members only so far as they have reference to morality and to the duties which he who professes them is bound to do to others. Each man may have, over and above, what opinions he pleases, without it being the Sovereign's business to take cognisance of them; for, as the Sovereign has no authority in the other world, whatever the lot of its subjects may be in the life to come, that is not its business, provided they are good citizens in this life[11]

Though any given person may or may not aspire to each and every aspect of this sinister philosophy, which forms a plethora of confusing isms, it is still nonetheless a homogenous one that eats at the very soul of our Liberty, and our nation as one.

As we have just read, there is no place in this philosophy for God or religion—Judeo-Christianity in particular! If, as Rousseau and Hobbes profess, we as helpless humans came into their Godless "society" seeking shelter and security from a lawless, Godless natural state with nothing, we then owe *all* we have and *all* we are to them and their society, which hath saved us from that state and hath given to us *all* our liberty by "forcing us to be free." How has any part of mankind ever been seduced by any part of that? Luckily for us, our founders were all well aware of the enslaving hypocrisy behind the lie. For just a taste of sanity, of what our founders knew well, compare this short piece of John Locke's 1690 *The Second Treaties of Civil Government*, section 6:

> Sec. 6. But though this be a state of liberty, yet it is not a state of licence: though man in that state have an uncontroulable liberty to dispose of his person or possessions, yet he has not liberty to destroy himself, or so much as any creature in his possession, but where some nobler use than its bare preservation calls for it. The state of nature has a law of nature to govern it, which obliges every one: and reason, which is that law, teaches all mankind, who will but consult it, that being all equal and independent, no one ought to harm another in his life, health, liberty, or possessions: *for men being all the workmanship of one omnipotent, and infinitely wise maker; all the servants of one sovereign mas-*

> *ter, sent into the world by his order, and about his business; they are his property, whose workmanship they are, made to last during his, not one another's pleasure*: and being furnished with like faculties, sharing all in one community of nature, there cannot be supposed any such subordination among us, that may authorize us to destroy one another, as if we were made for one another's uses, as the inferior ranks of creatures are for our's. *Every one, as he is bound to preserve himself, and not to quit his station wilfully, so by the like reason, when his own preservation comes not in competition, ought he, as much as he can, to preserve the rest of mankind, and may not, unless it be to do justice on an offender, take away, or impair the life, or what tends to the preservation of the life, the liberty, health, limb, or goods of another*[12] (emphasis added).

In just these few words, Locke unlocks what would otherwise be our earthly chains. Know that there is, and always has been, a brighter way. Thank God!

While on the subject of God, government, and our relationship with them, let us go to Max Stirner, who, in his 1845 *All Things Are Nothing to Me*, espouses the following:

> God cares only for what is his, busies himself only with himself, thinks only of himself, and has only himself before his eyes; woe to all that is not well-pleasing to him. He serves no higher person, and satisfies only himself. His cause is—a purely egoistic cause....

Mankind looks only at itself, mankind will promote the interests of mankind only, mankind is its own cause. That it may develop, it causes nations and individuals to wear themselves out in its service, and, when they have accomplished what mankind needs, it throws them on the dung-heap of history in gratitude. Is not mankind's cause—a purely egoistic cause?

Do truth, freedom, humanity, justice, desire anything else than that you grow enthusiastic and serve them? They all have an admirable time of it when they receive zealous homage. *Just observe the nation that is defended by devoted patriots. The patriots fall in bloody battle or in the fight with hunger and want; what does the nation care for that? By the manure of their corpses the nation comes to "its bloom"! The individuals have died "for the great cause of the nation," and the nation sends some words of thanks after them and—has the profit of it....*

God and mankind have concerned themselves for nothing, for nothing but themselves. Let me then likewise concern myself for *myself,* who am equally with God the nothing of all others, who am my all, who am the only one... Away, then, with every concern that is not altogether my concern! You think at least the "good cause" must be my concern? What's good, what's bad? Why, I myself am my concern, and I am neither good nor bad. Neither has meaning for me.

> The divine is God's concern; the human, man's. My concern is neither the divine nor the human, not the true, good, just, free, etc., but solely what is *mine*, and it is not a general one, but is—unique, as I am unique. Nothing is more to me than myself![13] (emphasis added).

If God is to exist, then why not be your own everything, your own alpha and your own omega—your own god? Are not egoism and humanism a contradiction in terms? One for the self and one for the collective? Yet they share a commonality in their hostility toward God. From whence could such a self-conflicting, anti-God philosophy originate?

As we have already seen, the concept of property and being able to hold claim to the fruits of your labor is also despised by this philosophy. In chapter 4 of his 1841 *What is Property?* French anarchist Pierre-Joseph Proudhon tells us the following:

> *Products say the economists, are bought only by products. This maxim is property's condemnation. The proprietor, producing neither by his own labor nor by his implement, and receiving products in exchange for nothing, is either a parasite or a thief. Then, if property can exist only as a right, property is impossible…*
>
> *The proprietor—an essentially libidinous animal, without virtue or shame—is not satisfied with an orderly and disciplined life. He loves property, because it enables him to do at leisure what he pleases and when he pleases. Having obtained the means of life, he gives himself up to trivialities and indolence; he enjoys, he fritters away his time,*

he goes in quest of curiosities and novel sensations. (emphasis added)

Proudhon is not talking about superrich billionaires out on their yachts here; he's talking about any business owner whatsoever who generates a profit. If you have a business, you must make a profit to stay in business. The proprietor is a self-made man or woman who—by taking some or all of the money they were to put a roof over their family's house with or food on their kid's table with—put it all at risk. They put it at risk not only on a whim or dreams or inspirations but to merely cover the cost of doing business. If all goes right, the job gets finished: the customer is happy; the employees are paid (along with their SSI, Workman's Comp, unemployment tax, reemployment tax, and disability insurance); the supplier, liability and vehicle insurances, and fuel bills are paid; the equipment doesn't need repair; the overhead is covered; licensing fees and permits are paid; and mandatory DOL, OSHA, DEC, and EPA standards are covered. Then after paying a 15 percent proprietor tax off the top and then paying the federal income and state income tax, what is left, if anything, is called profit.

Any owner of a well-run business knows that if a business isn't a growing business, it's a dying business. As such, a percentage of that profit must then be reinvested back into the business if it is to grow. And don't forget that the groceries still need to be bought and the roof still needs to be fixed. That's if it all goes good! How does one even gain by being a proprietor? As in many cases, all that work is done for nothing or, worse, at a loss. By definition, a proprietor is an entrepreneur. Whether or not you are suppressing employees or only suppressing yourself, owning a business where profits must be made is greed plain and simple. Profit is money and/or property kept by an individual business owner from the collective. Anybody who has owned and run so much as a Kool-Aid stand in business knows there is no such thing as punching out when you own a business. Until the day you pull the plug, it's 24-7-365. Kind of makes punching a clock for forty hours a week with a guaranteed profit no matter what sound like a cakewalk! I've done both, and comparatively, it is. But again, if having a job or getting paid for punching in and out is all that matters to you, then it's all you'll ever have.

> Property—to enjoy itself—has to abandon ordinary life, and busy itself in luxurious occupations and unclean enjoyments.
>
> His condition, whatever he may do, is an unproductive and *felonious* one; he cannot cease to waste and destroy without ceasing to be a proprietor"
>
> [*The proprietor is a foreigner to society*]; but, like the vulture, his eyes fixed upon his prey, he holds himself ready to pounce upon and devour it…property—after having robbed the laborer by usury—murders him slowly by starvation. Now, [*without robbery and murder, property cannot exist*]; with robbery and murder, it soon dies for want of support. [*Therefore it is impossible*]….(emphasis added)
>
> Every man who makes a profit has entered into a conspiracy with famine…Under the rule of property, the flowers of industry are woven into none but funeral wreaths. The laborer digs his own grave[14] (emphasis added).

To be a proprietor is to be a capitalist. The act of doing business, the exchange of property owned for property desired is capitalism. Capitalism is *the* famine causing conspiracy that any and every business owner has entered. This is a critical, fundamental of progressive collectivism that very few business owners who support it fail to understand.

Later, Errico Malatesta, in his 1891 work *Anarchy*, states:

> Having being born and bred in bondage, when the descendants of a long line of slaves started to think, they believed that slavery was an essential condition of life, and freedom seemed impossible to them. Similarly, workers who for centuries were obliged, and therefore accustomed, to depend for work, that is bread, on the goodwill of the master, and to see their lives always at the mercy of the owners of the land and of capital, ended by believing that it is the master who feeds them, and ingenuously ask one how would it be possible to live if there were no masters....
>
> There are two ways of oppressing men: either directly by brute force, by physical violence; or indirectly by denying them the means of life and thus reducing them to a state of surrender. The former is at the root of power, that is of political privilege; the latter was the origin of property, that is of economic privilege. Men can also be suppressed by working on their intelligence and their feelings, which constitutes religious or "universitarian" power; but just as the spirit does not exist except as the resultant of material forces, so a lie and the organisms set up to propagate it have no *raison d'être* except in so far as they are the result of political and

economic privileges, and a means to defend and to consolidate them....

The basic function of government...is always that of oppressing and exploiting the masses, of defending the oppressors and the exploiters; and its principle, characteristic and indispensable, *instruments are the police agent and the tax-collector, the soldier and the jailer*—to whom must be invariably added the trader in lies, be *he priest* or schoolmaster, remunerated or protected by the government to enslave minds and make them docilely accept the yoke....

The oppressed masses who have never completely resigned themselves to oppression and poverty, and who today more than ever show themselves thirsting for justice, freedom and well-being, are beginning to understand that they will *not be able to achieve their emancipation except by union and solidarity with all the oppressed, with the exploited everywhere in the world. And they also understand that the indispensable condition for their emancipation which cannot be neglected is the possession of the means of production, of the land and of the instruments of labour, and therefore the abolition of private property*[15] (emphasis added).

Here, Malatesta sums up the whole of the multifaceted Occupy movement in just one paragraph. Would they not agree? Employees are the "suppressed" and depicted as "slaves to capital," their minds "slaves to its agents" and their souls are "slaves to the priest." Go figure—Individual Liberty is so oppressive! And as it always does within the Philosophy, it all ends in the "abolition of private property"! Remember, with no private property, all is then held in common by the collective. The individual is powerless to keep or defend anything he or she may consider theirs but, in truth, belongs to the collective. This would include their very own lives because, as Rousseau has just explained to us, "his life is no longer a mere bounty of nature, but a gift made conditionally by the State." In such a philosophy where "the citizen is no longer the judge of the dangers to which the law-desires him to expose himself," where does any right to self-preservation, or any right contingent upon it (such as a right to bear arms), fit into such a philosophy? It doesn't. No Individual Right to property = no other Individual Right to anything, including any "pursuit of Happiness" or to "keep and bear Arms"! All that weakens property rights—including the redistribution of wealth, social justice, progressive tax, and sustainability—weakens the Second Amendment and the whole of our Individual Liberty!

After a series of gut checks and fighting back the urge to vomit, we can now begin to come, with at least some assurance, to the realization that this Philosophy is a polemic hostile to virtually all we as free Americans have known. Consider it, as I have, the necessary repulsive medicine needed to identify what it is that has targeted us for destruction—that we, for the sake of our children's Liberty, may have a chance to dig in our heels and bolster all our bulwarks (protective walls) against it.

Though there have been many writers from around the world who have labored to set the premise for this Philosophy, most notably Karl Marx and his *The Communist Manifesto* of 1848, America has not been exempt. I refer to what was commonly known as the *transcendentalist movement* of the nineteenth century. Allow me to introduce Henry David Thoreau: a favorite of academics, anarchists, anticolonialists around the world, the author of *Walden*. He penned his world-renowned essay "Civil Disobedience" in 1849 after being arrested and going to jail for tax evasion. In that essay, Thoreau puts forth:

> Part One
>
> "I HEARTILY ACCEPT the motto—"That government is best which governs least"; and I should like to see it acted up to more rapidly and systematically. Carried out, it finally amounts to this, which also I believe,— *"That government is best which governs not at all"*; and when men are prepared for it, that will be the kind of government which they will have. Government is at best but an expedient; but most governments are usually, and all governments are sometimes, inexpedient. The objections which have been brought against a standing army, and they are many and weighty, and deserve to prevail, may also at last be brought against a standing government. The standing army is only an arm of the standing government. The government itself, which is only the mode which the people have chosen to execute their will, is equally liable to be abused and perverted before the people can act through it....
>
> Government never of itself furthered any enterprise, but by the alacrity with which it got out of its way. *It* does not keep the country free. *It* does not settle the West. *It* does not educate. The character inherent in the American people has done all that has been accomplished; and it would have done somewhat more, if the government had not sometimes got in its way.

For government is an expedient by which men would fain succeed in letting one another alone; and, as has been said, when it is most expedient, the governed are most let alone by it. Trade and commerce, if they were not made of India rubber would never manage to bounce over the obstacles which legislators are continually putting in their way; and, if one were to judge these men wholly by the effects of their actions, and not partly by their intentions, they would deserve to be classed and punished with those mischievous persons who put obstructions on the railroads.

Law never made men a whit more just; and, by means of their respect for it, even the well-disposed are daily made the agents of injustice. A common and natural result of an undue respect for law is, that you may see a file of soldiers, colonel, captain, corporal, privates, powder-monkeys, and all, marching in admirable order over hill and dale to the wars, against their wills, ay, against their common sense and consciences, which makes it very steep marching indeed, and produces a palpitation of the heart. They have no doubt that it is a damnable business in which they are concerned; they are all peaceably inclined. Now, what are they? Men at all? or small movable forts and magazines, at the service of some unscrupulous man in power?...[*The mass of men serve the state thus, not as men mainly, but as machines, with their bodies. They are the standing army, and the mili-*

> *tia, jailers, constables, posse comitatus, etc.*] In most cases there is no free exercise whatever of the judgment or of the moral sense; but [*they put themselves on a level with wood and earth and stones; and wooden men can perhaps be manufactured that will serve the purpose as well. Such command no more respect than men of straw or a lump of dirt. They have the same sort of worth only as horses and dogs. Yet such as these even are commonly esteemed good citizens*]. (emphasis added)

Remember Stirner:

> Just observe the nation that is defended by devoted patriots. The patriots fall in bloody battle or in the fight with hunger and want; what does the nation care for that? By the manure of their corpses the nation comes to "its bloom"! The individuals have died "for the great cause of the nation," and the nation sends some words of thanks after them and—has the profit of it.[12]

Thoreau continues:

> Part 2
> Under a government which imprisons any unjustly, the true place for a just man is also a prison. The proper place to-day, the only place which Massachusetts has provided for her freer and less desponding spirits, is in her prisons,...It is there that the fugitive slave, and the Mexican prisoner on parole, and the Indian come to

plead the wrongs of his race, should find them; on that separate, but more free and honorable ground, where the State places those who are not with her, but against her—the only house in a slave State in which a free man can abide with honor. If any think that their influence would be lost there, and their voices no longer afflict the ear of the State, that they would not be as an enemy within its walls, they do not know by how much truth is stronger than error, nor how much more eloquently and effectively he can combat injustice who has experienced a little in his own person. It is there that the fugitive slave, and the Mexican prisoner on parole, and the Indian come to plead the wrongs of his race, should find them; on that separate, but more free and honorable ground, where the State places those who are not *with* her, but *against* her—the only house in a slave State in which a free man can abide with honor. Cast your whole vote, not a strip of paper merely, but your whole influence. A minority is powerless while it conforms to the majority; it is not even a minority then; but it is irresistible when it clogs by its whole weight. If the alternative is to keep all just men in prison, or give up war and slavery, the State will not hesitate which to choose. If a thousand men were not to pay their tax-bills this year, that would not be a violent and bloody measure, as it would be to pay them, and enable the State to commit violence and shed innocent blood."

"Cast your whole vote," *not* just a piece of paper! What a call for revolutionary action!

Part 3

The lawyer's truth is not truth, but consistency or a consistent expediency. Truth is always in harmony with herself, and is not concerned chiefly to reveal the justice that may consist with wrong-doing. *He well deserves to be called, as he has been called, the Defender of the Constitution.* There are really no blows to be given by him but defensive ones. He is not a leader, but a follower. His leaders are the men of '87. "I have never made an effort," he says, "and never propose to make an effort; I have never countenanced an effort, and never mean to countenance an effort, to disturb the arrangement as originally made, by which the various States came into the Union." *Still thinking of the sanction which the Constitution gives to slavery, he says, "Because it was a part of the original compact—let it stand."* Notwithstanding his special acuteness and ability, he is unable to take a fact out of its merely political relations, and behold it as it lies absolutely to be disposed of by the intellect—what, for instance, it behooves a man to do here in America to-day with regard to slavery, but ventures, or is driven, to make some such desperate answer as the following, while professing to speak absolutely, and as a private man—from which what new and singular code of social duties might be inferred?

> "The manner," says he, "in which the governments of those States where slavery exists are to regulate it is for their own consideration, under their responsibility to their constituents, to the general laws of propriety, humanity, and justice, and to God" (emphasis added).

Slavery ever being the chink in the armor of our founding has been, is being, and probably always will be relentlessly used by those within the Philosophy to discredit the whole of America's founding principles as hypocrisy, as if to pound into the mind-set of Black Americans specifically: "American freedom and American Liberty is not your freedom! It is not your Liberty to have! It's *their* Liberty, *white* liberty!" (More on this subject in the next chapters as well.) This, when, in truth, American Liberty is founded on the principle that "all Men are created equal" and for the whole of humankind!

But didn't slavery exist in the colonies under the *king's rule*, under which our founders had no say? From which our founders therefore declared our independence, just as much for the very reason of slavery as for any other? Yes, yes, yes, and yes! And upon our independence, did slavery end automatically upon the signing? No, there was no waving of a magic wand to end slavery upon the signing of either the Declaration or Constitution. It did, however, mark the beginning of the end of slavery. But wouldn't both Saul Alinsky and Michelle Obama agree that "it is necessary to begin where the world is if we are going to change it to what we think it should be"?

Thoreau concludes:

> The authority of government, even such as I am willing to submit to...It can have no pure right over my person and property but what I

> concede to it. The progress from an absolute to a limited monarchy, from a limited monarchy to a democracy, is a progress toward a true respect for the individual....Is a democracy, such as we know it, the last improvement possible in government? Is it not possible to take a step further towards recognizing and organizing the rights of man?[16]

Please allow me to a make note here as to what I have come to see as the enigma of Henry David Thoreau in "Civil Disobedience." Without taking a word of it out of context, I could split quotes from this essay into two separate columns. Each of which would represent to the other the very opposing contemporary political viewpoints that we now have before us today. However, it is the revolutionary left that has traditionally gained inspiration from it. This "speaking out of both sides of the mouth" is consistent with many writings from within the "New Left" (LaRouche) of the Philosophy's very own "alternative" or "alt-right" collectivism, seeking to deceivingly connect with the mainstream middle class. Remember Lenin and Alinsky regarding the role of the middle class.

As to a democracy as a "progress toward a true respect for the individual" and the seductive mantra of "this is what democracy looks like" coming out of the Occupy movement, these may deceivingly profess its origin in this context, but our founders knew it to be otherwise. Democracy is *not* Individual Liberty! A true democracy simply gives government the power to enforce the will of the majority or "general will." It is nothing more and nothing less than a true "dictatorship of the proletariat" as called for by Marx. F. A. Hayek reminds us of this in his *Road to Serfdom* ("Planning and Democracy"):

It is now often said that democracy will not tolerate "capitalism". If "capitalism" means here the competitive system based on free disposal of over private property, it is far more important to realize that *only within this system is democracy possible. When it becomes dominated by a collective creed, democracy will inevitably destroy itself* (emphasis added).

How is it then that Occupy, Union, and other socialist-cause-based protesters generally call for both "democracy" and an end to capitalism?

It cannot be said of Democracy, as Lord Acton truly said of liberty, that "it is not a means to a higher political end, *it is itself the highest political end.*"

A true "dictatorship of the proletariat", even if democratic in form, if undertook centrally to direct the economic system, would probably destroy personal freedom as completely as any autocracy has ever done.

The fashionable concentration on democracy as the main value threatened is not without danger. It is largely responsible for the misleading and unfounded belief that, so long as the ultimate source of power is the will of the majority, the power cannot be arbitrary...*it is not the source but the limitation of power* which prevents it from being arbitrary...If democracy resolves on a task which necessarily involves the

> use of power which cannot be guided by fixed rules, it must become arbitrary power[17] (emphasis added).

The Constitution, as established by our founders, *is that limit*! And as John Locke established, there can be no Liberty without "rule of law." The Constitution again, as founded, is also that rule of law. So before falling in lockstep with the likes of Occupiers or other such "democratic" revolutionaries, we need to ask ourselves, what is the end to which we aspire, Liberty or democracy? One does not equal the other—and one, as history has proven, is actually a threat to the other!

Another transcendentalist was Robert Dale Owen, the founder of English socialism who is said to have initiated the American left as we know it today. Where Nancy Pelosi progressively invoked the Declaration of Independence on its 237th anniversary to establish Obamacare as a "declaration of health independence" in 2013, in 1826, on its 50th anniversary, Owen hailed *A Declaration of Mental Independence* from the pulpit of his newly founded commune in New Harmony, Indiana, proclaiming:

> Yes, my friends, the Declaration of Independence, in 1776, prepared the way to secure to you MENTAL LIBERTY, without which man never can become more than a mere localized being, with powers to render him more miserable and degraded than the animals which he has been taught to deem inferior to himself....
>
> Are you prepared to achieve a MENTAL REVOLUTION, as superior in benefit and importance to the first revolution, as the mental powers of man exceed his physical powers?

I now DECLARE, to you and to the world, that Man, up to this hour, has been, in all parts of the earth, a slave to a TRINITY of the most monstrous evils that could be combined to inflict mental and physical evil upon his whole race.

I refer to PRIVATE, OR INDIVIDUAL PROPERTY—ABSURD AND IRRATIONAL SYSTEMS OF RELIGION—and MARRIAGE, FOUNDED ON INDIVIDUAL PROPERTY COMBINED WITH SOME ONE OF THESE IRRATIONAL SYSTEMS OF RELIGION.

It is difficult to say which of these grand sources of all crime ought to be placed first or last; for they are so intimately interlinked and woven together by time, that they cannot be separated without being destroyed:—each one is necessary to the support of the other two. This formidable Trinity, compounded of Ignorance, Superstition and Hypocrisy, is the only Demon, or Devil, that ever has, or, most likely ever will torment the human race. It is well calculated, in all its consequences, to produce the utmost misery on the mind and body of man of which his nature is susceptible. The division of property among individuals prepared the seeds, cultivated the growth, and brought to maturity all the evils of poverty and riches existing among a people at the same time; the industrious experiencing privations and the idle being overwhelmed and injured by wealth.

Religion, or Superstition,—for all religions have proved themselves to be Superstitions,—

by destroying the judgement, irrationalized all the mental faculties of man, and made him the most abject slave, through the fear of nonentities created solely by his own disorganized imagination. Superstition forced him to believe, or to say he believed, that a Being existed who possessed all power, wisdom and goodness—that he could do and that he did, everything—and yet, that evil and misery superabound; and that this Being, who makes and does all things, is not the direct or indirect author of evil or misery. Such is the foundation on which all the mysteries and ravings of Superstition are erected in all parts of the world. Its inconsistency and inconceivable folly have been such as to keep the world in continual wars, and massacres, to create private divisions, leading to every imaginable evil....

The forms and ceremonies of Marriage, as they have been hitherto generally performed, and afterwards supported, make it almost certain, that they were contrived and forced upon the people at the same period that property was first divided among a few leading individuals and Superstition was invented: This being the only device that could be introduced to permit them to retain their division of the public spoils, and to create to themselves an aristocracy of wealth, of power, and of learning.

To enable them to keep their children apart from the multitude who were to be kept in poverty, in ignorance, and consequently

> without power,—and to monopolize all wealth and power and learning to themselves,—some such contrivance as Marriage, with mysterious forms and ceremonies, to hide their real intentions from the ignorant, was absolutely necessary, that they might, through the influence of their wealth, learning and power, select the most beautiful and desirable women from among all the people,—and thus enslave and make them, in fact, a part of their private property.
>
> The revolution, then, to be now effected, is the DESTRUCTION of this HYDRA OF EVILS—in order that the many may be no longer poor, wretched beings, — dependent on the wealthy and powerful few…Upon the experience of a life devoted to the investigation of these momentous subjects, I fearlessly now declare to you, from a conviction, as strong as conviction can exist in the human mind, that this compound of ignorance and fraud, IS THE REAL AND ONLY CAUSE OF ALL THE CRIME, AND MISERY ARISING FROM CRIME, WHICH CAN BE FOUND IN HUMAN SOCIETY[18] (emphasis original).

And so here it is in this philosophy that it is the hated "trinity" of God, property and/or capitalism, and the family in the revolution that must be destroyed—as it is this "three-headed Hydra" that "is the real and only cause of all the crime, and misery arising from crime, which can be found in human society."

What makes presenting this philosophy so difficult is the unlimited number of tangents that spin off it. So many so that it becomes all too easy for me to go off on one and lose my place, which I am tempted to do to show you more here regarding "the real cause of all crime"; but all things in due time. Think of this philosophy as a web of which we are, for now, on a steadfast journey to the center of that we may find out to whom it is, that may be the spider. The strands, we shall touch on in the following chapters, so we continue.

Frederick Engels, coauthor with Karl Marx of *The Communist Manifesto*, expands our understanding of how it is that the family came to be so despised by this philosophy in his 1884 *The Origin of the Family, Private Property, and the State*:

> II. The Family
>
> 4. The Monogamous Family
>
> It is based on the supremacy of the man, the express purpose being to produce children of undisputed paternity; such paternity is demanded because these children are later to come into their father's property as his natural heirs.

The sole purpose for the origin of the "monogamous" marriage and "paternal" family was to establish "undisputed paternity" for heirs of private property.

> The man had his athletics and his public business, from which women were barred; in addition, he often had female slaves at his disposal and during the most flourishing days of Athens an extensive system of prostitution which the state at least favored.. The men, who would have been ashamed to show any love for

> their wives, amused themselves by all sorts of love affairs…
>
> This was the origin of monogamy as far as we can trace it back among the most civilized and highly developed people of antiquity. It was not in any way the fruit of individual sex-love, with which it had nothing whatever to do; marriages remained as before marriages of convenience. It was the first form of the family to be based, not on natural, but on economic conditions—on the victory of private property over primitive, natural communal property. The Greeks themselves put the matter quite frankly: the sole exclusive aims of monogamous marriage were to make the man supreme in the family, and to propagate, as the future heirs to his wealth, children indisputably his own.

Because of the concept of private property, there must be "indisputable" heirs to inherit it. In such a monogamous marriage, it is only the woman who needs to be monogamous to have such an "indisputable heir." Thus, Engels's bourgeois family is founded on the needs of private property and *not* the collective! In this sense, the wife is but property, a sex slave, to insure inheritance of property, but the man is free to be promiscuous. With the elimination of property, the woman would be emancipated from such monogamous slavery and free to be promiscuous as well. Where monogamy only benefits one man in his private concerns, the promise of emancipated, promiscuous wives benefits the whole of the collective. Such are the lures of propertyless collectivism; and as we will see in the coming chapters, such is the "morality" of the Philosophy.

Thus, wherever the monogamous family remains true to its historical origin and clearly reveals the antagonism between the man and the woman expressed in the man's exclusive supremacy....

In...marriage of convenience...the woman...does not let out her body on piece-work as a wage-worker, but sells it once and for all into slavery...Sex-love in the relationship with a woman becomes, and can only become, the real rule among the oppressed classes, which means today among the proletariat-whether this relation is officially sanctioned or not. But here all the foundations of typical monogamy are cleared away. Here there is no property, for the preservation and inheritance of which monogamy and male supremacy were established; hence there is no incentive to make this male supremacy effective. What is more, there are no means of making it so. Bourgeois law, which protects this supremacy, exists only for the possessing class and their dealings with the proletarians. The law costs money and, on account of the worker's poverty, it has no validity for his relation to his wife. Here quite other personal and social conditions decide. And now that large-scale industry has taken the wife out of the home onto the labor market and into the factory, and made her often the bread-winner of the family, no basis for any kind of male supremacy is left in the proletarian household.

Women can only truly be loved, truly be respected, and truly have equal status in a chronically poor classless communist society working in government factories.

> In the old communistic household, which comprised many couples and their children, the task entrusted to the women of managing the household was as much a public and socially necessary industry as the procuring of food by the men. With the patriarchal family, and still more with the single monogamous family, a change came. Household management lost its public character. It no longer concerned society. It became a private service; the wife became the head servant, excluded from all participation in social production. Not until the coming of modern large-scale industry was the road to social production opened to her again—and then only to the proletarian wife. But it was opened in such a manner that, if she carries out her duties in the private soervice of her family, she remains excluded from public production and unable to earn; and if she wants to take part in public production and earn independently, she cannot carry out family duties....
>
> The modern individual family is founded on the open or concealed domestic slavery of the wife, and modern society is a mass composed of these individual families as its molecules[19] (emphasis added).

Women must be freed from working for the benefit of their "private" families so they can be put to work for the collective.

How did such a patriarchal family come to be? Engels continues:

> IX. Barbarism and Civilization
>
> Here—the American Indians must serve as our example—we find the gentile constitution fully formed…The tribe itself breaks up into several tribes, in each of which we find again, for the most part, the old gentes. The related tribes, at least in some cases, are united in a confederacy. This simple organization suffices completely for the social conditions out of which it sprang….
>
> The population is extremely sparse; it is dense only at the tribe's place of settlement… The division of labor is purely primitive, between the sexes only. The man fights in the wars, goes hunting and fishing, procures the raw materials of food and the tools necessary for doing so. The woman looks after the house and the preparation of food and clothing, cooks, weaves, sews. They are each master in their own sphere: the man in the forest, the woman in the house. Each is owner of the instruments which he or she makes and uses: the man of the weapons, the hunting and fishing implements, the woman of the household gear. The housekeeping is communal among several and often many families. What is made and used in common is common property - the house, the garden, the long-boat. Here therefore, and here alone, there

still exists in actual fact that *"property created by the owner's labor"* (emphasis added).

But humanity did not everywhere remain at this stage. In Asia they found animals which could be tamed and, when once tamed, bred…A number of the most advanced tribes—the Aryans, Semites, perhaps already also the Turanians—now made their chief work first the taming of cattle, later their breeding and tending only. Pastoral tribes separated themselves from the mass of the rest of the barbarians: the first great social division of labor. The pastoral tribes produced not only more necessities of life than the other barbarians, but different ones. They possessed the advantage over them of having not only milk, milk products and greater supplies of meat, but also skins, wool, goat-hair, and spun and woven fabrics, which became more common as the amount of raw material increased. Thus for the first time regular exchange became possible…Originally tribes exchanged with tribe through the respective chiefs of the gentes; but as the herds began to pass into private ownership, exchange between individuals became more common, and, finally, the only form. Now the chief article which the pastoral tribes exchanged with their neighbors was cattle; cattle became the commodity by which all other commodities were valued and which was everywhere willingly taken in exchange for them—in short, cattle acquired a money function and already at this stage did the work of money. With such necessity and speed, even at the very beginning of commodity exchange, did the need for a money commodity develop....

Gold and silver were beginning to be used for ornament and decoration, and must already have acquired a high value as compared with copper and bronze. The increase of production in all branches—cattle-raising, agriculture, domestic handicrafts—gave human labor-power the capacity to produce a larger product than was necessary for its maintenance. At the same time it increased the daily amount of work to be done by each member of the gens, household community or single family. It was now desirable to bring in new labor forces. War provided them; prisoners of war were turned into slaves. With its increase of the productivity of labor, and therefore of wealth, and its extension of the field of production, the first great social division of labor was bound, in the general historical conditions prevailing, to bring slavery in its train. *From the first great social division of labor arose the first great cleavage of society into two classes: masters and slaves, exploiters and exploited* (emphasis added).

Here we have it from the coauthor of *The Communist Manifesto* that the *Communist* beginning of the "first great social division of labor" was the introduction of slavery. From that slave-based division of labor "arose the first great cleavage of society into two classes: masters and slaves, exploiters and exploited," otherwise referred to as the bourgeoisie or capitalists and the proletariat or worker classes. So we have it that per communist doctrine, regardless of the fundamental truth that it is capitalism, and only capitalism, that provides us *the* avenue of enterprise to freedom and the ability to provide for ourselves, capitalism is nonetheless founded in slavery! What better way to cloak the documented history of tyranny that is communism than as the false promise of a return of a preoppression, preslavery utopia? What better way for communists to get control over a people than to convince them that their only real avenue to dignity, freedom, and true Liberty—capitalism—is what once led them to slavery? But such is the great deception of the Philosophy!

> All the surplus which the acquisition of the necessities of life now yielded fell to the man; the woman shared in its enjoyment, but had no part in its ownership. The "savage" warrior and hunter had been content to take second place in the house, after the woman; the "gentler" shepherd, in the arrogance of his wealth, pushed himself forward into the first place and the woman down into the second. And she could not complain. The division of labor within the family had regulated the division of property between the man and the woman. That division of labor had remained the same; and yet it now turned the previous domestic relation upside down, simply because the division of labor outside the family had changed. The same cause which had ensured to the woman her previous supremacy in the house—that her activity was confined to domestic labor—this same cause now ensured the man's supremacy in the house: the domestic labor of the woman no longer counted beside

the acquisition of the necessities of life by the man; the latter was everything, the former an unimportant extra. *We can already see from this that to emancipate woman and make her the equal of the man is and remains an impossibility so long as the woman is shut out from social productive labor* and restricted to private domestic labor. *The emancipation of woman will only be possible when woman can take part in production on a large, social scale, and domestic work no longer claims anything but an insignificant amount of her time. And only now has that become possible through modern large-scale industry, which does not merely permit of the employment of female labor over a wide range, but positively demands it,* while it also tends towards ending private domestic labor by changing it more and more into a public industry.

The man now being actually supreme in the house, the last barrier to his absolute supremacy had fallen. This autocracy was confirmed and perpetuated by the overthrow of mother-right, the introduction of father-right, and the gradual transition of the pairing marriage into monogamy. But this tore a breach in the old gentile order; the single family became a power, and its rise was a menace to the gens.

The inequalities of property among the individual heads of families break up the. The transition old communal household communities wherever they had still managed to survive, and with them the common cultivation of the soil by and for these communities. The cultivated land is allotted for use to single families, at first temporarily, later permanently to full private property is gradually accomplished, parallel with the transition of the pairing marriage into monogamy. The single family is becoming the economic unit of society.[20] (emphasis added).

And so it is right there in their own words: the enterprising individual man has stolen the girl from the collective, and the communists want her back! And in that, we find the reasoning behind modern-day feminism. More on that in following chapters when we get to the strands, but for now, we continue to the center of the web.

Marx and Engels published their iconic *The Communist Manifesto* in 1848. "Marxism" helped make the following world-famous:

> II Proletarians and Communists:
>
> [T]he theory of Communists may be summed up in a single sentence: Abolition of private property.
>
> We Communists have been reproached with the desire of abolishing the right of personally acquiring property as a fruit of a man's own labour, which property is alleged to be the groundwork of all personal freedom, activity and independence...
>
> *And the abolition of this state of things is called by the bourgeois, abolition of individuality and freedom! And rightly so. The abolition of bourgeois individuality, bourgeois independence, and bourgeois freedom is undoubtedly aimed at* (emphasis added).

It is one thing for me or anybody else to tell you that the destruction of our property rights is the destruction of the very foundation upon which our free society stands and, therefore, *must* be preserved. But it is quite another for one to hear *the* enemies of our freedom and independence say in their own words that they want to destroy those same property rights for the very same reason we want to preserve them! Our very *freedom* and independence depend on them! Now, you know not only are the champions of Individual Liberty absolutely correct in this analogy but that *the* sworn enemies of that freedom and independence know it as well! *Any* assumption that property rights are in any way negotiable to a free people is of the philosophy that seeks to destroy them!

> You are horrified at our intending to do away with private property. But in your existing society, private property is already done away with for nine-tenths of the population; its existence for the few is solely due to its non-existence in the hands of those nine-tenths. You reproach us, therefore, with intending to do away with a form of property, the necessary condition for whose existence is the non-existence of any property for the immense majority of society. In one word, you reproach us with intending to do away with your property. Precisely so; that is just what we intend. From the moment when labour can no longer be converted into capital, money, or rent, into a social power capable of being monopolised, *i.e.*, from the moment when individual property can no longer be transformed into bourgeois property, into capital, from that moment, you say, indi-

viduality vanishes. [*You must, therefore, confess that by "individual" you mean no other person than the bourgeois, than the middle-class owner of property. This person must, indeed, be swept out of the way, and made impossible*]…(emphasis added) But don't wrangle with us so long as you apply, to our intended abolition of bourgeois property, the standard of your bourgeois notions of freedom, culture, law, &c. Your very ideas are but the outgrowth of the conditions of your bourgeois production and bourgeois property, just as your jurisprudence is but the will of your class made into a law for all, a will whose essential character and direction are determined by the economical conditions of existence of your class.

In the words of yet another one of its founders, all of what you have ever known to be you and yours is nothing short of *hated* by those who adhere to the Philosophy! You "must indeed, be swept away, and made impossible"! And the family?

> Abolition [*Aufhebung*] of the family! Even the most radical flare up at this infamous proposal of the Communists.
> On what foundation is the present family, the bourgeois family, based? On capital, on private gain. In its completely developed form, this family exists only among the bourgeoisie. But this state of things finds its complement in the practical absence of the family among the proletarians, and in public prostitution.

> The bourgeois family will vanish as a matter of course when its complement vanishes, and both will vanish with the vanishing of capital Do you charge us with wanting to stop the exploitation of children by their parents? To this crime we plead guilty. But, you say, we destroy the most hallowed of relations, when we replace home education by social. And your education! Is not that also social, and determined by the social conditions under which you educate, by the intervention direct or indirect, of society, by means of schools, &c.? The Communists have not invented the intervention of society in education; they do but seek to alter the character of that intervention, and to rescue education from the influence of the ruling class.
>
> The bourgeois clap-trap about the family and education, about the hallowed co-relation of parents and child, becomes all the more disgusting, the more, by the action of Modern Industry, all the family ties among the proletarians are torn asunder, and their children transformed into simple articles of commerce and instruments of labour.

All of our love, our values, our morals, and our traditions—along with the whole "honor thy mother and father" aspect of our traditional American family relationships—are to come to an abrupt end. The children must then, in the interest of "the collective," be taken from their parents at earlier and earlier ages (kindergarten and preschool) to be raised with allegiances not to their parents but to the state and the "general will" through "society education." More on this as well when we take a look at the Fabian Socialist John Dewey and his role as "the father" of modern education in a later chapter. In fact, if history is to be our guide, they will be trained to spy on and rat out not only neighbors but their parents as well!

> The bourgeois sees his wife a mere instrument of production. He hears that the instruments of production are to be exploited in common, and, naturally, can come to no other conclusion that the lot of being common to all will likewise fall to the women.
>
> He has not even a suspicion that the real point aimed at is to do away with the status of women as mere instruments of production.
>
> For the rest, nothing is more ridiculous than the virtuous indignation of our bourgeois at the community of women which, they pretend, is to be openly and officially established by the Communists....
>
> Our bourgeois, not content with having wives and daughters of their proletarians at their disposal, not to speak of common prostitutes, take the greatest pleasure in seducing each other's wives.
>
> Bourgeois marriage is, in reality, a system of wives in common and thus, at the most, what the Communists might possibly be reproached with is that they desire to introduce, in substitution for a hypocritically concealed, an openly legalised community of women. For the rest, it is self-evident that the abolition of the present system of production must bring with it the

abolition of the community of women springing from that system, *i.e.*, of prostitution both public and private.

[*The Communists are further reproached with desiring to abolish countries and nationality*].

It is the virtuous, monogamous woman and mother of the traditional family who is the whore; for it is they who, by giving birth, perpetuate the patriarchies of God, family, and the property of capitalism.

Without national sovereignty, we have no "We the People" constitution. We, along with any "right" we may profess, will be left to the mercy of the UN or other global overseer, whose doctrine would be comprised from this very philosophy!

The working men have no country. We cannot take from them what they have not got. Since the proletariat must first of all acquire political supremacy, must rise to be the leading class of the nation, must constitute itself *the* nation, it is so far, itself national, though not in the bourgeois sense of the word.

When the ancient world was in its last throes, the ancient religions were overcome by Christianity. When Christian ideas succumbed in the 18th century to rationalist ideas, feudal society fought its death battle with the then revolutionary bourgeoisie. The ideas of religious liberty and freedom of conscience merely gave expression to the sway of free competition within the domain of knowledge....

"Undoubtedly," it will be said, "religious, moral, philosophical, and juridical ideas have been modified in the course of historical development. But religion, morality, philosophy, political science, and law, constantly survived this change."

"There are, besides, eternal truths, such as Freedom, Justice, etc., that are common to all states of society. [*But Communism abolishes eternal truths, it abolishes all religion, and all morality*], instead of constituting them on a new basis; it therefore acts in contradiction to all past historical experience...."

IV

In short, the [*Communists everywhere support every revolutionary movement against the existing social and political order of things*]... (emphasis added)

The Communists....openly declare that their ends can be attained only by the forcible overthrow of all existing social conditions. Let the ruling classes tremble at a Communist revolution. The proletarians have nothing to lose but their chains. They have a world to win[21] (emphasis added).

And upon the rubble of our bourgeois capitalist system, before the "new normal" rises, shall "Year Zero" (Pol Pot) be declared and obeyed! All historical and "eternal truths" abolished forever! In the end, it is this philosophy that is behind the "revolution" to wipe the "three-headed Hydra" of *God, family,* and *capitalism* from the face of the earth! We have seen it in their own words! We have seen the reasoning behind their ongoing "revolution" to establish a "true dictatorship" of a Godless, moralless, propertyless, will-less, even wifeless proletariat. When you think about it, it only makes sense. As "family" embodies long-established relationships, traditions, love, and trust, it is the one aspect of humanity strong enough to resist the infiltration and propaganda of any offending doctrine and, by God's grace, even that of Satan himself!

Capitalism, which alone embodies both *Individual Liberty* and *property*, is none other than the one and only earthly avenue to the *freedom* of being able to provide for oneself and family, the *empowerment* of "free will" and the *dignity* of standing your own ground! Wherever we have these things, we have our independence, and no need for those of the Philosophy. Wherever we have no need for them, they are powerless! So it is in order to have their power over us they will stop at nothing to encourage, seduce, or force upon us that dependence. And with God, are not all things possible? But these are understandings of only one philosophy. We continue with the other:

From her 1911 *Anarchism and Other Essays*, further illustrating the topsy-turvy paradigm of this philosophy, there's this from *Mother Earth* magazine founder, Emma Goldman:

> "Prisons: A Social Crime and Failure"
> Says Havelock Ellis, the political criminal of our time or place may be the hero, martyr, saint of another age. Lombroso calls the political criminal the true precursor of the progressive movement of humanity....
> The occasional criminal "represents by far the largest class of our prison population, hence is the greatest menace to social well-be-

ing." What is the cause that compels a vast army of the human family to take to crime, to prefer the hideous life within prison walls to the life outside? Certainly that cause must be an iron master, who leaves its victims no avenue of escape, for the most depraved human being loves liberty....

There is close relation, says Havelock Ellis, between crimes against the person and the price of alcohol, between crimes against property and the price of wheat. He quotes Quetelet and Lacassagne, the former looking upon society as the preparer of crime, and the criminals as instruments that execute them. The latter find that "the social environment is the cultivation medium of criminality...*every society has the criminals it deserves*"....

Edward Carpenter estimates [*that five-sixths of indictable crimes consist in some violation of property rights; but that is too low a figure. A thorough investigation would prove that nine crimes out of ten could be traced, directly or indirectly, to our economic and social iniquities, to our system of remorseless exploitation and robbery*]. (emphasis added)

Again, we see that it is our property rights—*the* foundation of capitalism—that are, via the laws that protect them, *the* cause of, nine tenths, of all crime, as well as all "economic and social iniquities" and "exploitation." It would then follow that those who "support" and "uphold" the Constitution and enforce the ensuing laws protecting that right to property would then especially be despised by this philosophy.

> The "majesty of the law"…is of a "higher" nature…steeped in the theological muddle, which proclaims punishment as a means of purification, or the vicarious atonement of sin.
>
> Society might with greater immunity *abolish all prisons* at once, than to hope for protection from these twentieth-century chambers of horrors.…
>
> With the social conscience awakened, the average individual may learn to refuse the "honor" of being a bloodhound of the law. He may cease to persecute, despise, and mistrust the social offender…it might be possible to free the prison victims (or "human prey") from the brutality of prison officials, guards, and keepers.…
>
> Prisoners have always worked; only the State has been their exploiter, even as the individual employer has been the robber of organized labor…If, then the State can be instrumental in robbing their helpless victims of such tremendous profits is it not high time for organized labor to…insist on decent remuneration for the convict, even as labor organizations claim for themselves?
>
> An ex-convict has needs. Prison life has made them anti-social beings, and the rigidly closed doors that meet them on their release are not likely to decrease their bitterness. The inevitable result is that they form a favorable nucleus

out of which scabs, black legs, detectives and policemen are drawn, only too willing to do their masters bidding...the workingman should insist on the right of the convict to work, he should meet him as a brother, take him into his organization, and with his aid turn against the system which grinds them both."

"I am not very sanguine that...any real change in that direction can take place until the *conditions that breed both prisoner and the jailer will forever be abolished*"[22] (emphasis added).

Here, from Goldman, we learn that it is actually the criminal who is the victim of our suppressive capitalist bourgeois system. Their victimhood can never end until the whole of that system is "forever abolished"! Ellis, whom she quotes, is the Fabian Socialist, "sexologist"/eugenist author of *Sexual Inversion* (1897) and *The Task of Social Hygiene* (1912). He is largely credited for jump-starting the "sexual revolution."

Voltairine de Cleyre, in her 1903 *Crime and Punishment*, agrees, reiterating:

> Probably nine-tenths of all offenses committed...various forms of stealing,— robbery, burglary, theft, embezzlement, forgery, counterfeiting, and the thousand and one ramifications and offshoots of the act of taking what the law defines as another's. It is impossible to consider crimes of violence apart from these, because the vast percentage of murders and assaults committed by the criminaloid class are simply inci-

dental to the commission of the so-called lesser crime. A man often murders in order to escape with his booty, though murder was no part of his original intention. Why, now, have we such a continually increasing percentage of stealing?

Will you persistently hide your heads in the sand and say it is because men grow worse as they grow wiser? that individual wickedness is the result of all our marvelous labors to compass sea and land, and make the earth yield up her wealth to us? Dare you say that?

"THE REASON MEN STEAL IS BECAUSE THEIR RIGHTS ARE STOLEN FROM THEM BEFORE THEY ARE BORN."

Now do we see that all men eat,— eat well? You know we do not Some have so much that they are sickened with the extravagance of dishes, and know not where next to turn for a new palatal sensation. They cannot even waste their wealth. Some, and they are mostly the hardest workers, eat poorly and fast, for their work allows them no time to enjoy even what they have…stand[ing] in long lines waiting for midnight and the plate of soup…whole blocks of them,…Some die because they cannot eat at all. Pray tell me what these last have to lose by becoming thieves. And why shall they not become thieves? And is the action of the man who takes the necessities which have been denied to him really criminal? Is he morally worse than the man who crawls in a cellar and dies of starvation? I think not He is only a little more assertive. Cardinal Manning said: "A starving man has a natural right to his neighbor's bread." The Anarchist says: "A hungry man has a social right to read"....

"But" you will say, and say truly, "to begin by taking loaves means to end by taking everything and murdering, too, very often." And in that you draw the indictment against your own system. If there is no alternative between starving and stealing (and for thousands there is none), then there is no alternative between society's murdering its members, or the members disintegrating society. Let Society consider its own mistakes, then: let it answer itself for all these people it has robbed and killed : let it cease its own crimes first!

These are the things that make criminals, the perverted forces of man, turned aside by the institution of property, which is the giant social mistake to-day. It is your law which keeps men from using the sources and the means of wealth production... it is this, and nothing else, which is responsible for all the second class of crimes and all those of violence incidentally committed while carrying out a robbery (emphasis added)...

There is a class of crimes of violence which arises from another set of causes than economic slavery—acts which are the result of an antiquated moral notion of the true relations of men and women. These are the Nemesis of the institution of property in love. If every one would learn that the limit of his right to demand a certain course of conduct in sex relations is himself; that the relation of his beloved ones to others is not a matter for him to regulate, any more than the relations of those whom he does not love; if the freedom of each is unquestioned, and whatever moral rigors are exacted are exacted of oneself only; if this principle is accepted and followed, crimes of jealousy will cease. But religions and governments uphold this institution and constantly tend to create the spirit of ownership, with all its horrible consequences.

If it wasn't for God's "morality" in our bourgeoisie property-based society, the whole of humanity could be one giant global orgy? Although it may be a humorous question, my point is not, as they really do mean it. Again, it is the morals of biblical religion that have spawned the institutions of marriage and monogamy, which in turn have enslaved woman to man as his *property*. Of course, this is what leads to jealousy, which in turn leads to crimes against woman and all "crimes of passion"—which are, in reality, "crimes of property." It is in this context that *women must be emancipated*!

As for thieves, the great thief is within the law, or he buys it; and as for the small one, see what you do! To protect yourself against him, you create a class of persons who are sworn to the service of the club and the revolver; a set of spies; a set whose business it is to deal constantly with these unhappy beings, who in rare instances are softened thereby, but in the majority of cases become hardened to their work as butchers to the use of the knife; a set whose business it is to serve cell and lock and key; and lastly, the lowest infamy of all, the hangman. Does any one want to shake his hand, the hand that kills for pay?

So in the end, is the only real purpose for our law Enforcement officers to keep our property from the starving masses? Who would want to shake the hands of such "a class of persons"? And from here emanates the revolutionary cry "abolish all Prisons"! Also from Voltairine de Cleyre there's one more piece:

> It was an imperfect illumination of the intellect, such only as was possible in those less enlightened days,…They appealed to all they had, the Bible, the inner light, the best that they knew, to justify their faith. We to whom a wider day is given, who can appeal not to one book but to thousands, who have the light of science"[23] (emphasis added).

When researching this philosophy, it all eventually leads back to God and scripture. Why? What is it about God and scripture that they must demonize in the name of "illuminated intellect" and "science"? As it is again, in their own words, that they have—time, time, and time again—led us to God and scripture, I defer myself to the same for some insight toward the answer:

> [M[y speech and my preaching was not with enticing words of man's wisdom, but in demonstration of the Spirit and of power: That your faith should not stand in the wisdom of men, but in the power of God. Howbeit we

speak wisdom among them that are perfect: yet not the wisdom of this world, nor for the prince of this world, that come to naught.

But we speak the wisdom of God in a mystery, even the hidden wisdom which God ordained before the world unto our glory; Which none of the princes of this world knew : for if they knew it, they would not have crucified the Lord of glory....

Now we have received, not the spirit of the world, but the spirit which is of God, that we might know the things that are freely given to us of God. Which things also we speak, not in the words which man's wisdom teacheth, but which the Holy Ghost teacheth; comparing spiritual things with spiritual.

But the natural man receiveth not the things of the Spirit of God: for they are foolishness unto him, neither can he now them, because they are spiritually discerned (emphasis added).

Let no man deceive himself. If any man among you seemeth to be wise in this world, let him become a fool, that he may be wise. For the wisdom of this world is foolishness with God. For it is written, He taketh the wise in their own craftiness...Therefore let no man glory in men.[24] (1 Corinthians 2)

Is there a difference between knowledge of this world and true wisdom? What value is the knowledge of a thousand books if true wisdom is, as scripture indicates, "spiritually discerned"? How is it that, for generations now, few have been able to see any of the many aspects of this "philosophy," which is the elephant in the room trampling upon our God-given Liberty? Even when shown, they still don't see? When people do see it, they wonder why nobody else can see it. To see, one must know the truth. To know the truth, one must obtain the wisdom that is "spiritually discerned." One can only obtain "spiritually discerned" wisdom through scripture. And key to it all is that one must humble himself/herself before God, as our founding fathers were well-known to do, to ask for His guidance and an understanding of them. If the common knowledge or "general will" of a society holds that God and scripture are nothing but "superstition" and/or antiquated "wives' fables," then who among the people might come to see that which they have embraced has come to enslave them? These are the things that must be considered if our natural God-given Liberty is to be preserved. And so it is that we shall.

Continuing with the mind-set of "The reason men steal is because their rights are stolen from them before they are born," in their 1969 document *You don't Need a Weatherman to Know Which Way the Wind Blows*, our understanding of the Philosophy expands even further with this from Weather Underground:

> Submitted by Karin Asbley, Bill Ayers, Bernardine Dohrn, John Jacobs, Jeff Jones, Gerry Long, Home Machtinger, Jim Mellen, Terry Robbins, Mark Rudd and Steve Tappis.
>
> I - So the very first question people in this country must ask in considering the question of revolution is where they stand in relation to the United States as an oppressor nation, and where they stand in relation to the masses of people

throughout the world whom US imperialism is oppressing.

Before we hear more of the Weather Underground (TWU), let us look for a moment to Lenin's 1916 *Imperialism, the Highest Stage of Capitalism* for some insight into this "imperialism":

> VII. IMPERIALISM AS A SPECIAL STAGE OF CAPITALISM
> Imperialism is capitalism at that stage of development at which the dominance of monopolies and finance capital is established; in which the export of capital has acquired pronounced importance; in which the division of the world among the international trusts has begun, in which the division of all territories of the globe among the biggest capitalist powers has been completed.[25]

With that clarification, we continue with the TWU:

> The primary task of revolutionary struggle is to solve this principal contradiction on the side of the people of the world. It is the oppressed peoples of the world who have created the wealth of this empire and it is to them that it belongs; the goal of the revolutionary struggle must be the control and use of this wealth in the interests of the oppressed peoples of the world.
> It is in this context that we must examine the revolutionary struggles in the United States. We are within the heartland of a worldwide

monster, a country so rich from its worldwide plunder that even the crumbs doled out to the enslaved masses within its borders provide for material existence very much above the conditions of the masses of people of the world.

If this is true, what do any of America's suppressed "interior colonies" stand to gain from a revolution?

The US empire, as a worldwide system, channels wealth, based upon the labor and resources of the rest of the world, into the United States. *The relative affluence existing in the United States is directly dependent upon the labor and natural resources of the Vietnamese, the Angolans, the Bolivians and the rest of the peoples of the Third World. All of the United Airlines Astrojets, all of the Holiday Inns, all of Hertz's automobiles, your television set, car and wardrobe already belong, to a large degree to the people of the rest of the world* (emphasis added).

The "war on cops", and/or the underlying anti-law enforcement sentiment of much of the revolutionary progressive movement is not by happenstance! Again, this is the concept of property in this philosophy. It is not a national concept but a global one! The "redistribution of wealth" goals are not from rich to poor in America but, rather, from an *unsustainable* overrich America to the world!

Therefore, any conception of "socialist revolution" simply in terms of the working people of the United States, failing to recognize the full scope of interests of the most oppressed peoples of the world, is a conception of a fight for a particular privileged interest, and is a very dangerous ideology. While the control and use of the wealth of the Empire for the people of the whole world is also in the interests of The vast majority of the people in this country, if the goal is not clear from the start we will further the preservation of class society, oppression, war, genocide, and the complete emiseration of everyone, including the people of the US.

The goal is the destruction of US imperialism and the achievement of a classless world: world communism (emphasis added).

II
Not every colony of people oppressed by imperialism lies outside the boundaries of the US. Black people within North America, brought here 400 years ago as slaves and whose labor, as slaves, built this country, are an internal colony within the confines of the oppressor nation. What this means is that black people are oppressed as a whole people.

And here it is that race is rolled into the collective progressive "revolution"—*not* for the benefit of that race but, as we will see, for the benefit of the Philosophy!

III
The struggle of black people—as a colony—is for self-determination, freedom, and

liberation from US imperialism. Because blacks have been oppressed...Black self-determination does not simply apply to determination of their collective political destiny at some future time. It is directly tied to the fact that because all blacks experience oppression in a form that no whites do, no whites are in a position to fully understand...This is why it is necessary for black people to organize separately and determine their actions separately at each stage of the struggle... the struggle for self-determination has had two stages: (1) *a united front against imperialism and for New Democracy* [emphasis added] (which is a joint dictatorship of anti-colonial classes led by the proletariat, the content of which is a compromise between the interests of the proletariat and nationalist peasants, petit bourgeoisie and national bourgeoisie); and (2) developing out of the new democratic stage, *socialism* [emphasis added].

It's all about the numbers for votes; they need the middle class! Then after they achieve "democratic socialism," from that, they can create a true socialist "dictatorship of the proletariat"! Once seduced into the Philosophy, the middle class—be they black, white, red, or whatever—literally becomes the means to its own end!

However, *the black liberation struggle in this country* will have only one "stage"; the struggle for self-determination *will embody within it the struggle for socialism* (emphasis added).

As Huey P. Newton (co-founder of Black Panther Party) has said, "In order to be a revolutionary nationalist, you would of necessity have to be a socialist." This is because—given the caste quality of oppression-as-a-people-through-a-common-degree-of-exploitation—self determination requires being free from white capitalist exploitation in the form of inferior (lower caste) jobs, housing, schools, hospitals, prices. In addition, only what was or became in practice a socialist program for self-determination—one which addressed itself to reversing this exploitation—could win the necessary active mass support in the "proletarian colony."

Remember, a revolution for "self-determination" is a revolution for your own country!

Much of the black petit bourgeoisie is actually a "comprador" petit bourgeoisie (like so-called black capitalists who are promoted by the power structure to seem independent but are really agents of white monopoly capital), who would never fight as a class for any real self-determination; and secondly, because many black petit bourgeoisie, perhaps most, while not having a class interest in socialist self-determination, are close enough to the black masses in the oppression and limitations on their conditions that they will support many kinds of self-determination issues, and, especially when the movement is winning, can be won to support full (socialist) self-determination. For the black movement to work to maximize this support from the petit bourgeoisie is correct; but it is in no way a united front where it is clear that the Black Liberation Movement should not and does not modify the revolutionary socialist content of its stand to win that support.

Remember this from Lenin:

> We must combine the purely proletarian struggle with the general peasant struggle, but not confuse the two. We must support the general democratic and general peasant struggle, but not become submerged in this non-class struggle....
>
> While giving the utmost support to the most determined democratism, that party will not allow itself to be diverted from the revolutionary path by reactionary dreams and experiments in "equalisation" under the system of commodity production.[6]

Back to the TWU:

> IV
>
> "What is the relationship of the struggle for black self-determination to the whole worldwide revolution to defeat US imperialism and internationalize its resources toward the goal of creating a classless world-

> No black self-determination could be won which would not result in a victory for the international revolution as a whole…a revolutionary nationalist movement could not win without destroying the state power of the imperialists; and it is for this reason that the black liberation movement, as a revolutionary nationalist movement for self-determination, is automatically in and of itself an inseparable part of the whole revolutionary struggle against US imperialism and for international socialism.
>
> However, the fact that black liberation depends on winning the whole revolution does not mean that it depends on waiting for and joining with a mass white movement to do it. The genocidal oppression of black people must be ended, and does not allow any leisure time to wait; if necessary, black people could win self-determination, abolishing the whole imperialist system and seizing state power to do it, without this white movement.

A couple questions here for the suppressed "interior colonies" to consider: (1) Is it me, or do the calls for revolutionary action in this well-planned philosophy generally emanate from nonminority organizations directly or indirectly associated with the esteemed "ivory towers" of upper crust academia and/or those of privileged white backgrounds? (2) Is this your struggle that these revolutionaries support, or their revolution they want you to fight?

> When imperialism is defeated in the US,
> it will be replaced by socialism—nothing else…

> US imperialism is stronger, but also more vulnerable, than any imperialism of the past....
>
> *The strategy which flows from this is what Ché called "creating two, three, many Vietnams"* (emphasis added)—to mobilize the struggle so sharply in so many places that the imperialists cannot possibly deal with it all.

As nothing uses up our recourses and spends more of our money than the US military, there is no quicker way to drain them both from America than by keeping them activated and responding to multiple simultaneous crisis all around the world. Coincidentally, as reported by the *Washington Post* (June 4, 2010), "The Obama administration has significantly expanded a largely secret U.S. war against al-Qaeda and other radical groups...Special Operations forces have grown both in number and budget, and are deployed in 75 countries."[26] Any and all effort to demoralize our military would only serve to amplify the effect this strategy would have on our soldiers. And who quotes Che anyway?

> *Black people as a colony*...reflect the interests of the oppressed people of the world from within the borders of the United States; they *are part of the Third World* and part of the international revolutionary vanguard.

> VIII
> The crisis in imperialism has brought about a breakdown in bourgeois social forms, culture and ideology. The family falls apart, kids leave home, women begin to break out of traditional "female" and "mother" roles. There devel-

ops a "generation gap" and a "youth problem." *Our heroes are no longer struggling businessmen, and we also begin to reject the ideal career of the professional and look to Mao, Chef, the Panthers, the Third World, for our models.*

IX

Kids are ready for the full scope of militant struggle, and already demonstrate a consciousness of imperialism…to tell a kid in New York that imperialism tracks him and thereby oppresses him is often small potatoes compared to his consciousness that imperialism oppresses him by jailing him, pigs and all, and the only thing to do is break out and tear up the jail…*the breakdown of the family is crucial* to the woman question….

There must be a strong revolutionary women's movement, for without one it will be impossible for women's liberation to be an important part of the revolution. Revolutionaries must be made to understand the full scope of women's oppression, and the necessity to smash male supremacy.

X

We will only reach the high school kids who are in motion by being in the schoolyards, hangouts and on the streets on an everyday basis. From a neighborhood base, high school kids could be effectively tied in to struggles around other institutions and issues, and to the anti-imperialist move-

ment as a whole. We will try to involve neighborhood kids who aren't in high schools too; take them to anti-war or anti-racism fights, etc (emphasis added).

Again, the family is targeted: First by a "strong, revolutionary woman's movement" to "emancipate" mom from the family unit. Second, by their effort to use, or "involve neighborhood kids" and "high school kids". Nobody is safe from being utilized by this philosophy in their efforts to bring down the system that was "ordained" by our founders to be our free Constitutional Republic.

XI

The pigs are the capitalist state,… pigs are sweaty working-class barbarians who over-react and commit "police brutality"…understand pigs as the repressive imperialist State doing its job. Our job is not to avoid the issue of the pigs as "diverting" from anti-imperialist struggle, but to emphasize that they are our real enemy if we fight that struggle to win.

Pigs come down on people in everyday life in enforcing capitalist property relations, bourgeois laws and bourgeois morality; they guard stores and factories and the rich and enforce credit and rent against the poor. The overwhelming majority of arrests in America are for crimes against property.

The pigs will be coming down on the kids we're working with in the schools, on the streets, around dope; we should focus on them, point them out all the time, like the Panthers do. We should

> *relate the daily oppression by the pig to their role in political repression, and develop a class understanding of political power and armed force among the kids we're with.*
>
> As we develop a base these two aspects of the pig role increasingly Come together. In the schools, pig is part of daily oppression—keeping order...our job is to defeat the pigs and the army, and organize on that basis... *"political power comes out of the barrel of a gun"*[27] (emphasis added).

If you ever wondered why cops generally wind up having bottles or rocks chucked at them at most, if not all, anticapitalist, anti-imperialist, and Occupy Wall Street rallies, there's your answer.

Is any of this starting to sound a little familiar? As bad as what we have just read from the Weather Underground is, none of it is anything new philosophically from anything we have already heard so far.

The following is a transcript from a 1982 documentary titled *Nowhere to Hide*. In it, FBI Agent Larry Grathwohl presented the following after he had just infiltrated the Weather Underground:

> LARRY GRATHWOHL, FBI AGENT: I brought up the subject of what is going to happen after we take over the government. You know, we become responsible then for administrating 250 million people.
>
> And there was no answer. And no one had given any thought to economics, how are you going to clothe and feed these people. The only thing that I could get was that they expected

that the Cubans and the North Vietnamese and the Chinese and the Russians would all want to occupy different portions of the United States.

The immediate responsibility would be to protect against what they call against the counter-revolution.

And they felt that this counter-revolution could best be guarded against by creating and establishing reeducation centers in the Southwest, where we would take all the people who needed to be reeducated into the new way of thinking and teach them how things were going to be.

I asked, well, what is going to happen to those people that we can't reeducate, that are die-hard capitalists? And the reply was they would have to be eliminated. And when I pursued this further, they estimated that they would have to eliminate 25 million people in these reeducation centers. And when I say "eliminate," I mean kill—25 million people.[28]

Reality check: This is Communism. This is Socialism. This is the Philosophy!

The TWU was formed by members of "Students for a Democratic Society" (SDS) and the "Revolutionary Youth Movement" (RYM). Out of the roots of TWU came many new shoots including the Welfare Rights Organization, Acorn, and Project Vote. From the examiner.com:

> Keep in mind, ACORN is founded by these former Weather Underground. Even

Progressives for Obama is Ayers and Dohrn founded. Project vote was founded by Zach Pollett. Tom Hayden, Senator, founder of MoveOn.org, former husband of Jane Fonda, is former Weather Underground. Wade Rathke, founder of Acorn, is another one. So is Drummond Pike. Pike founded Tides.

The following excerpt is a reference excerpt that was taken from "Weather Underground, ACORN and Obama; The Ties That bind" by Mondoreb on 1,000 Papercuts.com The excerpt was originally taken from *ACORN: Who Funds the Weather Underground's Little Brother?* by Matthew Vadum:

> Zach Pollett, for instance, was Project Vote's executive director and Acorn's political director, until July, when he relinquished the former title. Mr. Pollett continues to work as a consultant for Project Vote through another Acorn affiliate.

Obama's Fight the Smears website says:

> Obama has admitted to working for Project Vote in 1992 when he ran a "successful voter Registration drive." He continues to say, "ACORN was not part of Project Vote."
>
> Mr. Obama is right; but *Project Vote was part of ACORN* (emphasis added). It is also no secret that Mr. Obama was once the attorney for ACORN in 1995 and was known as a rather

large attraction for speaking engagements at ACORN functions.[29]

Members of the Weather Underground and SDS; Tides Foundation; Center for American Progress; Van Jones's communist revolutionary organization, STORM; Black Radical Congress, SEIU, and AFL-CIO; Democratic Socialists of America (DSA); and the pro-Soviet, anti-American Institute for Policy Studies would all go on to become the Apollo Alliance, which openly and proudly authored Obama's first stimulus bill.

Be it as it may, it is not my objective here to go into the details of identifying how each of the strands of the web connect to each other and to the Obama administration, not only because the multitude of them would take a huge book all of its own to decipher and document but because it has already been done by others. And in reality, as sad as it sounds, it's rooted much deeper in America today than just the Obama administration and some revolutionaries. Consider them the mushroom caps but not the fungus itself that has become systemic, integrated throughout the whole of our being so completely that this could very well be mankind's *last call for liberty*! A parasitic fungus that is rooted so tenaciously that if man alone were to attempt to pull it out by its roots, it would quite literally turn us inside out, leaving nothing from which to rebuild.

Anyway, point being, from the TWU, the Philosophy pervasively blooms in many forms and in many directions. It is my objective, however, to present to you some of the different shades of the Philosophy behind the infestation in its own words that you might recognize it for what it is, no matter where, when, or how it blooms. And so we continue.

From Raymond Franklin and Solomon Resnik's 1973 *The Political Economy of Racism*, we not only get more clarification of anti-imperialism and anticolonialism but of the source of the predetermined philosophy behind why the Tea Party has to be racist:

> P107- "The black tragedy is that black Americans constitute a quasi-colony. They suffer from recourse drain without serious hope of transforming their homeland, a permanent ghetto, into a self-propelling, self-developing nation or community."
>
> P109- "Put simply, no solution to the black predicament is possible until issues of our empire are properly reduced by the defeat of American imperialism, and that cannot be accomplished only by (third world) peasants and guerilla armies. It must be undertaken here at home in a battle for a decent and meaningful existence. But her-in lies the danger: it will produce a stream of frustrated right wing cadre of considerable size in all parts of the country whose energies will increasingly be devoted to politics. This demagogic cadre will have roots among middle-class whites (white & blue collar alike). Their fears and hatred of blacks will find political expression"
>
> P113- (quoting Stokley Carmichael from speech in Cuba 1967) "In these cities we do not control our recourses, we do not control the land, the houses or the stores. These are controlled by whites who live outside the community. These very real colonies, as their capital and cheap labor are exploited by those who live outside the cities. White power makes laws with

guns and nightsticks in the hands of white racist policeman and black mercenaries."[30]

Then there was the Maoist International Movement or MIM, which published this in their Notes 162, May 15, 1998 issue:

> *By a MIM comrade*
> Washington, D.C., the U.$. capital city and the city with the greatest number of police officers per capita in the country, has had the highest (illegal) murder rate of any large city over the past 10 years. Police-state zealots conclude from this that D.C., like other cities, needs more and more pigs policing the streets. Revolutionaries know increased numbers of police are not the answer to crime. In fact, the proliferation of Amerikkka's police force only increases the violence which is committed against the masses.
> Amerikkka is at war with its internal semi-colonies. Amerikkka systematically denies oppressed nations the right to self-determination and control over political, economic and military affairs. The Amerikkkan police state enforces the oppressive relationship between the white nation and internal semi-colonies through its illegitimate INjustice system. Amerikkkan domination depends on its ability to control the oppressed through massive round ups by the Amerikkkan pigs into the ever-increasing prison system.

The high number of illegal murders mostly result from current systematic poverty and inequality. And it is the occupying settler police army which enforces national oppression. Above all, more pigs does not mean that the causes for crime are eradicated. Increasing the number of agents of Amerikka's police state will only strengthen Amerikkka's war against oppressed nations....

MIM refers to "illegal murders" in this case because the biggest murderers—the imperialists, their corporations and their armies—aren't doing anything illegal by bourgeois standards, and their crimes go unreported in official crime statistics.

Washington, D.C. is the murder capital of the world in more ways than one. Besides the illegal murder rates, D.C. is the seat of power for the most murderous imperialist power in the world: the United Snakes of Imperialism....

This is also the police state that murderously crushed the Maoist revolutionary Black Panther Party of the late 1960s, whose plan for self-reliance and self-determination for the Black nation would have...countered (the) economic isolation of the urban lumpenproletariat, all of which fuel today's illegal murder rate. Just as all nations oppressed by imperialism throughout the world, oppressed nations within the illegitimate U.$. borders need self determination and national liberation. These are the products of revolutionary struggle, not a stronger occupying army of police.[31]

No, Obama's Reverend Jeremiah Wright was not the first to refer to America as *AmeriKKKa*. For its implications, MIM Notes No. 200 (December 15, 1999) clarifies:

> MIM takes the spelling of Amerika with a "k" from the revolutionary movements of the 1970s. The term "United States" is inappropriate for a country that occupies thousands of First Nations, the Black nation, Aztlan and Puerto Rico. This country is not in fact "United" but is a substantial empire extending throughout u.$. borders and beyond….
>
> We use angry language because the oppressed and exploited have a lot to be angry about, these are the people in whose interests we work. If you want an organization that uses calm tones, the Democratic Party or the Greens might be for you. Our middle-class critics are inclined to believe that there is a neutral educational tone appropriate for all communications. In reality, a neutral tone is not appropriate for the emergency situation that exists today.[32]

Wherever one sees America spelled *Amerika* or *Amerikkka*, it is code, a statement of revolutionary significance declaring her racist illegitimacy! For even a better understanding of what MIM is and about, we go to their August 1996 Program of the Maoist Internationalist Movement:

JOE MARSHALL

"WHAT WE WANT
WHAT WE BELIEVE"

1. We want communism.

We believe that communism is the elimination of all oppression-the power of groups over other groups. This includes national oppression, class oppression, and gender oppression.

2. We want socialism.

We believe that socialism is the path to communism. We believe that the current dictatorship of the bourgeoisie oppresses the world's majority. We believe that socialism—the dictatorship of the proletariat and peasantry—is a necessary step towards a world without inequality or dictatorship—a communist world. We uphold the USSR under Lenin and Stalin (1917–953) and China under Mao (1949–1976) as models in this regard.

3. We want revolutionary armed struggle.

We believe that the oppressors will not give up their power without a fight. Ending oppression is only possible by building public opinion to seize power through armed struggle. We believe, however, that armed struggle in the imperialist countries is a serious strategic mistake until the bourgeoisie becomes really helpless. Revolution will become a reality for North America as the U.S. military becomes over-extended in the government's attempts to maintain world hegemony.

"We are advocates of the abolition of war, we do not want war; but war can only be abolished through war, and in order to get rid of the gun it is necessary to take up thegun."—Mao Zedong

4. We want organization.

We believe that democratic-centralism, the system of unified application of majority decisions, is necessary to defeat the oppressors. This system includes organization, leadership, discipline and hierarchy. The oppressors use these weapons, and we should, too. By building a disciplined revolutionary communist vanguard party, we follow in the tradition of comrades Lenin, Mao and Huey Newton.

5. We want independent institutions of and for the oppressed.

We believe that the oppressed need independent media to build public opinion for socialist revolution. We believe that the oppressed need independent institutions to provide land, bread, housing, education, medical care, clothing, justice and peace. We believe that the best independent institution of all is a self-reliant socialist government.

6. We want continuous revolution.

We believe that class struggle continues under socialism. We believe that under socialism, the danger exists for a new bourgeoisie to arise within the communist party itself. We believe that these new oppressors will restore capitalism unless they are stopped. We believe that the bourgeoisie seized power in the USSR after the death of Stalin in 1953; in China it was after Mao's death and the overthrow of the "Gang of Four" in 1976. We believe that China's Great Proletarian Cultural Revolution (1966–1976) is the farthest advance towards communism in human history, because it mobilized millions of people against the restoration of capitalism.

7. We want a united front against imperialism.

We believe that the imperialists are currently waging a hot war—a World War III—against the world's oppressed nations, including the U.S. empire's internal colonies. We seek to unite all who can be united under proletarian and feminist leadership against imperialism, capitalism and patriarchy.

We believe that the imperialist-country working classes are primarily a pro-imperialist labor aristocracy at this time. Likewise, we believe that the biological-wimmin of the imperialist countries are primarily a gender aristocracy. Thus, while we recruit individuals from these and other reactionary groups to work against their class, national and gender interests, we do not seek strategic unity with them. In fact, we believe that the imperialist-country working-classes and imperialist-country biological-wimmin, like the bourgeoisies and petit-bourgeoisies, owe reparations to the international proletariat and peasantry. As such, one of the first strategic steps MIM will take upon winning state power will be to open the borders.

We believe that socialism in the imperialist countries will require the dictatorship of the international proletariat and that the imperialist-country working-classes will need to be on the receiving end of this dictatorship.

8. We want New Democracy for the oppressed nations. We want power for the oppressed nations to determine their destinies.

We believe that oppressed people will not be free until they are able to determine their destinies. We look forward to the day when oppressed people will live without imperialist police terror and will learn to speak their mind without fear of the consequences from the oppressor. When this day comes, meaningful plebiscites can be held in which the peoples will decide for themselves if they want their own separate nation- states or some other arrangement.

9. We want world revolution.

We believe it is our duty to support Marxism- Leninism-Maoism everywhere, though our principal task is to build public opinion and independent institutions in preparation for Maoist revolution in North America. The imperialists think and act globally—we must do the same.

10. We want politics in command.

We believe that correct tactics flow from correct strategies, which flow from a correct ideological and political line. We believe that the fight against imperialism, capitalism and patriarchy goes hand-in-hand with the fight against revisionism, chauvinism, and opportunism.

"The correctness or otherwise of the ideological and political line decides everything. When the Party's line is correct, then everything will come its way. If it has no followers, then it can have followers; if it has no guns, then it can have guns; if it has no political power, then it can have political power." —Mao Zedong[33]

By now, we get the picture. It is the whole of our very being that is not only despised but hated. From the Constitution, the Republic it establishes, its military, and its laws down to the law enforcement officers who enforce them, God, capitalism, family, and the individual—all must be destroyed! Every bit of it is of bourgeois, by bourgeois, and for bourgeois!

Fire To The Prisons (*FTTP*), in their No. 11 Spring 2011 issue, brings it all home:

This society seeks to suppress, we want to bring all of ourselves to… our conflict with this society aimed at its destruction, so that we struggle with all the strength necessary to accomplishing our aim. It is in this light, as anarchists, that *we would best understand the place of hatred... We have an immense task before us: the destruction of the present social order. Hatred of the enemy--of the ruling order and all who willfully uphold it.*

We are all involved in a class conflict which politics cannot contain. Police violence doesn't happen in a vacuum; it happens because there is a capitalist economy based on property and the circulation of commodities, which the police defend and enforce on behalf of the rich. For the rest of us—the exploited and excluded classes - riots and sabotage will be the weapons we use. *The one upside to the world being colonized by the state/capital system is that there are targets everywhere, so conspire with your friends!* We are free only when we revolt; we won't be truly free until we totally destroy the current system. Pull back the iron curtain of law and order, and nurture the capacities of rebellious community...Breaking things at night is somewhere to start...Solidarity means attack!

"DEATH TO THE POLICE AND THE CLASS THAT HOLDS THEIR LEASHES!"

"DEATH TO THE WORLD OF WAGE SLAVERY AND WORK!" (capitalization original)

It is important to recognize that most people are currently in jail for financially driven crimes. We don't mean white-collar crimes. But crimes that stem from trying to overcome pov-

> erty or survive capitalism…It is understandable that given the opportunity, legal or not, those who were born into poverty would look for any chance to get out of it…Bank Robbers, grand theft auto, kidnapping, prostitution, or shoplifting are a few other examples…that *stem from the struggle to overcome the poverty of capitalism*[34] (p. 5, emphasis added).

Until presented and seen in this context, the importance and magnitude of what the Michael Brown/Officer Darren Wilson case in Ferguson, Missouri, and the Trayvon Martin/Zimmerman case in Florida represent cannot be fully comprehended. Racism is not *the* problem but merely a symptom of the real problem—the *whiteness* of property!

In April 2012, MIM (Prisons) posted an article titled "Travon Martin Murder One More Case of Imperialist Oppression" that included the following:

> Here we are in this endless cycle of genocide inflicted on the internal semi-colonies… As in the Trayvon Martin murder,…We know Amerika *is* Zimmerman! Zimmerman is only a physical manifestation of imperialism. Imperialism, like Zimmerman, travels the world stalking Third World nations and then attacking the oppressed nation, latching on and sucking the blood, the resources, leaving a lifeless corpse in its place….
>
> Racism is generally understood by revolutionaries first and foremost as an outgrowth of the ruling class, which nurtures these white

> supremacists into fascist foot soldiers. They are imperialism's reserve army and are intertwined with the state apparatus. They have a mutual interest in keeping things "the way they are... These bourgeois politicians serve the ruling class, they serve capital, they serve Wall Street. Our justice may not come tomorrow but it will surely come, and until then let us prepare the people for the cold reality in Amerika."[35]

MIM Prisons and *Fire to the Prisons* are just a couple of a number of revolutionary "prison-activist and political prisoner support movements" sending revolutionary works into our prisons, without which this writer would never have heard of them. So much for rehabilitation! Others include the Real Cost of Prisons Project (RCPP); the National Jericho Movement and Queers United in Support of Political Prisoners; the Prisoner Revolutionary Literature Fund (PRLF), "an educational literature fund that fills requests from U.S. prisoners for revolutionary literature"; and the Anarchist Black Cross that seeks "the total abolition of prisons"—all of which are organized against "the system" and what is referred to as the Prison Industrial Complex of the United States. And then there's the Labor Action Committee to Free Cop Killer Mumia Abu-Jamal, whose website states "is a group of union activists dedicated to educating workers about Jamal's case and promoting labor action in solidarity with his struggle." Their founding statement includes:

> We recognize that the persecution and death-row incarceration of Mumia Abu-Jamal is a blatant attack on the working class and all victims of oppression, for whom Jamal is such an eloquent spokesman. We also recognize that

relief for Mumia cannot be expected from the biased and racist so-called "justice" system in this country. Furthermore, workers have the power to free political prisoners such as Jamal through class-struggle action against the bosses and their state.[36]

The extent to what the revolutionaries of this philosophy consider legitimate tangible resistance is spelled out for us first in this also published by *FTTP* as they continue:

All action which impede Prison's aim of Social Control can be considered tangible Resistance.

- Chronology of Resistance -

-10/1/10 Santa Barbara, CA, USA – A Santa Barbara County jail Deputy suffered a broken nose and bruises to their head and torso after they were punched and kicked by an inmate

- 10/6/10 Florence, CO, USA – A United States Penitentiary Administrative Maximum Facility guard was stabbed three times with a homemade weapon.

- 10/26/10 Martinez, CA, USA – An inmate at Contra Costa County Jail faked a seizure and hit a nurse over the head with a lamp. The nurse later died from her injuries.

-11/13/10 Monticello, NY, USA – A Sullivan County Corrections Officer was punched in the mouth while trying to restrain an inmate who refused to enter their cell.

-12/18/10 Toronto, Ontario, Canada – An inmate being booked into the Toronto West Detention Center attacked two guards with a roofing hammer and "uttered death threats" as he smashed computers and furniture in the prison admissions area.

- 1/29/11 Seattle, WA, USA – A State Corrections Officer was found strangled with a microphone cord in the prison chapel at Washington State Prison.[34] (*FTTP* 11 [Spring 2011], 61; emphasis added)

And then again, by King Samir Shabaaz of the New Black Panther Party in this July 6, 2010, transcript:

>Samir: "My job is to educate black people, whether they want to be educated or not. I don't give a damn what they may think about white people, *I hate white people. All of them. Every last iota of a cracker I hate him*. Because we are still in this condition.
>
>We didn't come out here to play. There is to much serious business going on in your black community to be sliding through south street with *white, dirty cracker whores* on your arms.

> What's a matter with you black man, you got a doomsday with a white woman on your arm.
>
> We keep begging white people for freedom. No wonder we're not free. Your enemy can not make you free fool. You want freedom *you're going to have to kill some crackers. You're going to have to kill some of their babies*[37] (emphasis added).

The hatred within this philosophy for America and American society, her laws, law enforcement officers, and any and "all that is in any way connected" to the "laws about property"—the very foundation upon which our freedom and independence stands—is so great that even the death of a nurse is considered "tangible resistance"? You bet! It's a hard but necessary pill to swallow, but as jarring as a revelation this wake-up call is, our understanding of both the breadth and depth of this philosophy is still incomplete. There is still one more stop to make.

Now that we have come this deep into the realm of this philosophy, are not all things up, down? All things wrong, right? All things good, bad? And all things true, false? Who is it that could even conceive of such a place that holds so much hate? Is it a coincidence that all things considered an "injustice" here are eventually laid at the feet of God? Bakunin leaves little room for doubt in this from his 1871 work *God and the State*, where he brings us at once to our primary objective—the center of the web—that we might find by whom that it has been cast:

> Chapter I
>
> The Bible, which is a very interesting and here and there very profound book when considered as one of the oldest surviving manifes-

tations of human wisdom and fancy, expresses this truth very naively in its myth of original sin. Jehovah, who of all the good gods adored by men was certainly the most jealous, the most vain, the most ferocious, the most unjust, the most bloodthirsty, the most despotic, and the most hostile to human dignity and liberty—Jehovah had just created Adam and Eve, to satisfy we know not what caprice; no doubt to while away his time, which must weigh heavy on his hands in his eternal egoistic solitude, or that he might have some new slaves. He generously placed at their disposal the whole earth, with all its fruits and animals, and set but a single limit to this complete enjoyment. He expressly forbade them from touching the fruit of the tree of knowledge. He wished, therefore, that man, destitute of all understanding of himself, should remain an eternal beast, ever on all-fours before the eternal God, his creator and his master. But here steps in Satan, the eternal rebel, the first freethinker and the emancipator of worlds. He makes man ashamed of his bestial ignorance and obedience; he emancipates him, stamps upon his brow the seal of liberty and humanity, in urging him to disobey and eat of the fruit of knowledge.[38]

Alinsky, likewise, opens his book *Rules for Radicals* with the following:

> Lest we forget at least an over-the-shoulder acknowledgment to the very first radical: from all our legends, mythology, and history (and who is to know where mythology leaves off and history begins—or which is which), the first radical known to man who rebelled against the establishment and did it so effectively that he at least won his own Kingdom—Lucifer.[4]

If the Philosophy boils down to a revolution against the hated "three-headed Hydra," as it has been shown that it does, then their revolution against it can be reduced even further to just three words: "good against evil." And considering all we have just read, it only makes sense that it is none other than Satan who is held by this philosophy as its great "emancipator of worlds."

Also with Bakunin's forthright confirmation, we come to the humbling realization that we, as free Americans, *cannot* undo by our efforts alone that which *has not* been spun and cast upon us by man alone. We must, as a humble people, remember, as is declared in the Declaration of Independence and throughout the writings of our founders, what we have always known—that our very Independence and freedom would not and could not have ever even been hard-won and "secured" for us to begin with but for "a firm reliance on the protection of Divine Providence."

Endnotes

Chapter 1: To the Center of the Web

1. Obama, Roanoke, Virginia 7/13/12 - http://www.washingtontimes.com/blog/watercooler/2012/jul/15/picketvideo-obama-if-youve-got-business-you-didnt-/
2. Elizabeth Warren, September of 2011 in Andover, Massachusetts - http://www.businessinsider.com/the-viral-video-of-elizabeth-warren-going-after-gop-on-class-warfare-2011-9
3. Kropotkin- Law & Authority 1886 http://dwardmac.pitzer.edu/anarchist_archives/kropotkin/lawauthority.html
4. Saul Alinsky – "Rules For Radicals" 1969
5. Michelle Obama- Democrat National Convention, August 28, 2008 http://articles.cnn.com/2008-08-25/politics/michelle.obama.transcript_1_multiple-sclerosis-mom-greatest-gift/5?_s=PM:POLITICS
6. Vladimir Lenin. In his 1905 piece on "Petty-Bourgeois and Proletarian Socialism" http://www.marxists.org/archive/lenin/works/1905/oct/25.htm
7. Lenin -"Left-Wing Communism: an Infantile Disorder Should we Participate in Bourgeois Parliaments?" 1920 http://www.marxists.org/archive/lenin/works/1920/lwc/ch07.htm
8. "Remarks by President Obama at Young African Leaders Initiative Town Hall University of Johannesburg-Soweto Johannesburg, South Africa," June 29, 2013

http://www.whitehouse.gov/the-press-office/2013/06/29/remarks-president-obama-young-african-leaders-initiative-town-hall
9. Michael Bakunin - 1871 "Man, Society, Freedom
http://www.marxists.org/reference/archive/bakunin/works/1871/man-society.htm
10. Thomas Hobbes, "Leviathan" in 1651
http://archive.org/stream/hobbessleviathan00hobbuoft/hobbessleviathan00hobbuoft_djvu.txt
11. Jean Jacques Rousseau, "THE SOCIAL CONTRACT OR PRINCIPLES OF POLITICAL RIGHT" 1762,
12. Locke, "Second Treaties", Section 6 1690
http://www.constitution.org/jl/2ndtr02.txt
13. Max Stirner, "The Ego And His Own", "All Things Are Nothing To Me" 1845
http://flag.blackened.net/daver/anarchism/stirner/theego1.html#pp7
14. Pierre-Joseph Proudhon, "What is Property?" 1841
http://www.marxists.org/reference/subject/economics/proudhon/property/index.htm
15. Errico Malatesta, "Anarchy" 1891
http://robertgraham.wordpress.com/2010/02/28/errico-malatesta-anarchy-1891/
16. Henry David Thoreau, "Civil Disobedience" 1849
http://thoreau.eserver.org/civil.html
17. Friedrich A. Hayek, "The Road To Serfdom" 1944 (The Definitive Edition 2007) pg 110–111
18. Robert Dale Owen, "A Declaration of Mental Independence" 1826
http://www.atheists.org/content/declaration-mental-independence-robert-owen

(Transcendentalists-A Patriots Guide of the United States, Schweikart/Allen p 224–23)

19. Frederick Engels - "Origins of the Family, Private Property, and the State" 1884 II. The Family, 4. The Monogamous Family
http://www.marxists.org/archive/marx/works/1884/origin-family/ch02d.htm
20. Engels - Origins of the Family, Private Property, and the State" - IX. "Barbarism and Civilization"
http://www.marxists.org/archive/marx/works/1884/origin-family/ch09.htm
21. Karl Marx & Fredrick Engels, "Communist Manifesto" 1848
http://www.marxists.org/archive/marx/works/1848/communist-manifesto/ch02.htm
22. Emma Goldman, "Anarchism and Other Essays" 1911
http://dwardmac.pitzer.edu/anarchist_archives/goldman/aando/prisons.html
23. Voltairine de Cleyre, "Crime and Punishment" 1903
http://raforum.info/spip.php?article5577
24. King James Bible
25. Lenin, "Imperialism, the Highest Stage of Capitalism",
http://www.marxists.org/archive/lenin/works/1916/imp-hsc/ch07.htm
26. The Washington Post, 6/4/2010 –
http://www.washingtonpost.com/wp-dyn/content/article/2010/06/03/AR2010060304965.html
27. The Weather Underground, "You don't Need a Weatherman to Know Which Way The Wind Blows" 1969
http://www.rrpec.org/documents/weather%5B1%5D.pdf
28. "Nowhere to Hide", FBI Agent Larry Grathwohl, 1982

http://www.examiner.com/libertarian-in-fort-worth/obama-s-radical-ties-the-weather-underground

29. Examiner.com, "Obama's Radical Ties: The Weather Underground" JUNE 11, 2011 By: ANDREW CURTISS http://www.examiner.com/article/obama-s-radical-ties-the-weather-underground

30. Raymond Franklin & Solomon Resnik's 1973 "The Political Economy of Racism"

31. MIM, Maoist International Movement, MIM Notes 162, May 15, 1998 issue
http://www.prisoncensorship.info/archive/etext/dc/DCmurder.html

32. "MIM Notes" No. 200 December 15, 1999
http://www.prisoncensorship.info/archive/etext/faq/amerika.html

33. MIM, "Program of the Maoist Internationalist Movement": "What We Want What We Believe" August 1996
http://www.prisoncensorship.info/archive/etext/wim/program.html

34. "Fire To The Prisons" (FTTP), #11 Spring 2011 issue
http://zinelibrary.info/files/ftp11.pdf

35. MIM (Prisons), "Travon Martin Murder One More Case of Imperialist Oppression" April 2012
http://www.prisoncensorship.info/news/natlopp/

36. Labor Action Committee to Free Mumia Abu-Jamal January 1999
http://www.laboractionmumia.org/whoweare.html

37. FTTP, King Samir Shabaaz of "The New Black Panther Party" July 6, 2010
http://www.theblaze.com/stories/new-black-panther-field-marshal-whites-should-be-thankful-were-not-hanging-crackers-by-nooses-yet-yet-yet/

38. Michael Bakunin, "God and the State" 1871
http://www.marxists.org/reference/archive/bakunin/works/godstate/ch01.htm

CHAPTER 2

From the Strands of Order, Relativism, and the Frameworks of Sustainability to a Dictatorship of the Proletariat

In the first chapter, we came to know that the main objective of the Philosophy is to destroy what we have come to know as the three-headed "Hydra": God, capital or property, and the family. We learned of its web, that it's been cast upon us, and of its nefarious purpose in snaring our Liberty. And we have been told by its champions who it is they say they are *in their own words*. However, as revealing as our journey to the center of the web was, our understanding remains incomplete as the web has many strands, all emanating from the same source, all sharing a common objective. Sooner or later, they all interconnect. In this chapter, it is my hope to shed some light upon these strands that we may come to recognize not only what that objective is but the immediate and direct threat that objective poses to our Constitution, our republic, our faith, our happiness, our prosperity, and freedom itself. If and when their common objective were to be achieved—upon the whole of the earth, the moon, throughout the solar system, the galaxy, into the whole of the known universe and beyond—shall our sacred Liberty be outlawed for all time! Again, not in my words but theirs!

Not all that comes from the Philosophy is as direct, offensive, or in-your-face revolutionary as some of those presented in chapter 1. Some of it is downright seductive. Some of it is elusive, and some of it is accusatory, fishing for guilt. Some of it may appear to be philosophically neutral in meaning or relative to the general beliefs of most, if not all of us. However, no matter its demeanor, it is still nonetheless the same philosophy. As Van Jones says, they "drop the radical pose for the radical ends." For a nation unaware of the whole meaning lingering beneath all the nice sounding words and phrases, these may be the most detrimental of all; in short, candy-coated poison happily gobbled up. Keeping this, along with all we have learned so far in mind, in this chapter, let us take a closer look not only at what is being said, but a look through it to its whole meaning in the fuller context of the Philosophy from which it is spoken.

As we have already seen, one of the mainframe concepts of the Philosophy is that no individual part of any collective has any value of its own other than that value that it adds to the collective, or which "the whole" gives it. In any organic or living "organism," the cells have no value individually. What value does, say, a skin cell or liver cell have, stand-alone? They cannot do the job of any organ by themselves. In addition, without all the other cells and organs of the body, and the respiratory and vascular systems sustaining it, and the central nervous system controlling it all, any individual cell would most assuredly die. It couldn't have even ever come into existence without all the other cells of the "organism" from which it came. No individual cell can have a mind, will, or "personality" of its own. Therefore, no given cell can have any value except when working as part of its pertaining collective, according to its purpose in the "central plan" of the organism. Imagine if our cells were to go rogue and do according to their own will. We as an "organism" would die a certain death. It is in this context that the individual in society is viewed by the Philosophy. The referencing of the earth and/or human society as an organic organisms is a concept brought into mainstream political philosophy by Auguste Comte, first in his 1830–1842, *The Course in Positive Philosophy*; then later, in his 1851–1854, *Système de politique positive*. According to the *New World Encyclopedia* (*NWE*), Comte's work in *positivism* was based on "the development of the individual human organism," the whole of humankind being a single organism. The NWE says that Comte:

> [D]eveloped a philosophy he called "*Positivism*," in which he described human society as having developed through three stages, the third of which he called the "positive" stage, dominated by scientific thought. *He was the first to apply the scientific method to the social world, and coined the term sociology* to describe the scientific study of human society. It was his hope that through such endeavors, an understanding of human society could be achieved that would enable humankind to *progress to a higher level, in which the entire human race could function together as one*. He also coined the term "*altruism*," (as apposed to egoism) advocating that *people should live for the sake of others*[1] (emphasis added).

Positive science oversimplified is the scientific study of human society through three stages of *social evolution* from the *theological* to the *metaphysical*, and finally, on to the *scientific* or *positive*.

Theological societies having a belief in God or supernatural beings are just an early primitive stage of human sociological evolution that we must eventually grow out of. Conveniently for the positivist but to the detriment of "Individual Liberty," without the absolutism that God had previously provided, mankind as a single organism is then free to "evolve" into the earthly "sciences" of humanism, such as environmentalism and relativism. Individuals are said to be of no significance whatsoever to Comte's sociology, the family being the smallest recognized unit. According to Anthony Harrison-Barbet of Philosophical Connections at Philosophos.com:

> Corresponding to each of the three periods are also, Comte says, three kinds of social organizations (though again he allows for a degree of flexibility in the application of his classification).
>
> (1) In the Ancient world and the Middle Ages we find an acceptance of an absolute authority, divine right of kings, or militarism. The ethos of such societies might be said to be conquest.
>
> (2) The Enlightenment era is characterized by belief in abstract rights, popular sovereignty, the rule of law. The emphasis is on defence.
>
> (3) The modern period is that of the industrial society, in which the emphasis is on a centralized economy *organized by a 'scientific' elite. The key word is now "labour."*
>
> If this third (and for Comte final) type of society is to be developed so as to ensure its mutually peaceful qualities are exhibited, *a new science of man will be required. This is sociol-*

ogy. See further *System of Positive Philosophy*. It is needed to formulate the basic laws which underlie human society, *a knowledge of which will enable man to reorganize society* so that it will satisfy his needs *and enable him to maximize his progress*....

Comte regards sociology as the ultimate synthesizing science. He says this is achieved by reference to the idea of humanity and human needs; sociology determines each science's contribution in this respect. He also distinguishes between [social statics] and [social dynamics]. Social statics examines the general laws which relate to [*social cohesion or order*]. The latter is concerned rather with [*what is needed for the development of order, that is, progress*]....

Moreover, the historical laws themselves must be understood in the light of our understanding of human nature. Thus, while operating within broad historical constraints, [*social planning is entirely possible, indeed required*].

As for the forms of government society should have, Comte favoured [*rule by the knowledgeable experts*] (positivist scientists and philosophers) [*whose decisions, exercised through government, would have to be obeyed by the people because the rulers know best. There is thus no place in his scheme for rights of individuals*] in so far as [*they are subordinate to society*], indeed humanity as a whole; and [*it is therefore only in this context, which emphasizes duties, that the concept of 'rights' can have any application. Humanity, the*

*"Great Being", takes the place of God, and is the basis of all morality]*² (emphasis added).

"Progress" is the fundamental mantra of "progressive" social philosophy. In the context of Comte's sociology, Harrison-Barbet finally clarifies for us what, in a philosophical sense, progressive "progress" is actually progressing to—"order"! All that I am about to show you in the following chapter begins with the purpose of "order"!

Before we continue, a clarification, if I may, on the critical difference between *order* and *rule of law*. *Rule of law* is a free people already at full Liberty ordaining a *limited* "constitutional government" to preserve the sanctuary needed for their Liberty to thrive. All government officers are *sworn* to the preservation, protection, and defense of the Constitution, which establishes that "limited government" to preserve the Liberty of the people. Society is the result of a free and enterprising people. *Order*, on the other hand, is whatever the all-powerful governing body and its elite panel of "planners" want it to be. Society and all its members are both subject to and at the mercy of the whims of unchecked government. Society is the result of the collective submission and obedience to government's will. Big difference!

Harrison-Barbet's observation here that "it is therefore only in this context, which emphasizes duties, that the concept of 'rights' can have any application" is a warning to all in the free world who will hear. Understand the difference between positive "rights," which can only be emphasised in the context of an individual's "duties" to his/her society of "order," and our unalienable Individual Rights, endowed to each of us by our Creator! It is a warning not to be taken lightly and, while reading what follows, a warning to be kept close at hand.

Comte's new social science is needed as the "queen" of all sciences because as the "ultimate synthesizing science…sociology determines each science's contribution" necessary to form the "knowledge...which will enable man to reorganize" and *transform society from a free society into a planned society*—where "social planning," as *the standard*, is "indeed required." And remember also that "there is...no place in his scheme for rights of individuals." On what scientific foundation will the "knowledgeable experts (positivist scientists and philosophers) whose decisions, exercised through government, would have to be obeyed by the people because the rulers know best" be based on? Well, not only is the positivism of sociology based on relativism, it is "directed" relativism. Or as Comte himself says:

> The next great hindrance to the use of observation *is the empiricism* which is introduced into it by those who, in the name of impartiality, would interdict the use of any theory whatever. No logical dogma could be more thoroughly irreconcilable with the spirit of the positive philosophy, or with its special character in regard to the study of social phenomena, than this. *No real observation of any kind of phenomena is possible, except in as far as it is first directed*[3] (emphasis added).

In regard to Comte and the "evolutionary progress" of society in sociology, Lewis A. Coser, in his 1977 *Masters of Sociological Thought: Ideas in Historical and Social Context*, adds two final and very important points from Comte: population and "division of labor":

> Furthermore, Comte...admits...[*increases in population...are seen as a major determinant of the rate of social progress*]. The "progressive con-

densation of our species, especially in its early stages" brings about

> *such a division of employment...as could not take place among smaller numbers;...individuals are stimulated to find subsistence by more refined methods...By creating new wants and new difficulties, this gradual concentration develops new means, [not only of progress but of order, by neutralizing physical inequalities, and affording a growing ascendancy to those intellectual and moral forces which are suppressed among a scanty population]* [Coser, 1977:7–8]

Beyond language and religion, there is a third factor that links man to his fellows: [*the division of labor*]. Men are

> *bound together by the very distribution of their occupations; and it is this distribution which causes the extent and growing complexity [of the social organism].*
>
> *The [social organization] tends more and more to rest on an exact estimate of individual diversities, by so distributing employments [as to appoint each one to the destination he is most fit for], from his own nature..., from his education and his position, and, in short, from all his qualifications; so that [all individual organizations, even the most vicious and imperfect..., may finally be made use of for the general good.*[4]
> [Coser, 1977:10–12; added emphasis in brackets]

In a smaller population, there is less of a chance of unsavory quirks popping up in the ranks of the people's DNA that could cost society not only in their care but in their unemployability. As we will see, population control plays a sinister but vital role within the Philosophy. And that "social organization tends more and more to rest on an exact estimate of individual diversities, by so distributing employments as to appoint each one to the destination he is most fit for, from his own nature...so that all individual organizations, even the most vicious and imperfect...may finally be made use of" not for the benefit of the individual but "for the general good", is something to remember when considering our children's education. As it is no less than *the* founding principle behind the "data mining" of today's progressive Common Core education. Such are the aspects of Comte's *Plan of the Scientific Operations Necessary for Reorganizing Society*. Such is the foundation of the "science" of sociology. Such is the scientific basis for evolution, global warming, and a sustainable New World Order!

In such an altruistic, "we're all in this together" society, all individuals must carry out their "shared responsibility" according to the "central plan" of the "organism" for their "shared prosperity" of all in the body politic. At the 2012 Democratic National Convention, President Bill Clinton gave America what amounted to an ultimatum for the upcoming November election, stating:

> We think the country works better with *a strong middle class*, with real opportunities for poor folks to work their way into it—(cheers, applause)—with a relentless focus on the future, with business and government actually working together to promote growth and broadly *share prosperity*. You see, we believe that *"we're all in this together"* is a far better philosophy than

"you're on your own"...Democracy does not... have to be a blood sport, it can be an honorable enterprise that *advances the public interest.*

When we vote in this election, we'll be deciding what kind of country we want to live in. If you want a *winner-take-all, you're-on-your-own society*, you should support the Republican ticket. But if you want a country of *shared opportunities and shared responsibility, a we're-all-in-this-together society*, you should vote for Barack Obama and Joe Biden[5] (emphasis added).

Key, remember here what Alinsky, Kropotkin, Lenin, Engels, and Marx revealed to us about their plan for the middle-class family within the Philosophy and their "revolution." Note also that Clinton offers opportunity for the poor to "work their way into it," but not one to work through it to higher achievements.

Above, we just went over the concept of how "shared responsibility for shared prosperity" fits into advancing the collective "public interest," but what of the "you're on your own" aspect of what Clinton is referring? For a clarification, we go to the 2008 Democratic National Convention, where then candidate Obama said this:

> That old, discredited Republican philosophy: Give more and more to those with the most and hope that prosperity trickles down to everyone else.
>
> In Washington, they call this the "*Ownership Society*," but what *it really means is that you're on your own*. Out of work? Tough luck, you're on your own. No health care? The market will fix it. You're on your own. Born

> into poverty? Pull yourself up by your own bootstraps, even if you don't have boots. You are on your own...It's time for us to change America....
>
> That's the promise of America, the idea that we are responsible for ourselves, but that we also rise or fall as one nation, *the fundamental belief that I am my brother's keeper, I am my sister's keeper*[6] (emphasis added).

Here, Obama reveals what "ownership society" really means: "it really means is that you're on your own." Ownership is private property, is it not? With no property to own, there can be no "ownership." Therefore, "on your own" equals private property! It all sounds nice until you know the whole meaning of what they're saying. If Clinton was to say what is truly meant, he would have had to say, "If you want to have property, you should vote for the Republican ticket." Of course, as a Democrat, he can't say that, so he must speak to us in a code in which he knows the true meaning and Obama knows the true meaning, but most of "we the people" until now anyway have been clueless to. Though we may only see, smell, and taste the candy, the poison is most assuredly there. With that, we continue our journey; this time, to the strands of the web, that the poison may come to be known:

In 1945, at the close of World War II, Stuart Chase released his book *Democracy Under Pressure*. In it, he put forth the following:

> Chapter-1 pg 4 - Will It Be Peace?
> We are a people with many freedoms and we glory in them. Are we so free that we lack the cement which holds a nation together in crisis?

Taking and Giving For three hundred years Americans have been taking from their land and natural resources without giving an equivalent back. Now almost half our arable land has been damaged or destroyed by erosion. Too many of us have thought of our country as something to be mined and exploited, not something to be loved and maintained. The people who now go to black markets with a knowing wink are carrying on the same tradition. Not only individuals but powerful groups have been operating on what might be called the Me First principle.

We were too free! So the stage is set for all of what follows that it all can be traced back to this: the wayward "me first" individualist, capitalist earth exploiters.

For a few stirring months after Pearl Harbor we really had national unity. We buried our differences in an almost universal desire to serve the nation. Many were ready to sit up all night spotting planes, to work all day for nothing at menial jobs in hospitals, to give unlimited time as air-raid wardens and shore patrols. We were Americans all, in a dangerous world. But as the shock wore off, the unity wore off too. By the early summer of 1943, there were days when it seemed as if the country were falling apart in a welter of strikes, crackdowns, threats, seizures, black-market operations, name-calling, bad blood, double-crossing.

Without war "cementing" us all together into a single collective being, expressing only our "general will," standing against our common enemy, and our Liberty secure, we start to go about our individual lives. What now? As under war conditions, the whole of the populous can very easily be manipulated and herded as directed by the planners toward their common predetermined end. We all want to win the war! But now that it was ending, how could the planners, such as Chase, conspire to win the peace?

> Of course, you say; good old human nature. Then where was our human nature right after Pearl Harbor?...Human nature is not something that goes on and off like a faucet. Again, it may be objected that pressure group politics is a good old American custom. No one can gainsay it. So was marching off to war with a squirrel rifle an old American custom. Customs change. The Great Society The need for developing a sense of the whole community does not arise alone from the war. We cannot operate a high-energy economy without it.

One way to begin destroying the "individual," the whole concept of every body having their own life and their own thing to get back to doing after the war, would be the systematic belittlement of our identity with our strong "free" American history, including the "folklore" surrounding the "Don't Tread On Me" rugged individualism and "Liberty or Death" resolve of our Citizen's Militia, unyieldingly fighting for our very independence and freedom—which, by the way, thanks at least in part to the "squirrel guns," we won! That stalwart image of independence and self-sufficiency must be destroyed! It must be replaced, or our view and respect for it must be destroyed. To do that, though, would take generations of reeducation. Such an education, however, is a strand all to its own we will cover next time around the web.

On the subject of "pressure group politics," is it fair that only the squeaky wheel gets the grease? No, not really, but why can't we hear the other wheels? Remember Kropotkin when he wrote about when "the law establishes Mr. So-and-So's right to a house, it is not establishing his right to a cottage he has built for himself, or to a house he has erected with the help of some of his friends. In that case, no one would have disputed his right."[7] As the Philosophy only recognizes property and proprietorships in this light, so does it only recognize your voice as "stand-alone" and separated from others of like voice. As it is near impossible to build a house or multi-million-dollar business alone, so it is as near impossible that, stand-alone, our individual voices would ever be heard.

However, Citizens United have a much louder voice. By limiting the heights to which we may aspire financially to the labor of one, "social planners" can keep us all poor or, at least, without any real financial clout. By limiting our political voice to that of the volume of one, they keep our voices dismissably low or, at least, without any real political clout. In the Citizens United case, the Supreme Court, at least for now, found that citizens do have the "right to unite" and to corporately pool their recourses for both financial and political causes. Beware, holders of the Philosophy will stop at nothing to once again take that power back away from the people!

> As the power age advances, every man jack of us becomes more dependent on the community. Yet the com munity is so large that we are seldom aware of this dependence. Only when the electric power goes off in a blizzard, or the milk train breaks down, do we realize for a few minutes how the community bears us in its

arms. From San Diego to Aroostook County, we are our brothers' keepers. *All the Main Streets merge into one great society.*

The pressure groups seem to be largely led by men who are ignorant of the fact that we are our brothers' keepers. They think such talk is Sunday School stuff. They are wrong (emphasis added).

Excuse me, but if I may, I am *not* my brother's "keeper"! As my brother is not my "keeper" *if* we are both free men! Neither am I the "keeper" of my wife—God forbid! However, I am the "keeper" of my livestock and my pets! As I am no man's pet, neither is no man or woman a pet of mine! Social justice is not charity!

Back to Chase:

It is the first law of modern technology. The self-sufficiency of the individual farmer or the small local group, which was characteristic of the handicraft age, has been sacrificed to the superior output of quantity production. *Each worker, manager, establishment, now performs a single small operation in a vast national assembly line. Every citizen is dependent for his food and shelter on millions of other citizens. Nobody can go it alone any more.* Your great-grandfather could get three square meals a day from his own farm, if a little salt were thrown in. Can you? Figure out where the items for a simple breakfast come from, and how many people are involved, directly and indirectly, in producing and delivering them. The men who run pressure groups seem to assume that their crowd can go it alone. They act largely on the principle of Me First and the public be damned. If their special interest and the public interest happen to coincide, it is probable they did not plan it that way....

The depression should have provided proof enough that Americans are tied together *in a single organism* (emphasis added).

"Nobody can go it alone anymore"! We're all just "workers" in a "vast national assembly line"! Remember Obama from Roanoke, Virginia:

Look, if you've been successful, you didn't get there on your own. You didn't get there on your own. I'm always struck by people who think, well, it must be because I was just so smart. There are a lot of smart people out there. It must be because I worked harder than everybody else. Let me tell you something—there are a whole bunch of hardworking people out there. (Applause.)

If you were successful, somebody along the line gave you some help.

There was a great teacher somewhere in your life. Somebody helped to create this unbelievable American system that we have that allowed you to thrive. Somebody invested in roads and bridges. If you've got a business—you didn't build that. Somebody else made that happen. The Internet didn't get invented on its own. Government research created the Internet so that all the companies could make money off the Internet.

The point is, is that when we succeed, we succeed because of our individual initiative, but also because we do things together.[8]

Chase continues:

> If the idea is every man for himself and the devil take the hindmost, the devil in no time at all works right up to the front of the line. The pressure boys act as though they had never heard of this state of affairs. They think they can still obtain three squares a day off the old farm. They think they can kick their way through the delicate veins, nerves, tendons of an interdependent community, and get theirs.

Remember Hobbes's comparison of a social society to parts of a single organic organism:

> Why may we not say, that all Automata (Engines that move themselves by springs and wheeles as doth a watch) have an artificiall life? For what is the Heart, but a Spring; and the Nerves, but so many Strings; and the Joynts, but so many Wheeles, giving motion to the whole Body, such as was intended by the Artificer? goes yet further, imitating that Rationall and most excellent worke of Nature, Man. For by Art is created that great LEVIATHAN called a COMMON-WEALTH, or STATE.

> The Wealth and Riches of all the particular members, are the Strength...Equity and Lawes, an artificiall Reason and Will. Lastly, the acts and Covenants, by which the parts of this Body Politique were at first made...and united...[9]

And Chase continues:

> If this spirited free-for-all actually persists after Demobilization Day, nobody will get anything, especially the rest of us. There will be no safe little shelf for anybody. With interdependence...of new mass production facilities, the dominoes ought to go down even more rapidly. There will be no peace on Main Street.

Chapter 6: The Great Transformation

Pg 62 - In our perplexity let us turn to the economic historian Karl Polanyi. He has a theory which tries to explain the enigma. After a superbly documented analysis, he concludes that the formation of monopolies was due not so much to human waywardness as to a revolt of society against the stony rigors of the automatic market. Let us briefly examine his thesis, for it may help us in trying to find an answer to the paradox. (The Great Transformation, Farrar and Rinehart, 1944.) The Great Transformation Polanyi describes how the market economy started with bright Utopian promises, and how by subordinating everything to a maximum output of goods, its leaders hoped to solve mankind's economic problems. He traces the steady deterioration of that ideal until the final collapse of the world Free Market in the early 1930's, *and the adoption of managed economies by every state on earth.* Why did such a logical conception come to such a sad end? Polanyi is the first, as far as I am concerned, ever to answer this question satisfactorily. *The chief trouble with the Market,* he says, was not that *it exploited people* which of course it did from time to time but that it *dissolved society. It broke up the family and made people spiritually homeless.* It wrenched them out of their farms, their crafts, their ancient ties, and herded them, rootless, into the dark, Satanic mills. It offered a mechanical institution depending on *money prices to supersede the organic human institutions* which mankind had always known. For thousands of years, markets had been dependent on society, defined in this sense. Men came first and money second. The 19th century reversed the process, and the resulting tensions finally exploded in the disorders, wars, revolutions of our time (emphasis added).

Here, Chase equates the Free Market where, and only where, true wealth can be created by enterprising entrepreneurs meeting the natural (versus unnaturally imposed) demand for things and where, and only where, people are free to vote with their dollars on the value of those things with slavery. And far from destroying society, free enterprise allowed us as individuals families and, as a nation, the historically rare and humane opportunity to prosper—and so we did!

The "market breaking up the family"? This is a typical deceptive, progressive contradiction, just another example of the Philosophy speaking out of both sides of its mouth. Follow me here: Property ownership is unique to each individual. Individualism is capitalism. Capitalism is *the* market. The market is capitalism. Property, however, is the essence, the very foundation, of all three. Don't forget what we have already been told in chapter 1 by Fredrick Engels in his 1884 *Origins of the Family, Private Property, and the State*:

> II. The Family
>
> 4. The Monogamous Family
> It is based on the supremacy of the man, the express purpose being to produce children of undisputed paternity; such paternity is demanded because these children are later to come into their father's property as his natural heirs.[10]

Far from destroying the family, here again, you have it in their own founders' words that, according to their own philosophy, the market, property, and capitalism are what actually created the family! And in addition, remember Robert Dale Owens's 1826 "Declaration of Mental Independence," where he reminds us:

> Man, up to this hour, has been, in all parts of the earth, a slave to a TRINITY of the most monstrous evils that could be combined to inflict mental and physical evil upon his whole race.
>
> I refer to PRIVATE, or INDIVIDUAL PROPERTY—ABSURD AND IRRATIONAL SYSTEMS OF

RELIGION—and MARRIAGE, FOUNDED ON INDI-
VIDUAL PROPERTY COMBINED WITH SOME ONE
OF THESE IRRATIONAL SYSTEMS OF RELIGION.

The revolution, then, to be now effected, is the DESTRUCTION of this HYDRA OF EVILS.[11]

As it has been shown, the Philosophy stands against the "three-headed Hydra" of God, family, and property as a whole. So again, what Chase is actually showcasing here is yet another example of the level of deceit woven throughout the web that defines this philosophy. He goes on to tell us:

> The era of mercantilism, which preceded the Market, was one of expanding trade routes, but they were controlled by the state, often elaborately controlled. At the time of the industrial revolution, the middle classes revolted against these controls. Their revolt was so determined that it swung the pendulum all the way over to the ideal of no control at all. Instead of a series of little regulated markets set against the background of organic society, there was to be one big Market, self-regulating and automatic, to which all social behavior should be subservient. Everything a Commodity In order to have a truly self-regulating and flexible system, Polanyi points out, everything must obviously be included, because everything must be treated as a commodity with a price. Otherwise the mechanism will not work automatically. Labor must become a commodity; so must land; so must money. As a result, industrial workers,

> with nothing but the Market to depend upon, were stripped of human dignity, to be disposed of like so much pig iron. Their less negotiable qualities tended to disappear. *Similarly the buying and selling of natural resources, removed from the ancient protection of society,* amounted to summoning the demons of flood, fire, erosion, dust storm, stream pollution (emphasis added).

In what sense do we obtain any "dignity" by the government, the sovereign, being the sole owner and controller of not only all the fruits of our labor but our labor itself? Who holds and controls the value of a slave's labor: the slave, or the slave owner? If I am a free man, I am the sole owner of my labor. Though the market or all the other free people may dictate its true value, it is I alone who chooses at what price I am willing to work! If I am a free man, nothing—be it government or labor union—has a monopoly on either the value of my labor or the price I choose to work. And if I am truly a free man, I am the sole owner of its fruit! Is America to be "the land of the free" or not? But if we do submit, willingly or otherwise, at least "the demons of flood, fire, erosion, dust storm, stream pollution" will all be held at bay.

> Money was made a commodity by tying it to gold. Gold was bought and sold like anything else, at so much an ounce. Its behavior was naturally uncertain, with alternate gluts and shortages. This caused recurring shocks to the money supply, and threatened the stability of industry. Businessmen, according to Poknyi, were the first victims of the money-commodity theory. "The Market required that the individ-

ual respect economic law even if it happened to destroy him."

- Society versus the Market-

Almost immediately society moved to protect itself against this logical Moloch. The first reaction was the factory legislation of the 1830's in Britain. In due course came legislation for public health, public schools, food and drug laws, municipal trading, subsidies, embargoes, tariffs, and other "government interference." The most drastic interference, however, did not come from the government at all, but from the trusts, monopolies, and trade associations of the businessman, and from the labor unions of the workers. The guardians of the market theory roared their disapproval, but the reaction continued with little interruption down to the crowning debacle when Britain went off gold in 1931. The guardians steadily claimed it all a plot of the radicals…Something very deep and very powerful was obviously at work. To fit this historical development into the theory of the class struggle, into fights between radicals and reactionaries, or into standard theories of property, is impossible. The facts come running out of all the cracks. But they fit easily into a flesh-and-blood social structure spontaneously trying to protect itself against the ravages of a cold mathematical Market. For example, according to market philosophy nothing must be undertaken unless it "pays."

First, as far as "guardians of the market theory" roaring their disapproval of our currency being taken off the "gold standard"—who doesn't want their money to be worthless? Not to mention the effect that it has in allowing governments to spend more money than there is gold in the world. And the effect that this had in governments then being allowed to spend more money—than there was money! And then there's the effect that has in the newly extra–constitutionally empowered government printing, printing, and printing until they need to print some more! And the effect that then has in government not only making our money even more worthless but enslaving us all, for generations, to the ensuing debt, hyperinflation, and eventual ruin! As of 2014, some four trillion dollars in new money had been printed/digitized by the US Federal Reserve, with another trillion dollars or so being added annually—all resulting in our noses being held to the grindstone working overtime, two, or even three, jobs chasing a dollar that's worth less and less to pay bills that are higher and higher! Who doesn't want that? No wonder we no longer have the time to "waste" babysitting our wayward politicians and out-of-control government or, as it were, to watch the "dish runaway with the spoon"!

Second, monopolies *cannot* happen without government being an active supporter. Capitalism is, by definition, a competition between competitors. No matter how successful my competitors, they *cannot* control my cost but only affect my efficiency, lest they own not only all my suppliers but all my labor and all the demand for my product and/or service. Only government can do that! Only government can affect my cost via mandates, regulation, licenses, and taxes that not only impede my profitability but that of my suppliers and my competitors as well. Only government has the power to either enforce all these equally or to subsidize with favor. Only government makes the rules! Only government has the power to pick winners and losers. I am not a smaller and poorer business because my competition is bigger and richer.

Third, I don't undertake the obligation of a garden unless it pays with food or fauna. I don't undertake the effort of the hunt unless it might pay with meat for my freezer. I don't even undertake the drinking of a glass of water or of my next breath unless they pay with the quenching of my thirst or my need for air! Why would I bother to exert laborious effort, be it in my own business or after punching a clock for my employer, unless it is to pay? Why would anyone bother to invest any time, effort, or capital into an idea or inspiration if there were no potential for it to "pay"? Even a labor camp prisoner who is forced to work for no pay works in hope that it might pay with his life being spared.

Unemployed persons can rot by the thousands if it does not pay some enterpriser to hire them. Clearly no society can long tolerate such a destructive taboo. It is worse than foot-binding or child marriage. It is a form of human sacrifice.

The monopoly movement thus appears in a strange new light, as a natural human defense. Monopolies were formed to protect businessmen from the violent ups and downs of the Market, precisely as trade unions were developed to protect workers from the howling blizzards of the Free Market in labor. If monopolies are part of this social defense mechanism, clearly they cannot be liquidated blindly. If they are broken up in a flood of cease and desist orders, they will surely form again as soon as the government lawyers go home to get a little sleep.

If the Market was destructive to that vague but powerful entity which we call society, then it followed naturally that we should have government interference, labor unions, and business monopolies Big Business, Big Unions, Big Government[12].

If the market offered liberation from tyranny, what would the tyrant do to crush it? If the subtlety of Chase's eloquence has left you any room to question his meaning or allegiance to the Philosophy, maybe the following from page 163 of his 1932 book *A New Deal* will clear things up for you:

> Best of all, the new regime would have the clearest idea of what an economic system was for. The sixteen methods of becoming wealthy *would be proscribed—by firing squad if necessary*—ceasing to plague and disrupt the orderly process of production and distribution. Money would no longer be an end, but would be thrust back where it belongs as a labor-saving means. The whole vicious pecuniary complex would collapse as it has in Russia. *Money making as a career would no more occur to a respectable young man than burglary, forgery or embezzlement.* "Everyone," says Keynes, "will work for the community and, *if he does his duty,* the community will uphold him." Money making and money accumulating cannot enter into the life calculations of a rational man in (communist)

Russia. A society of which this is even partially true is a tremendous innovation[13] (emphasis added).

Keynes, whom he quotes, is none other than John Maynard Keynes, the famed Fabian Socialist namesake of Keynesian economics.

A New Deal would go on to become the namesake of President Franklin D. Roosevelt's New Deal. And per Mr. Zygmund Dobbs (Keynes at Harvard), Chase would then go to be "appointed to the National Resources Committee, and a year later further rewarded by appointment to the Resettlement Administration. He quickly climbed to the Securities & Exchange Commission (1939) the TVA (Tennessee Valley Authority) (1940) and finally settled in U.N.E.S.C.O."

In a 2001 interview on WBEZ Chicago 91.5 FM, then Senator Obama said this:

> "If you look at the victories and failures of the civil rights movement and its litigation strategy in the court, I think where it succeeded was to vest formal rights in previously dispossessed peoples. So that I would now have the right to vote, I would now be able to sit at the lunch counter and order and *as long as I could pay for it* I'd be okay. But *the Supreme Court never ventured into the issues of redistribution of wealth* and sort of more basic issues of political *and economic justice in this society*. And to that extent as radical as people tried to characterize the Warren court, it wasn't that radical. *It didn't break free from the essential constraints that were placed by the founding fathers in the Constitution,*

at least as it's been interpreted, and the Warren court interpreted it in the same way that generally the Constitution is a charter of negative liberties. It says what the states can't do to you, it says what the federal government can't do to you, but it doesn't say what the federal government or the state government must do on your behalf. And that hasn't shifted. One of the I think tragedies of the civil rights movement was because the civil rights movement became so court focused, I think that there was a tendency to lose track of the political and community organizing and activities on the ground that are able to put together the actual coalitions of power through which you bring about redistributed change and in some ways we still suffer from that. Maybe I'm showing my bias here as a legislator as well as a law professor, but I'm not optimistic about bringing about *major redistributive change* through the courts. The institution just isn't structured that way. You just look at very rare examples during the desegregation era the court was willing to for example order changes that cost money to a local school district. The court was very uncomfortable with it. It was very hard to manage, it was hard to figure out. You start getting into all sorts of separation of powers issues in terms of the court monitoring or engaging *in a process that essentially is administrative* and takes a lot of time. The court's just not very good at it and politically it's very hard to legitimize opinions from the court in that regard. So I think that *although you can craft theoretical justifications for it* legally. Any three of us sitting here could come up with a rational for bringing about economic change through the courts[14] (emphasis added).

Though he starts out with a statement we can all agree on, this is a fundamental break from all that our Constitution stands for and counter to all that the founders secured in it. The courts venturing into "redistributive change" alone holds huge implications. The constraints he refers to, set by our founders, are the very essence of our Constitutional republic. We will be coming back to these "restraints" again. You *cannot* distribute or redistribute that which is not yours. For the government to redistribute a thing, it must first confiscate or otherwise take possession of it from its rightful owner. For an example, if you tell me that you have a right to an education, house, heat, vacation, food, stove, refrigerator, transportation, phone, or healthcare—whether you can pay for any of them or not, what you are really saying is that you have a right to somebody else's property to pay for them with. If I am from the government, knowing that, because of the Constitution, I am constrained from redistributing such property to you, but I say to you, "Give me the power to take that property from its rightful owners so I that I can give those things to you, that social justice can be done" and then you give me that power? What you may not realize is that in giving me, the government, that power, you have also given me the power to make sure that you can never ever have such property for yourself. For before you can have or "horde" such property for yourself, I will then redistribute it from you to somebody else. The promise of social justice, which is the promise of redistribution, is *not* the promise of prosperity—it is a *lie*! It is a lie founded in jealousy and the coveting of what rightfully belongs to another! Redistribution, by its definition, undermines the whole of our free society by universally undermining the property rights of all. Consider federalist Noah Webster, who wrote this in his 1787 *An Examination Into the Leading Principles of the Federal Constitution*:

> Wherever we cast our eyes, we see this truth, that *property* is the basis of *power*; and this being established as a cardinal point, directs us to the means of preserving our freedom.[15]

Referring to the Constitution, "at least as it has been interpreted," as a "Charter of negative liberties" is also diabolically apposed to the Constitution as written. Leaving us in such a perplexed state with so many questions, we might be tempted to just drop the whole issue and go back about our business. Don't do it! Regarding Obama's "as interpreted" clause, things relative are things with no meaning, except that meaning which is breathed into the meaningless words by the reader. Does the Constitution have meaning or not? Do the words of the Constitution set forth its meaning, or does the reader? If words have no meaning, what meaning does any written document or contract have? So what does the Constitution mean?

Justice William J. Brennan Jr. served as a Supreme Court justice from 1956 to 1990. In a speech given at the Text and Teaching Symposium at Georgetown University on October 12, 1985, he said this about his duties as a Supreme Court justice:

> The Constitution embodies the aspiration to social justice, brotherhood, and human dignity that brought this nation into being....
>
> Like every text worth reading, it is not crystalline. The phrasing is broad and the limitations of its provisions are not clearly marked. Its majestic generalities and ennobling pro-

nouncements are both luminous and obscure. This ambiguity of course calls forth interpretation, the interaction of reader and text....

Thus I will attempt to elucidate my approach to the text as well as my substantive interpretation....

When Justices interpret the Constitution they speak for their community, not for themselves alone. The act of interpretation must be undertaken with full consciousness that it is, in a very real sense, the community's interpretation that is sought...Because judicial power resides in the authority to give meaning to the Constitution, the debate is really a debate about how to read the text, about constraints on what is legitimate interpretation.

(1) Do you realize this is coming from a former Supreme Court justice? Social justice? Really? How is it that I never knew Karl Marx was one of our founding fathers? As we have shown, "social justice" is the *forced* confiscation of, and subsequent redistribution of, any or all personal wealth and/or private property that the "supreme sovereign" decrees should be taken from its rightful owner then, with extreme prejudice, given with favor to someone else. Ask yourself, how does that fit in with Individual Liberty, which requires the protection of property rights?

Another problem with the whole social justice theory is that it is "We the People" who, according to James Madison in Federalist Essay 49, are supposed to be the "legitimate fountain of power." To say our government has the arbitrary power to confiscate the people's private property at will would be to say, as Alexander Hamilton puts it in Federalist Essay 78, that "the servant is above the master." Not only that, but if you look at society as a series of railcars, full of people freely moving and mingling by their own accord from one car to another—all on the same track of opportunity to potential success, all being pulled by the same engine that is free enterprise—a simpler truth becomes evident.

As coal is a fuel for train engines, property and capital are fuel for free enterprise, which is *the* engine of our economy and *only* creator of new wealth. That being said, you *cannot* tax the engine redistributing the coal, the fuel, from the engine to the caboose and expect the train to run long even on level ground; for as the load being pulled gets heavier and heavier, the engine runs lower and lower on fuel. Through the eyes of the Philosophy as prescribed by Karl Marx, our free society is said to resemble more of a class-based layer-cake society, where the top layers weigh heavily upon the bottom layers, keeping them down and eternally suppressed. However, as America was founded to be a society of free individuals, all created equal and endowed with the same unalienable Rights, we are, in truth, a one-class society. Compare the layer-cake society of Marx to say that of a lava lamp, where all are in a single class—some at the top, some at the bottom, some rising, some sinking. Any at the bottom can go to the top; any at the top, at any moment, could go straight to the bottom. The energy source giving motion to it all? Liberty!

(2) Does judicial power really reside in his "authority to give meaning to the Constitution"? How does anybody from any part of any branch of government obtain the "power and authority" to "give meaning" to that which binds them? Only through hostile interpretation! If a given entity has the "power and authority" to interpret that which binds it, how, may I ask, can it possibly be bound?

(3) When Justices interpret the Constitution, they don't speak for themselves or their community; they act on behalf of a philosophy counter to Individual Liberty and in violation of the very specific enumerated constraints placed upon them by our founders,

as set forth "in writing" in the Constitution. And because judicial power resides only in the authority to *"ascertain"* the meaning of the Constitution, any rogue reinterpretation of it by enterprising judges of their supreme directive is counter to its ordained purpose and of the highest insubordination.

Supreme Court judges holding the Liberty of a people in one hand and the Constitution in the other are supposed to be the most steadfast bulwarks of that Liberty, not subject it to hostile reinterpretations. Following Brennan's philosophy of relativism can only leave his interpretations wide open to further reinterpretations and so on and so forth. Where would it all end? In something akin to relative nihilist existentialism? Or maybe existential relativist nihilism? What difference does it make when meaning is meaningless? We, as free Americans, hold our Constitution to a higher standard than just a bunch of words doomed to inevitable irrelevance.

(4) If "the debate is really a debate on how to read" the Constitution, may I offer….. in English. Brennan continues:

> Those who would restrict claims of right to the values of 1789 specifically articulated in the Constitution turn a blind eye to social progress and eschew adaptation of overarching principles to changes of social circumstance.

No, it is "social progress" that has turned a blind eye to Individual Liberty, and any judicial collaboration in favor of their wayward interpretation of the Constitution is at least counter to its fundamental principle of securing our Individual Rights, Liberty, and property. The Supreme Court was not established to construe an overarching "society" superior to the Constitution with liberty of tyranny. That's happened once before in our history, and it resulted in a civil war.

We current Justices read the Constitution in the only way that we can: as Twentieth Century Americans. We look to the history of the time of framing and to the intervening history of interpretation. But the ultimate question must be, what do the words of the text mean in our time. For *the genius of the Constitution rests not in any static meaning it might have had in a world that is dead and gone, but in the adaptability of its great principles to cope with current problems and current needs....*

Interpretation must account for the transformative purpose of the text. Our Constitution was not intended to preserve a preexisting society but to make a new one....

Having discussed at some length how I, as a Supreme Court Justice, interact with this text, I think it time to turn to the fruits of this discourse. For the Constitution is a sublime oration on the dignity of man....

As augmented by the Bill of Rights and the Civil War Amendments, this text is a sparkling vision of the supremacy of the human dignity of every individual...It is a vision that has guided us as a people throughout our history, although the precise rules by which we have protected fundamental human dignity have been transformed over time in response to both transformations of social condition and evolution of our concepts of human dignity." (emphasis added).

(1) The Constitution did not promote the welfare of America by securing the "Blessings of Liberty" to our founders' generation only. Our founders specifically secured them in the preamble "to ourselves and our Posterity." Note, it is "P*osterity*" that is emphasized with capitalization. Therefore, they are the rightful inheritance of "our Posterity" in perpetuity. They are not this or any generation's to interpret away. There is no expiration date on American freedom!

(2) What is "transformative purpose" of text? The text of the Constitution, having a specific meaning of purpose, preserves the fundamental transformation of America from the preexisting state of tyranny under the king to one of Individual Liberty in perpetuity, or at least until the Constitution is no more.

(3) If what Justice Brennan says is true and the "rules by which we have protected fundamental human dignity have been transformed over time in response to both transformations of social condition and evolution of our concepts of human dignity," under what interpretation of such "transformation of social condition" would we cease to be free altogether? Any and all concepts of dignity allowed us by the courts are now, of course, also relative and subject to the same hostile reinterpretation.

> As government acts ever more deeply upon those areas of our lives once marked "private," there is an even greater need to see that individual rights are not curtailed or cheapened in the interest of what may temporarily appear to be the "public good." And as government continues in its role of provider for so many of our disadvantaged citizens, there is an even greater need to ensure that government act with integrity and consistency in its dealings with these citizens. To put this another way, the possibil-

ities for collision between government activity and individual rights will increase as the power and authority of government itself expands.

If I am a free man or a free woman, I am free to be my own provider. Regardless, under what circumstance do you or I have the right to surrender our children's Liberty?

It was not until the Thirteenth and Fourteenth Amendments were added, in 1865 and 1868, in response to a demand for national protection against abuses of state power, that the Constitution could be interpreted to require application of the first eight amendments to the states.

What interpretation is needed for Article VI of the Constitution, which directs:

This Constitution, and the Laws which shall be made in pursuance thereof; and all Treaties made, or which shall be made, under the Authority of the United States, shall be the Supreme Law of the Land; and the judges *in every state*, shall be bound thereby, *any Thing in the Constitution or Laws of any State to the contrary notwithstanding.*
The Senators and Representatives before mentioned, and the *Members of the several State Legislatures, and all executive and judicial Officers, both of the United States and of the Several States,*

> *shall be bound by Oath or Affirmation, to support this Constitution?* (emphasis added).
>
> I mentioned earlier the judge's role in seeking out the community's interpretation of the Constitutional text. Yet, again in my judgment, when a Justice perceives an interpretation of the text to have departed so far from its essential meaning, that Justice is bound, by a larger constitutional duty to the community.

Where Justice Brennan here states that, as a Supreme Court justice, his "larger constitutional duty" is to the "community's interpretation of the Constitution," Alexander Hamilton tells us in Federalist 78:

> It is far more rational to suppose, that the courts were designed to be an intermediate body between the people and the legislature, in order, among other things, *to keep the latter within the limits assigned to their authority. The interpretation of the laws is the proper and peculiar province of the courts. A constitution is, in fact, and must be regarded by the judges, as a fundamental law. It therefore belongs to them to ascertain its meaning*, as well as the meaning of any particular act proceeding from the legislative body. If there should happen to be an irreconcilable variance between the two, *that which has the superior obligation and validity ought, of course, to be preferred*; or, in other words, *the Constitution ought to be preferred* to the statute, *the intention of the*

> *people to the intention of their agents*[16] (emphasis added).

The Constitution is the "intention of The People"! The Constitution as "fundamental" is, per *Webster's* dictionary, "the basis," "the foundation," "the original and primary source" and "underlying principle, rule, law, that serves as the groundwork" from which all other laws are to be pursuant to. If that foundation is inconvenient to "designing men," then it has served its purpose! If "the community" wants it to be otherwise, they'll change their Constitution the constitutional way—through amendments!

> This public encounter with the text, however, has been a profound source of personal inspiration. The vision of human dignity embodied there is deeply moving. It is timeless. It has inspired Americans for two centuries and it will continue to inspire as it continues to evolve. That evolutionary process is inevitable and indeed, it is the true interpretive genius of the text.[17]

To whom do our judges swear an oath: a yet-to-be-determined utopian collective or the Constitution?

Nothing is timeless but God. No vision is timeless if left open to interpretation. Any process that is evolutionary is, by definition, a Godless process. Being that all men are created equal and we are all endowed by our Creator with certain unalienable Rights and only God is timeless, nothing evolutionary can possibly preserve them. As God is absolute, neither can our Liberty be preserved by anything relative.

However, what we do get from Justice Brennan is an idea of what, if any, meaning the Constitution holds from the perspective of the Philosophy. With the Constitution placed into such a weakened state from this relativism, the door has been left wide open for all that follows in this chapter, and then some.

When Obama, in his WBEZ interview, referred to how the Warren court interpreted the Constitution as a "charter of negative liberties," that "it says what the states can't do to you, it says what the federal government can't do to you, but it doesn't say what the federal government or the state government must do on your behalf"—do we understand the implications of such a philosophy? If our Constitution is a charter of negative liberties, what would a Constitution of *positive liberties*, one telling us what government "must do on your behalf," look like?

On January 11, 1944, President Franklin D. Roosevelt said this in his message introducing his Second Bill of Rights to the Congress of the United States on the State of the Union:

> It is our duty now to begin to lay the plans and determine the strategy for the winning of a lasting peace and the establishment of an American standard of living higher than ever before known. We cannot be content, no matter how high that general standard of living may be, if some fraction of our people—whether it be one-third or one-fifth or one-tenth—is ill-fed, ill-clothed, ill-housed, and insecure.
>
> This Republic had its beginning, and grew to its present strength, under the protection of certain inalienable political rights—among them the right of free speech, free press, free worship, trial by jury, freedom from unreason-

able searches and seizures. They were our rights to life and liberty.

As our nation has grown in size and stature, *however—as our industrial economy expanded—these political rights proved inadequate to assure us equality in the pursuit of happiness.*

We have come to a clear realization of the fact that true individual freedom cannot exist without economic security and independence. "Necessitous men are not free men." People who are hungry and out of a job are the stuff of which dictatorships are made.

In our day these economic truths have become accepted as self-evident. We have accepted, so to speak, *a second Bill of Rights under which a new basis of security and prosperity can be established for all*—regardless of station, race, or creed.

Among these are:
The right to a useful and remunerative job in the industries or shops or farms or mines of the nation;

The right to earn enough to provide adequate food and clothing and recreation;

The right of every farmer to raise and sell his products at a return which will give him and his family a decent living;

The right of every businessman, large and small, to trade in an atmosphere of freedom from unfair competition and domination by monopolies at home or abroad;

> The right of every family to a decent home;
>
> The right to adequate medical care and the opportunity to achieve and enjoy good health;
>
> The right to adequate protection from the economic fears of old age, sickness, accident, and unemployment;
>
> The right to a good education.
>
> *All of these rights spell security.* And after this war is won we must be prepared to move *forward*, in the implementation of these rights, to new goals of human happiness and well-being[18] (emphasis added).

Essentially, our Individual Liberty and God-given unalienable Rights, after bringing our country to its most powerful and most prosperous state yet, were now to be considered obsolete. The government would now turn to issuing positive security to counter the antiquated Individual Liberty. On December 10, 1948, these "positive rights" would be incorporated into the United Nations Universal Declaration of Human Rights:

> Article 1.
>
> All human beings are born free and equal in dignity and rights. They are endowed with reason and conscience and should act towards one another in a spirit of brotherhood.
>
> Article 3.
>
> Everyone has the right to life, liberty and security of person.

So far, it sounds real familiar, almost exactly like our own Declaration of Independence, right? Almost, however, the difference being no Right to pursue our own happiness! Beware to all those who would let the difference between "Happiness" and "security of person" slide by uninvestigated. With one, there is the freedom of Individual Liberty; with the other, only serfdom.

> Article 22.
>
> Everyone, as a member of society, has the *right to social security* and is entitled to realization, through national effort and international co-operation and in accordance with the organization and resources of each State, of the economic, social and cultural rights indispensable for his dignity and the free development of his personality.
>
> Article 23.
>
> (1) Everyone has the *right to work*, to free choice of employment, to just and favourable conditions of work and to protection against unemployment.
>
> (2) Everyone, without any discrimination, has the *right to equal pay* for equal work.
>
> (3) Everyone who works has the *right to just and favourable remuneration* ensuring for himself and his family an existence worthy of human dignity, and *supplemented*, if necessary, by other means of *social protection*.
>
> (4) Everyone has the *right to form and to join trade unions* for the protection of his interests (emphasis added).

Why would we ever need a "right" to union protection? No Individual Right or Liberty is protected by unions. They are a collective anti-individual, antifree-enterprise Marxist concept. There is no place for a meritocracy "in the membership." The "slugs" are equal in every way to anyone dumb enough to excel. Upon joining a union, you surrender your individuality, as well as ownership of the value of your labor, over to the collective "of the membership." Our Constitution was ordained to protect our Individual Liberty.

Article 24.

Everyone has the *right to rest and leisure*, including reasonable limitation of working hours and periodic holidays with pay.

Article 25.

(1) Everyone has the *right to a standard of living* adequate for the *health* and well-being of himself and of his family, including *food, clothing, housing and medical care and necessary social services, and the right to security in the event of unemployment, sickness, disability, widowhood, old age or other lack of livelihood in circumstances beyond his control.*

(2) Motherhood and childhood are entitled to *special care and assistance.*

Article 26.

(1) Everyone has the *right to education.* Education *shall be free*, at least in the elementary and fundamental stages. Elementary education shall be compulsory. Technical and professional education shall be made generally available and

higher education shall be equally accessible to all on the basis of merit.

(2) *Education shall be directed* to the full development of the human personality and to the strengthening of respect *for human rights* and fundamental freedoms. It shall promote understanding, tolerance and friendship among all nations, racial or religious groups, *and shall further the activities of the United Nations* for the maintenance of peace (emphasis added).

Human rights include the right to "directed education"? We will be getting to education, including John Dewey, in another chapter, but know that it does not include independence, self-sufficiency, rugged individualism, or the teaching "of facts and absolutes" as "there is no social gain thereat"!

Article 27.
(1) Everyone has *the right* freely to participate in the cultural life of the community, to enjoy the arts and *to share* in scientific advancement and its benefits.
(2) Everyone has the *right to the protection* of the moral and material interests resulting from any scientific, literary or artistic production of which he is the author.

Article 28.
Everyone is entitled to a social and international order in which the rights and freedoms set forth in this Declaration can be fully realized.

Article 29.

(1) *Everyone has duties to the community in which alone the free and full development of his personality is possible*[19] (emphasis added).

Let us consider for a moment some ramifications of such a "social and international order." Where do we know that just such an "order" already exists both domestically and internationally? Where do we know that positive rights are already an everyday reality, including right here in the good ol' USA? Think about it! Where do we already know that housing, a standard of living, food, clothing, health care, dental care, education, a program (excuse me, a mean a job), protection, and a right to recreation are all rights guaranteed by law?

After a career in law enforcement as a corrections officer, the answer to me is painfully obvious—that's right, *prison*! Why are such positive rights needed in prison? Because all those in prison have already lost, surrendered, or otherwise forsaken the Liberty necessary to provide such things for themselves! FDR was exactly right when he said, "All of these rights spell security." This is the "progress" they want us, as free Americans, to move "forward" to? Know that in reality, the security of such collective civil/human rights are not but the "rights" and "security" of prisoners!

And again, as we saw in Bakunin collectivism in chapter 1, we see here a reference to the same "personality" in the fuller context of "everyone" having "duties to the community." Such a *personality* can only be *the* measure of an individual's compliance to those government-mandated programs or "duties." Now, remember Anthony Harrison-Barbet explaining Comte's positive evolutionary sociology:

> As for the forms of government society should have, Comte favoured *rule by the knowl-*

edgeable experts (positivist scientists and philosophers) *whose decisions, exercised through government, would have to be obeyed by the people because the rulers know best. There is thus no place in his scheme for rights of individuals* in so far as *they are subordinate to society*, indeed humanity as a whole; and *it is therefore only in this context, which emphasizes duties, that the concept of 'rights' can have any application. Humanity, the "Great Being", takes the place of God, and is the basis of all morality*[2] (emphasis added).

Only through your "duties to the community" is it possible for your individual personality to be developed. *Human rights are not individual rights.* They are positive collective rights, all with correlating "duties" in harmony with the central plan. They are *not* to be undermined by any wayward individuality.

On October 22, 2012, Governor Romney made the following statement from his third debate against Obama:

> Well, I—I absolutely believe that America has a—a responsibility and the privilege of helping defend freedom and promote the principles that—that make the world more peaceful. *And those principles include human rights*, human dignity, *free enterprise*, freedom of expression[20] (emphasis added).

It is only within the context of this analysis of Obama's "negative liberties" transforming into the "redistributive change" of positive rights and Individual Liberty versus human rights that Romney's statement can be recognized for the colossal mistake that it is. Has the Philosophy become so ingrained into our system that even those who espouse to champion the Individual Liberty necessary for "free enterprise" know not that the "human rights" they simultaneously champion are the antithesis of them?

Chapter 7 of the 1977 communist Constitution of the Soviet Union (USSR) looked like this:

> Chapter 7: THE BASIC RIGHTS, FREEDOMS, AND DUTIES OF CITIZENS OF THE USSR
>
> Article 39. Citizens of the USSR enjoy in full the social, economic, political and personal rights and freedoms proclaimed and guaranteed by the Constitution of the USSR and by Soviet laws. *The socialist system ensures enlargement of the rights and freedoms of citizens and continuous improvement of their living standards as social, economic, and cultural development programmes are fulfilled.*
>
> Enjoyment by citizens of their *rights and freedoms must not be to the detriment of the interests of society or the state,* or infringe the rights of other citizens.
>
> Article 40. Citizens of the USSR have the right to work (*that is, to guaranteed employment* and pay in accordance wit the quantity and quality of their work, and not below the state-established minimum), including the right to choose their trade or profession, type of job and work in accordance with their inclinations, abilities,

training and education, *with due account of the needs of society.*

This right is ensured by the socialist economic system, steady growth of the productive forces, free vocational and professional training, improvement of skills, training in new trades or professions, and development of the systems of vocational guidance and job placement.

Article 41. Citizens of the USSR have *the right to rest and leisure.*

This right is ensured by the establishment of *a working week not exceeding 41 hours,* for workers and other employees, a shorter working day in a number of trades and industries, and shorter hours for night work; by the provision of paid annual holidays, weekly days of rest, extension of the network of cultural, educational, and health-building institutions, and the development on a mass scale of sport, physical culture, and camping and tourism; *by the provision* of neighborhood recreational facilities, and of other opportunities *for rational use of free time.*

The length of collective farmers' working and leisure time is established by their collective farms.

Article 42. Citizens of the USSR have the *right to health protection.*

This right is ensured by *free,* qualified *medical care provided by state health institutions*; by extension of the network of therapeutic and health-building institutions; by the development and improvement of safety and hygiene in industry; by carrying out broad prophylactic measures; by measures to improve the environment; by special care for the health of the rising generation, including *prohibition of child labour*, excluding the work done by children as part of the school curriculum; and by developing research to prevent and reduce the incidence of disease and ensure citizens a long and active life.

Article 43. Citizens of the USSR have *the right to maintenance in old age, in sickness*, and in the event of complete or partial disability or loss of the breadwinner.

The right is guaranteed by social insurance of workers and other employees and collective farmers; by allowances for temporary disability; by the provision by the state or by collective farms of *retirement pensions*, disability pensions, and pensions for loss of the breadwinner; by providing employment for the partially disabled; by care for the elderly and the disabled; and by other forms of *social security* (emphasis added).

Under Such "improved" conditions, all the children will be protected from any exploitation for profits in family businesses, that from what I don't see here, in the form of a "positive right' allowing proprietorships, aren't allowed anyway. Any of these Communist "rights" starting to look familiar?

> Article 44. Citizens of the USSR have *the rights to housing.*
>
> *This right is ensured by the development and upkeep of state and socially-owned housing;* by assistance for co-operative and individual house building; *by fair distribution, under public control,* of the housing that becomes available *through fulfilment of the programme of building well-appointed dwellings, and by low rents and low charges for utility services. Citizens of the USSR shall take good care of the housing allocated to them* (emphasis added).

For housing, you'll get what you get and you'll be happy by order and decree once there has been "fulfillment of the programs"—both to be "as determined" by the state. But you have a right to a house once you get it, whatever it is, whenever you get it. Remember, no property rights are recognized in socialism. All property is government property to be distributed and redistributed upon whim of government will. The list goes on:

> Article 45. Citizens of the USSR have the *right to education.*
>
> This right is ensured by free provision of all forms of education, by the institution of universal, compulsory secondary education, and broad development of vocational, specialised secondary, and higher education, *in which instruction is oriented toward practical activity and production*; by the development of extramural, correspondence and evening courses, by the provision of state scholarships and grants and privileges for

students; by the free issue of school textbooks; by the opportunity to attend a school where teaching is in the native language; and by the provision of facilities for self-education.

Article 46. Citizens of the USSR have the *right to enjoy cultural benefits.*
This rights is ensured by broad access to the cultural treasures *of their own land and of the world that are preserved in state and other public collections; by the development and fair distribution of* cultural and educational institutions throughout the country; by developing television and radio broadcasting and the publishing of books, newspapers and periodicals, and by extending the free library service; and by expanding cultural exchanges with other countries.

Article 47. Citizens of the USSR, *in accordance with the aims of building communism, are guaranteed freedom* of scientific, technical, and artistic work. This freedom is ensured by broadening scientific research, encouraging invention and innovation, and developing literature and the arts. *The state provides the necessary material conditions for this and support for* voluntary societies and unions of workers in the arts, organises introduction of inventions and innovations in production and other spheres of activity.

> The rights of authors, inventors and innovators are protected by the state (emphasis added).

All "positive rights" are micromanaged by the state as they are owned by the state. Hence, the term *positive*! As there is no market to determine demand or value of things "positive," what and where "fair distribution" is by decree only, whether wanted or not, and then only what and where any "right" is beneficial, not to the people but to the state. One needs only to remember Joseph Stalin's "famine" caused by the "redistribution" of grain and food in the Ukraine that resulted in the forced slow starvation of seven to nine million middle-class peasants or "Kulaks" to know what happens time and time again when government has control of what we need to survive! On the subject of "the famine," Eric Margolis, contributing foreign editor of the *Toronto Sun*, tells us:

> Socialist luminaries like Bernard Shaw, Beatrice and Sidney Webb and PM Edouard Herriot of France, toured Ukraine during 1932–33 and proclaimed reports of famine were false. Shaw announced: "I did not see one under-nourished person in Russia." New York Times correspondent Walter ("In order to make an omelet you have to break a few eggs.") Duranty, who won a Pulitzer Prize for his Russian reporting, wrote claims of famine were "malignant propaganda." Seven million people were dying around them, yet these fools saw nothing. The New York Times has never repudiated Duranty's lies. Modern leftists do not care to be reminded their ideological and

historical roots are entwined with this century's greatest crime—the inevitable result of enforced social engineering and Marxist theology.

Western historians delicately skirt the sordid fact that the governments of Britain, the U.S. and Canada were fully aware of the Ukrainian genocide and Stalin's other monstrous crimes. Yet they eagerly welcomed him as an ally during World War II. Stalin, who Franklin Roosevelt called "Uncle Joe," murdered four times more people than Adolf Hitler.[21]

We continue with the Soviet Constitution:

Article 48. Citizens of the USSR have the right to take part in the management and administration of state and public affairs and in the discussion and adoption of laws and measures of All-Union and local significance.

This right is ensured by the opportunity to vote and to be elected to Soviets of People's Deputies and other elective state bodies, to take part in nationwide discussions and referendums, in people's control, in the work of state bodies, public organisations, and local community groups, and in meetings at places of work or residence.

Permission has been granted to the proletarian peasants to not only have their powerless voices heard but for them to have meaningless participation. To "take part in the management of the State" is not the same things as "to manage the State."

> Article 49. Every citizen of the USSR has *the right* to submit proposals to state bodies and public organisations for improving their activity, and *to criticise shortcomings in their work.*
>
> Officials are obliged, within established time-limits, to examine citizens' proposals and requests, to reply to them, and to take appropriate action.
>
> Persecution for criticism is prohibited. Persons guilty of such persecution shall be called to account (emphasis added).

Didn't Mao say the same thing in his Hundred Flowers Campaign? In 1957, Mao invited intellectuals to participate in open discussion and criticism of the Communist government, as "where 100 flowers bloom—100 schools of thought contend." Only five weeks later, after coaxing "the snakes out of their dens so they could chop off their heads," the "antirightist campaign" began lasting through 1960, beginning over a decade of political persecutions. Half a million people were targeted and sent to labor camps where they labored all day and were subject to "self-criticism" meetings at night, leading to mass depression, divorce, and suicide.

Several articles and books, including Xianhui Yang's *Woman from Shanghai: Tales of Survival from a Chinese Labor Camp*, document what transpired. Three thousand or so prisoners were sent to the Jiabiangou Labor Camp for "reeducation through labor," where only around five hundred would survive. It was closed in 1961. The only real archives available on Jiabiangou are its survivors.[22]

On August 25, 2008, Howard W. French wrote an article for *The New York Times*, where he quoted what it was like there, including "the exposure to bitter cold; hunger so intense as to cause inmates to eat human flesh; the familiar sequence of symptoms, beginning with edema, that lead down the path to death; the toolbox of common survivor techniques, from toadyism to betrayal, from stealthy theft to making use of the vestiges of privilege." Other "stories depict unimaginable and viscerally disgusting acts of self-survival: cannibalism, eating vomit, picking undigested food from animal feces, excavation of fellow prisoner's plugged intestines in desperate attempts to forestall death."[23]

A positive "right" is no unalienable Individual Right! There is no criticizing communism under communist rule!

> Article 50. In accordance with the interests of the people and *in order to strengthen and develop the socialist system,* citizens of the USSR are *guaranteed* freedom of speech, of the press, and of assembly, meetings, street processions and demonstrations.
>
> Exercise of these political freedoms is ensured by putting public buildings, streets and squares at the disposal of the working people and their organisations, by broad dissemination of information, and by the opportunity to use the press, television, and radio.
>
> Article 51. *In accordance with the aims of building communism,* citizens of the USSR have the right to associate in public organisations that promote their political activity and initiative and satisfaction of their various interests.
>
> Public organisations *are guaranteed conditions* for successfully performing the functions defined in their rules.

Article 52. Citizens of the USSR *are guaranteed* freedom of conscience, that is, the right to profess or not to profess any religion, and to conduct religious worship or atheistic propaganda. Incitement of hostility or hatred on religious grounds is prohibited.

In the USSR, *the church is separated from the state*, and the school from the church.

Article 53. The family *enjoys* the protection of the state.

Marriage is based on the free consent of the woman and the man; the spouses are completely equal in their family relations.

The state helps the family by providing and developing a broad system of childcare institutions, by organising and improving communal services and public catering, by paying grants on the birth of a child, by providing children's allowances and benefits for large families, and other forms of family allowances and assistance (emphasis added).

Without the Liberty to provide anything for themselves, the Russian people under this positive Constitution are at the mercy of the state for them. With no power to check government abuse, "positive rights" become empty "positive promises." What faith would you put in a Communist promise?

Article 54. Citizens of the USSR are *guaranteed* inviolability of the person. No one may be arrested except by a court decision or on the warrant of a procurator.

Article 55. Citizens of the USSR are *guaranteed* inviolability of the home. No one may, without lawful grounds, enter a home against the will of those residing in it.

Article 56. The privacy of citizens, and of their correspondence, telephone conversations, and telegraphic communications is protected by law.

Article 57. Respect for the individual and protection of the rights and freedoms of citizens are *the duty of all state bodies, public organisations, and officials.*
    Citizens of the USSR have the right to protection by the courts against encroachments on their honour and reputation, life and health, and personal freedom and property.

Article 58. Citizens of the USSR have the right to lodge a complaint against the actions of officials, state bodies and public bodies. Complaints shall be examined according to the procedure and within the time-limit established by law.
    Actions by officials that contravene the law or exceed their powers, and infringe the rights of citizens, *may be appealed* against in a court in the manner prescribed by law.
    Citizens of the USSR have the right to compensation for damage resulting from unlaw-

ful actions by state organisations and public organisations, or by officials in the performance of their duties.

Article 59. *Citizens' exercise of their rights and freedoms is inseparable from the performance of their duties and obligations.*

Citizens of the USSR are obliged to observe the Constitution of the USSR and Soviet laws, comply with the standards of socialist conduct, and uphold the honour and dignity of Soviet citizenship.

Article 60. *It is the duty of, and matter of honour for, every able-bodied citizen of the USSR to work conscientiously in his chosen, socially useful occupation, and strictly to observe labour discipline. Evasion of socially useful work is incompatible with the principles of socialist society.* (emphasis added)

Under a positive constitution, the citizens are not free to pursue their own happiness, only "obligated" to work for the happiness of the state. Fabian Socialist George Bernard Shaw agreed that, indeed, "evasion of socially useful work is incompatible with the principles of socialist society" when he stated the following:

> You must all know half a dozen people at least who are no use in this world, who are more trouble than they are worth. Just put them there and say Sir, or Madam, now will you be kind enough to justify your existence? If you cant

justify your existence, if youre not pulling your weight in the social boat, if youre not producing as much as you consume or perhaps a little more, then, clearly, we cannot use the organizations of our society for the purpose of keeping you alive, because your life does not benefit us and it cant be of very much use to yourself.[24]

Article 61. *Citizens of the USSR are obliged to preserve and protect socialist property. It is the duty of a citizen of the USSR to combat misappropriation and squandering of state and socially-owned property and to make thrifty use of the people's wealth.*

Persons encroaching in any way on socialist property shall be punished according to the law.

Article 62. *Citizens of the USSR are obliged to safeguard the interests of the Soviet state, and to enhance its power and prestige.*

Defence of the Socialist Motherland is the sacred duty of every citizen of the USSR.

Betrayal of the Motherland is the gravest of crimes against the people.

Article 63. *Military service in the ranks of the Armed Forces of the USSR is an honorable duty of Soviet citizens.*

Article 64. *It is the duty of every citizen of the USSR to respect the national dignity of other cit-*

izens, and to strengthen friendship of the nations and nationalities of the multinational Soviet state.

Article 65. A citizen of the USSR is obliged to respect the rights and lawful interests of other persons, *to be uncompromising toward anti-social behaviour, and to help maintain public order.*

Article 66. *Citizens of the USSR are obliged to concern themselves with the upbringing of children, to train them for socially useful work, and to raise them as worthy members of socialist society.* Children are obliged to care for their parents and help them.

Article 67. Citizens of the USSR are obliged to protect nature and conserve its riches.

Article 68. *Concern for the preservation of historical monuments and other cultural values is a duty and obligation of citizens of the USSR.*

Article 69. *It is the internationalist duty of citizens of the USSR to promote friendship and co-operation with peoples of other lands and help maintain and strengthen world peace*[25] (emphasis added).

This is what it leads to. Under a "positive" constitution, "positive rights" including "human rights" are, by permission, only given out with an accompanying "duty" to the state. What is owned by the state and then allowed by the state can and will be revoked by the state at the state's convenience. Under a positive constitution, what is moral or honorable is not for you to decide; you are told. Under a positive constitution, your children are not yours to raise and educate as you see fit. They are the state's to be raised and educated by you how you are told, to "train them for socially useful work, and to raise them as worthy members of socialist society."

The Constitution of the United States does not include such positive liberties for a reason. We don't get our Rights from government! We are born with them! They are natural and inherent, endowed to us by our Creator! For us to accept any redistributed right or liberty from a government, we must first surrender them or have them confiscated from us in order to receive our allowed ration of them back from government. What we surrender to the government, we are no longer free to do for ourselves!

In 1925, Adolf Hitler said this in his *Mein Kampf*:

> Volume One - A Reckoning
> Chapter II: Years of Study and Suffering in Vienna
>
> The environment of my youth consisted of petty-bourgeois circles, hence of a world having very little relation to the purely manual worker....
>
> The reason for this hostility, as we might almost call it, lies in the fear of a social group, which has but recently raised itself above the level of the manual worker, that it will sink back into the old despised class, or at least become identified with it. To this, in many cases, we must add the repugnant memory of the cultural poverty of this lower class, the frequent vulgarity of its social intercourse; the petty bourgeois' own position in society, however insignificant it

may be, makes any contact with this outgrown stage of life and culture intolerable.

Consequently, the higher classes feel less constraint in their dealings with the lowest of their fellow men than seems possible to the 'upstart.'

For anyone is an upstart who rises by his own efforts from his previous position in life to a higher one.

Ultimately this struggle, which is often so hard, kills all pity. Our own painful struggle for existence destroys our feeling for the misery of those who have remained behind.

In this respect Fate was kind to me. By forcing me to return to this world of poverty and insecurity, from which my father had risen in the course of his life, it removed the blinders of a narrow petty-bourgeois upbringing from my eyes. Only now did I learn to know humanity, learning to distinguish between empty appearances or brutal externals and the inner being.

Volume One - A Reckoning
Chapter X: Causes of the Collapse

The first consequence of gravest importance was the weakening of the peasant class. Proportionately as the peasant class diminished, the mass of the big city proletariat increased more and more, until finally the balance was completely upset.

Now the abrupt alternation between rich and poor became really apparent. Abundance and poverty lived so close together that the saddest consequences could and inevitably did arise. Poverty and frequent unemployment began to play havoc with people, leaving behind them a memory of discontent and embitterment. The consequence of this seemed to be political class division. Despite all the economic prosperity....

In proportion as economic life grew to be the dominant mistress of the state, money became the god whom all had to serve and to whom each man had to bow down.

Volume One - A Reckoning
Chapter XII: The First Period of Development of the National Socialist German Workers' Party

No resurrection of the German people can occur except through the recovery of outward power. But the prerequisites for this are not arms, as our bourgeois 'statesmen' keep prattling, but the forces of the will. The German people had more than enough arms before. They were not able to secure freedom because the energies of the national instinct of self-preservation, the will for self-preservation, were lacking. The best weapon is dead, worthless material as long as the spirit is lacking which is ready, willing, and determined to use it. Germany became defenseless, not because arms were lacking, but because the will was lacking to guard the weapon for national survival....

To win the masses for a national resurrection, no social sacrifice is too great.

> Whatever economic concessions *are made to our working class* today, they stand in no proportion to the gain for the entire nation if they help to give the broad masses back to their nation (emphasis added).

Or, as Rousseau says, "As he yields others over himself, he gains an equivalent for everything he loses, and an increase of force for the preservation of what he has."[26]

> Only pigheaded short-sightedness, such as is often unfortunately found in our employer circles, can fail to recognize that *in the long run there can be no economic upswing for them and hence no economic profit*....
> *If during the War the German unions had ruthlessly guarded the interests of the working class, if even during the War they had struck a thousand times over and forced approval of the demands of the workers they represented on the dividend-hungry employers...the War would not have been lost.*...
> The national education of the broad masses can only take place indirectly through a social uplift, since thus exclusively can those general economic premises be created which permit the individual to partake of the cultural goods of the nation...a people cannot be made 'national' in the sense understood by our present-day bourgeoisie....
> In the blood alone resides the strength as well as the weakness of man...Peoples which

> renounce the preservation of their racial purity renounce with it the unity of their soul in all its expressions....
>
> Without the clearest knowledge of the racial problem and hence of the Jewish problem there will never be a resurrection of the German nation....
>
> *Organizing the broad masses of our people which are today in the international camp into a national people's community does not mean renouncing the defense of justified class interests* (emphasis added).

As we will see later, the purification of blood or eugenic aspect of Hitler's version of the Philosophy is not without company. Neither is the confiscation of proprietor profits or call for unionized labor uprisings. Also note that though he wants to "organize" the international camp or Communists into a National Socialists camp, he does not renounce their commonality, defending "class interests," that "social justice" be done.

> The integration of an occupational group which has become a class with the national community, or merely with the state, is not accomplished by the lowering of higher dasses but by uplifting the lower dasses. This process in turn can never be upheld by the higher class, but only by the lower class fighting for its equal rights. The present-day bourgeoisie was not organized into the state by measures of the nobility, but by its own energy under its own leadership....

> *Unions with a fanatical national leadership in political and national matters would make millions of workers into the most valuable members of their nation....*

Just as surely as a worker sins against the spirit of a real national community when, without regard for the common welfare and the survival of a national economy, he uses his power to raise extortionate demands, *an employer breaks this community to the same extent when he conducts his business in an inhuman, exploiting way, misuses the national labor force and makes millions out of its sweat. He then has no right to designate himself as national, no right to speak of a national community; no, he is a selfish scoundrel who induces social unrest* and provokes future conflicts which whatever happens must end in harming the nation.

Thus, the reservoir from which the young movement must gather its supporters will primarily be the masses of our workers. Its work will be to tear these away from the international delusion, to free them from their social distress, to raise them out of their cultural misery and lead them to the national community as a valuable, united factor, national in feeling and desire....

Clear position must express itself in the propaganda of the movement (emphasis added).

Volume Two - The National Socialist Movement
Chapter I: Philosophy and Party

Democracy is exploited by the Marxists for the purpose of paralysing their opponents and gaining for themselves a free hand to put their own methods into action. When certain groups of Marxists use all their ingenuity for the time being to make it be believed that they are inseparably attached to the principles of democracy...*Marxism will march shoulder to shoulder with democracy until it succeeds indirectly in securing for its own criminal purposes even the support of those whose minds are nationally orientated and whom Marxism strives to exterminate...Instead of appealing to the democratic conscience, the standard bearers of the Red International would immediately send forth a furious rallying-cry among the proletarian masses and the ensuing fight would not take place in the sedate atmosphere of Parliament but in the factories and the streets. Then democracy would be annihilated forthwith.* And what the intellectual prowess of the apostles who represented the people in Parliament had failed to accomplish would now be successfully carried out by the crow-bar and the sledge-hammer of the exasperated proletarian masses...At a blow they would awaken the bourgeois world to see the madness of thinking that the Jewish drive towards world-conquest can be effectually opposed by means of Western Democracy (emphasis added).

It isn't the antibourgeois, anticapitalist, or "pro-proletarian revolution" aspects of what define Communism or socialism that Hitler is against. He is a socialist! It is the *delay* of justice, the two-step process, specifically the "democratic step," of their revolution that he hates. It's not the exploitation of the middle class—that they be deceitfully seduced into becoming the means to their own *eventual* end—that he hates; *it is that it is eventual!* Unlike the Communists of the Inter-National Socialist Camp, Hitler and his National Socialist Camp would "send forth a furious rallying-cry among the proletarian masses and the ensuing fight would not take place in the sedate atmosphere of Parliament but in the factories and the streets. Then democracy would be annihilated forthwith."

> The word 'religious' acquires a precise meaning only when it is associated with a distinct and definite form through which the concept is put into practice....But, *since the masses of the people are not composed of philosophers or saints, such a vague religious idea will mean for them nothing else than to justify each individual in thinking and acting according to his own bent...* But all these ideas, no matter how firmly the individual believes in them, may be critically analysed by any person and accepted or rejected accordingly, until the emotional concept or yearning has been transformed into an active service that is governed by a clearly defined doctrinal faith. Such a faith furnishes the practical outlet for religious feeling to express itself and thus opens the way through which it can be put into practice.

> *Without a clearly defined belief, the religious feeling would not only be worthless for the purposes of human existence but even might contribute towards a general disorganization, on account of its vague and multifarious tendencies....*
>
> Every philosophy of life, even if it is a thousand times correct and of the highest benefit to mankind, will be of no practical service for the maintenance of a people as long as its principles have not yet become the rallying point of a militant movement. And, on its own side, this movement will remain a mere party until is has brought its ideals to victory and transformed its party doctrines into the new foundations of a State which gives the national community its final shape (emphasis added).

Hitler is all for religion as long as it is "clearly defined" by his terms benefitting his ends, but not allowing any other that might lead to or "justify each individual in thinking and acting according to his own bent." Like Hobbes says:

> [A] covenant, made, not with men, but with God; this also is unjust: for there is no Covenant with God, but by mediation of some body that representeth Gods Person; which none doth but Gods Lieutenant, who hath the Soveraignty under God. But this pretence of Covenant with God, is so evident a lye, even in the pretenders own consciences, that it is not onely an act of an unjust, but also of a vile, and unmanly disposition. Because the Right of bear-

ing the Person raigne of them all, is given to him they make Soveraigne, by Power of Covenant onely of one to another, and...cannot be forfeited. there can happen no breach of Covenant on the part of the Soveraigne; and consequently none of his Subjects, by any pretence of forfeiture, can be freed from his Subjection.[9]

Hitler continues:

> The current political conception of the world is that the State, though it possesses a creative force which can build up civilizations, has nothing in common with the concept of race as the foundation of the State. The State is considered rather as something which has resulted from economic necessity, or, at best, the natural outcome of the play of political forces and impulses. Such a conception of the foundations of the State, together with all its logical consequences, not only ignores the primordial racial forces that underlie the State, but it also leads to a policy in which the importance of the individual is minimized.

This is another example here of duplicity in meaning or in the understanding of meaning implied versus the meaning understood. This is a very common tactic used by most, if not all, progressive politicians today. Though it is probably not Hitler's intention here, as this was meant for German ears, you need to become aware of it so that you might be able to recognize it, not if but when it occurs. Example, when we as Americans, who have been raised in a society that traditionally upholds rugged "individualism" against the collectivism of Marxism, hear Hitler speak ill of Marxism because it "leads to a policy in which the importance of the individual is minimized," it lends to confusion. That confusion then allows for us to accept that Hitler and, therefore, fascism as being synonymous with "right wing" individualism. Not so!

As you have already read above, he is about "nationalizing" the people under a "general will," prohibiting, as he says, "each individual in thinking and acting according to his own bent." What matters to Hitler is that the bloodlines of each and every individual who has submitted to the "general will" of his state be pure. Not like under Marxism, where they *need* all suppressed races, genders, and classes, in addition to the petty bourgeoisie/middle class, in order to win elections in their "eventual" democratic revolution toward a "dictatorship of the proletariat" and the "utopia" of socialism/communism.

So in hearing Hitler speak of the importance of the individual, he may mean one thing (bloodlines of each in the collective), but we hear another—"the importance of each individual." They are not the same; they are opposite! Beware the progressive politicians who have engaged in this "duplicity" of meaning with their words, which mean *not* what you understand! Beware the progressive politician who holds "right wing" individualism and capitalism synonymous to Hitler's *collectivist* fascism!

> Thus the Marxist doctrine is the concentrated extract of the mentality which underlies the general concept of life today. For this reason alone it is out of the question and even ridiculous to think that what is called our bourgeois world can put up any effective fight against Marxism. For this bourgeois world is permeated with all those same poisons and its conception

of life in general differs from Marxism only in degree and in the character of the persons who hold it. The bourgeois world is Marxist but believes in the possibility of a certain group of people—that is to say, the bourgeoisie—being able to dominate the world, while Marxism itself systematically aims at delivering the world into the hands of the Jews.

Over against all this, the völkisch concept of the world recognizes that the primordial racial elements are of the greatest significance for mankind. In principle, the State is looked upon only as a means to an end and this end is the conservation of the racial characteristics of mankind. Therefore on the völkisch principle we cannot admit that one race is equal to another. By recognizing that they are different, the völkisch concept separates mankind into races of superior and inferior quality. On the basis of this recognition it feels bound in conformity with the eternal Will that dominates the universe, to postulate the victory of the better and stronger and the subordination of the inferior and weaker. And so it pays homage to the truth that the principle underlying all Nature's operations is the aristocratic principle and it believes that this law holds good even down to the last individual organism. It selects individual values from the mass and thus operates as an organizing principle, whereas Marxism acts as a disintegrating solvent.

There you have it: Hitler bases his theory of racial superiority on the theory of evolution! What philosophy promotes evolution?

> Volume Two - The National Socialist Movement
> Chapter II: The State
> We National Socialists, who are fighting for a new philosophy of life must never take our stand on the famous 'basis of facts', and especially not on mistaken facts. If we did so, we should cease to be the protagonists of a new and great idea and would become slaves in the service of the fallacy which is dominant today. We must make a clear-cut distinction between the vessel and its contents. The State is only the vessel and the race is what it contains. The vessel can have a meaning only if it preserves and safeguards the contents. Otherwise it is worthless.
> Hence the supreme purpose of the folkish State is to guard and preserve those original racial elements which, through their work in the cultural field, create that beauty and dignity which are characteristic of a higher mankind. *We, as Aryans, can consider the State only as the living organism of a people*, an organism which does not merely maintain the existence of a people, but functions in such a way as to lead its people to a position of supreme liberty by the progressive development of the intellectual and cultural faculties (emphasis added).

Comte's positive sociology, being "a knowledge of which will enable man to reorganize society so that it will satisfy his needs and enable him to maximize his progress"—along with his "social dynamics…what is needed for the development of order, that is, progress"—is evidently here hard at work under Hitler.²

> It will be the task of the People's State to make the race the centre of the life of the community. It must make sure that the purity of *the racial strain will be preserved.* It must proclaim the truth that *the child is the most valuable possession a people can have. It must see to it that only those who are healthy shall beget children; that there is only one infamy, namely, for parents that are ill or show hereditary defects to bring children into the world* and that in such cases it is a high honour to refrain from doing so. But, on the other hand, it must be considered as reprehensible conduct to refrain from giving healthy children to the nation. In this matter the State must assert itself as the trustee of a millennial future, in face of which the egotistic desires of the individual count for nothing and will have to give way before the ruling of the State. In order to fulfil this duty in a practical manner *the State will have to avail itself of modern medical discoveries. It must proclaim as unfit for procreation all those who are inflicted with some visible hereditary disease or are the carriers of it; and practical measures must be adopted to have such people rendered sterile.* On the other hand, provision must be made for the normally fertile woman so that she will not be restricted in child-bearing through the financial and economic system operating in

a political regime that looks upon the blessing of having children as a curse to their parents. The State will have to abolish the cowardly and even criminal indifference with which the problem of social amenities for large families is treated, and it will have to be the supreme protector of this greatest blessing that a people can boast of. Its attention and care must be directed towards the child rather than the adult.

Those who are physically and mentally unhealthy and unfit must not perpetuate their own suffering in the bodies of their children. From the educational point of view there is here a huge task for the People's State to accomplish. But in a future era this work will appear greater and more significant than the victorious wars of our present bourgeois epoch. Through educational means the State must teach individuals that illness is not a disgrace but an unfortunate accident which has to be pitied, yet that it is a crime and a disgrace to make this affliction all the worse by passing on disease and defects to innocent creatures out of mere egotism. And the State must also teach the people that it is an expression of a really noble nature and that it is a humanitarian act worthy of admiration if a person who innocently suffers from hereditary disease refrains from having a child of his own but gives his love and affection to some unknown child who, through its health, promises to become a robust member of a healthy community. *In accomplishing such an educa-*

> *tional task the State integrates its function by this activity in the moral sphere. It must act on this principle without paying any attention to the question of whether its conduct will be understood or misconstrued, blamed or praised.*
>
> If for a period of only 600 years those individuals would be sterilized who are physically degenerate or mentally diseased, humanity would not only be delivered from an immense misfortune but also restored to a state of general health such as we at present can hardly imagine. If the fecundity of the healthy portion of the nation should be made a practical matter in a conscientious and methodical way, we should have at least the beginnings of a race from which all those germs would be eliminated which are today the cause of our moral and physical decadence[27] (emphasis added).

Yeah, just imagine all the benefits. However, Hitler was in no way the only one envisioning a eugenically pure utopia.

Thomas Robert Malthus, an ordained minister, first published his work *An Essay on the Principle of Population* in 1798. He put forth a simple but controversial observation that set the precedent for much of what the progressive movement would later adopt as justification for central planning, population control, prostitution, family planning, birth control, and the moral bankruptcy of society through "unnatural," nonprocreational promiscuity and sexual liberation. In it, he correlates virtuous monogamous relationships of "one man, one woman" with undesirable exponential increases in population. If society doesn't partake in the "vice" of promiscuousness, then the "greater evils" of poverty, starvation, and disease most assuredly await us. As part of his essay, Malthus put forth:

> Book I - Chapter I
>
> I.I.1 In an inquiry concerning the improvement of society, the mode of conducting the subject which naturally presents itself, is,
>
> 1. *To investigate the causes that have hitherto impeded the progress of mankind towards happiness*; and,
>
> 2. To examine the probability *of the total or partial removal of these causes in future*.
>
> I.I.6 In plants and irrational animals, the view of the subject is simple. They are all impelled by a powerful instinct to the increase of their species; and this instinct is interrupted by no doubts about providing for their offspring. Wherever therefore there is liberty, the power of increase is exerted; and the superabundant effects are repressed afterwards by want of room and nourishment.
>
> I.I.7 The effects of this check on man are more complicated. Impelled to the increase of his species by an equally powerful instinct, *reason interrupts his career, and asks him whether he may not bring beings into the world, for whom he cannot provide the means of support*. If he attend to this natural suggestion, the restriction too frequently produces vice. If he hear it not, the human race will be constantly endeavouring to increase beyond the means of subsistence. But as, by that law of our nature which makes food

> necessary to the life of man, *population can never actually increase beyond the lowest nourishment capable of supporting it, a strong check on population, from the difficulty of acquiring food, must be constantly in operation.* This difficulty must fall somewhere, and must necessarily be severely felt in some or other of the various forms of misery, or the fear of misery, by a large portion of mankind.
>
> I.I.10 Whether the law of marriage be instituted, or not, *the dictate of nature and virtue seems to be an early attachment to one woman*; and where there were no impediments of any kind in the way of an union to which such an attachment would lead, and no causes of *depopulation* afterwards, the *increase of the human species would be evidently much greater than any increase which has been hitherto known* (emphasis added).

The earth can only provide a good, healthy high standard of living for so many people. Once the limit point is reached, the standard of living begins to decline. In game conservation, it's referred to as the "carrying capacity." However, Malthus does not take into account man's ever-expanding abilities to provide through technology and markets, an ever-increasing amount of varied provisions, more than adequate to sustain higher and higher populations. He also points out the specific troublesome human trait of moral virtue—which, if left unchecked without some kind of "impediment" or constraint, would lead to an "increase of the human species" that "would be evidently much greater than any increase which has been hitherto known": the virtue of "an early attachment to one woman."

Chapter II

I.II.1 *The ultimate check to population appears then to be a want of food*, arising necessarily from the different ratios according to which population and food increase. But this ultimate check is never the immediate check, except in cases of actual famine.

I.II.4 The preventive check, as far as it is voluntary, is peculiar to man, and arises from that distinctive superiority in his reasoning faculties, which enables him to calculate distant consequences. The checks to the indefinite increase of plants and irrational animals are all either positive, or, if preventive, involuntary. But man cannot look around him, and see the distress which frequently presses *upon those who have large families*; he cannot contemplate his present possessions or earnings,... if he follow the bent of his inclinations, he may be able to support the offspring which he will probably bring into the world. *In a state of equality, if such can exist, this would be the simple question. In the present state of society other considerations occur.* Will he not lower his rank in life, and be obliged to give up in great measure his former habits? Does any mode of employment present itself by which he may reasonably hope to maintain a family? Will he not at any rate subject himself to greater difficulties, and more severe labour, than in his single state? Will he not be unable to transmit to his children the same advantages of education and improvement that he had himself

> possessed? Does he even feel secure that, *should he have a large family, his utmost exertions can save them from rags and squalid poverty, and their consequent degradation in the community?* And may he not be reduced to the grating necessity of forfeiting his independence, and *of being obliged to the sparing hand of Charity for support?* (Emphasis added)

As the population increases, men with "an early attachment to one woman," procreating large families, do so to the detriment of not only themselves but to the whole of society. In a "we're all in this together," where all things are "equal" in everybody's house/society with "shared responsibility for a shared prosperity," everybody might suffer only a little. In a bourgeois or capitalist society with a "property class," the lower class and poor bear the brunt of the misery.

> I.II.5 *These considerations are calculated to prevent, and certainly do prevent, a great number of persons in all civilized nations from pursuing the dictate of nature in an early attachment to one woman.*
>
> I.II.7 When this restraint produces *vice*, the evils which follow are but too conspicuous. *A promiscuous intercourse to such a degree as to prevent the birth of children*, seems to lower, in the most marked manner, the dignity of human nature. It cannot be without its effect on men, and nothing can be more obvious than its tendency to degrade the female character, and to destroy all its most amiable and distinguishing characteristics....

I.II.8 *When a general corruption of morals, with regard to the sex, pervades all the classes of society, its effects must necessarily be, to poison the springs of domestic happiness, to weaken conjugal and parental affection, and to lessen the united exertions and ardour of parents in the care and education of their children*—effects which cannot take place without a decided diminution of the general happiness and virtue of the society....

I.II.11 Of the preventive checks, the restraint from marriage which is not followed by irregular gratifications may properly be termed moral restraint.

I.II.12 Promiscuous intercourse, unnatural passions, violations of the marriage bed, and improper arts to conceal the consequences of irregular connexions, are preventive checks that clearly come under the head of vice.

I.V.1 Of the ancient state of the British isles, and of islanders in general..."It is among these people that we trace the origin of that multitude of singular *institutions which retard the progress of population. Anthropophagy, the castration of males, the infibulation of females, late marriages; the consecration of virginity, the approbation of celibacy, the punishments exercised against girls who become mothers at too early an age*"....

I.V.7 Eareeoie societies...have been so often described, that little more need be said of them here, than that *promiscuous intercourse and infanticide* appear to be their fundamental laws…"so agreeable is this licentious plan of life to their disposition, that the most beautiful of both sexes thus commonly spend their youthful days, habituated to the practice of *enormities that would disgrace the most savage tribes*. When an Eareeoie woman is delivered of a child, a piece of cloth dipped in water is applied to the mouth and nose, which suffocates it….

I.V.14 *The great checks to increase appear to be the vices of promiscuous intercourse, infanticide, and war*, each of these operating with very considerable force….

I.V.22 Prostitution is extensively diffused, and prevails to a great degree among the lower classes of women; which must always operate as a most powerful check to population….

I.V.24 In the island of Formosa, it is said that the women were not allowed to bring children into the world before the age of thirty-five. If they were with-child prior to that period, *an abortion* was effected by the priestess"[28] (emphasis added).

Who could argue against sexual liberation as population control? Malthus observes that copious society-wide engagement of promiscuousness in not just sex but in unnatural passions of non-procreational (homosexuality? bestiality?) sex—along with infanticide, abortion, castration—could save us from a worse end than mere moral depravity. Though Malthus himself sees that a "general corruption of morals, with regard to the sex" serves only "to lessen the… virtue of the society" to those who would destroy the three-headed Hydra of our long held faith in God, our love of family, the concept of private property, and free enterprise, upon which our Individual Liberty stands. Malthusianism is the perfect premise upon which to kill two birds with one stone: Individual Liberty, which our own founding fathers warned was for a "moral people only," and population control, that their own privileged standard of living be preserved.

Margaret Sanger, the Fabian Socialist, eugenist founder of Family Planning agrees. In her 1920 book *Women and the New Race*, Sanger says the following:

> I. Woman's Error and Her Debt
> THE MOST far-reaching social development of modern times is the revolt of woman against sex servitude....
>
> No period of low wages or of idleness with their want among the workers, no peonage or sweatshop, no child-labor factory, ever came into being, save from the same source. Nor have famine and plague been as much "acts of God"...all students know, have their basic causes in over-population.

From the get-go, Sanger correlates the liberation of women from their sex servitude to that of both overpopulation and their liberation from the capitalist, imperialist exploiters and their sweatshops!

> II. Women's Struggle for Freedom
> Women in all lands and all ages have instinctively desired family limitation...It has been manifested in such horrors as infanticide, child abandonment and abortion....
>
> Society must recognize the terrible lesson taught by the innumerable centuries of infanti-

cide and foeticide. If these abhorrent practices could have been ended by punishment and suppression, they would have ceased long ago....

What is that lesson? It is this: woman's desire for freedom is born of the feminine spirit, which is the absolute, elemental, inner urge of womanhood. It is the strongest force in her nature; it cannot be destroyed; it can merely be diverted from its natural expression into violent and destructive channels,

If women cannot be liberated from their inherently slavish role as mothers, then via their "desire for freedom...born of the feminine spirit," which "cannot be destroyed," they will simply continue to kill their babies either through abortion or infanticide.

V. The Wickedness of Creating Large Families

THE MOST serious evil of our times is that of encouraging the bringing into the world of large families. The most immoral practice of the day is breeding too many children....

The immorality of large families lies not only in their injury to the members of those families but in their injury to society... Large families make plentiful labor and they also provide the workers for the child-labor factories as well as the armies of unemployed. That *population, swelled by overbreeding, is a basic cause of war,* we shall see in a later chapter. Without the large family, not one of these evils could exist to any considerable extent, much less to the extent that they exist to-day. The large family—especially the family

> too large to receive adequate care—is the one thing necessary to the perpetuation of these and other evils and is therefore a greater evil than any one of them....
>
> The average mother of a baby every year or two has been forced into unwilling motherhood, so far as the later arrivals are concerned. It is not the less immoral when *the power which compels enslavement is the church*, state or the propaganda of well-meaning patriots... *The wrong is as great as if the enslaving force were the unbridled passions of her husband. The wrong to the unwilling mother, deprived of her liberty, and all opportunity of self-development, is in itself enough to condemn large families as immoral* (emphasis added).

The role of wife and mother are slavery, and the resulting family is immoral. Large families take even more of the mother's time, depriving her of her liberty and, more importantly, self-development. Motherhood is slavery!

> *The most merciful thing that the large family does to one of its infant members is to kill it.* The same factors which create the terrible infant mortality rate, and which swell the death rate of children between the ages of one and five, operate even more extensively to lower the health rate of the surviving members...
>
> *Large families among the rich are immoral* not only because they invade the natural right of woman to the control of her own body, to

self-development and to self-expression, but *because they are oppressive to the poorer elements of society*. If the upper and middle classes of society had kept pace with the poorer elements of society in reproduction during the past fifty years, the working class to-day would be forced down to the level of the Chinese whose wage standard is said to be a few handfuls of rice a day.

The woman who has escaped the chains of too great reproductivity will never again wear them…Being free, we have a right to expect much of her. We expect her to give still greater expression to her feminine spirit—we expect her to enrich the intellectual, artistic, moral and spiritual life of the world. We expect her to *demolish old systems of morals, a degenerate prudery, Dark-Age religious concepts*, laws that enslave women by denying them the knowledge of their bodies, and information as to contraceptives.

VI. Cries of Despair and Society's Problems

Each and every unwanted child is likely to be in some way a social liability. It is only the wanted child who is likely to be a social asset. If we have faith in this intuitive demand of the unfortunate mothers, if we understand both its dire and its hopeful significance, we shall dispose of those social problems which so insistently and menacingly confront us to-day.…

Can a mother who would "rather die" than bear more children serve society by bearing still others? Can children carried through nine months of dread and unspeakable mental anguish and born into an atmosphere of fear and anger, to grow up uneducated and in want, be a benefit to the world?

VII. When Should a Woman Avoid Having Children?

To the woman who wishes to have children, we must give these answers to the question when not to have them....

By all means there should be no children when either mother or father suffers from such diseases as tuberculosis, gonorrhea, syphilis, cancer, epilepsy, insanity, drunkenness and mental disorders. In the case of the mother, heart disease, kidney trouble and pelvic deformities are also a serious bar to childbearing....

The jails, hospitals for the insane, poorhouses and houses of prostitution are filled with the children born of such parents, while an astounding number of their children are either stillborn or die in infancy.

Sanger, believing in the science of eugenics, here lists some unwanted elements among us that might be "bred out" of the human race, if only they weren't allowed to breed. Look for her "wanted child" versus the "unwanted child" to show up again.

The woman of the workers knows what society does with her offspring. Knowing the bitter truth, learned in unspeakable anguish, what shall this woman say to society? The power is in her hands. She can bring forth more children to perpetuate these conditions, *or she can withhold the human grist from these cruel mills which grind only disaster.*

Shall she say to society that she will go on multiplying the misery that she herself has endured? Shall she go on breeding children who can only suffer and die? Rather, shall she not say that until society puts a higher value upon motherhood she will not be a mother? Shall she not sacrifice her mother instincts *for the common good* and say that *until children are held as something better than commodities upon the labor market, she will bear no more? Shall she not give up her desire for even a small family*, and say to society *that until the world is made fit for children to live in, she will have no children at all?* (Emphasis added)

In the end, until we have a full-blown utopian, socialist society where there can be no profit by the labor of her progeny, any family, even the small family, must be viewed as continuing to "perpetuate these conditions."

XII. Will Birth Control Help the Cause of Labor?

LABOR seems instinctively to have recognized the fact that its servitude springs from numbers... *The basic principle of craft unionism is limitation of the number of workers in a given trade....*

> The weakness of craft unionism is that it does not carry its principle far enough. It applies its policy of limitation of numbers only to the trade. In his home, the worker, whether he is a unionist or non-unionist, goes on producing large numbers of children to compete with him eventually in the labor market....
>
> That enemy (of labor) is the reproductive ability of the working class which gluts the channels of progress with the helpless and weak, and stimulates the tyrants of the world in their oppression of mankind [emphasis added].

Here, again, her concern is the effect of children born on the proletariat class. Overproduction is a common accusation against capitalism in so to keep the value of labor low. But why would a company, any company, or even all companies in some vast right-wing conspiratorial agreement purposefully "overproduce" just to keep the market value of labor down when to do so would simultaneously force the values of all their products and bottom lines down as well? It's an accusation that makes no real-world sense whatsoever. Here, Sanger actually blames the family for that overproduction by flooding the market with workers, thereby lowering the value of labor. But wouldn't such an increase in population also increase the numbers of potential customers and, therefore, a potential expansion of the market via a higher demand for both products and labor? Nevertheless, two of the big problems here for Sanger are family and free-market capitalism.

XIII. Battalions of Unwanted Babies the Cause of War

As soon as the country becomes overpopulated, these reactionaries proclaim loudly its moral right to expand. They point to the huge population, *which in the name of patriotism they have previously demanded* should be brought into being.

The "need of expansion" is only another name for overpopulation...Behind all war has been the pressure of population.

Robert Thomas Malthus, formulator of...the relation of overpopulation to war. He showed that mankind tends to increase faster than the food supply. He demonstrated that were it not for the more common diseases, for plague, famine, floods and wars, human beings would crowd each other to such an extent that the misery would be even greater than it now is...*If we do not exercise sufficient judgment to regulate the birth rate, we encounter disease, starvation and war* (emphasis added).

We do not have to connect the dots from Malthusianism's population control to Sanger; she tells us of the connection herself. In addition to the imperialist exploitation of the capitalists and their market, there is also the "unwanted-baby-fed war machine of the Patriot." Remember what Max Stirner said about patriots in his 1845 *All Things Are Nothing to Me*:

> Just observe the nation that is defended by devoted patriots. The patriots fall in bloody battle or in the fight with hunger and want; what

does the nation care for that? By the manure of their corpses the nation comes to "its bloom"! The individuals have died "for the great cause of the nation," and the nation sends some words of thanks after them and—has the profit of it.²⁹

XIV. Woman and the New Morality

UPON the shoulders of the woman conscious of her freedom rests the responsibility of creating a new sex morality....

We get most of our notions of sex morality *from the Christian church...* The church has generally defined the "immoral woman" as one who mates out of wedlock. Virtually, it lets it go at that. In its practical workings, *there is nothing in the church code of morals to protect the woman, either from unwilling submission to the wishes of her husband, from undesired pregnancy*, nor from any other of the outrages only too familiar to many married women. Nothing is said about *the crime of bringing an unwanted child into the world*, where often it cannot be adequately cared for and is, therefore, condemned to a life of misery. *The church's one point of insistence is upon the right of itself to legalize marriage and to compel the woman to submit to whatever such marriage may bring.* It is true that there are remedies of divorce in the case of the state, but the church has adhered strictly to the principle that marriage, once consummated, is indissoluble. Thus, in its operation, *the church's code of sex morals has nothing to do with the basic sex rights*

> *of the woman, but enforces, rather, the assumed property rights of the man to the body and the services of his wife.* They are man-made codes; their vital factor, as *they apply to woman, is submission to the man*....
>
> Church and state have forbidden women to leave their legal mates, or to refuse to submit to the marital embrace, *no matter how filthy, drunken, diseased or otherwise repulsive the man might be—no matter how much of a crime it might be to bring to birth a child by him*....
>
> Let it be realized that this creation of new sex ideals is a challenge to the church. Being a challenge to the church, it is also, in less degree, a challenge to the state...Imperialists and exploiters will fight hardest in the open, but the ecclesiastic will fight longest in the dark[30] (emphasis added).

As we saw in chapter 1, here again, from the suffering, unfairness, and overpopulation to "the assumed property rights of the man to the body and the services of his wife," it all eventually gets laid at the feet of God. Sanger's "new sex morality" of unfettered consequenceless promiscuity challenging both the church and the state is also an extremely effective challenge to the morality necessary for true Liberty to stand or, as Charles Carroll, signer of the Declaration of Independence (Maryland) put it in November of 1800:

> Without morals a republic cannot subsist any length of time; they therefore who are decrying the Christian religion whose morality is so sublime and pure...are undermining the

solid foundation of morals, the best security for the duration of free governments.[31]

In 1946, famed Fabian Socialist Julian Huxley wrote *UNESCO: Its Purpose and Its Philosophy* on behalf of the United Nations Educational, Scientific and Cultural Organization. In it, he declares its mission and agenda as such:

> From acceptance of certain principles or philosophies, Unesco is obviously debarred. Thus, while fully recognising the contribution made to thought by many of their thinkers, it cannot base its outlook on one of the competing theologies of the world as against the others, whether Islam, Roman Catholicism, Protestant Christianity, Buddhism, Unitarianism, Judaism, or Hinduism. Neither can it espouse one of the politico-economic doctrines competing in the world to-day to the exclusion of the others-the present versions of capitalistic free enterprise, Marxist communism, semi-socialist planning, and so on. It cannot do so, partly because it is contrary to its charter and essence to be sectarian, partly for the very practical reason that any such attempt would immediately incur the active hostility of large and influential groups, and the non-cooperation or even withdrawal of a number of nations…. (p. 6–7)
> Nor, with its stress on democracy and the principles of human dignity, equality and mutual respect, can it adopt the view that the State is a higher or more important end than

the individual; or any rigid class theory of society. And in the preamble to its Constitution it expressly repudiates racialism and any belief in superior or inferior "races," nations, or ethnic groups.

And finally, with its stress on the concrete tasks of education, science and culture, on the need for mutual understanding by the peoples of the world, and on the objectives of peace and human welfare on this planet, it would seem debarred from an exclusively or primarily other-worldly outlook. (p. 7)

An otherworldly outlook, of course, being a reliance upon or belief in God. As we have seen, it is prevalent within the Philosophy to start a statement, as Huxley does here, with a favorable view of the apposing philosophy consisting of Individual Liberty and its three pillars of happiness, God, family, and property. Then comes the appearance of neutrality. However, as it always does, it ends here, as well, with extreme prejudice.

Pay special close attention to what comes next, for it is the basis set by Comte expanded on by Huxley, which is the premise for all that follows and what comprises the strands of order and sustainability.

> Accordingly its outlook must, it seems, be based on some form of *humanism*. Further, that humanism must clearly be *a world humanism*... It must also be a scientific *humanism*....
>
> Finally it must be an evolutionary as opposed to a static or ideal humanism. *It is essential for Unesco to adopt an evolutionary approach.* If it does not do so, its philosophy will be a false

humanism." It not only shows us man's place in nature and his relations to the rest of the phenomenal universe, not only gives us a description of the various types of evolution and the various trends and directions within them, but allows us to distinguish desirable and undesirable trends, and to demonstrate the existence of progress in the cosmos. *And finally it shows us man as now the sole trustee of further evolutionary progress*, and gives us important guidance as to the courses he should avoid and those he should pursue if he is to achieve that progress. (p. 7–8)

An evolutionary approach provides the link between natural science and human history ; it teaches us the need to think in the dynamic terms of speed and direction rather than in the static ones of momentary position or quantitative achievement; it not only shows us the origin and biological roots of our human values, but gives us some basis and external standards for them among the apparently neutral mass of natural phenomena....

Thus the general philosophy of Unesco should, it seems, be a scientific world humanism, global in extent and evolutionary in background. (p. 8, emphasis added)

Again, Comte's social dynamics being "what is needed for the development of order, that is, progress." Thus, "social planning is... indeed required."

The evolutionary aspect is critical to understanding the importance of environmentalism and the protection of biodiversity to the

Philosophy. Humanism and evolutionism are both fundamentally anti-God. With no God, there is no creation and no God-given unalienable Individual Rights. Also, with no God and no creation, we are only here because of evolution. It now becomes our "shared responsibility" to protect the biodiversity of earth so that future evolution has the largest "primordial soup," if you will, from which to evolve into the future. Again, this is the social premise of all environmentalism, all biodiversity, and the positive rights of "order"!

III. UNESCO AND HUMAN PROGRESS

Our first task must be to clarify the notion of desirable and undesirable directions of evolution....

Evolution in the human sector consists mainly of changes in the form of society; in tools and machines, in new ways of utilising the old innate potentialities, instead of in the nature of these potentialities, as in the biological sector. (p. 9)

The ethical values may be limited and primitive, such as unquestioning loyalty to a tribe, or high and universal, like those which Jesus first introduced into the affairs of the world: the point is that only in the human sector do they become a part of the mechanism of change and evolution.... (p. 11)

Of special importance in man's evaluation of his own position in the cosmic scheme and of his further destiny is *the fact that he is the heir, and indeed the sole heir, of evolutionary progress to date.*

When he asserts that he is the highest type of organism, he is not being guilty of anthropocentric vanity, but is enunciating a biological fact. Furthermore, *he is not merely the sole heir of past evolutionary progress, but the sole trustee for any that may be achieved in the future.* From the evolutionary point of view, the destiny of man may be summed up very simply: it is to realise the maximum progress in the minimum time. That is why the philosophy of Unesco must have an evolutionary background, and why the concept of progress cannot but occupy a central position in that philosophy.

Even knowledge that appears to be wholly beneficent can be applied in such a way that it does not promote progress. Thus, the application of medical science may increase the number of human beings in a given area but lower their quality or their opportunities for enjoyment of life: and if so, in the light of our basic criterion of evolutionary direction, it is wrong. (p. 12, emphasis added)

Modern medicine with all its advances and benefits to mankind must be strictly controlled because, if left unregulated in an unchecked market, it would lead to overpopulation. And with too many people sucking up all the air, food, water, and natural resources, it will decrease the standard of living for everybody. So that the planners can continue to live the good life, some or many of us must die. Being that God is absent from the Philosophy, all emphasis and hope for the future of mankind and nature all depend on evolutionary direction; therefore, the ensuing need to try and control it—*not* for the benefit of us but of the Philosophy, in the name of evolutionary progress in "minimum time."

QUALITY AND QUANTITY

There is, however, an optimum range of size for every human organisation as for every type of organism...there is an optimum range of human population density, and of total population in the world. (p. 14, emphasis added)

Meanwhile, Unesco must devote itself not only to raising the general welfare of the common man, but also to raising the highest level attainable by man. (p. 15)

The first pre-requisite is to make the world realise that proper social organisation can be made to promote, and is indeed the only adequate means of promoting, both the degree and the variety of individuation among the members of society. In the present phase of.history, the tendency has been to regard efficiency of social organisation and high degree of individuality as an inevitable opposition. At one extreme we have the exaggerated *individualism, found mostly in the U.S.A.*, which still looks on "government" and all organisation of society as somehow inimical to the people as individuals. At the other extreme we have the philosophy of Fascism, in which the State is regarded as embodying the highest values, and any undue development of the individual is suppressed as inimical to the State. However, this apparent contradiction is a false one, and the "opposites" of society and the individual can be reconciled. Though that reconciliation will not be easy, it is, with the prevention of war, the most important task now before existing humanity. (p. 15–16, emphasis added)

SOME GENERAL PRINCIPLES

And this at once makes it equally obvious that the opposed thesis of unrestricted individualism is equally erroneous. *The human individual is, quite strictly, meaningless in isolation; he only acquires significance in relation to some form of society* (emphasis added).

All UNESCO quality and quantity is set forth from here in the context of the Malthusian principle of optimum population.

As individuals, we are, "quite strictly, meaningless." We "only acquire significance" from society! Remember Hobbes in his 1651 *Leviathan*:

> To this (State of Nature) warre of every man against every man, this Warre...nothing can be Unjust. The nothing is notions of Right and wrong, Justice and Injustice have there no place. Where there is no common Power, there Is no Law: where no Law, no Injustice...Justice, and Injustice are none of the Faculties neither of the Body, nor Mind. If they were, they might be in a man that were alone in the world, as well as his Senses, and Passions. They are Qualities, that relate to men in Society, not in Solitude.[9] (p. 100)

If we, as individuals, are meaningless, our Individual Rights are meaningless, and our voice is meaningless! How could a representative republic of a free people work that way? Hobbes makes the point that justice is a quality obtainable only from society. The whole pretence of Plato's utopian *Republic*, written sometime between 380 and 360 BC, is essentially a dialogue "of the nature and origin of justice" between Socrates and some of his contemporaries of reason. Plato, who was the "originator" according to editor Louise Ropes Loomis—"of the theory of governments began first with social contracts by which bands of men pledged themselves to refrain from harming one another in order to make possible an advantageous life together"—says this of justice:

> They say that to do injustice is, by nature, good; to suffer injustice, evil; but that the evil is greater than the good. And so when men have both done and suffered injustice and have had experience of both, not being able to avoid the one and obtain the other, they think that they had better agree among themselves to have neither; *hence there arise laws and mutual covenants*; and *that which is ordained by law is termed by them lawful and just. This they affirm to be the origin and nature of justice*—it is a mean or compromise, between the best of all, which is to do injustice and not be punished, and *the worst of all, which is to suffer injustice without the power of retaliation*; and justice, being at a middle point between the two, is tolerated not as a good, but as the lesser evil, and honoured by reason of the inability of men to do injustice. For no man who is worthy to be called a man would ever

> submit to such an agreement if he were able to resist; he would be mad if he did. Such is the received account, Socrates, of the nature and origin of justice.
>
> Now that those who practise justice *do so involuntarily* and because they have not the power to be unjust will best appear if we imagine something of this kind: having given both to the just and the unjust power to do what they will, let us watch and see whither desire will lead them; then we shall discover in the very act the just and unjust man to be proceeding along the same road, following their interest, which all natures deem to be their good, *and are only diverted into the path of justice by the force of law.*[32] (p 255–256, emphasis added)

As Huxley says, the individual "only acquires significance in relation to some form of society", and Hobbes says justice and injustice are "qualities, that relate to men in Society, not in solitude", Plato says, "Those who practise justice do so involuntarily...only diverted into the path of justice by the force of law." Remember, Rousseau, in his 1762 *Social Contract*, says:

> In order then that the social compact may not be an empty formula, it tacitly includes the undertaking, which alone can give force to the rest, that whoever refuses to obey the general will shall be compelled to do so by the whole body. This means nothing less than that *he will be forced to be free...(emphasis added)*

> *We might, over and above all this, add, to what man acquires in the civil state, moral liberty, which alone makes him truly master of himself; for the mere impulse of appetite is slavery, while obedience to a law which we prescribe to ourselves is liberty*[25] (emphasis added).

And remember Michael Bakunin in his 1871 *Man, Society and Freedom*, who wraps it up this way:

> Emerging from the state of the gorilla, man has only with great difficulty attained the consciousness of his humanity and his liberty....He was born a ferocious beast and a slave, and has gradually humanized and emancipated himself only in society, which is necessarily anterior to the birth of his thought, his speech, and his will. *He can achieve this emancipation only through the collective effort of all the members, past and present, of society, which is the source, the natural beginning of his human existence...Man completely realizes his individual freedom as well as his personality only through the individuals who surround him, and thanks only to the labor and the collective power of society. Without society he would surely remain the most stupid and the most miserable among all the other ferocious beasts*[33] (emphasis added).

Therefore, as Obama says, "You didn't get there on your own.... If you've got a business—you didn't build that. Somebody else made that happen." Point being, there are serious fundamental philosophical implications to what Huxley, as well as Obama, is saying when referring to the meaninglessness of the individual. "Thus," as Huxley continues, "UNESCO's activities, while concerned primarily with providing richer development and fuller *satisfactions for the individual, must always be undertaken in a social context*" (p. 16).

A social context remember, as we have just seen, where Huxley himself has just pointed out, that "the human individual is, quite strictly, meaningless."

> THE PRINCIPLE OF EQUALITY AND THE FACT OF INEQUALITY
>
> There are instances of biological inequality which are so gross that they cannot be reconciled at all with the principle of equal opportunity. Thus low-grade mental defectives cannot be offered equality of educational opportunity, nor are the insane equal with the sane before the law or in respect of most freedoms. However, the full implications of the fact of human inequality have not often been drawn and certainly need to be brought out here, as they are very relevant to Unesco's task. (p. 18)
>
> At the outset, let it be clearly understood that we are here sneaking only of biological inequality-inequality in genetic endowment. Social inequality, due to accident of birth or upbringing, is something wholly different....
>
> Secondly, there is difference in quality or level. *Human beings are not equal in respect of various desirable qualities.* Some are strong, others weak; some healthy, others chronic invalids; *some long-lived, others short-lived; some bright,*

> *others dull; some of high, others of low intelligence; some mathematically gifted, others very much the reverse; some kmd and good, others cruel and selfish. It is usually not so easy to say how much of this second sort of inequality is due to heredity and therefore relevant for our purpose....* (p. 19)
>
> *Already considerable progress has been made, though largely on an empirical basis as yet, in fitting the right man to the right job....*
>
> This has quite other implications; for, whereas variety is in itself desirable, the existence of weaklings, fools, and moral deficients cannot but be bad. It is also much harder to reconcile politically with the current democratic doctrine of equality. In face of it, indeed, the principle of equality of opportunity must be amended to read *"equality of opportunity within the limits of aptitude."* (p. 20, emphasis added).

Note Huxley's "fitting the right man to the right job" and "progress…on an empirical basis" are virtually identical to Comte's sociology, positivism, population, and "division of labor," where "the social organization tends more and more to rest on an exact estimate of individual diversities, by so distributing employments *as to appoint each one to the destination he is most fit for*"[4] (emphasis added). Look for this to show up yet again in the next chapter.

> *Biological inequality is, of course, the bedrock fact on which all of eugenics is predicated. But it is not usually realised that the two types of inequality have quite different and indeed*

contrary eugenic implications. *The inequality of mere difference is desirable, and the preservation of human variety should be one of the two primary aims of eugenics.* But the inequality of level or standard is undesirable, and the other primary aim of eugenics should be the raising of the mean level of all desirable qualities. While there may be dispute over certain qualities, there can be none over a number of the most important, such as a healthy constitution, a high innate general intelligence, or a special aptitude such as that for mathematics or music.

At the moment, it is probable that the indirect effect of civilisation is dysgenic instead of eugenic; and in any case it seems likely that the dead weight of genetic stupidity, physical weakness, mental instability, and disease-proneness, which already exist in the human species, will prove too great a burden for real progress to be achieved.

Thus even though it is quite true that any radical eugenic policy will be for many years politically and psychologically impossible, it will be important for Unesco to see that the eugenic problem is examined with the greatest care, and that the public mind is informed of the issues at stake so that much that now is unthinkable may at least become thinkable." (p. 21, emphasis added)

Again, you have it in their own words, their own doctrine, that Huxley's "biological inequality" in "fitting the right man to the right job" and/or Comte's "division of labor," as well as eugenics, are all here being established as the official policy of UNESCO.

It can also be said then that it is Comte's positive sociology, which includes the "division of labor," that is effectively "the bedrock fact on which all of eugenics is predicated." It is also the very same sociology being taught to our children in our schools today. With government-controlled and run health care now looming large over a justifiably hesitant America, how long before eugenics, once again, rears its ugly head? A legitimate question considering both eugenics and universal health care emanate from the very same philosophy. As such, beware that the "unthinkable" may soon again become the "thinkable" in order to retard the ever-increasing costs associated with tending to a "dysgenic" population.

> THE APPLICATION OF SCIENCE AND ART
> It is possible to exploit new agricultural methods in a way that is in the long run technically disastrous to agriculture itself, by causing soil exhaustion or erosion, but it is also possible to do so in *a way which is technically sound but socially wrong-by causing over-population*...or by ruining natural beauty or causing the extinction of striking or interesting species of animals and plants, or by creating a depressed agricultural class with unduly low standards. (p. 28, emphasis added)

The "science" of food production then, according to such progressivism—though wholly capable of meeting the demand of more and more people—is to deny to the masses the "socially wrong" production of the food necessary to meet that demand as to not "cause overpopulation"! Overpopulation damages vistas and force extinctions in biodiversity those spec'd out to be living by the planners would otherwise get to enjoy. How is it that *more* food for everybody creates *more* depressed classes? But such is the "directed science" of progressive collectivism's sociological sustainable development.

> EDUCATION
> *Education has a social as well as an individual function*: it is one of the means by which society as a whole can become conscious of its traditions and its destiny, can fit itself to make adjustment to new conditions, and can inspire it to make new efforts towards a fuller realisation of its aims....
>
> Further, *since the world to-day is in process of becoming one, and since a major aim of Unesco must be to help in the speedy and satisfactory realisation of this process, that Unesco must pay special attention to international education....*
>
> *This would mean an extension of education backwards from the nursery school to the nursery itself.* (p. 30, emphasis added)

Again, the children are to be "educated" socially, beginning from "the nursery itself" on, not to enable them to become productive and fruitful members of society but for a "speedy and satisfactory realization" of Huxley's and UNESCO's planned vision of the world "becoming one."

> NATURAL SCIENCE
> Still another and quite different type of borderline subject is that of eugenics. It has been on the borderline between the scientific and the

unscientific, constantly in danger of becoming a pseudoscience based on preconceived political ideas or on assumptions of racial or class superiority and inferiority. It is, however, essential Still another and quite different type of borderline subject is that *eugenics should be brought entirely within the borders of science, for?* as already indicated, *in the not very remote future the problem of improving the average quality of human beings is likely to become urgent; and this can only be accomplished by applying the findings of a truly scientific eugenics.* (p. 37–38)

The application of genetics in eugenics immediately raises the question of Values what qualities should we desire to encourage in the human beings of the future? But many are indirect. To take but one example, industrialism has not only transformed and largely destroyed the old way of life in the countries where it has taken its rise, but is also doing so in the remotest and most primitive countries, with whose life it is now coming into contact. In conjunction *with laisser-faire and capitalist economic systems it has not only created a great deal of ugliness (much of it preventable), but has turned men away from the consideration of beauty and of art, and of their significance and value in life-partly by its insistence on money values, partly by the fascination exerted on the young mind by the products of mechanical invention. Thus Unesco, which is concerned with all the higher activities of man,* are endeavour to see such science is tempered with art, that the classical tradition in education is not replaced by some new system, equally rigid and one-sided, based on natural science, and, in general, *that society is imbued with a proper scale of values.* (p. 38, emphasis added)

"Scientific eugenics" is to be incorporated into the new social education of children to replace the "rigid" old, classical capitalist-based tradition of education "that society is imbued with a proper scale of values."

HUMAN VALUES: PHILOSOPHY AND THE HUMANITIES

The Christian emphasis on the spiritual worth of the individual soul, the medieval discovery of the enhancement of the personality through romantic love, *and the exaggerated individualism* of the Renaissance, to modern times, *where the conflict between the development of individuality and the function of the individual as a cog in the social machine has posed itself in new and acute ways.* (p. 43, emphasis added)

As capitalism is individualism, and individualism is spawned from the "individual soul" *myth* of Christianity, they all pose an acute problem to the Philosophy. Where every individual in a free society is wholly autonomous with stand-alone intrinsic God-given value, in such a Godless collective, his or her greatest obtainable significance is but a dispensable "cog in the social machine." Such is the order to which the Philosophy progresses.

THE SOCIAL SCIENCES

In general, we need a new approach, at the same time social and evolutionary, to many basic problems of existence, an approach in which aesthetic and moral values are considered as well as objective facts within scientific analysis.... This would bring out historical facts, such as the Christian introduction of the idea of general altruism as opposed to tribal solidarity, the emergence of the ideal of romantic love between the sexes in medieval times, and still more recently that of the love of nature and of landscape beauty.

It would relate these to the general process of enlarging the emotional capacity of mankind and increasing the possibilities of emotional satisfaction; and it would also draw certain practical conclusions, concerning the means for providing such satisfaction in a modern society-through drama and painting, through national parks and nature preservation, through the beauty of tine architecture and good planning, through world community. (p. 44)

Social science increases the "emotional satisfaction" of mankind beyond the superstitions of Christian thought through science, environmentalism, planning, and globalism to a controlled and planned society, as apposed to a free one preserving Individual Liberty.

However, if Unesco is to have a real social policy, it must not confine itself to such general studies, but must also face up to particular problems which press on the modern world. Simply as illustrative examples, I will mention *population*, the *conservation of wild life*, and semantics. *The recognition of the idea of an optimum population-size* (of course *relative* to technological and social conditions) *is an indispensable first step towards that planned control of populations which is necessary if man's blind reproductive urges* are not to wreck his ideals and his plans for material and spiritual betterment. *The recognition of the fact that the wild life of the world is irreplaceable, but that it is being rapidly destroyed*, is necessary if we are to realize in time that areas must be set aside where, in the ultimate interests of mankind as a whole, the spread of man must take second place to the conservation of other species. (p. 45, emphasis added)

This speaks for itself: out of Malthusian principles shall evolve Comte's "order," a planned eugenic population control of our "blind reproductive urges" in order to save irreplaceable wildlife? Biodiversity preservation first, people concerns second? The scary thing is they mean it!

THE CREATIVE ARTS

The physical provision of beauty and art must, in the world of to-day, be largely an affair of government, whether central or local. (p. 50)

The physical provision of *aesthetic* satisfaction must include at least fine architecture, *town planning*, landscape beauty, and good design of everyday objects. (p. 51) (emphasis added)

And to insure "that society is imbued with a proper scale of values," art, or "the physical provision of beauty," must "be largely an affair of government"—that the funding of such "imbuing art" as Andres Serrano's *Piss Christ*, awarded $15,000 through the National Endowment of the Arts, shall be assured.[34]

This is where the whole concept of "planning committees" comes from: to enact or enable a "planned society"! Almost every state has one. Most counties, towns, and cities now have appointed planning or "steering" committees centrally planning every inch of "progress" right down to the aesthetics, including what flowers are blooming on the street corners; that our submission to their plan, our servitude, may appear to be but a bed of roses. We will be returning to this, so remember it.

MASS MEDIA

The possibility of a much wider dissemination of information of every sort, both within and across national boundaries. This means that public opinion can be built up more rapidly and can be better informed than ever before. There is, however, another side to this picture. National public opinion can also be built up by means of propaganda, on the basis of false, distorted or incomplete information, and though the mass media, as I have said, provide the possibility of spreading information across national boundaries, this possibility is often not realised, and indeed often deliberately fought against, *by means of censorship, official control of press and radio, and the creation of psychological barriers in the minds of the people...* the mass media provide the first agencies in history through which peoples may speak to peoples, instead of communication between countries being limited to small minorities, yet it is also true that what they say to each other through these agencies may be false, and what they hear may be limited by man-made barriers or its effect distorted by previous propaganda Accordingly, as one of its earliest aims in this field, Unesco must seek to discover what are the various barriers to free, easy, and undistorted dissemination of news and knowledge between nations, and to see that they are lowered or if possible removed. (p. 58, emphasis added)

Scientific discovery has at last made it possible to satisfy the basic needs of all humanity, thus establishing a foundation on which we can proceed to build a superstructure nearer to the heart's desire. Reminding people that one of the basic needs of men is the need for giving, for devotion to something other than self, for service and love of others (emphasis added).

It's not nature or nature's God which provides our "basic" human needs, but our own "scientific discovery". If so, how did we ever exist long enough to discover science? The "devotion to something other than self, for service and love of others" is coincidentally, by definition, none other than Comte's "altruism."

In case you missed it, "nearer to the heart's desire" comes directly from the Fabian Socialist's famous Fabian Window. The stained glass window in England depicts founding Fabians George Bernard Shaw and Sidney Webb swinging sledgehammers onto the earth that sits on an anvil over a hot billowed fire. Behind them on the wall is the

Fabian Shield depicting a wolf in sheep's clothing. Over them, their banner reads, "REMOULD IT NEARER TO THE HEARTS DESIRE." This line comes from a poem by Omar Khayyam, a Persian poet out of the Middle Ages. Here is the same line in a fuller context of the poem from which it was taken, "The Rubayyat" of Omar Khayyam:

> LXXXVIII.
> Ah, love! could thou and I with Fate conspire
> To grasp this sorry Scheme of Things entire,
> Would not we shatter it to bits—and then Remold it nearer to Heart's Desire![35]

Huxley finishes:

> Taking the techniques of persuasion and information and true propaganda that we have learnt to apply nationally in war, and deliberately bending them to the international tasks of peace, if necessary utilising them, as Lenin envisaged, to "overcome the resistance of millions" to desirable change.[36] (p. 60)

Invoking Lenin, UNESCO intends to deliberately bend the true propaganda of war toward globalism and the New World Order! All media will be made available to forward the agenda of the Philosophy.

If you're thinking, *Yeah, but that was way back in 1946*, you might want to read the following NGO position paper from the United Nations' 1994 International Conference on Population and Development (ICPD):

> *Population, development and environment are inextricably linked and are critical to determining quality of life on Earth, now and for generations to come.* The 1994 International Conference on Population and Development (ICPD) must address these paramount issues together, with foresight well into the next century.
>
> *Increasing poverty, overconsumption of resources in the North, low status of women, inappropriate economic policies, rapid population growth and unsustainable use of natural resources are all interconnected. One quarter of the world's population—predominantly in the industrialized nations—consumes over 70% of the earth's resources and is responsible for most of the global environmental degradation. In addition, the implications of adding 95 to 100 million people annually to the world's current population of 5.4 billion people are staggering and will place tremendous stress on the earth's ability to provide for basic human needs* (emphasis added).

Here, you have the classic theory of the rich 25 percent *unsustainably* soaking the poor 75 percent of the world, being directly tied by UN NGOs (nongovernment organizations) to "increasing poverty, overconsumption of resources in the North, low status of women, inappropriate economic policies, rapid population growth and unsustainable use of natural resources." What are industrialized nations? Predominately capitalist nations! It is all one and the same problem, and America, as the quintessential industrialized nation of greedy capitalists in the world, would then be, of course, the quintessential perpetrator to be targeted by such a philosophy. And weren't we just told that it's not the earth, nature, or God, but our own "scientific discovery" that provides for "our basic human needs" anyway?

Regarding the "low status of women," how does it even fit in here? Where could they be coming from to somehow make the confusing connection between that and sustainability? According to the Philosophy, in the paternalism of capitalism, women are considered property as well. Remember Fredrick Engels in *Origins of the Family, Private Property, and the State*: "The 'savage' warrior and hunter had been content to take second place in the house, after the woman; the 'gentler' shepherd, in the arrogance of his wealth, pushed himself forward into the first place and the woman down into the second."

Remember Voltairine de Cleyre in *Crime and Punishment*, saying, "There is a class of crimes of violence which arises from another set of causes than economic slavery—acts which are the result of an antiquated moral notion of the true relations of men and women. These are the Nemesis of the institution of property in love."[37] The "antiquated moral notion" is the implied moral notion of God. And remember Engels and Marx in *The Communist Manifesto*: "The bourgeois family will vanish as a matter of course when its complement vanishes, and both will vanish with the vanishing of capital."[38] If the rights of women were really their concern and not the destruction of the three-headed Hydra—all aspects of which have herein been incorporated into the social accusatory—wouldn't they be more focused on the Muslim Brotherhood, the statism of ISIS, or communist China's gender-based eugenics? What then is their true focus?

> Clearly, current patterns of consumption and *distribution of people*, wealth and natural resources are as much to blame for widespread environmental degradation as is the sheer number of people. *Efforts to address population* should

focus on the root causes of poverty, migration and high fertility rates, such as low status of women and girls, *early ages of marriage*, lack of education and health care, high child mortality rates, lack of *access to family planning* information and services for women, men and teenagers, etc. Addressing the consumption *lifestyles of peoples and societies* is equally important.

Alleviating poverty, empowering women, increasing access to family planning and health care, ensuring human rights, developing more sustainable lifestyles in the North and improving international development policies are all critical to providing a decent quality of life for future generations, *without causing irreversible damage to the environment* (emphasis added).

RECOMMENDATIONS

A. Improve the status of women. Women's empowerment/ability to control their own lives is the foundation for all action linking population, environment and development. Women are agents for environmental and economic change worldwide, and should be recognized for their role in managing resources and families. As the status of women improves, they become empowered to make independent decisions concerning their lives, fertility, and contributions to development processes.

ACTIONS

1. All governments should strive for universal access of women to primary health care that includes reproductive health, maternal and child health and *family planning* information and services through programs that are women-managed and women-centered. *In the effort to meet these goals, governments should follow the United Nations Development Program's recommendation to dedicate 20% of total spending to the satisfaction of basic human needs.*

6. Governments should promote public education campaigns to improve social perceptions of women's roles in society and to raise awareness of the value of women's work and welfare to families and societies.

7. ICPD should recognize the fundamental role of women in regulating the relationship between humans and their environment, and should call for increased targeting of development projects toward a better quality of life for women and their children.

B. Increase and improve international *family planning* and health assistance programs. Current international population assistance is far from sufficient to meet the demand for voluntary *family planning* and comprehensive health care. *Some of the most effective population programs are those which integrate family planning with comprehensive health care and education....*

C. Reduce overconsumption and poverty. As population and/or consumption in any given area increases, more demands are placed on natural resources. In the industrialized countries of the North, these demands are excessive and overconsumption has led to inequities in resource use. *One fifth of the world's population is consuming a majority of the world's resources, leading to global climate change, deforestation, loss of biodiversity, perpetuation of poverty, and local and national environmental degradation.* In many regions of the South, a vicious cycle of poverty combined with *inappropriate development policies, inequitable land distribution, lack of education and choices, and increasing concentrations of populations drives people to exhaust the very resources on which their livelihood depends, and thereby leads to environmental degradation.*

ACTIONS

1. All governments, *especially in the North*, should adopt natural resource and population policies that take into consideration population growth, demographic patterns (such as migration), access to and availability of resources.

2. Northern governments should take action to reduce CO_2 emissions in their countries by at least 25% from 1990 levels by the year 2005; to take appropriate measures to reduce substantially emissions of other greenhouse gases; and to take steps to ultimately reduce greenhouse gases by 60% (emphasis added).

Family planning is population control! A controlled population is a sustainable populations, as it appears that not just our own "scientific discovery", but at least "20%" of our "total" government spending will now be needed to satisfy those same "basic human needs".

In their 2007 *Massachusetts v. EPA* ruling, the US Supreme Court found the EPA could regulate carbon. US EPA Administrator (2009) Lisa Jackson proclaimed greenhouse gasses, including carbon dioxide, to be an official "endangerment." In 2010 came the EPA's "tailpipe rule" regulating car emissions. In June 2012, it was upheld by the US Court of Appeals, District of Columbia Circuit. As reported by The Christian Science Monitor:

> Today's ruling by the court confirms that EPA's common sense solutions to address climate pollution are firmly anchored in science and law," *Fred Krupp, president of Environmental Defense Fund* (emphasis added), said in a statement. "Today is a good day for climate *progress* in America and for the thin layer of atmosphere that sustains life on Earth."[39]

Coincidentally, the Environmental Defense Fund is a signer of this very document.

We continue with the 1994 ICPD:

> 3. Northern governments should urge the development and implementation of programs and policies promoting energy efficiency, *the use of renewable energy sources, and the transfer of environmentally sound technologies to developing countries.*

4. Governments, especially Northern, should encourage community efforts to *implement educational programs on the social and environmental impacts of overconsumption and production* and to build awareness of consumer responsibility to global environmental well-being.

5. Governments should promote conversion to equitable and ecologically *sustainable* economies and take responsibility for the needs of those whose livelihoods are negatively affected.

6. Governments should support *fair trade* (not free trade) *land redistribution, debt alleviation,* equitable tax systems, *regulation of transnational corporations,* an end to structural adjustment policies and the *integration of social and environmental costs into product prices.*

7. Governments should support and enforce legislation to strengthen consumer rights, especially to ensure environmentally *sustainable,* safe and healthy products, and establish the "right to know" laws which enable people to make informed consumption choices.

8. *Northern governments should ensure access to safe and effective means of family planning* for both men and women citizens in their own countries.

D. Increase participation of local organizations and indigenous people in the design and implementation of programs. *As is the case with all programs for sustainable development,* health and family planning programs must be built with, not for, local

people. *Consulting with and working through local organizations assures appropriate design of programs,* and the quality and effectiveness of service delivery.

ACTIONS

1. Countries should commit to increasing the decision- making role of local groups and communities *in the design and implementation of population assistance* projects.

2. *Governments should establish or strengthen procedures for regular consultations with non-governmental organizations representing local, national and global interests in designing, implementing and evaluating development plans, programs and projects.* (emphasis added)

Here, you have a collective of NGOs, all of whom have the ear of the UN directly, requesting that the UN press governments into giving them more power of influence in the central planning of sustainable development. You be the judge of whether or not, since 1994, you have been witness to any of these things being implemented in the United States.

3. Donor nations should direct support to non- governmental organizations that design and implement community programs.

E. Preparation of ICPD national reports. *All nations* participating in ICPD should assess interlinkages among population, development and environment in their countries and *should strive to coordinate national population policies with their environment and development strategies.*

ACTIONS

1. *Each national report should delineate the ways in which rapid growth, population migration and resource consumption are affecting development plans* and poverty and make projections for the future. *Such assessments should include relationships to availability of basic human needs, including health care, education, food and employment.*

2. *Each national report should assess population within the context of sustainability,* including where and how demographic pressures are interacting most with natural resources and *ecologically sensitive areas,* i.e., including population-environment dynamics such as: Soil erosion and desertification; deforestation; water scarcity; *urbanization; production of greenhouse gases;* extinction of species from habitat destruction; and coastal resource depletion due to increased demands for water, *conversion of wetlands* for agriculture and housing, and *unsustainable* fishing.

Special focus should be on the so-called *"ecologically endangered zones"*: coastal agricultural areas, upland forests, urban squatter settlements, arid and semi-arid grazing areas, etc.

F. *Institution-building for integrating population into environmental decision-making. The institutional framework needed to assess the implications of population growth and distribution, especially their potential impact on natural resources and sustainable development, must be strengthened in all countries.*

ACTIONS

The institutions available for policy analysis and project implementation have been useful to those governments which have invested in *long-term planning.*

1. Governments and *multilateral institutions should require an analysis of the effects of population growth and rate of consumption of natural resources in all planning documents* and Environmental Impact Assessments. (emphasis added)

All that is listed here in this UN NGO document is essentially listed as some of the many strands that make up but a single web, including family planning, population control, consumption control, lifestyle control, environmentalism, biodiversity, comprehensive health care, women's fertility, cultural diversity, right-to-know laws, renewable energy, consumer rights, central planning, global warming, sustainable development, resource control, institution building, human rights, wealth redistribution, land redistribution, the status of women, education, and CO2-emissions control.

JOE MARSHALL

U.S. SIGNATORIES:

ALLIANCE FOR CHILD SURVIVAL -- U.S.A.
ASSOCIATION FOR VOLUNTARY SURGICAL CONTRACEPTION -- U.S.A.
DEVELOPMENT STRATEGIES FOR FRAGILE LANDS -- U.S.A.
DIANNE DILLON-RIDGLEY, YOUNG WOMEN'S CHRISTIAN ASSOCIATION (YWCA) * -- U.S.A.
ENVIRONMENTAL DEFENSE FUND -- U.S.A.
GENERAL FEDERATION OF WOMEN'S CLUBS -- U.S.A.
GILBERTE VANSINTEJAN -- U.S.A.
JANICE MIANO, AUDUBON INTERNATIONAL NETWORK * -- U.S.A.
KATHRYN CAMERON PORTER, CONSERVATION INTERNATIONAL * -- U.S.A.
KIRSTEN B. MOORE, THE POPULATION COUNCIL * -- U.S.A
NATIONAL AUDUBON SOCIETY -- U.S.A.
NATIONAL ENVIRONMENTAL LAW CENTER -- U.S.A.
NATIONAL WILDLIFE FEDERATION -- U.S.A.
PANOS INSTITUTE -- U.S.A.
POPULATION COMMUNICATIONS -- U.S.A.
POPULATION ACTION INTERNATIONAL -- U.S.A.
RAINFOREST ALLIANCE -- U.S.A.
SIERRA CLUB -- U.S.A.
WEEDEN FOUNDATION -- U.S.A.
WOMEN OF COLOR -- NASSAU NOW (NATIONAL ORGANIZATION OF WOMEN) -- U.S.A.

LAST CALL FOR LIBERTY

ZERO POPULATION GROWTH -- U.S.A.

OTHER SIGNATORIES OF NOTE:

FAMILY PLANNING ASSOCIATION OF TRINIDAD AND TOBAGO
INDONESIAN PLANNED PARENTHOOD ASSOCIATION -- INDONESIA
INTERNATIONAL FEDERATION OF SOCIAL WORKERS -- NORWA
PLANNED PARENTHOOD ASSOCIATION OF ZAMBIA --
WILARSA BUDIHARGA, INDONESIAN PLANNED PARENTHOOD
ASSOCIATION * -- INDONESIA
WORLD POPULATION FOUNDATION -- NETHERLANDS[40]

A 1976 Marquette University report, "Habitat: A Festive Air, Serious Business" by Curtis Carter, tells us that from May 31 through June 11, 1976, in Vancouver, Canada:

> Some 930 delegates representing 132 nations met to act on the recommendations which had been prepared in advance by the U. N. Habitat Secretariat....
> Heading the U.S. delegation were Carla Hills, Secretary of the Department of Housing and Urban Development, and Russell Peterson, chairman of the Council on Environmental Quality....
> Two complementary gatherings paralleling the official U.N. Conference were the Habitat

> Forum-a conference of *nongovernmental organizations* and the Vancouver Symposium-a closed conference of 24 scientists, *planners*, and *Humanists* (emphasis added).

Carter then points out a couple of themes at the forefront:

> "The Arts and Human Settlements," and "Social Justice and Human Settlement Policy", The third component of Habitat, the Vancouver Symposium, convened prior to the official conference to prepare a set of recommendations for the U.N. delegates.
> The symposium was sponsored by the International Institute for Environment and Development (IIED), the National Audubon Society, and the Population Institute. Among the 24 symposium participants were Mead, Fuller, Barbara Ward, president of IIED, and *Maurice Strong*, former secretary-general of the U.N. Conference on the Human Environment.[41]

Three things I want to point out here are, (1) Maurice Strong, whose influence on the push for global governance is unparalleled; (2) humanists; (3) nongovernment organizations or NGOs. Who is Maurice Strong? What are NGOs, and who or what are humanists? The humanist question is going to have to wait until a little later. We'll get to know them a little better when we get to *The Humanist Manifesto*, their involvement in education, and church infiltration. For now, remember Huxley when he declared, "Thus the general philosophy of Unesco should, it seems, be a scientific world humanism, global in extent and evolutionary in background."[36] On Strong and NGOs, they are inseparable. In 1997, Henry Lamb—whose extensive work exposing Strong, NGOs, and the agenda behind "sustainable development" has been unmatched—explains:

> U.N. Secretary General, Kofi Annan… announced [Strong]…also a member of the Commission on Global Governance…as Senior Advisor, "to assist planning and executing a far-reaching reform of the world body"….
>
> As a Senior Advisor to Kofi Annan, Strong will have a free hand to do what he wants while Annan takes the heat—or the praise. Strong prefers to operate in the background. He, perhaps more than any other single person, is responsible for the development of a global agenda now being implemented throughout the world. Although various components of the global agenda are associated with an assortment of individuals and institutions, Maurice Strong is, or has been, the driving force behind them. *It is essential that Americans come to know this man* who has been entrusted with the task of "reforming" the U.N.—this man Maurice F. Strong "(emphasis added)."

Not only do I wholeheartedly agree with Mr. Lamb that America should get to know Maurice F. Strong, I believe that what he has to tell us about Strong and his NGO concept is vital to fully comprehending the force of their impact in what remains in this chapter. So before we continue, I yield to Mr. Lamb:

Strong is also closely aligned with Mikhail Gorbachev and was a participant in Gorbachev's State of the World Forum in San Francisco in 1995.[2] His organization, Earth Council, and Gorbachev's organization, Green Cross International, are currently developing a new "Earth Charter" for presentation to the U.N. General Assembly and ratification by all U.N. members before the year 2000. *He served on the Brundtland Commission, headed by Gro Harlem Brundtland, then-Vice President of the World Socialist Party.* Strong's love for socialist ideas is scattered throughout his professional life—as they apply to everyone else. For himself, he is quite the capitalist....

Strong's first exposure to the U.N. came in 1947 when, at 18, he went to New York to take a job as assistant pass officer in the Identification Unit of the Security Section. He lived with Noah Monod, then treasurer of the U.N....

Strong wanted to become an international ambassador for the YMCA, but settled for a position on the International Committee of the U.S.A. and Canada which raised funds for the YMCA.

This experience may have been the genesis of Strong's realization that NGOs (non-government organizations) provide an excellent way to use NGOs to couple the money from philanthropists and business with the objectives of government. In 1959, Strong created his own company, MF Strong Management. While serving as executive vice-president of Canada's Power Corporation, he also ran his own company, Alberta gas company, another company called Ajax, and elevated his role in the international YMCA and Canada's Liberal Party....

By 1966, Strong had moved up again in government. He became Director General of Canada's External Aid. *He also became President of Canada's YMCA....*

External Aid was transformed from a one-man operation to the Canadian International Development Agency (CIDA) in 1968, which Strong headed. His mentor, Lester Pearson, created another institution called the International Development Research Center (IDRC). *The IDRC was a quasi-government agency that had unique authority to receive charitable donations—and issue tax deductible certificates—and give money directly to individuals, governments, and private organizations.* Strong became its head in 1970.

The 1972 Stockholm Conference on Human Environment (Earth Summit I) had far more international significance than was ever reported. *NGO's* (non-government organizations) *were funded by the Canadian government* to attend the conference to *give the appearance of participation by the general public.* Of course, only those NGOs personally selected by Strong received funding. One such NGO was headed by William Turner, Strong's protege who then headed the Power Corporation which Strong once headed....

The 1972 Stockholm Conference institutionalized the environment as a legitimate concern of government, and it institutionalized NGOs as the instruments through which government could varnish its agenda with the appearance of public support. The primary outcome of the conference was a recommendation to create *the United Nations Environment Programme (UNEP) which became a reality in 1973 with Maurice Strong as its first Executive Director.* Not surprisingly, Nairobi, Strong's headquarters twenty-years earlier, was chosen for the permanent headquarters of the UNEP....

Strong became a Vice President of the World Wildlife Fund (WWF), a post he held until 1981. In 1983, Strong was appointed to the U.N.'s World Commission on Environment and Development, headed by Gro Harlem Brundtland, Vice President of the World Socialist Party. Strong also had a colleague appointed as Executive Director, Warren "Chip" Lindner, an American lawyer, based in Geneva who had handled an intricate merger for Strong and who later went to work for the World Wildlife Fund in Gland, Switzerland. *[Strong, and the World Wildlife Fund, were largely responsible for the content of the Brundtland Commission's final report],* Our Common Future (emphasis added).

On a note of interest, the Fabian Socialist president of the British Eugenics Society, the founding secretary general of UNESCO and founder of the International Union for Conservation of Nature and Natural Resources (IUCN), *Julian Huxley*, —along with *Prince Philip* of England; *Prince Bernard*, the ex-Nazi SS Officer; and *Max Nicholson*, founder of EarthWatch and founding director general of Britain's Nature Conservancy—were all the cofounders of the World Wildlife Fund, founded in 1961.

> He asked [Bella Abzug] to schedule a special conference in Miami for women through her recently formed NGO called Women's Environment and Development Organization (WEDO). Another NGO formed by Abzug in 1981, the Women's USA Fund, had been almost dormant until 1991, when the NGO received nearly $1 million. *He arranged for the creation of the Business Council on Sustainable Development.* Strong's long-time colleague, and former cabinet minister to Pierre Trudeau, J. Hugh Faulkner, was asked to leave his post as Executive Director of the International Chamber of Commerce to take charge of the new organization. The new organization was immediately accredited to the Rio Conference and designated to advise Strong... *The Canadian Participatory Committee for UNCED (CPCU) was entirely funded by the Canadian government* and consisted of carefully selected individuals who represented various NGOs.
>
> *The practice started by Strong at the 1972 conference, of cloaking the agenda in the percep-*

tion of public grassroots support from NGOs, culminated in Rio in 1992, with the largest collection of NGOs ever assembled in support of Agenda 21. Only those NGOs that were "accredited" by the U.N. Conference were permitted to attend. And only those which had demonstrated support for the agenda were funded....

Strong has influence with the major Foundations which provide the funding for NGOs and he has influence with the major international NGOs *that coordinate the activities of the thousands of smaller NGOs* around the world. *Strong has served, or is currently on the Board of Directors of the International Union for the Conservation of Nature (IUCN); the World Wide Fund for Nature (WWF); and the World Resources Institute (WRI); the three international NGOs that have developed and advanced the global agenda since the early 1970s. Strong also served on the U.N.-funded Commission on Global Governance,* co-chaired by Ingvar Carlsson, and Shirdath Ramphal, former President of the IUCN. The Commission's final report, *Our Global Neighborhood,* sets forth detailed plans to achieve what is called "Global Governance." In 1991, Strong wrote the introduction to a book published by the Trilateral Commission, called *Beyond Interdependence: The Meshing of the World's Economy and the Earth's Ecology,* by Jim MacNeil. (David Rockefeller wrote the foreword). Strong said this:

> "*This interlocking...is the new reality of the century*, with profound implications for the shape of our institutions of governance, national and international. *By the year 2012, these changes must be fully integrated into our economic and political life*" (emphasis added).

Has he accomplished his goal?

He told the opening session of the Rio Conference (Earth Summit II) in 1992, that industrialized countries have:

> developed and benefited from the *unsustainable patterns of production and consumption* which have produced our present dilemma. It is clear that current *lifestyles and consumption patterns of the affluent middle class*—involving *high meat intake, consumption of large amounts of frozen and convenience foods, use of fossil fuels, appliances, home and work-place air-conditioning, and suburban housing—are not sustainable.* A shift is necessary toward lifestyles less geared to environmentally damaging consumption patterns (emphasis added).

Remember Michelle Obama when asked by *Parade* magazine what she hoped to accomplish in her second term: "We still need to find a way to impact the nature of food in grocery stores, in terms of sugar, fat, and salt."

Lamb continues:

In an essay by Strong entitled *Stockholm to Rio: A Journey Down a Generation*, he says:

> The concept of national sovereignty has been an immutable, indeed sacred, principle of international relations. It is a principle which will yield only slowly and reluctantly to the new imperatives of global environmental cooperation. What is needed is recognition of the reality that in so many fields, and this is particularly true of environmental issues, *it is simply not feasible for sovereignty to be exercised unilaterally by individual nation-states, however powerful.* The global community must be assured of environmental security[42] (emphasis added).

Now with that under our belts, we can now go on to the report of Habitat: United Nations Conference on Human Settlements Vancouver, Canada, 31 May to 11 June, 1976 (Habitat I), that resulted in part with this:

> II. GENERAL PRINCIPLES
>
> 10. Land is one of the fundamental elements in human settlements. *Every State has the right to take the necessary steps to maintain under public control the use, possession, disposal and reservation of land. Every State has the right to plan and regulate use of land, which is one of its most important resources, in such a way that the growth of population centres both urban and rural are based on a comprehensive land use plan....*
>
> 13. All persons *have the right and the duty* to participate, individually and collectively in

the elaboration and implementation of policies and programmes of their human settlements.

14. To achieve universal progress in the quality of life, a fair and balanced structure of the economic relations between States has to be promoted. *It is therefore essential to implement urgently the New International Economic Order*, based on the Declaration and Programme of Action approved by the General Assembly in its sixth special session, and on the Charter of Economic *Rights and Duties* of States (emphasis added).

This statement alone, as subtle as it may seem, is in direct conflict—a 180-degree override and rewrite to the complete opposite—of the American founding understanding of property and property rights. It is diabolically apposed to our free Constitution. If you are the *owner* in fee simple, of your property, then that property is yours to do with according to your plan, whatever is best for you, your family, and your property, not what the state says you must do according to theirs. If you have bought some land or are a homeowner in America today, are you the tenant, or do you own it? For that matter, do you really own any item you may consider to be "your property"?

A. Settlement policies and strategies
(Agenda item 10 (a))
Preamble

2. These strategies must then be incorporated in the general planning framework....

4. Population growth and rapid changes in the location of human activities proceed at such a pace that, *by the end of the century we shall*

> *have to build "another world on top of the present one"....*
>
> 5. In fact, the very construction of the physical components of human settlements—be they rural or urban, in the form of dwellings or roads, with traditional or modern technologies—in sufficient volume to meet the needs of society, could become a leading sector of the economy and a major generator of meaningful employment, instead of being treated as a residual of so-called "productive" activities.

For infrastructure to be built, there must be a demand for it to be done by some natural driving force that is mutually beneficial to the owners, the investors, industry benefactors, the local community, and the labor hired to build it. Otherwise, it is simply by unnatural decree at the expense of all. Sure, the labor will get their pay, which will also be by decree; but under such a global government system, that's all they'll ever be allowed to be: just "the workers."

> Recommendation A.1 A national settlement policy
>
> (b) ALL COUNTRIES SHOULD ESTABLISH AS A MATTER OF URGENCY A NATIONAL POLICY ON HUMAN SETTLEMENTS, EMBODYING THE DISTRIBUTION OF POPULATION, AND RELATED ECONOMIC AND SOCIAL ACTIVITIES, OVER THE NATIONAL TERRITORY.
>
> c) Such a policy should
>
> v) Be devised to facilitate population redistribution to accord with the availability of resources.

Yes, this does say "to facilitate population redistribution" according to recourses! Not only will there be redistribution of wealth, food, and services, there's going to be a need to redistribute people!

> B. Settlement planning
> (Agenda item 10 (b))
> Preamble
> 1. Planning is a process to achieve the goals and objectives of national development through the rational and efficient use of available resources. Thus plans must include clear goals and adequate policies, objectives and strategies along with concrete programmes.
> 3. Planning decisions taken at one level must be related and complementary to those taken at other levels, both "above" and "below", and appropriate machinery must be devised to resolve potential conflicts between them.

In order for anything, especially a "plan," to be "related and complementary" at all levels, it must be a homogenous one originating from a single source, must it not? If so, then all "decisions" made orchestrating such a plan must also originate from, and/or at least be approved by, a single all-powerful overseeing central source. Who or what might they be? What is their plan for us, or for you?

> Recommendation B.12 Neighbourhood planning
> (b) NEIGHBOURHOOD PLANNING SHOULD GIVE SPECIAL ATTENTION TO THE SOCIAL QUALITIES, AND PROVISION OF FACILITIES, SERVICES

AND AMENITIES, REQUIRED FOR THE DAILY LIFE OF THE INHABITANTS.

Recommendation B.16 Planning processes

(b) PLANNING AT ALL SCALES MUST BE A CONTINUING, PROCESS REQUIRING CO-ORDINATION, MONITORING EVALUATION AND REVIEW, BOTH FOR DIFFERENT LEVELS AND FUNCTIONS AS WELL AS FEEDBACK FROM THE PEOPLE AFFECTED.

Who or what is it that is to do all the "coordination," "evaluating," "reviewing," and "monitoring" of all the "social qualities" of the all the "affected," all the "facilities" and "services" provided, and all the "provisions" provided for everything that is needed for their "daily lives"? What real weight or effect would any "feedback," if dared to be offered at all, have on the orchestrators of such a plan?

D. Land
(Agenda item 10 (d))
Preamble

1. *Land…cannot be treated as an ordinary asset, controlled by individuals and subject to the pressures and inefficiencies of the market. Private land ownership is also a principal instrument of accumulation and concentration of wealth and therefore contributes to social injustice; if unchecked, it may become a major obstacle in the planning and implementation of development schemes. Social justice, urban renewal and development, the provision of decent dwellings-and healthy conditions for the people can only be*

> *achieved if land is used in the interests of society as a whole* (emphasis added).

Everything from within this philosophy, as we have already been shown, is contingent upon government control of all property. The whole of the concept of private property, including our unalienable Right to it and the Constitution that preserves those Rights, is exactly what they just said it is: "a principal instrument of accumulation and concentration of wealth and therefore contributes to social injustice…a major obstacle in the planning and implementation of development schemes." As shocking and revolting the above paragraph is, it's nothing new to the Philosophy. As property is part of the three-headed Hydra, holders of the Philosophy will do anything and everything in their power to destroy it!

> 2. Instead, the pattern of land use should be determined by the long-term interests of the community…*Public control of land* use is therefore indispensable to its protection as an asset and the achievement of the long-term objectives of human settlement policies and strategies.
>
> 3. *To exercise such control effectively, public authorities require detailed knowledge of the current patterns of use and tenure of land*; appropriate legislation defining the boundaries of individual rights and public interest; and *suitable instruments* for assessing the value of land and *transferring to the community*, inter alia through taxation, *the unearned increment* resulting from changes in use (emphasis added).

Again, Alinsky would agree that "public authorities require detailed knowledge of the current patterns of use and tenure of land" is a necessary step as "we must begin from where we are if we are to build power for change." Then the "suitable instruments" of government can transfer over "to the community…the unearned increment" or profits in land value. If the market value of your property goes up while you own it, that is *not* your gain; it belongs to the collective, to "society." Why? Because like Obama said, "You didn't build that. Somebody else made that happen"!

4. Above all, Governments must have the political will to evolve and implement innovative and adequate urban and rural land policies, as a corner-stone of their efforts.

Recommendation D.1 Land resource management

(a) *Public ownership or effective control of land in the public interest is the single most important means…achieving a more equitable distribution of the benefits or development* whilst assuring that environmental impacts are considered.

(b) LAND IS A SCARCE RESOURCE WHOSE MANAGEMENT SHOULD BE *SUBJECT TO PUBLIC SURVEILLANCE OR CONTROL IN THE INTEREST OF THE NATION*

c) This applies in particular to land required for:

(ii) The implementation of programmes of urban renewal and land-assembly, schemes;

(iv) The preservation and improvement of valuable components of the man-made environment, such as historic sites and monuments and other areas of unique and aesthetic social and cultural value;

d) Land is a natural resource fundamental to the economic, social and political development of peoples and therefore *Governments must maintain full jurisdiction and exercise complete sovereignty over such land* with a view to freely planning development of human settlements throughout the whole of the natural territory.

Recommendation D.2 Control of land use changes

(a) Agricultural land, particularly on the periphery of urban areas, is an important national resource.

5. *Without public control land is a prey to speculation and urban encroachment.* (emphasis added)

Market value means nothing to land that can only be owned and controlled by the government. If nobody can own it, what market value can it possibly have? What value does the market have without the concept of property?

(b) CHANGE IN THE USE OF LAND, ESPECIALLY FROM AGRICULTURAL TO URBAN, SHOULD BE SUBJECT TO PUBLIC CONTROL AND REGULATION.

(c) Such control may be exercised through:

(i) Zoning and land-use planning... or control of land-use changes in particular;

(ii) Direct intervention, e.g. the *creation of land reserves* and land banks, *purchase*, compensated expropriation and/or *pre-emption, acquisition of development rights*, conditioned leasing of public and communal land, *formation of public and mixed development enterprises*;

(v) A planned co-ordination between orderly urban development and the promotion and location of new developments, *preserving agricultural land.*

Recommendation D.3 Recapturing plus value

(a) Excessive profits resulting from the increase in land value due to development and change in use are one of the principal causes of the concentration of wealth in private hands. Taxation should not be seen only as a source of revenue for the community but also as a powerful tool to encourage development of desirable locations, *to exercise a controlling effect on the land market and to redistribute to the public at large the benefits of the unearned increase in land values.* (emphasis added)

(b) THE UNEARNED INCREMENT RESULTING FROM THE RISE IN LAND VALUES RESULTING FROM CHANGE IN USE OF LAND, FROM PUBLIC INVESTMENT OR DECISION OR DUE TO THE GENERAL GROWTH OF THE COMMUNITY MUST BE SUBJECT TO APPROPRIATE RECAPTURE BY PUBLIC BODIES (THE COMMUNITY),

UNLESS THE SITUATION CALLS FOR OTHER ADDITIONAL MEASURES SUCH AS NEW PATTERNS OF OWNERSHIP, THE GENERAL ACQUISITION OF LAND BY PUBLIC BODIES.

Nothing is to remain of property rights. Nobody other than the government is to be allowed to profit from property investments. With this philosophy, *no private investment is safe*. All you have to do is ask the GM bondholders what it felt like to have what has been reported as 90 percent of their $27 billion in private investments confiscated from them by the Obama administration and the federal government of the United States of America and redistributed to the UAW via some sort of never-before-heard-of executive declaration that grossly expanded all previously known legal conceptions of eminent domain to include any and all private investments held by any company determined by government to be too big, too small, or too cute to fail.

In reality, many "secure" bondholders, including schoolteacher Debra June, lost big. In a June 1, 2009 CNN interview, she said she lost over 90 percent of her investment. After the "bailout," June, who had invested $70,000 in "secured bonds," was forced to accept 140 shares of regular GM stock now worth less than $200 in total. If so, that's only a 0.29 percent return or a 99.71 percent loss![44] How does a schoolteacher recover from that? What future can free enterprise, capitalism, and our property rights ever have in a country where any and all investments into them could all be confiscated without a moment's notice by "the common Power that keeps us all in Awe"? What kind of future awaits America and the world under such "new patterns of ownership"?

(c) Specific ways and means include:

(i) Levying of appropriate taxes, e.g. capital gains taxes, land taxes and betterment charges, and particularly taxes on unused or under-utilized land;

(ii) Periodic and frequent assessment of land values in and around cities, and determination of the rise in such values relative to the general level of prices:

(iii) Instituting development charges or permit fees and specifying the time-limit within which construction must start;

(iv) Adopting pricing and compensation policies relating to value of land prevailing at a specified time *rather than its commercial value* at the time of acquisition by public authorities;

(v) Leasing of publicly owned land in such a way that future increment which is not due to the efforts by the new user is kept by the community;

(vi) Assessment of land suitable for agricultural use which is in proximity of cities mainly at agricultural values.

Recommendation D.4 Public ownership

(a) *Public ownership of land cannot be an end in itself; it is justified in so far as it is exercised in favour of the common good rather than to protect the interests of the already privileged.*

(b) PUBLIC OWNERSHIP, TRANSITIONAL OR PERMANENT, SHOULD BE USED, WHEREVER APPROPRIATE, *TO SECURE AND CONTROL AREAS*

OF URBAN EXPANSION AND PROTECTION; AND TO IMPLEMENT URBAN AND RURAL LAND REFORM PROCESSES, AND SUPPLY SERVICED LAND AT PRICE LEVELS WHICH CAN SECURE *SOCIALLY ACCEPTABLE PATTERNS OF DEVELOPMENT.*

Recommendation D.5 Patterns of ownerships

(a) *Many countries are undergoing a process of profound social transformation; a review and restructuring or the entire system of ownership rights is,* in the majority of cases, *essential to the accomplishment of new national objectives.*

(b) PAST PATTERNS OF OWNERSHIP RIGHTS SHOULD BE TRANSFORMED TO MATCH THE CHANGING NEEDS OF SOCIETY AND BE COLLECTIVELY BENEFICIAL.

(c) Special attention should be paid to:

(i) Redefinition of legal ownership including the rights of women and disadvantaged groups and usage rights for a variety of purposes;

(ii) Promoting land reform measures *to bring ownership rights into conformity with the present and future needs of society*;

(iii) Clear definition of public objectives and private ownership *rights and duties* which may vary with time and place;

(iv) Transitional arrangements to change ownership from traditional and customary patterns to new systems, especially in connexion with communal lands, whenever such patterns are no longer appropriate (emphasis mine).

Plain and simple, private property rights, the way we have always known them, all have to be vanquished. Destroy property rights, and you destroy the whole of capitalism, free enterprise, the pursuit of happiness, and Individual Liberty. The Constitution itself, as a binding document, would accordingly also be effectively rendered useless in the protection of Liberty—reinterpreted to meaninglessness.

Note that, again, the essence of Comte's positive sociology is ever present as it is "only in this context, which emphasizes duties, that the concept of 'rights' can have any application."

And finally, one last item from Vancouver:

> (v) Methods for the separation of land ownership rights from development rights, the latter to be entrusted to a public authority.[44]

Remember this was back in 1976. Though our farms had pretty much been nationalized by 1930's, via such progressive collectivism as the "New Deal", NYS Milk Control, and it's ensuing favorable Supreme Court decision in *Nebbia –vs- NY-*(1934).

In 1983, Gro Harlem Brundtland was asked by the United Nations to head an investigative commission, and the Brundtland Commission was established. Brundtland—a founder of the "socialist pupils" at Hegdehaugen, leader of the Labour Party, former multiterm socialist Norwegian prime minister, and the then serving vice president of the World Socialist Party—along with fellow commission member Maurice Strong, released their *Brundtland report* or *Our Common Future: From One Earth to One World* in 1987:

> A Threatened Future
> 3. The failures that we need to correct arise both from poverty and from the short-

sighted way in which we have often pursued prosperity....

4. The growth in economic interaction between nations amplifies the wider consequences of national decisions. Economics and ecology bind us in ever-tightening networks. Today, many regions face risks of irreversible damage to the human environment that threaten the basis for human progress.

1. Poverty

10. This Commission should give attention on how to look into the question of more participation for those people who are the object of development. Their basic needs include the right to preserve their cultural identity, and their right not to be alienated from their own society, and their own community. So the point I want to make is that *we cannot discuss environment or development without discussing political development. And you cannot eradicate poverty, at least not only by redistributing wealth or income, but there must be more redistribution of power."*

    Aristides Katoppo
    Publisher
    WCED Public Hearing
    Jakarta, 26 March 1985

24. *The 'greenhouse effect', one such threat to life support systems, springs directly from increased resource use. The burning of fossil fuels and the cutting and burning of forests release carbon diox-*

ide (CO2). The accumulation in the atmosphere of CO2 and certain other gases traps solar radiation near the Earth's surface, causing global warming[45] (emphasis added).

It comes in no simpler terms: capitalism and/or globalization is the cause of worldwide poverty and global warming. This from back in 1987! Who heard of global warming in 1987? As such, capitalism, free enterprise, the "pursuit of prosperity," and the nations that enable or allow it must all be destroyed. A mere distribution of wealth won't cut it; "there must be more redistribution of power"! For those who think that the distribution of wealth in the United States stops at our borders, think again! Remember that the poorest in America are among the richest in the world. After there is no "rich" left here, if the Philosophy is ever to realize what its holders are calling for here, America's internally redistributed wealth, property and power will then all be redistributed yet again to the whole of the world, as fertilizer for their new social world order! Think *middle class* and how Alinsky, Marx, and Lenin all deceptively called for seducing them all into being *the* redistributive means to not only their own demise but that of a whole country.

Make no mistake, this is social justice! This is sustainable development! What better than a calamitous, exploitive, greedy capitalism-induced global warming or cooling, to gel the masses of the world together into faction for "change"? If what they say is true, then what they say we need to do to fix it must be true too; and if so, we must make it happen like now to save us, right? But again, jumping on the man-caused global-warming bandwagon here isn't going to happen in a vacuum without consequence, as to do so is to sign on to the same revolutionary "social causes" of the very same progressive collectivism of Marx, Lenin, and Alinsky—if not in cause, at least in effect. It is *not* a coincidence! Is not the "science" behind the very concept of "man-caused" climate change/global warming a product of the very same "directed" social science that spawned the population-controlling "science" of eugenics, the new property-rights-robbing "frameworks" of "sustainable development," and the evolution "proving" the fallacy of God Himself?

Such social "science" has led to official calls in the US government for anti-organized crime RICO laws to be used in the prosecution of noncompliant skepticism, even where scientifically rebuked. How long before that same "science" and those same laws are used by that same government to prosecute skeptics of any or *all* that "science" determines we must believe? Does any other science do that? Something to think about as *the* people who brought you the concept of man-caused climate change *and* the concept of sustainable development are here telling us in their own words: "We cannot discuss environment…without discussing political development. And you cannot eradicate poverty, at least not only by redistributing wealth or income, but there must be more redistribution of power." Environmentalism is *not* conservation!

> From One Earth to One World
> 1. From space, we see a small and fragile ball dominated not by human activity and edifice but by a pattern of clouds, oceans, greenery, and soils. Humanity's inability to fit its activities into that pattern is changing planetary systems, fundamentally. Many such changes are accompanied by life-threatening hazards. This new reality, from which there is no escape, must be recognized—and managed.
> 2. From space, we can see and study *the Earth as an organism whose health depends on the health of al its parts*. We have the power to rec-

oncile human affairs with natural laws and to thrive in the process (emphasis added).

Remember that Hobbes, Comte, and the implied insignificance of any and all individual aspects of any "organism" and "the earth as an organism" coming from the same philosophy begin to make sense as well.

>3. *Our Common Future*…must be based on policies that sustain and expand the environmental resource base. And we believe such growth to be absolutely essential to relieve the great poverty that is deepening in much of the developing world
>
>4 …hope for the future is conditional on decisive political action now to begin managing environmental resources to ensure both *sustainable human progress and human survival*…the time has come to take the decisions needed to secure the resources to sustain this and coming generations.

>I. The Global Challenge
>
>5. The proportion of the world's adults who can read and write is climbing; the proportion of children starting school is rising; and *global food production increases faster than the population grows.*
>
>6. But the same processes that have produced these gains have given rise to trends that the planet and its people cannot long bear…

> *The gap between rich and poor nations is widening.* (emphasis added)

I realize that, by now, you're probably picking up on these things on your own, but again, this is yet another instance of *the* collectivist source of the whole 99 percent versus the 1 percent. And its correlating "Bourgeois capitalists are getting richer while the oppressed are getting poorer".

> 7. *The burning of fossil fuels puts into the atmosphere carbon dioxide, which is causing gradual global warming....*
>
> 8. Poverty is a major cause and effect of global environmental problems. It is therefore futile to attempt to deal with environmental problems without a broader perspective that encompasses the factors underlying world poverty and international inequality.
>
> 9. These concerns were behind the establishment in 1983 of the World Commission on Environment and Development by the UN General Assembly....
>
> 10. We came to see that a new development path was required, one that sustained human progress not just in a few pieces for a few years, but for the entire planet into the distant future. Thus 'sustainable development' becomes a goal not just for the 'developing' nations, but for industrial ones as well.

2. The Interlocking Crises

11. Until recently, the planet was a large world in which human activities and their effects were neatly compartmentalized within nations...*These compartments have begun to dissolve...an environmental crisis, a development crisis, an energy crisis. They are all one.*

13. Economic activity has multiplied to create a $13 trillion world economy, and this could grow five to tenfold in the coming half century. Industrial production has grown more than fiftyfold over the past century, four-fifths of this growth since 1950. Such figures reflect and presage profound impacts upon the biosphere, as the world invests in houses, transport, farms, and industries. Much of the economic growth pulls raw material from forests, soils, seas, and waterways.

14. A mainspring of economic growth is new technology...including new forms of pollution and the introduction to the planet *of new variations of life forms that could change evolutionary pathways....*

17. Life-threatening environmental concerns have surfaced in the developing world. Countrysides are coming under pressure from increasing numbers of farmers and the landless. *Cities are filling with people, cars, and factories* (emphasis added).

Let's think this one through from a commonsense standpoint. As city populations rise, planning mandates building up not out and stacking all the people up in little "sustainable living cubes." The cost of infrastructure and distributing provisions is cheaper that way. How many times have we heard about the smog and congestion of "inner-city traffic." In Ithaca, New York, it's simply been referred to as *Carmageddon*. Public transportation becomes just short of mandatory, and with no vehicles of our own, we can only go where they take us, when they take us, if they take us, and Liberty is lost. So it is that personal vehicles are "unsustainable" in multiple aspects!

> The *resources gap between most developing and industrial nations is widening,* in which *the industrial world dominates in the rule-making of some key international bodies and in which the industrial world has already used much of the planet's ecological capital. This inequality is the planet's main 'environmental' problem; it is also its main 'development' problem.* (emphasis added)

Remember Errico Malatesta in *Anarchy*:

> The oppressed masses who have never completely resigned themselves to oppression and poverty, and who today more than ever show themselves thirsting for justice, freedom and well-being, are beginning to understand that they will not be able to achieve their emancipation except by union and solidarity with all the oppressed, with the exploited everywhere in the world. And they also understand that the indispensable condition for their emancipation which cannot be neglected is the possession of the means of production, of the land and of the

instruments of labour, and therefore the abolition of private property.[46]

24. The arms race—in all parts of the world—pre-empts resources that might be used more productively to diminish the security threats created by environmental conflict and the resentments that are fuelled by widespread poverty.

3. Sustainable Development

27. The concept of sustainable development does imply limits - not absolute limits but limitations imposed by the present state of technology and social organization on environmental resources and *by the ability of the biosphere to absorb the effects of human activities*....

29. *Sustainable global development requires that those who are more affluent adopt life-styles within the planet's ecological means—in their use of energy, for example. Further, rapidly growing populations can increase the pressure on resources and slow any rise in living standards; thus sustainable development can only be pursued if population size and growth are in harmony with the changing productive potential of the ecosystem.*

30. Yet in the end, *sustainable development is not a fixed state of harmony, but rather a process of change in which the exploitation of resources, the direction of investments, the orientation of technological development, and institutional change are made consistent with future as well as present needs*. We do not pretend that the process is

easy or straightforward. Painful choices have to be made. Thus, in the final analysis, *sustainable development must rest on political will* (emphasis added).

Sustainable development "is [*not*] a fixed state of harmony"! Not in my words but theirs! It is, however, an obvious expansion of both Comte's positivism and Malthusian principles of population control, that the privileged few planners calling the shots continue their "rise in living standards" while the rest of us are forced to "adopt life-styles within" their social interpretation of "the planet's ecological means," consistent, of course, with the future needs of their master plan.

> 32. Those responsible for managing natural resources and protecting the environment are institutionally separated from those responsible for managing the economy. The real world of interlocked economic and ecological systems will not change; *the policies and institutions concerned must.*
>
> 36. *The present challenge is…to give the environmental agencies more power to cope with the effects of unsustainable development.*
>
> II. The Policy Directions
> 40. The Commission has focused its attention in the areas of population, food security, the loss of species and genetic resources, energy, industry, and human settlements—*realizing that all of these are connected and cannot be treated in isolation one from another.*

1. Population and Human Resources

41. In many parts of the world, the population is growing at rates that *cannot be sustained by available environmental resources*, at rates that are outstripping any reasonable expectations of improvements in housing, health care, food security, or energy supplies.

42. Thus the 'population problem' must be dealt with....

43. Urgent steps are needed to limit extreme rates of population growth. Choices made now will influence the level at which the population stabilizes next century within a range of 6 billion people....

44. *Governments that need to do so should develop long-term, multifaceted population policies and a campaign to pursue broad demographic goals: to strengthen social, cultural, and economic motivations for family planning*, and to provide to all who want them the education, contraceptives, and services required (emphasis added).

"Family planning" and population-control policies as interdependent "demographic goals"? Sure, but it's all so the women can have a "right to choose," right? Sure, it is. Just remember from UNESCO's philosophy: "In the ultimate interests of mankind as a whole, the spread of man must take second place to the conservation of other species."[34]

2. Food Security: Sustaining the Potential

51. Food security requires attention to questions of distribution, since hunger often

arises from lack of purchasing power rather than lack of available food. It can be furthered by land reforms.

3. Species and Ecosystems: Resources for Development

53. *The diversity of species is necessary for the normal functioning of ecosystems and the biosphere as a whole....*

56. *The network of protected areas that the world will need in the future must include much larger areas brought under some degree of protection. Therefore, the cost of conservation will rise - directly and in terms of opportunities for development foregone....*

57. Governments should investigate the prospect of agreeing to a 'Species Convention'... to support the implementation of such a convention.

4. Energy: Choices for Environment and Development

58. Today, the average person in an industrial market economy uses more than 80 times as much energy as someone in sub-Saharan Africa....

59. To bring developing countries' energy use up to industrialized country levels by the year 2025 would require increasing present global energy use by a factor of five. The planetary ecosystem could not stand this, *especially*

> *if the increases were based on non-renewable fossil fuels....*
>
> 62. Energy efficiency can only buy time for the world to develop 'low-energy paths' based on renewable sources, which should form the foundation of the global energy structure during the 21st Century...However, achieving these use levels will require a programme of coordinated research, development, and demonstration projects *commanding funding necessary to ensure the rapid development of renewable energy....*
>
> 70. Many essential human needs can be net only through goods and services provided by industry, and *the shift to sustainable development must be powered by a continuing flow of wealth from industry* (emphasis added).

Note again: "Sustainable development must be powered by a continuing flow of wealth from industry"! Sustainable development is not self-sufficient! It can only survive by feeding upon or, as it were, "exploiting" the fruits of another's labor!

> 78. The present level of debt service of many countries, especially in Africa and Latin America, is not consistent with sustainable development....
>
> 82. *Traditional forms of national sovereignty raise particular problems in managing the 'global commons'* and their shared ecosystems—the oceans, outer space, and Antarctica....

> 83. *The UN Conference on the Law of the Sea was the most ambitious attempt ever to provide an internationally agreed regime for the management of the oceans. All nations should ratify the Law of the Sea Treaty as soon at possible*[47] (emphasis added).

The Law of the Sea Treaty and the Small Arms Treaty both directly threaten our sovereignty. Both have been high on the Obama administration's to-do list. How much more power will it give them to accomplish their objective? The concept of "global commons" may seem nice enough, but we'll take a closer look when we get to chapter 10 of "Our Common Future."

> Our Common Future, Chapter 2: Towards Sustainable Development
>
> I. The Concept of Sustainable Development
> 4. *Sustainable development requires meeting the basic needs of all and extending to all the opportunity to satisfy their aspirations for a better life.*
> 6. Sustainable development...can be consistent with economic growth, *provided the content of growth reflects the broad principles of sustainability and non-exploitation of others* (emphasis added).

What is it in a collective that might be meant by the "exploitation of others"? Remember Pierre Kropotkin from the first chapter. In his 1886 *Law and Authority*, he reminds us again:

> The history of *the genesis of capital has already been told* by Socialists many times. They have described how it was born of war and pillage, of slavery and serfdom, of modern fraud *and exploitation*. They have shown how it is nourished by the blood of the worker, *and how little by little it has conquered the whole world*. The same story, concerning the genesis and development of law has yet to be told....
>
> *Law, in its quality of guarantee of the results of pillage, slavery and exploitation*, has followed the same phrases of development as capital; *twin brother and sister, they have advanced hand in hand, sustaining one another with the suffering of mankind'* (emphasis added).

Exploitation within the Philosophy is synonymous with both capitalism and the laws that protect private property. Both stand in the crosshairs of the planners planning for our future in a collectivist, socialist society. Therefore—along with free enterprise—our Individual Liberty, private property, and laws that protect them are all unsustainable and must, therefore, all be *annihilated*!

> But growth by itself is not enough. High levels of productive activity and widespread poverty can coexist, and can endanger the environment. Hence *sustainable development requires that societies meet human needs*....
>
> 7. Sustainable development can only be pursued if demographic developments are in harmony with the changing productive potential of the ecosystem.

8. A society may in many ways compromise its ability to meet the essential needs of its people in the future—*by overexploiting resources,* for example...ill-considered development.

A communications gap has kept environmental, population, and development assistance groups apart for too long, preventing us from being aware of *our common interest and realizing our combined power.* Fortunately, the gap is closing. We now know that what unites us is vastly more important than what divides us.

We recognize that poverty, environmental degradation, and population growth are inextricably related and that none of these fundamental problems can be successfully addressed in isolation. We will succeed or fail together.

Arriving at a commonly accepted definition of 'sustainable development' remains a challenge for all the actors in the development process.

'Making Common Cause'
U.S. Based Development, Environment, Population NGOs
WCED Public Hearing
Ottawa, 26–27 May 1986

II. Equity and the Common Interest

16. *How are individuals in the real world to be persuaded or made to act in the common inter-*

> est? *The answer lies partly in education, institutional development, and law enforcement.*
>
> 24. Internationally, *monopolistic control over resources* can drive those who do not share in them to excessive exploitation of marginal resources....
>
> 26. Our inability to promote the *common interest* in sustainable development is often a product of the *relative neglect of economic and social justice within and amongst nations* (emphasis added).

Again, the concept of "social justice" is the concept of forced "redistribution of property." It is needed because of the neglect of the greedy capitalists to share most, if not all, their earnings, as I noted earlier, with the global collective. Monopolists within the Philosophy are capitalists. Kropotkin, continuing from *Law and Authority*, also reminds us this about laws:

> The major portion have but one object—to protect private property, i.e., wealth acquired by the exploitation of man by man. Their aim *is to open out to capital fresh fields for exploitation*, and to sanction the new forms which that exploitation continually assumes...They exist to keep up the machinery of government, which *serves to secure to capital the exploitation and monopoly of the wealth produced*. Magistrature, police, army, public instruction, finance, all serve one God- capital; all have but one object—to facilitate the exploitation of the worker by the capitalist[7] (emphasis added).

Like we went over in the beginning of this chapter, it may all sound good until you know the meaning of what they're saying in the fuller context of the Philosophy from which it emanates. Nothing coming out of the collectivism of this philosophy is stand-alone. No matter what aspect, all of them have a plethora of further implications lurking beneath the surface—every single one of them being hostile, by design, to our Constitution, our sovereignty, and the whole of our Individual Liberty.

> 27. The world must quickly design strategies that will allow nations to move from their present, often *destructive, processes of growth and development* onto sustainable development paths. This will require policy changes *in all countries*, with respect both to their own development and to their impacts on other nations'....
>
> Box 2-1 Growth, Redistribution, and Poverty
> *The poverty line is that level of income below which an individual or household cannot afford on a regular basis the necessities of life. The percentage of the population below that line will depend on per capita national income and the manner in which it is distributed.* How quickly can a developing country expect to eliminate absolute poverty? The answer will vary from country to country, but much can be learned from a typical case.
> Consider a nation in which half the population lives below the poverty line and where the distribution of household incomes is as fol-

lows: the top one-fifth of households have 50 per cent of total income, the next fifth have 20 per cent, the next fifth have 14 per cent, the next fifth have 9 per cent, and the bottom fifth have just 7 per cent. This is a fair representation of the situation in many low-income developing countries.

In this case, if the income distribution remains unchanged, per capita national income would have to double before the poverty ratio drops from 50 to 10 per cent. *If income is redistributed in favour of the poor, this reduction can occur sooner.* Consider the case in which *25 per cent of the incremental income* of the richest one-fifth of the population *is redistributed equally to the others....*

The aim is to ensure that the world is well on its way towards sustainable development by the beginning of the next century, *it is necessary...to pursue vigorous redistributive policies.*

33. *The very logic of sustainable development implies an internal stimulus to Third World growth.*

39. Sustainability requires views of human needs and well-being that incorporate such non-economic variables as education and health enjoyed for their own sake, clean air and water, and the protection of natural beauty. It must also work to remove disabilities from disadvantaged groups (emphasis added).

As was pointed out earlier, that stimulus is the redistribution of America to the world! Sustainability can be whatever they want it to be when it is they who have full control of all our money and property to pay for it with! Remember what you're reading here about all that encompasses the true nature of what sustainable is. And know that this very United Nations document is *the* genesis of the concept of "sustainable development."

> 48. *A child born in a country where levels of material and energy use are high places a greater burden on the Earth's resources than a child born in a poorer country.*

Remember what key aspect of the philosophy that Lewis A. Coser showed us particularly pertains here from Comte's "science" of sociology:

> Furthermore, Comte...admits...*increases in population...are seen as a major determinant of the rate of social progress.*[4]

Being that "the average person in an industrial market economy uses more than 80 times as much energy," every child born in America is at least unsustainable (times eighty)! Reason enough for some population control in the old USA ASAP!

> 51. *Population policies should be integrated with other economic and social development programmes* female education, health care, and the expansion of the livelihood base of the poor. But time is short, and developing countries will also have to promote *direct measures to reduce fertil-*

ity...In fact, increased access to *family planning services is itself a form of social development*...

62. Industrialized countries must recognize that their energy consumption *is polluting the biosphere and eating into scarce fossil fuel supplies*...Changing these patterns *for the better will* call for new policies in *urban development, industry location, housing design, transportation systems, and the choice of agricultural and industrial technologies* (emphasis added).

What do "direct measures to reduce fertility" have to do with "family" planning? "Family planning" is *family control* for the sake of biodiversity, in the name of sustainable development! Any Individual Liberty expressed in home designs, business investments, transportation choices, and/or private property developments cannot be allowed in a sustainable, centrally planned and controlled world. Therefore, all Individual Liberty and "individual will" must be crushed, sacrificed "for the better will" of the collective! Remember Hobbes, that where men "have no other Law but their own Appetites, there can be no generall Rule of Good"! And Remember Rousseau from his 1762 *Social Contract*:

> [Each of us puts his person and all his power in common under the supreme direction of the general will], and, in our corporate capacity, we receive each member as an indivisible part of the whole.....
>
> Each individual, as a man, may have a particular will contrary or dissimilar to the general will which he has as a citizen. His particular interest may speak to him quite differently

from the common interest: his absolute and naturally independent existence may make him look upon what he owes to the common cause as a gratuitous contribution, the loss of which will do less harm to others than the payment of it is burdensome to himself; and, regarding the moral person which constitutes the State as a *persona ficta*, because not a man, *[he may wish to enjoy the rights of citizenship without being ready to fulfil the duties of a subject. The continuance of such an injustice could not but prove the undoing of the body politic]*....

In order then that the social compact may not be an empty formula, it tacitly includes the undertaking, which alone can give force to the rest, that whoever refuses to obey the general will shall be compelled to do so by the whole body. *[This means nothing less than that he will be forced to be free]*.[26] (emphasis added)

Sustainable development *is* the Philosophy! However, being able to identify its camouflaged attributes is not always easy. And by design, they can rarely be exposed in short explanations. But hopefully, by the grace of God, piece by piece, strand by strand, humbly praying that they be not "spiritually discerned," we can begin to see the web of deceit for what it is from wherever, whenever, and whomever it emanates.

67. Most technological research by commercial organizations is devoted to product and process innovations that have *market value*. *Technologies are needed that produce 'social goods',*

> *such as improved air quality or increased product life, or that resolve problems normally outside the cost calculus of individual enterprises.*

This is the context in which both the Bush and Obama administrations have justified subsidizing "green" corporations like A123 Systems with huge sums of taxpayers' money. According to US Department of Energy (DOE) Office of Public Affairs, director Dan Leistikow in an October 16, 2012, release:

> Under this Administration, the Department of Energy, with strong bipartisan support, awarded $2 billion in grants to 29 companies to build or retool 45 manufacturing facilities spread across 20 states to build advanced batteries, engines, drive trains and other key components for electric vehicles.[48]

Actually, the total cost to the American taxpayers from the Obama administration's subsidization of the "green" market has been estimated to be as high as $90 billion. From the Heritage Foundation, there is this from an October 2012 report:

> It is no secret that President Obama's and green-energy supporters' (from both parties) foray into venture capitalism has not gone well....
>
> So far, 34 companies that were offered federal support from taxpayers are faltering—either having gone bankrupt or laying off workers or heading for bankruptcy....

The 2009 stimulus set aside $80 billion to subsidize politically preferred energy projects. Since that time, *1,900 investigations have been opened* to look into stimulus waste, fraud, and abuse (although not all are linked to the green-energy funds), and nearly 600 convictions have been made. Of that $80 billion in clean energy loans, grants, and tax credits, at least 10 percent has gone to companies that have since either gone bankrupt or are circling the drain.[49]

From Fisker and the Chevy Volt, to Solyndra, and all the subsidized anaerobic manure digesters in between, there are many technologies/products that the "planners" in the DOE have decreed as "social goods" with "social values." They are, therefore, needed, regardless of the fact that there is little to no market demand for them—yet. As they are, in real life, so cost prohibitive that their costs are "normally outside the cost calculus of individual enterprises", they have little to no *Free* Market value. Herein steps the planners to force a "sustainable" *fair* market for them anyway, using our tax dollars and the power and force of the United States government to force out competing choices thereby forcing us into compliance with their collective vision of a "planned" sustainability. Where's the freedom of choice in that?

> 76. *Sustainability requires…changes in the legal and institutional frameworks that will enforce the common interest…* Such a view places the right to use public and private resources in its proper *social context* and provides a goal for more specific measures[50] (emphasis added).

This gets right to the heart of what, in this writer's observation, makes sustainable development so completely devastating to a free people. It "requires...changes in the legal and institutional frameworks that will enforce the common interest." Our Constitution does not enforce the common good collectively; it protects the Individual Liberty we all have in common. Therefore, it must be destroyed and replaced with an "institutional framework" that will!

Without private property, there can be no free enterprise as it entails the exchange of property owned for property desired. Where "market values" are applied to any given item, idea, or service by an "unchanneled" people freely voting with their dollars on what they are willing or not willing to pay for them—"social values" in their "social context" are decreed by the planners the supreme sovereign or, as Hobbes says, by "the common power" that "keeps us all in awe"!

> Our Common Future
> Chapter 5: Food Security: Sustaining The Potential
>
> 1. The world produces more food per head of population today than ever before in human history....
>
> 3. Between 1950 and 1985, cereal production outstripped population growth....
>
> 5. *Demand for milk and meat is growing as incomes rise in societies that prefer animal protein. and much agricultural development in the industrialized nations has been devoted to meeting these demands.* In Europe, meat production more than tripled between 1950 and 1984, and milk production nearly doubled./5 Meat production for exports increased sharply, particularly in the rangelands of Latin America and Africa. World

meat exports have risen from around 2 million tons in 1950–52 to over 11 million tons in 1984.

6. To produce this milk and meat required in 1984 about 1.4 billion cattle and buffaloes, 1.6 billion sheep and goats, 800 million pigs, and a great deal of poultry—all of which weigh more than the people on the planet./7 Most of these animals graze or browse or are fed local plants collected for them. However, rising demands for livestock feedgrains led to sharp increases in the production of cereals such as corn, which accounted for nearly two-thirds of the total increase in grain production in North America and Europe between 1950 and 1985.

11. The food surpluses in North America and Europe result mainly from subsidies and other incentives that stimulate production even in the absence of demand. Direct or indirect subsidies, which now cover virtually the entire food cycle, have become extremely expensive. In the United States, the cost of farm support has grown from $2.7 billion in 1980 to $25.8 billion in 1986 (emphasis added).

Food subsidies being a progressive policy, as is usually the case with progressive policies, is here proving to be an obstacle to not only free-market enterprise and Individual Liberty but to their own progressive policies as well! Progressivism is not only incompatible with Liberty; it is inconsistent with itself! Such inconsistencies, like they are here, are generally projected from the progressive collectivism from which they originate on to capitalism, our founding, or some other aspect of our Individual Liberty.

> 14. A particular area of concern is the impact of these policies on developing countries. They depress international prices of products, such as rice and sugar, that are important exports for many developing countries and so reduce exchange earnings of developing countries. They increase the instability of world prices.
>
> 30. Growing populations and the decreasing availability of arable land lead poor farmers in these countries to seek new land in forests to grow more food… often forests are cleared without forethought or planning.
>
> 39. Global food security also depends on ensuring that all people, even the poorest of the poor, can get food…on the world scale this challenge requires a reappraisal of global food distribution.…
>
> 40. *Countries that are subsidizing food exports are increasing unemployment in food-importing countries.* This marginalizes people, and marginalized people are forced to destroy the resource base to survive. Shifting production to food-deficit countries and to the resource-poor farmers within those countries is a way of securing sustainable livelihoods. (emphasis added)

So here we have it—food justice! Sustainable food is job security for the third world. This will mean more and more of our food being grown there instead of here at home. Have you noticed that many of the fresh fruits and vegetables at the grocery store are now grown in Mexico, Chili, Guatemala, Vietnam, or Argentina? Add to that the elimination of food production here in the United States for "environmental" reasons such as the threat imposed by irrigation to the Delta Smelt in California. The impact this philosophy can have our food supply is nothing short of totalitarian.

> 45. *Government intervention in agriculture is the rule in both industrial and developing countries, and it is here to stay...* In fact, the real problem in many developing countries is the weakness of these systems.
>
> 46. Many governments regulate virtually the entire food cycle—inputs and outputs, domestic sales, exports, public procurement, storage and distribution, price controls and subsidies—as well as imposing various land use regulations: acreage, crop variety, and so on.
>
> 3.1 Land Use
>
> 57. The initial task in enhancing the resource base will be to delineate broad land categories: enhancement areas...intensive areas... and restoration areas....
>
> 59. Selection of land for each category could be made *the responsibility of a board or commission representing the interests involved,* especially the poor and more marginalized segments of the population. *The process must be public in character... Classifying land according to best use* will determine variations in infrastruc-

ture provision, support services, promotional measures, regulatory restrictions, fiscal subsidies, and other incentives and disincentives.

62. Restoration may *require limits on human activities*...The state...could protect these areas *by declaring them national reserves.*

65. In some areas excessive use of ground-water is rapidly lowering the water table—usually *a case where private benefits are being realized at society's expense.*

5.1 Land Reforms

92. Given institutional and ecological variations, a universal approach to land reform is impossible. Each country should work out its own programme of land reform *to assist the land-poor* and to provide a base for coordinated resource conservation. *The redistribution of land is particularly important* where large estates and vast numbers of the land-poor coexist....

96. The traditional rights of subsistence farmers, particularly shifting cultivators, pastoralists. and nomads, must therefore be protected from encroachments. Land tenure rights and *communal rights in particular must be respected*[51] (emphasis added).

Land and property rights, as we have always known them as a free People and how they were preserved in the Constitution, are under attack by the Philosophy! Why? As Federalist Noah Webster explained, They are the "fountain" from which the "stream" of Liberty flows! Sustainable development is its chosen weapon! Once our property rights have been assumed by the government, the people will most probably never get them back!

>Our Common Future
>Chapter 7: Energy: Choices for Environment and Development
>
>5. The period ahead must be regarded as transitional from an era in which energy has been used in an unsustainable manner. A generally acceptable pathway to a safe and sustainable energy future has not yet been found....
>
>6. The growth or energy demand in response to industrialization, urbanization, and societal affluence has *led to an extremely uneven global distribution of primary energy consumption./1* The consumption of energy per person in industrial market economies, for example, is more than *80 times greater* than in sub-Saharan Africa. (See Table 7–1.) And *about a quarter of the world's population consumes three-quarters of the world's primary energy.*
>
>13. A 50 percent fall in per capita primary energy consumption in industrial countries and a 30 per cent increase in developing countries... But this path would require huge structural changes to allow market penetration of efficient technologies.
>
>16. Many forecasts of recoverable oil reserves and resources suggest that oil production will level off by the early decades of the next century and then gradually fall during a period of reduced supplies and higher prices.

Gas supplies should last over 200 years and coal about 3.000 years at present rates of use. These estimates persuade many analysts that the world should immediately embark on a vigorous oil conservation policy.

87. *Renewable* energy sources require a much higher priority in national energy programmes...The technological challenges of renewables are minor compared with the challenge of creating the social and institutional frameworks that will ease these sources into energy supply systems.

88. The Commission believes that every effort should be made to develop the potential for renewable energy, which should form the foundation of the global energy structure during the 21st Century. A much more concerted effort must be mounted if this potential is to be realized. But a major programme of renewable energy development will involve large costs and high risks, particularly massive-scale solar and biomass industries. Developing countries lack the resources to finance all but a small fraction of this cost although they will be important users and possibly even exporters. Large-scale financial and technical assistance will therefore be required.

96. *Energy pricing policies play a critical role in stimulating efficiency....*

109. Nations intervene in the 'market price' of energy in a variety of ways. Domestic taxes (or subsidies) on electrical power rates,

oil, gas and other fuels are most common. They vary greatly between and even within countries where different states, provinces, and sometimes even municipalities have the right to add their own tax...taxes on energy...can...cause energy prices to rise beyond a certain level—a level that varies greatly among jurisdictions.

110. Some nations also maintain higher than market prices on energy through duties on imported electricity, fuel, and fuel products. Others have negotiated bilateral pricing arrangements with oil and gas producers in which they stabilize prices for a period of time[52] (emphasis added).

This taxing government intervention, manipulation, and controlling of fuel costs—punishing us for, say, purchasing fossil fuels and rewarding us with subsidy for purchasing the central planner's designated green, renewable, or sustainable fuels—is what is collectively referred to as a *green economy*. This "intervention" is exactly what Obama was promising when he warned us that under his "plan of a cap and trade system, electricity rates would necessarily skyrocket." It was what self-proclaimed revolutionary communist Van Jones was appointed to be in charge of as Obama's first "green-jobs czar."

Our Common Future
Chapter 9: The Urban Challenge
1. By the turn of the century, almost half the world will live in urban areas - from small towns to huge megacities./1 The world's economic system is increasingly an urban one,

with overlapping networks of communications, production, and trade./2 This system, with its flows of information, energy, capital, commerce, and people, provides the backbone for national development. A city's prospects - or a town's - depend critically on its place within the urban system, national and international. So does the fate of the hinterland, with its agriculture, forestry, and mining, on which the urban system depends.

10. In most Third World cities, the enormous pressure for shelter and services has frayed the urban fabric. Much of the housing used by the poor is decrepit. Civic buildings are frequently in a state of disrepair and advanced decay. So too is the essential infrastructure of the city; public transport is overcrowded and overused, as are roads, buses and trains, transport stations, public latrines, and washing points. Water supply systems leak, and the resulting low water pressure allows sewage to seep into drinking water. A large proportion of the city's population often has no piped water, storm drainage, or roads./7

31. *A national urban strategy could provide an explicit set of goals and priorities for the development of a nation's urban system and the large, intermediate, and small centres within it. Such a strategy must go beyond physical or spatial planning, it requires that governments take a much broader view of urban policy than has been traditional.*

32. With an explicit strategy, nations can begin to reorient those central economic and major sectoral policies that now reinforce megacity growth, urban decline, and poverty. They can likewise promote more effectively the development of small and intermediate urban centres, the strengthening of their local governments, and the establishment of services and facilities needed to attract development initiatives and investment. *Ministries of Planning, Finance, Industry, Agriculture, and so on would have clear goals and criteria against which to assess the effects of their policies and expenditures on urban development.* Contradictory policies and programmes could be changed. At the very least, the spatial biases inherent in macroeconomic and fiscal policies, annual budgets, pricing structures, and sectoral investment plans could be exposed and assessed. Within such a strategy, the traditional tools of urban policy, including *land use planning and control*, would stand a better chance of being effective (emphasis added).

Just who will be the "ministers of planning" planning such an "urban strategy"?

33. The formulation of such a strategy *is clearly a central government responsibility*. Beyond this, however, the role of central governments should be primarily to strengthen the capacity of local governments to find and carry

through effective solutions to local urban problems and stimulate local opportunities.

39. To become key agents of development, city governments need enhanced political, institutional, and financial capacity, *notably access to more of the wealth generated in the city*. Only in this way can cities adapt and deploy some of the vast array of tools available to address urban problems - tools such as land title registration, land use control, and tax sharing.

49. Landownership structures and the inability or unwillingness of governments to intervene in these structures are perhaps the main factors contributing to 'illegal' settlements *and chaotic urban sprawl*. When half or more of a city's workforce has no chance of obtaining a legal plot on which a house can be built, let alone of affording to buy or rent a house legally, *the balance between private landownership rights and the public good must be quickly rethought* (emphasis added).

This is yet another warning shot across the bow of private property rights and, therefore, Individual Liberty! Both are to become subordinate to the central plan or general will of the collective. Again, private property owners with the power and right to have "their own appetite" to do with their property as they see fit stand in the way of sustainable development!

51. Most cities urgently need a large and continuous increase in the availability of cheap housing plots convenient to the main centres

of employment. *Only government intervention can achieve this*, but no general prescriptions are possible. Societies differ too much *in how they view private landownership and land use rights*, in how they use different instruments such as direct grants, tax write-offs, or *deduction of mortgage interest*, and in *how they treat land speculation, corruption, and other undesirable activities* that often accompany processes of this kind.

54. Many poor people rent accommodation; half or more of a city's entire population may be tenants. Increasing the availability of house sites, materials, and credits does little for those who must rent. One possibility *is financial support to non-governmental, non-profit organizations to purchase end develop property* specifically for rental units. A second is support for tenants to buy out landlords and *convert tenancy into cooperative ownership*.

57. The available resources in or close to cities are often underused. Many landowners leave well-located sites undeveloped in order to benefit later from their increasing value as the city grows. Many *public agencies have land that could be put to better use*, such as the area next to stations and harbours controlled by railway and port authorities (emphasis added).

Whatever plans, ideas, or hopes you may have had for your property, the Liberty to pursue any of them, along with the property itself, will all be taken from you and put to "better use" in the name of sustainable development! How they plan to do it is even more devastating as it undermines our very republic—the same republic guaranteed to us in Article IV Section 4 of the Constitution! How? By using appointed comprehensive sustainable-development (steering) committees of "professionals," "stakeholders," and other "local" interests (which may include a farmer, a business owner, and even a sympathetic legislator or two) with the power to secure huge sums of pumped-in funding and grants, the authority of our constitutionally limited elected officials is systematically undermined. With the appointed new frameworks of the new normal in place and quickly putting forth their approval of ready-made "plans" for "sustainability", by the collective consensus of the few appointed "stakeholders" that seemingly reap huge monetary rewards locally, the slow process of lawmaking set forth by our founders in the Constitution is overrun and made "obsolete." Such local "sustainable" planning/steering committees actively crush property rights and free enterprise development locally, via a plethora of redistributive cross jurisdictional regulations and mandates, which actually qualify them for copious funds in federal and state grants to do so.

Lawmaking is supposed to be by elected representatives only and is slow for a reason—that our Liberty be protected from "designing men" with the time we might need to see and understand their treachery. With our voice removed from the government, we the people lose our vote, along with any and all power we ever had from it. We lose the power to hold our representatives accountable! "Planners" are not our representatives. They represent their agenda and their "vision" of the new normal by channeling, nudging, directing, or otherwise forcing us to submit to it by stripping of us of our Liberty one Right at a time!

> Several countries have introduced special programmes to *encourage public and private cooperation in the development of such lands*, a trend

that should be encouraged. There is a general need to find innovative and effective ways of *pooling land for the common good.* Most cities have mechanisms for acquiring land either at market rates (which means that schemes are never implemented), or at *arbitrarily low confiscatory rates* (where the alliance of political forces and landlords blocks the acquisition anyway)[53] [emphasis added].

Our Common Future
Chapter 10: Managing The Commons
1. *The traditional forms of national sovereignty are increasingly challenged by the realities of ecological and economic interdependence. Nowhere is this more true than in shared ecosystems and in 'the global commons'*—those parts of the planet that fall outside national jurisdictions. Here, sustainable development can be secured only through international cooperation and agreed regimes for.

7. Only the high seas outside of national jurisdiction are truly 'commons'; but fish species, pollution, and other effects of economic development do not respect these legal boundaries. *Sound management of the ocean commons will require management of land-based activities as well.* Five zones bear on this management: inland areas, which affect the oceans mostly via *rivers; coastal lands—swamps, marshes, and so on*—close to the sea, where human activities can directly affect the adjacent waters; coastal

waters—estuaries, lagoons, and shallow waters generally—where the effects of land-based activities are dominant; offshore waters, out roughly to the edge of the continental shelf; and the high seas, surveillance, development, and management in the common interest....

10. Other threats are more concentrated. The effects of pollution and land development are most severe in coastal waters and semi-enclosed seas along the world's shore-lines. The use of coastal areas for settlement, industry, energy facilities, and recreation will accelerate, as will the upstream manipulation of estuarine river systems through dams or diversion for agriculture and municipal water supplies. These pressures have destroyed estuarine habitats as irrevocably as direct dredging, filling, or paving. Shore-lines and their resources will suffer ever increasing damage if current, business-as-usual approaches to policy, management, and institutions continue.

20. The Commission believes that a number of actions are urgently needed to improve regimes for oceans management. Thus the Commission proposes measures to: advance the *Law of the Sea.*

2.5 The Law of the Sea

53. *The Convention also defines the waters, sea bed, and subsoil beyond the limits of national jurisdiction, and recognizes this as international. Over 45 per cent of the planet's surface, this sea-*

bed area and its resources are declared to be the 'common heritage of mankind', a concept that represents a milestone in the realm of international cooperation. *The Convention would bring all mining activities in the sea-bed under the control of an International Seabed Authority.*

54. By early 1987, the Convention had been signed by 159 nations, and 32 countries had ratified it. However, a small number of significant states had indicated that they were unlikely to ratify it./18 The reasons for this rest largely with the regime proposed to manage the common sea bed.

II. Space: A Key to Planetary Management

56. *This Commission, in view of these developments, considers space as a global commons and part of the common heritage of mankind.*

1. Remote Sensing from Space

58. If humanity is going to respond effectively to the consequences of changes human activity has induced—the build-up of atmospheric carbon dioxide, depletion of stratospheric ozone, acid precipitation, and tropical forest destruction - better data on the Earth's natural systems will be essential.

59. Today several dozen *satellites contribute to the accumulation of new knowledge* about the Earth's systems....

61. Recently, an international and interdisciplinary group of scientists has proposed

a major new initiative—the International Geosphere-Biosphere Programme (IGBP) to be coordinated through ICSU. It would investigate the biosphere using many technologies, including satellites....

62. The primary frustration about this wealth of data is that the information is dispersed among governments arid institutions, *rather than being pooled. UNEP's Global Environment Monitoring System* is a modest effort to pool space data relevant to the Earth's habitability....

63. The primary responsibility for action rests initially with national governments, cooperating to pool, store and exchange data. In time, *international efforts might be funded through some direct global revenue source*[54] (emphasis added).

The implications of global commons including biodiversity corridors, rivers, estuaries, swamps, coastal areas, the sky, the weather, the sea, sea floor and subsoil, Antarctica, outer space, the moon, other planets, their moons, and beyond have huge devastating consequences for America, our sovereignty, and our sacred Liberty. If, as "global commons and part of the common heritage of mankind," these areas were to come under the ownership of the organism of mankind and policed by a "global monitoring system" for the collective benefit of the world—(1) any of the revenues and profits earned within those areas would not and could not ever be realized by any enterprising entrepreneur, company, or nation-state as the fundamental principle of capitalism, commerce, and free enterprise is simply the exchange of private property owned for private property desired. There can be no enterprise, no commerce, and therefore no market where there is no concept of private property allowed.

In a global common, private property is effectively outlawed as ownership of everything has already been relinquished to the "collective" of the whole of mankind. (2) As such, any food, minerals, or energy resources to be harvested from these areas could never be the private property of the harvesters. As there is no property and no commerce in a global common, there can be no keeping the fruits (which are property) of your labor. Where it is unlawful to keep the fruits of your labor, there can be neither "pursuit of happiness" nor any hope of prosperity. Where there is no prosperity, there can only be poverty and therefore no Liberty. (3) If and when the United States signs on to the Law of the Sea Treaty, those who do sign the agreement will be the individuals guilty in blatant violation of their sworn oath to the Constitution of effectively outlawing Individual Liberty everywhere outside the sovereign borders of America forever! Not to mention many such decreed "global commons" within our borders as well!

If, in the distant future, we were to ever gain the ability to draw energy from, or even live on, the moon or any of the planets in our solar system or beyond, no property, no real estate, and no Liberty will be allowed anywhere as the Law of the Sea will have already given ownership of them all as global commons to the organism of mankind. As such, the Law of the Sea not only outlaws Liberty here on earth today but throughout the whole of the known universe and beyond for all conceivable time! However, while the United States maintains at least some degree of sovereignty, Liberty will have at least one teeny-tiny sanctuary left—America. And upon her last remaining *reservation* shall Liberty have her last gleaming, and there shall the once fiercely independent and noble free American have their last measure of sovereignty and freedom! (4) Remember, nation-state sovereignty is unsustainable!

> Our Common Future
> Chapter 12: Towards Common Action: Proposals For institutional and Legal Change
>
> 3. All nations will also have a role to play in…changing trends, and *in* righting *an international economic system that increases rather than decreases inequality, that increases rather than decreases numbers of poor and hungry.*
> 4. *Security must be sought through change*[55] (emphasis added).

The "international economic system" to which the Brundtland Commission refers, as we have seen over and over throughout this work, refers to globalization or international capitalism. *Globalism* and *globalization* may sound similar, but they are generally defined by the Philosophy as polar opposites, just another effort designed to throw off readers not steeped in the Philosophy as capitalism is property, and without property, there is no Individual Liberty. The "system" also includes the laws that protect property. In agreeing with that assessment, the Brundtland Commission report, "Our Common Future," here states that "security must be sought through change" from the system of capitalist globalization to their system of international socialism. Remembering Hitler's National Socialism is Nazism, and Nazism is fascism, you may be relieved to know that International Socialism, on the other hand, is only Communism.

The 1992 Earth Summit II, the UN Conference on Environment and Development, in Rio de Janeiro resulted in the United Nation's *Agenda 21*. Agenda 21 includes four sections and forty chapters of the many different aspects of sustainable development. In section II, chapter 10, "Integrated Approach to the Planning and Management of Land Resources," the frameworks of the "new system of sustainability" is put forth as follows:

1. Land is normally defined as a physical entity in terms of its topography and spatial nature; a broader integrative view also includes natural resources: the soils, minerals, water and biota that the land comprises. These components are organized in ecosystems which provide a variety of services essential to the maintenance of the integrity of life-support systems and the productive capacity of the environment. Land resources are used in ways that take advantage of all these characteristics. Land is a finite resource, while the natural resources it supports can vary over time and according to management conditions and uses. *Expanding human requirements and economic activities* are placing ever increasing pressures on land resources, creating competition and conflicts and resulting in *suboptimal use of both land and land resources.* If, in the future, human requirements are to be met in a *sustainable* manner, *it is now essential to resolve these conflicts* and move towards more effective and efficient use of land and its natural resources. Integrated physical and land-use planning and management is an eminently practical way to achieve this…*link social and economic development with environmental protection and enhancement, thus helping to achieve the objectives of sustainable development.…*

3. Land resources are used for a variety of purposes which interact and may compete with one another; therefore, *it is desirable to plan and manage all uses in an integrated man-*

ner. Integration should take place at two levels, considering, on the one hand, all environmental, social and economic factors (including, for example, impacts of the various economic and social sectors on the environment and natural resources) and, on the other, all environmental and resource components together (i.e., air, water, biota, land, geological and natural resources). Integrated consideration facilitates appropriate choices and trade-offs, thus *maximizing sustainable productivity and use.* Opportunities to allocate land to different uses arise in the course of major settlement or development projects or in a sequential fashion *as lands become available on the market.*

4. A number of *techniques, frameworks,* and *processes* can be combined to facilitate an integrated approach. *They are the indispensable support for the planning and management process,* at the national and local level, ecosystem or area levels and for the development of specific plans of action. Many of its elements are already in place but need to be more widely applied, further developed and strengthened. This programme area is concerned primarily with *providing a framework that will coordinate decision-making...of Agenda 21* (emphasis added).

Agenda 21 is the "frameworks" of the new normal! The new normal is central planning mandating what is optimal in lifestyle, land use, and social development while eliminating what is suboptimal! "Exploitation," as capitalism is defined by the Philosophy, is, of course, suboptimal! Central planning is socialism! As Agenda 21 is a centrally planned International Socialism, Agenda 21 is a centrally planned global/world communism!

Objectives

5. *The broad objective is to facilitate allocation of land to the uses that provide the greatest sustainable benefits and to promote the transition to a sustainable and integrated management of land resources....*

6. Governments *at the appropriate level, with the support of regional and international organizations, should ensure that policies and policy instruments support the best possible land use and sustainable management of land resources.* Particular attention should be given to the role of agricultural land. To do this, they should:

Review the *regulatory framework*, including laws, regulations and enforcement procedures, in order to identify improvements needed to *support sustainable land use and management* of land resources and *restricts the transfer of productive arable land to other uses; Strengthening planning and management systems.*

7. Governments *at the appropriate level, with the support of regional and international organizations,* should review and, if appropiate, revise planning and management systems to facilitate an integrated approach. To do this, they should:

a. *Adopt planning and management systems that facilitate the integration of environmental components such as air, water, land and other natural resources, using landscape ecological planning (LANDEP) or other approaches that focus on, for example, an ecosystem or a watershed* (emphasis added).

With such fundamentally transforming "improvements" to our current constitutional "regulatory framework" in place, "strengthening planning and management systems" to "restrict" the free enterprise of market-based property exchanges, usage, and/or developments, the long "integrated" list of "environmental components" becomes the bottomless social bucket from which the planners will be then empowered to pull an endless supply of legal "green" excuses; with which to declare any and all pursuit of profit or "Happiness" exploitive, unfair, unsustainable, and therefore no longer legal or allowed!

Enhancing education and training

16. Governments *at the appropriate level*, in collaboration with the *appropriate local authorities, non-governmental organizations* and *international institutions, should promote the development of the human resources that are required to plan and manage land and land resources sustainably.* This should be done by providing incentives for local initiatives and by enhancing local management capacity, *particularly of women*, through:

a. Emphasizing interdisciplinary and integrative approaches *in the curricula of schools and technical, vocational and university training*;

    b. Training all relevant sectors concerned to deal with land resources in an integrated and sustainable manner;

    c. Training communities, relevant extension services, community-based groups and non-governmental organizations on land management techniques (emphasis added).

What will be the appropriate level of "international institutions" that will develop and oversee this intergovernmental collaboration, if not the very United Nations that released this document? Again, we see the call for NGO involvement; this time, in promoting "the development of the human resources that are required to plan and manage land and land resources sustainably."

And what better way to plan and "develop" these "required human recourses" for the new normal than through a new curriculum for our children? Remember Julian Huxley in *UNESCO: Its Purpose and Its Phlosophy*:

> EDUCATION
>
> *Education has a social as well as an individual function: it is one of the means by which society as a whole can become conscious of its traditions and* its destiny, can fit itself to *make adjustment to new conditions*, and can inspire it to make new efforts towards a fuller realisation of its aims…..
>
> Further…the world to-day is in process of becoming one…This would mean an extension of education backwards from the nursery school to the nursery itself.[36] (p. 30, emphasis added)

Chapter 29
Strengthening The Role Of Workers And Their Trade Unions

1. Trade unions are vital actors in facilitating the achievement of sustainable development in view of their experience in addressing industrial change, the extremely high priority they give to protection of the working environment and the related natural environment, and their promotion of socially responsible and economic development. The existing network of collaboration among trade unions and their extensive membership provide important channels through which the concepts and practices of sustainable development can be supported.

2. The overall objective is poverty alleviation and full and sustainable employment, which contribute to safe, clean and healthy environments - the working environment, the community and the physical environment. *Workers should be full participants in the implementation and evaluation of activities related to Agenda 21.*

4. For workers and their trade unions to play a full and informed role in support of sustainable development, *Governments and employers should promote the rights of individual workers to freedom of association and the protection of the right to organize* as laid down in ILO conventions. Governments should consider ratifying and implementing those conventions, if they have not already done so.

> 6. Trade unions, employers and Governments should cooperate to ensure that the concept of sustainable development is equitably implemented.
>
> 7. Joint (employer/worker) or *tripartite* (employer/worker/Government) collaborative mechanisms at the workplace, community and national levels should be established to deal with safety, health and environment, including *special reference to the rights and status of women* in the workplace.
>
> 9. Trade unions should continue to define, develop and promote policies on all aspects of sustainable development[56] (unless otherwise noted—emphasis added).

Though the language of Agenda 21 is somewhat muted from the 1987 Brundtland Report, the message is not! Private property, Free Market, free-enterprise principles, and the unalienable Rights and Liberties of the individual must be neutralized. Most, if not all, private property and any profits from it must be forcefully extracted from the rightful owners and liberally redistributed to the chosen among the collective. Unions, already being an extra market, if not an antimarket collectivist concept, make for the perfect partner in sucking the life out of free-market enterprise and, therefore, out of the whole of our Individual Liberty.

None of the threats posed by "sustainability" to our Individual Liberty and property rights could ever be realized by those who seek to destroy them without a compromised Constitution. All of what we have just examined previously here—including collectivism, relativism, positivism, humanism, unionism, evolutionism, globalism, central planning, environmentalism, social justice, eugenics, biodiversity, and sustainable development—have each played their own role in destroying *the* fundamental principles of our only true earthly freedom—Individual Liberty. Each represents yet another strand in the web of the Philosophy that has been cast upon us and our freedom. None could succeed in their endeavor alone. Woven together, however, they wield a great and alluring strength and tenacity in their common purpose.

Everything we just went over has very real global implications, including in the United States. But the United States having a Constitution (at least in theory) protecting our Individual Rights, including property rights, how does it become specifically applicable to America and pertain to each of us as Americans? For the answer to that question, we must go to President Bill Clinton's 1993 Executive Order 12852 establishing the President's Council on Sustainable Development:

> Introduction
>
> The President's Council on Sustainable Development (PCSD) was established by President Clinton in June 1993 to advise him on sustainable development and develop "bold, new approaches to achieve our economic, environmental, and equity goals." Formally established by Executive Order 12852, the PCSD was administered as a federal advisory committee under the Federal Advisory Committee Act.[57]

Members of the PCSD included but were not limited to the following:

Jonathan Lash, President, *World Resources Institute*

John H. Adams, Executive Director, *Natural Resources Defense Council*

Andrew Cuomo, Secretary, *U.S. Department of Housing and Urban Development*

Carol M. Browner, Administrator, *U.S. Environmental Protection Agency*

Samuel C. Johnson, Chairman, *S.C. Johnson & Son, Inc.*

Dianne Dillon-Ridgley, Executive Director, *Women's Environment and Development Organization*

Dan Glickman, Secretary, *U.S. Department of Agriculture*

Fred D. Krupp, Executive Director, *Environmental Defense Fund*

Kenneth L. Lay, Chairman and CEO, *Enron Corporation*

Rodney Slater, Secretary, *U.S. Department of Transportation*

Michelle Perrault, International Vice President, *Sierra Club*

Bill Richardson, Secretary, *U.S. Department of Energy*

Richard W. Riley, Secretary, *U.S. Department of Education*

John C. Sawhill, President, *The Nature Conservancy*[58]

Here again, as on the 1994 United Nations NGO position document, we see Fred Krupp from the Environmental Defense Fund listed alongside multiple other NGOs and New York State's current governor, Andrew Cuomo.

> Task Forces:
> In order to look at specific issue areas in greater detail, The President's Council On Sustainable Development has created the following task forces:
> Climate Change Task Force International Task Force
> Environmental Management Task Force (EMTF)
> Metropolitan and Rural Strategies Task Force[59]

In addition to these, but for some reason not listed with the other task forces, is the *Population and Consumption Task Force*. Let us take a look one at a time:

> Climate Change Task Force
> The Task Force on Climate Change was created to advise the President on domestic policy options and activities that could reduce greenhouse gas emissions using approaches that maximize *societal benefits*, minimize economic impacts, *and are consistent with U.S. international agreements* (emphasis added).

Any domestic policy options and *activities* maximizing *collective* "societal benefits" are to be consistent not with the Constitution but with "international agreements"! This is another task force member of note in addition to those above:

Jay D. Hair, National Wildlife Federation

Climate Change Principles:

3. Global climate change policies should be based on national commitments and accountability to produce predictable results... United States policies to address climate change should *be based on the integration of environmental, economic and social goals.*

4. Development and Dissemination of Improved Technologies

To protect the climate cost effectively, technology breakthroughs, technology incentives, and the elimination of barriers for the deployment of existing technologies are needed. Broad-based cooperative programs to stimulate markets and develop and disseminate new and existing technology to industrialized and developing countries, must be a high priority[60] (emphasis added).

Environmental Management Task Force (EMTF)

The purpose of the Environmental Management Task Force was to advise the President on the next steps in building the new environmental management framework of the 21st Century.

This is not conservation! As we have seen, the specified purpose of the United Nation's Habitats, Brundtland Report, and Agenda 21 is to establish central planning on a global-scale period. To do that, everything that stands in its way has been declared "unsustainable" and targeted for destruction. The purpose of this task force is essentially the same: to advise on the establishment of "the next steps in building the new environmental management framework of the 21st Century," to override the framework already set forth in our Constitution right here in the good ol' USA!

>Co-Chairs:
>Carol Browner, Environmental Protection Agency
>Harry J. Pierce, General Motors Corporation
>Michael McClosky, Sierra Club

>Overview
>The need for better ways to protect the environment is now well documented. In short, *many traditional* and emerging *regulatory* and non-regulatory tools *have inherent limitations* for addressing the sources of current and future environmental problems (emphasis added).

The "inherent limitations" in past regulation as well as the implementation of a centrally planned regulatory "sustainable development," as it has been defined by those who developed it, are the Constitution, the representative republic it establishes, and the unalienable Individual Rights and Liberty of the people they were ordained to protect.

>*Sustainable America*, the PCSD's consensus report to the President issued in March 1996, recommended steps that could be taken to improve environmental management, but

stopped short of characterizing *the nature of a more fully integrated environmental management framework* to foster sustainable development.

One of the most important revelations of *Sustainable America* was that meaningful and long term solutions for environmental, economic and social equity problems will require new strategies that address the source of problems, create mutual benefit throughout society....

The PCSD provides a unique service at this important period in the discussion on the environmental management paradigm shift by moving it beyond regulatory reform to the more integrative goals of sustainable development. Development and agreement on an environmental *management framework* that better aligns economic, environmental and social factors[60] (emphasis added).

As the Constitution, *the* framework of our republic and property-based free society, stands in the way of sustainable development by protecting our property rights from infringement by the government, an "environmental management paradigm shift" is required to establish a new "framework" to move the enforcement of sustainability "beyond regulatory reform." This alone should scare the hell out of every freedom-loving American alive! Remember President Obama in his 2001 radio interview:

> *The essential constraints* that were placed by the founding fathers in the Constitution, *at least as it's been interpreted*, and the Warren court

interpreted it in the same way that generally *the Constitution is a charter of negative liberties.* It says what the states can't do to you, it says what the federal government can't do to you, *but it doesn't say what the federal government or the state government must do on your behalf*[4] (emphasis added).

"Sustainable development" or "smart growth" is just such another effort to empower the government into the position and power of imposing "what the federal government or the state government must do on your behalf."

> International Task Force
>
> *The purpose of the International task force was to advise the President on policies that foster U.S. leadership in sustainable development internationally. Specifically, it shall promote the creation and continuation of national sustainable development councils around the world.*

It all sounds nice in theory, but are all those "national sustainable development councils around the world" to be freely elected and unelected at the will of the people, or appointed and imposed on them without elections? Who pays for it?

> Forum presenters included:...*John Audley, National Wildlife Federation*; Steve Canner, US Council on International Business; Antonio Parr, World Bank; *David Schorr, World Wildlife Fund*[61] (emphasis added).

Population and Consumption Task Force: Executive Summary:

The President's Council on Sustainable Development (PCSD) was created in June 1993 to develop recommendations to help move the United States toward sustainable development—simultaneous economic, social, and *environmental progress* that enables current generations to attain a high quality of life without compromising the ability of future generations to do so....

The U.S. population is 263 million, *growing among the highest rates of any industrialized country* (one percent per year). *Unparalleled anywhere, is U.S. consumption*—which includes goods as well as services, waste products, and raw materials; in short, the total mass of materials and energy sources that make its way through our economy. *For America's future, the United States must strive to manage its resources, reduce waste products, and stabilize population so that the total impact of its activity is sustainable.*

With the world's largest economy, the United States consumes enormous amounts of resources and still generates more wastes of all kinds. In addition, steady *population growth has been a major force driving up the use of many resources*....

The Task Force believes that the two most important steps the United States must take toward sustainability are: 1) to stabilize U.S. population promptly; and 2) to move toward

> greater material and energy efficiency *in all production and use* of goods and services.
>
> STABILIZING U.S. POPULATION
>
> America's population now grows by three million each year—the equivalent of another Connecticut each year, or a California each decade. U.S. population is likely to reach 350 million by the year 2030; *a level that would place even greater strain on our ability to increase prosperity,* clean up pollution, alleviate congestion, manage sprawl, and reduce the overall consumption of resources.

Optimum population for an optimum collective prosperity is a Malthusian principle that is here being redefined as "sustainable." How does any government increase prosperity when each and every government activity represents a real financial cost to the people? And as we know, the higher the population, the higher cost for a "controlling government" to maintaining them. Keep in mind what Julian Huxley said earlier "must" be UNESCO's philosophy:

> The recognition of the idea of an optimum population-size… planned control of populations which is necessary if man's blind reproductive urges…The recognition of the fact that the wild life of the world is irreplaceable,… the spread of man must take second place to the conservation of other species.[36] (p. 45, emphasis added)

> Fortunately, the United States can stabilize its population by addressing the determinants of growth with the sensitivity....
>
> Every year, almost 60 percent of all pregnancies and 40 percent of all births in the United States are either *mistimed or unwanted*. Some 30 million American women are estimated to be *at risk for an unintended pregnancy*. One third of these women do not use contraceptives, *and the unhappy consequence* is that half of all unintended pregnancies occur to these women. Most vulnerable are sexually active teens. More than 80 percent of the one million teen pregnancies every year are unintended....
>
> *If all pregnancies were planned*, America would be able to lower its infant mortality rate, enhance economic hope and make the demand for abortion scant indeed....
>
> Finally, one-third of U.S. population growth comes from legal and illegal immigration, now at an all-time high. This is a sensitive issue, but reducing immigration levels is a necessary part of population stabilization and the drive toward sustainability (emphasis added).

Though both my children were "planned," if "all pregnancies were planned," neither my wife nor myself would have ever been born to plan our children. Note as well that the concept of Sanger's "unwanted" child has here been expanded to include the "mistimed."

POPULATION POLICY RECOMMENDATIONS

Increase and improve public outreach, educational efforts, and access to related contraceptive methods and reproductive health....

A national commission should report on changes in national *population distribution* that affect sustainable development prospects.

CURBING U.S. CONSUMPTION

U.S. consumption is not usually seen as a problem but rather as a model for the world. *However, without a change in U.S. consumption habits, stabilizing population will not have the desired effect of moving the country toward a sustainable economy.*

In the late 1980s, the world's industrialized nations had 20 percent of the global population but consumed 85 percent of all aluminum and synthetic chemicals; 80 percent of paper, iron, and steel; 75 percent of timber and energy; 65 percent of meat, fertilizer, and cement; half the world's fish and grain; and 40 percent of the fresh water. The United States is the world's largest single consumer and the greatest producer of wastes.

Sounds like a simple listing of generic stats, but are they? Remember the "context" in which the Weather Underground in their 1969 "You Don't Need a Weatherman to Know Which Way the Wind Blows" called for their "revolution" against the imperialist suppressor nation of "Amerika"!

The primary task of revolutionary struggle is to solve this principal contradiction on the side of the people of the world. It is the oppressed peoples of the world who have created the wealth of this empire and it is to them that it belongs; the goal of the revolutionary struggle must be the control and use of this wealth in the interests of the oppressed peoples of the world. *It is in this context* that we must examine the revolutionary struggles in the United States. We are within the heartland of a worldwide monster, *a country so rich from its worldwide plunder* that even the crumbs doled out to the enslaved masses within its borders provide for material existence very much above the conditions of the masses of people of the world....

The relative affluence existing in the United States is directly dependent upon the labor and natural resources... of the Third World. All of the United Airlines Astrojets, all of the Holiday Inns, all of Hertz's automobiles, your television set, car and wardrobe already belong, to a large degree to the people of the rest of the world....

The goal is the destruction of US imperialism and the achievement of a classless world: world communism[62] (emphasis added).

U.S. per capita consumption is not rising except in plastic and paper, *but because of population growth,* its total resource consumption is still increasing. Yet studies show that U.S. *quality of life* is not keeping pace.

Appropriate incentives and policy tools can change the efficiency with which Americans use materials and energy. *One way is to raise the price of natural resource use* and waste generation *to reflect their true environmental costs—* by *imposing charges* and reducing subsidies for harmful practices...with care for broad public involvement and for descriptions and analyses, so as to avoid misunderstanding about "winners" and "losers."

Only government makes the rules and enforces regulation. In a "planned society," favoritism must necessarily be imposed to enforce the plan! That favoritism being forcefully imposed is "social justice"! As by definition, social justice is, always has been, and always will be *the* choosing by the "planners" of society's winners and its losers!

Polls find consumers eager to help make a difference for the environment with their own actions, and increasingly concerned with the concept of global stewardship. However, even experts have a hard time making informed choices in a clamorous marketplace....

Each American now produces 4.5 pounds of trash per day, by far the world's highest level. Each year, 180 million gallons of motor oil are improperly sent to landfills or poured down U.S. drains—an amount equal to 16 Exxon Valdez oil spills.

If polluting technologies are priced in accord with their environmental costs, clean technologies will be able to compete more effectively.

CONCLUSION

The Population and Consumption Task Force, *with an agenda of "everything under the sun,"* sought to strike a balance between individual and government actions, between action at the federal and local levels, between providing individuals with information for making sustainable decisions and creating conditions that make those decisions good sense, and between actions that affect our numbers and actions that affect our resource use and waste production....

The Population and Consumption Task Force urges readers of this report to join with us in the challenging task of striking this new balance and of creating a sustainable way of life in the United States[63] (emphasis added).

With an agenda of "everything under the sun," what aspect of our life would they not seek to control? When considering this "new balance" between the increasing costs of traditional energy sources such as coal and oil and the now subsidized lower costs of "clean technologies," remember what Obama told the *San Francisco Chronicle* in January of 2008:

> Under my plan of a cap-and-trade system, electricity rates would necessarily skyrocket... Coal-powered plants, you know, natural gas, you name it, whatever the plants were, whatever the industry was, they would have to retro-

fit their operations. That will cost money. They will pass that money on to consumers.[64]

Population Issues.
Title X

Some 4,000 clinics and other agencies nationwide will receive $193.4 million in fiscal year 1995 and provide services to more than four million clients…85 percent are low income… Title X reaches fewer than half of those eligible for the services it provides…

Family planning is dramatically cost-effective. *For every dollar spent on publicly funded family planning services of any kind, $4.40 is saved that the federal government would otherwise be obliged by law to spend on medical care, welfare benefits, and other social services.*

When Mitt Romney wrongly sited the 49 percent of Americans on public assistance as only 47 percent, he probably wasn't thinking of it in this context. However, the real cost of dependency upon government is reflected here in its tragic effect on the loss of both liberty and life. As the cost of medical care, welfare, and "other social services" can only be attributed to government-dependent babies born and allowed to live, in what kind of world *are we to live where the government seeks to terminate our unborn children based on the justification that dead babies are statistically cheaper $4.40 to 1?*

Private Insurance

Almost two-thirds of women of reproductive age in the United States do not rely on publicly provided family planning because

> they have private-sector, employment-related insurance. But private insurance does not uniformly offer good coverage for family planning services....
>
> Thus, an important strategy for reducing the number of unintended pregnancies and births in the United States is to expand access, particularly for poor women, to contraception and related reproductive health services. Contraception is cost-effective, assists women in having the number of children they want when they want them, prevents abortions, and works toward the goal of having every child born in the United States be *a wanted child*.

When seen in the context of population control, Obama forcing the Catholic Church to provide contraception can be seen for what it is: a stand-up triple furthering the Philosophy's cause in at least three ways: population control, private business control, and God control! And once again, we have a return of Margaret Sanger's "wanted" versus unwanted child.

> Population Distribution
>
> The uneven distribution and movement of people also has important national implications. The destruction of coastal areas, the massing of population in areas that would suffer from rising sea levels and severe storms due to climate change, the loss of prime farmland, and concentrated stress on scarce water resources are all issues of interest to the national government.

> *Unevenly distributed economic activity is at the root of uneven population distribution*—both as a cause and an effect[65] (emphasis added).

Is this not in the same spirit of the 1976 (Habitat I) United Nations Conference on Human Settlements?

> ALL COUNTRIES SHOULD ESTABLISH AS A MATTER OF URGENCY A NATIONAL POLICY ON **HUMAN SETTLEMENTS, EMBODYING** *THE DISTRIBUTION OF POPULATION*, **AND RELATED** ECONOMIC *AND SOCIAL ACTIVITIES*, **OVER THE NATIONAL TERRITORY.**
>
> c) Such a policy should
> v) Be devised to facilitate *population redistribution* to accord with the availability of resources[44] (emphasis added).

Population distribution controls where we can and cannot live, compromising our property rights and Individual Liberty. *Population redistribution* is our forced removal and relocation from where we already live. Do we really want to revisit what hasn't been official US policy since President Andrew Jackson's progressive Indian Removal Act of 1830, which ultimately resulted in the death of thousands on the Trail of Tears? Where is the Liberty in that?

> Metropolitan and Rural Strategies Task Force
> The mission of the Metropolitan and Rural Strategies Task Force was to encourage and support local and *regional collaboration* among Federal, State, and local government agencies; public interest and community groups; and

businesses to advance sustainable development in metropolitan and rural communities.

GOALS:

Promote supportive policies that provide incentives and dismantle disincentives and barriers to institutional cooperation on sustainable community development in metropolitan and rural areas; *advance a holistic vision of sustainable community* development...*develop national and community frameworks* of indicators and metrics to evaluate progress on sustainable community development.

Sustainable America - A New Consensus for the Prosperity, Opportunity and a Healthy Environment for the Future[66] (emphasis added).

The key "disincentive" to the "sustainable development" of a "planned society" is capitalism, along with the Free Market and our Individual Rights to property that it embodies. The number one barrier to "sustainable development" is the Constitution. As such, they must be "dismantled," and upon the "old world" shall the "frameworks" and "holistic vision of sustainable community development" of the new consensus of the new normal be built!

A few ways businesses around the world are being lured to "evolve" from their state of exploitation toward one of "sustainable conscientiousness" is through low-profit, limited liability companies (L3C), community interest companies (CIC), or public benefit corporations otherwise known as B corporations. Public benefit companies have emerged as a "hybrid" between for-profit and not-for-profit businesses to foster that evolution. The difference from traditional profit-based corporations is a change in the legal corporate framework from one where the sole priority is maximum profit to one of a collective purpose of "people, planet, and profit."

With the demonization of capitalism, property, free enterprise, prosperity, profit, and Individual Liberty, being the driving force behind sustainable development, the greedy capitalists are effectively offered the compromise of easing their social guilt by 1/3 in B corporations seeking to "help build a global movement to redefine success in business."[67] B corporations represent the "planned" evolutionary "progress" of society, from one of egoist, capitalist greed toward one of Comte's globalist altruism, or more simply, the phasing out of Liberty.

> Definition and Vision Statement
> The Council adopted the Brundtland Commission's definition of sustainable development. The vision statement articulates the Council's broad concept of the benefits of sustainability for the nation[68].

This paragraph is what applies everything in the "broad concept" of all we have just gone over to the United States and every single American! We *don't* have to connect the dots of Clinton's sustainable development to the Brudtland Commission's "definition of sustainable development." They shamelessly tell us here that they have "adopted" it not only for themselves but, like it or not, for every one of us as well.

> Chapter 1: National Goals Toward Sustainable Development
> This common set of goals emerged from the Council's vision. *These goals express in concrete terms the elements of sustainability.*

Alongside the goals are suggested indicators that can be used to help measure progress toward achieving them.

GOAL 1: HEALTH AND THE ENVIRONMENT

Ensure that every person enjoys the benefits of clean air, clean water, and a healthy environment at home, at work, and at play.

GOAL 2: ECONOMIC PROSPERITY

Sustain a healthy U.S. economy that grows sufficiently to create meaningful jobs, reduce poverty, and provide the opportunity for a high quality of life for all in an increasingly competitive world.

GOAL 3: EQUITY

Ensure that all Americans are afforded justice and have the opportunity to achieve economic, environmental, and social well-being.

GOAL 4: CONSERVATION OF NATURE

Use, conserve, protect, and restore natural resources—land, air, water, and biodiversity—in ways that help ensure long-term social, economic, and environmental benefits for ourselves and future generations.

GOAL 5: STEWARDSHIP

Create a widely held ethic of stewardship that strongly encourages individuals, institutions, and corporations to take full responsibility for the economic, environmental, and social consequences of their actions.

GOAL 6: SUSTAINABLE COMMUNITIES

Encourage people to work together to create healthy communities where natural and historic resources are preserved, jobs are available, sprawl is contained, neighborhoods are secure, education is lifelong, transportation and health care are accessible, and all citizens have opportunities to improve the quality of their lives.

GOAL 7: CIVIC ENGAGEMENT

Create full opportunity for citizens, businesses, and communities to participate in and influence the natural resource, environmental, and economic decisions that affect them.

GOAL 8: POPULATION

Move toward stabilization of U.S. population.

GOAL 9: INTERNATIONAL RESPONSIBILITY

Take a leadership role in the development and implementation of global sustainable development policies, standards of conduct, and trade and foreign policies that further the achievement of sustainability.

GOAL 10: EDUCATION

Ensure that all Americans have equal access to education and lifelong learning opportunities that will prepare them for meaningful work, a high quality of life, and an understanding of the concepts involved in sustainable development[69] (emphasis added).

Chapter 2: Building A New Framework for A New Century

Future progress requires that the United States broaden its commitment to environmental protection to embrace the essential components of sustainable development: environmental health, economic prosperity, and social equity and well-being. This means reforming the current system of environmental management and building a new and efficient framework....

The nation should pursue two paths in reforming environmental regulation. The first is to improve the efficiency and effectiveness of the current environmental management system. The second is to develop and test innovative approaches and create a new alternative environmental management system that achieves more protection at a lower cost. To help achieve this, the administrator of *the U.S. Environmental Protection Agency (EPA)*, working in partnership with other federal agencies and other stakeholders, *should have the authority to make decisions* that will achieve environmental goals efficiently and effectively.

Besides improving the cost-effectiveness of the current system, the Council believes that the nation needs to develop policy tools that meet the following broad criteria:

> *Make Greater Use of Market Forces.* Sustainable development objectives must harness market forces through policy tools, such as emissions trading deposit/refund systems and tax and subsidy reform. This approach can [*substantially influence the behavior*] of firms, governments, and individuals.

> *Use Intergovernmental Partnerships.* Federal, state, and tribal governments need to work together [*in partnership with local communities to develop place-based strategies*] that integrate economic development, environmental quality, and social policymaking with broad public involvement.

POLICY RECOMMENDATION 3

ACTION 1. Companies, trade associations, wholesalers, retailers, consumer groups, and other private sector parties can develop models of shared product responsibility.....

ACTION 2. A joint committee involving the private and nonprofit sectors should recommend to the President individuals to be *appointed* to a Product Responsibility Panel... *The Product Responsibility Panel* should help identify means of conducting effective monitoring, evaluation, and analysis of the projects' progress and possible links with other sustainable development initiatives. It should also help coordinate sound economic and environmental analyses to assist in transferring the lessons from local demonstration projects to *regional* and national policies. The panel should have a balanced representation of *stakeholders* with interests in the life cycle of a product, including its supply, procurement, consumption, and disposal. By immediately identifying product categories for demonstration projects, U.S. industry, in cooperation with government agencies *and the environmental community*, could begin to carry out *the new models of shared responsibility*....

ACTION 3. Following evaluation of the projects, the federal government, private companies, and individuals should voluntarily adopt practices and policies that have been successfully demonstrated to carry out extended product responsibility on a regional and national scale. *The Product Responsibility Panel should recommend any legislative changes needed to remove barriers* to extending product responsibility (emphasis added).

The bottom line is the call for *a new framework* of *appointed* "intergovernmental partnerships" working "in partnership with local communities to develop place-based strategies." In Article IV, Section 4, the Constitution *guarantees* us a representative republic, stating, "The United States shall guarantee to every State in this Union a Republican Form of Government," wherein "We The People," as the true source of power in a free society, maintain our voice in holding our representatives accountable. With "appointed committees," we lose our voice; and where we lose our voice, we lose our republic!

On a sidenote, wasn't Obamacare legislation left open-ended, leaving the door open for its frameworks of appointed committees or "panels" to propagate themselves, their regulations, and their authoritative bureaucracies indefinitely? Considering that the much-smaller country of England's government health-care system is somewhere between the fifth and third largest employer in the world, Obamacare promises to far surpass them in bureaucratic weight alone!

FROM THE TOP OF A MOUNTAIN TO THE HEART OF THE CITY

For businesses...*stewardship* extends beyond products and *includes a strong commitment to the communities* in which they are located.

Stewardship ultimately comes back to growth policy and land use planning.

TOOLS FOR EXTENDED PRODUCT RESPONSIBILITY

Government Subsidies, Tax Credits, and Procurement Preference:

Direct subsidies or tax credits can encourage sustainable processes and products. Because a *national priority is usually the justification for a subsidy or tax credit*, these tools should not conflict with the goals of sustainability...

Greater Use of Market Forces

The marketplace's power to produce desired goods and services at the lowest cost possible is

> *driven by the price signals that result from this decentralized decision process* (emphasis added).

The Free Market is "decentralized" because we are at Liberty to conduct business naturally. To become "sustainable," our freedom to choose must then be manipulated by imposed unnatural costs, channeling our actions into their vision of sustainable development through enforcement of their centralized plan. Every subsidy and regulatory expense represents another monkey wrench thrown into the market, the balance of which costs every one of us not only in dollars but in our sacred Liberty as well!

> Despite the nation's commitment to a Free Market economic system, governmental policy substantially influences the workings of the marketplace. For example, *tax levels on different products and activities lower or raise their market prices and artificially encourage or discourage their use*...At other times, government tax and spending subsidy programs may be essential if the short-term rewards of the marketplace do not coincide with the long-term goals (emphasis added).

This is *the* "artificial" progressive planner's market-manipulating monkey wrench exposed! And once again, not in my words but theirs! There can be no freedom of choice in a planned sustainable society.

PRESERVING THE LONG ISLAND PINE BARRENS

In 1993, weary of litigation and stung by a real estate recession, the parties to the dispute and other stakeholders, aided by the Suffolk County Water Authority, joined together to help *the state legislature draft a bill that led to the creation of the Pine Barrens Commission.* The commission promotes a distinctive management plan for the region.... It will achieve this not only through outright purchase of some land but through an innovative market-oriented method to preserve vital areas. *Under the plan, landowners in the core area whose property is not acquired outright but who cannot build on it, can sell their development rights* for use in outlying areas that are suitable for higher density development than local zoning currently allows. *The plan* has identified three types of receiving areas: areas where residential development may increase modestly, areas where commercial density may increase, and *planned development districts* where densities may increase substantially. The result is a program that offers a cost-effective and equitable way to preserve land with the potential to improve the future shape of communities on the periphery of the Pine Barrens.

Across the United States, communities are struggling to save ecologically important areas while also allowing for growth and development. *The use of transfer of development rights* helps address this challenge by harnessing market incentives to allow developers, environmentalists, and local citizens *to implement new methods for long-term community planning* (emphasis added).

The freely elected state legislature here creates an unelected commission to promote a "management plan." Where in the Constitution was any part of our legislative branch of government ordained the power to, in turn, ordain another branch of unelected authority? If Congress, our state and local legislators were all given that power, then might the commissions appointed have the power to appoint commissions of their own, and so on and so forth? Luckily for us, for what it's worth, the very first words of the Constitution after the Preamble read, "All legislative Powers here in granted shall be vested in a Congress of the United States, which shall consist of a Senate and House of Representatives." My lying eyes just aren't seeing anything there about any unelected and unsworn commissions or committees, replacing our Liberty to pursue our own happiness with the "shared responsibility" of a forced collective compliance to the centrally planned utopian "vision" of others!

> Building Intergovernmental Partnerships
> *Two related reforms are now in order to help shift the focus from the narrow goal of environmental protection to the broader goal of sustainable development.* The first reform is to move from a federally focused governmental decision-making structure *to a collaborative design that shares responsibility among levels of government.* The second reform is to shift the focus from centralized environmental regulation organized around separate programs to protect air, water, and land *to a comprehensive place-based approach.* It should be designed to integrate economic, environmental, and social policies to meet the needs and aspirations of localities while protecting national interests.

> *To accomplish these reforms, the new system will need to rely heavily on partnerships among federal, regional, state, local, and tribal levels of government.* These partnerships will require *unprecedented cooperation* and communication within and among levels of government in a geographic area. For example, *carrying out a community-designed sustainable development strategy may depend on close collaboration by a local economic development agency, a regional transportation authority*, a state housing department, and a federal environmental agency....
>
> This shift in focus to place-based partnerships will require major changes in the roles and responsibilities of federal and state regulatory agencies in communities interested in accepting new local responsibilities. The agencies should help build local decision-making capacity *so that communities can begin to develop integrated economic, environmental, and social equity strategies themselves* (emphasis added).

This is it! The royal sustainable extraconstitutional "I dub thee the power" to appoint unelected committees with the power to "develop integrated economic, environmental, and social equity strategies themselves." Economics within the Philosophy, as we have seen, includes social justice, which is redistribution of wealth and property. Sustainability also includes social equity strategies forcing collectivism's socialist values onto Americans, which are in direct conflict with our founding values and Individual Liberty.

POLICY RECOMMENDATION 7
INTERGOVERNMENTAL PARTNERSHIPS

ACTION 1. Federal agencies should develop effective partnerships with state governments to administer environmental regulatory programs...States should also share in the increased flexibility when using federal grant monies, conditioned on performance-based measures of environmental results agreed upon by federal and state agencies.

ACTION 2. Federal and state agencies should enter into partnerships with communities that wish to develop and carry out sustainable development strategies designed to address local circumstances.

TRANSPORTATION AND SUSTAINABLE DEVELOPMENT

Transportation choices, land use patterns, community design, and pollution are inherently linked. Further, transportation affects national and economic security as it increasingly accounts for the largest share of oil consumed in the United States...

This report outlines many steps that can be taken by government at all levels, communities, businesses, and residents to address the challenge of a sustainable transportation system.

Improve *community design to contain sprawl* better, expand transit options, and make efficient use of land within a community to *locate homes* for people of all incomes, places of work, schools, businesses, shops, and transit in close proximity and in harmony with civic spaces[70] (emphasis added).

Chapter 4: Strengthening Communities

Creating a better future depends, in part, on the knowledge and involvement of citizens and on a decision-making process that embraces and encourages differing perspectives of those affected by governmental policy. Steps toward a more sustainable future include developing community-driven strategic planning and collaborative regional planning; improving community and building design; decreasing sprawl; and creating strong, diversified local economies while increasing jobs and other economic opportunities.

In sustainable communities, people use a participatory approach to make conscious decisions about design. The concepts of efficiency and liveability guide these decisions. Development patterns promote accessibility, decrease sprawl, reduce energy costs, and foster the creation of built environments on a human scale....

In sustainable communities, partnerships involving business, government, labor, and employees promote economic development and jobs. *Participants cooperatively plan and carry out development strategies... buffering it from the effects of national and international economic trends...*

Much of what is needed to create more sustainable communities is within reach if people and their community institutions join forces. Many communities are beginning *to use sustainable development as a framework* for thinking about their future. The big institutions in society—including federal and state governments, businesses, universities, and national organizations—can and should provide support for local community efforts. *And in some cases, these institutions need to review the barriers they sometimes inadvertently have erected that diminish the ability of communities to pursue sustainable development* (emphasis added).

Again, sustainable development is an apposing force against all that is ordained and protected in the Constitution—the Constitution is that barrier!

Building A Community Together
The Council believes that one of the best ways to strengthen communities is to ensure that people have greater power over and responsibility for the decisions that shape their communities. Time and time again, community leaders told us that a fundamental component of implementing sustainable development locally is having people come together to identify a community's needs and then work toward collaborative solutions. Accomplishing this requires both political leadership and citizen involvement. *They also told us that creat-*

> *ing mechanisms for communities to work together cooperatively is necessary to deal with problems that cross political jurisdictions.*
>
> The integration of local decisionmaking offers a way to improve the economy, the environment, and social equity in communities.
>
> *Broad-based action is needed because local government alone cannot accomplish long-term solutions to community problems. Nor can individuals, businesses, community groups, or state and federal agencies do so by working in isolation. Lasting solutions are best identified when people from throughout a community—as individuals; elected officials; or members of the business community, environmental groups, or civic organizations—are brought together in a spirit of cooperation to identify solutions to community problems* (emphasis added).

Only through our submission to a larger regional-appointed collective, with a regional plan for us, can we hope to achieve sustainability.

> By listening to the stories of communities throughout the country, the Council learned that there are fundamental steps to a community-driven strategic planning process. *A critical first step is to assemble a broad cross section of the community to participate in an open, public process. Through a series of meetings and events, the community develops a vision for its future. It then conducts an inventory and assessment of its*

> *economic, natural, and human resources. Specific economic, environmental, and social goals are determined; these build on the community's vision, resources, and needs. Next, the community sets priorities for its goals, identifies specific actions, and establishes indicators or benchmarks to measure progress toward the goals. If successful, the strategic planning process results in a clear sense of direction and timing. It specifies the actions and responsibilities to be undertaken by business, residents, government, and community groups* (emphasis added).

It is *not* the vision of our communities that is to be "determined" at these "meetings" but rather their vision for us as determined by them. In a free society, community visions are determined individually by community members at the voting booth. There is *no* community-wide vote at these meetings. Neither are there any elected representatives to be held accountable by the community in the next election. It's a subtle but colossal difference in realities with devastating consequences to be paid, all of which will come at the cost of our representative republic, our Individual Rights, and Liberty. Nevertheless, with a "strategic plan" being all planned out for us, our corresponding duties can be assigned. As we have learned from such collectivism, it is "only in this context which emphasizes duties, that the concept of 'rights' can have any application."

> *By working together, communities can tackle issues—like transportation planning—that affect, and whose resolution can benefit, an entire region. This collaborative approach is not only an opportunity, it is a necessity.* Community leaders who

> met with the Council emphasized that *without regional approaches* to solve many critical problems that affect communities—such as economic development, transportation, land use, sprawl, and water quality—little long-term progress can be made[71] (emphasis added).

This is the function of the new "frameworks" referred to over and over again throughout what we have just gone over that are needed to "fundamentally transform" a free America from its founding state of Constitutional rule of law to one that, by definition, is a soviet system of rule by panel or committee.

What is a soviet? According to the *Random House Webster's College Dictionary*, it is "a governmental council, being part of a hierarchy of councils at various levels of government, culminating in the Supreme Soviet."

The "regional" aspect of such sustainability committees is also *not* benign as it dismisses both local autonomy and local representation. Again, this is the very heart of how sustainable development, and all that it entails, is and has been undermining the whole of our representative republic! What I have previously mentioned regarding unelected "assembled" and/or appointed committees subverting our elected officials is so established here in writing for you to read for yourself, not in my words but theirs! This is how, by "building a community together," that sustainable development is destroying our republic!

> Chapter 5: Natural Resources Stewardship
> Stewardship is an essential concept that helps to define appropriate human interaction with the natural world. An ethic of stewardship builds on collaborative approaches; ecosystem

integrity; and incentives in such areas as agricultural resources management, sustainable forestry, fisheries, restoration, and biodiversity conservation.

Remember why biodiversity preservation is so important to the Philosophy: preserve the biodiversity of the evolutionary primordial soup from which, in a Godless state of nature, all present life "evolved" and all future life will emerge. As such, the protection of biodiversity must take precedence, even over the needs of both humanity and freedom itself.

> *As the population increases*, so too will demands for fertile soil, clean and abundant water, healthy air, diverse wildlife, food, fuel, and fiber....
>
> *Privately owned lands*...are most often delineated by boundaries that differ from the geographic boundaries of the natural system of which they are a part. In some cases, therefore, *individual or private decisions can have negative ramifications*. For example, *private decisions are often driven by strong economic incentives that result in severe ecological or aesthetic consequences* to both the natural system and to communities outside landowner boundaries (emphasis added).

The whole of the concept of private property and the freedom of private decision-making that goes with it is wholly unsustainable!

> Although much remains to be done, the United States has made major strides in achieving a healthier environment and better protection of its natural resources. For example, *by 1994, 14 million acres across the United States were protected through regional, state, and local land trusts.* These private and voluntary efforts have produced a 49-percent increase in conservation acreage since 1990....
>
> How can society best develop and maintain a commitment to stewardship? The answer is multifaceted, but it starts with understanding *the dynamics at work in the environment* and the connection among environmental protection, economic prosperity, *and social equity and well-being.* It depends on *the processes* by which individuals, institutions, and government at all levels can work together toward protecting and restoring the country's inherited natural resource base...Also important is the widespread understanding that people, *bonded by a shared purpose, can work together to make sustainable development a reality* (emphasis added).

Therefore, in order to achieve "a healthier environment and better protection of its natural resources," all efforts should be made to neutralize, if not eliminate, the concepts of private property and self-determination, which are the very essence of Individual Liberty. The objective of "land trusts" is the objective of sustainable development, which is the forced submission of the individual to the general will or central plan of a single global organism: the organism of mankind!

Using Collaborative Approaches to Manage Natural Resources

Collaborative approaches can apply both to public and private resources when the decisions made on their use have broad implications for the whole community. What has become clear is that the conflicts over natural resources increasingly are *exceeding the capacity of institutions, processes, and mechanisms to resolve them....*

What is usually missing from the process is a mechanism to enable the many *stakeholders* to work together to identify *common goals*, values, and areas of interest...The Council endorses the concept of collaborative approaches to resolving conflicts.

Groups are discovering and demonstrating that collaborative approaches, *based on a framework of natural systems or defining land forms such as watersheds*, offer useful tools *for identifying common visions and goals*...Experience is showing that they can *serve as reliable means for addressing...social considerations; building from but moving beyond the limits of narrow jurisdictions and authorities*...Collaborative approaches envisioned here can give impetus to stakeholders...and exercise collective responsibility[72] (emphasis added).

This "frameworks of natural systems...such as watersheds" is the scheme that necessitates the "regional" approach to "addressing...social considerations."

Collaborative approaches sound nice, but who is collaborating? Are we to be a representative republic or a republic of collaborative soviets?

Remember this from the Brundtland Report: "Conflicts over natural resources are exceeding the capacity, processes, and mechanisms to resolve them." The main "mechanism" being the Constitution, the main "process" being our constitutional representative republic, the main "capacity" being exceeded is the *limited* capacity of government ordained in the Constitution! Therefore, we must move "beyond the limits of narrow jurisdictions and authorities" of constitutional government if we are to achieve sustainability under a whole new "frameworks."

> Chapter 6: U.S. Population and Sustainability
>
> Population growth, especially when coupled with current consumption patterns, affects sustainability. A sustainable United States is one *where all Americans have access to family planning and reproductive health services, women enjoy increased opportunities* for education and employment, and responsible immigration policies are fairly implemented and enforced.
>
> It is possible for more people to have a smaller impact but only if—*through changes in lifestyle*....
>
> Production and consumption in the United States together form the critical link between population and sustainability. National quality of life derives in large part from the unprecedented scale of U.S. production and consumption...

> This high standard of living is also reflected in a high level of consumption -- a level amplified by growth in population...*the size of the population and the scale of consumption impinge significantly on American society's ability to achieve sustainability....*
>
> Managing population growth, resources, and wastes is essential to ensuring that the total impact of these factors is within the bounds of sustainability. *Stabilizing the population without changing consumption and waste production patterns would not be enough, but it would make an immensely challenging task more manageable. In the United States, each is necessary; neither alone is sufficient.*
>
> Family planning is highly cost-effective compared with the social and public costs of unintended pregnancy, and it helps ensure that every child is a wanted child[73] (emphasis added).

Within the Philosophy, eugenic population control and population distribution control are not only necessary for planned sustainable development and the preservation of the biodiversity; they are interdependent.

As far as insuring every child is a wanted child, remember Margaret Sanger's "Each and every unwanted child is likely to be in some way a social liability. It is only the "wanted" child who is likely to be a social asset."

So when it is professed by academics, as it is on page 26 of the October 2012 issue of *Popular Science* in an article titled *Can We Reengineer Ourselves to Cope with the Effects of Climate Change?* that

NYU bioethics philosophy Professor S. Mathew Liao and colleagues proposed a new way to deal with climate change; reengineer humans to make to make us less of a burden on the planet. Their paper proposed that doctors could use in-vitro fertilization to select for embryos with genes for short stature, making future generations physically smaller and thus less carbon intensive. Drugs could induce meat allergies, reducing consumption of carbon intensive beef. These approaches, Liao and his co-authors say, could encourage people to make the eco-friendly choices many seem unable to make on their own.

The ideas are, as the authors admit preposterous.[74]

Then we know that, one, there is nothing "new" in their "new way to deal with climate change." And, two, the only thing preposterous here is the claim that they consider their own science "preposterous." They really do count on us being ignorant of what we are learning here in *Last Call for Liberty*. However, let the Philosophy be put on notice that, in the spirit of Chief Joseph from where the sun now stands, *we will be ignorant no more forever*!

Chapter 7: International Leadership

The United States has both reason and responsibility to develop and carry out global policies that support sustainable development. Because of its history and power, the United States is inevitably a leader and needs to be an active participant in cooperative international efforts to encourage democracy, support scientific research, and enhance economic development that preserves the environment and protects human health.

With one of the highest standards of living in the world, the United States is the largest producer and consumer in history: with fewer than 5 percent of the world's population, the nation consumes nearly 25 percent of the planet's resources. This high standard of living and huge economy also have made the United States the world's largest producer of wastes....

Issues of development, environment, and human security are as surely related globally as they are locally. This country will not prosper, nor will freedom thrive, in a violent and unstable world. Poverty, inequity, and environmental destruction corrode the bonds that hold stability and progress together. The peoples of the world can only achieve their legitimate aspirations for economic betterment within the context of environmental protection *and a more equitable distribution of the fruits of that progress* (emphasis added).

It is the success and prosperity of United States that is the cause of global poverty. Poor nations and poor people don't have prosperity because we have it all. Therefore, after the thrill of redistributing all the wealth in America is gone, there remains both the "reason and responsibility" of redistributing it all from the United States to the world!

> Certain problems can only be addressed through global cooperation...Previous chapters of this report emphasize the importance of local communities and individual responsibility in moving the United States toward a more sustainable path....
>
> *Falling short of its own goals may signal to the world the ineffectiveness of free institutions to create environmentally sound economic development that equitably distributes the benefits of growing prosperity. If the United States believes that free institutions are the best means for pursuing human aspirations, it must show that these institutions can respond to the great changes taking place.*
>
> More than 100 nations have established national councils on sustainable development similar to the U.S. President's Council on Sustainable Development; they seek to create consensus and shape policies to bring together economic, environmental, and equity goals. Some, like the Canadian and Australian Roundtables, began their work several years before the U.S. Council. Most have been organized *in response to the 1992 Earth Summit, the United Nations Conference on Environment and Development.*

As "free-institutions" are not at all compatible with the central planning totalitarianism of sustainable development, how might the United States "show that these institutions can respond to the great changes taking place"? There are only two ways. They could, via relativism, breath a whole new meaning into what "free institutions" are, making them compatible. Or, if the free institutions of our free society are to survive intact, the only real choice we have is by first exposing then destroying the lie of sustainable development! The "exposing" part has been put forth for decades now by such great defenders of Liberty as Henry Lamb and Tom DeWeese. Their grand efforts continue, though I might add in a far humbler way, right here as you read this work. Why do our elected representatives not see the frameworks of the new normal being constructed beneath their very noses that *by design* will make them and our republic as a whole obsolete? Pray that free America humbles herself before her Creator that she might see the sustainable elephant in the room before it crushes her and her freedom forever!

Again, we don't have to connect the dots of Clinton's PCSD to the United Nations or Agenda 21 as they tell us here in their own words of that connection to *the* 1992 Earth Summit or Agenda 21 specifically!

GLOBAL CLIMATE CHANGE

The most important greenhouse gas influenced by human activity is carbon dioxide. Concentrations of carbon dioxide have increased by about 30 percent over preindustrial levels. *Buildup of this gas results primarily from the burning of fossil fuels and deforestation.*

The buildup of greenhouse gases in the atmosphere is expected to lead to an enhanced greenhouse effect popularly referred to as global warming. Carbon dioxide accounts for the great majority of global warming....

Since the world depends on fossil fuels (which account for most carbon dioxide emissions) for 90 percent of its energy, the implications of global warming could be profound. If the risks of warming are judged to be too great, then nothing less than a *drastic reduction in the burning of coal, oil, and natural gas would be necessary.*

POLICY RECOMMENDATION I

ACTION 2. The federal government should cooperate in key international agreements—from *ratifying the U.N. Convention on Biological Diversity* to taking the lead in achieving full implementation of specific commitments made in international environmental agreements to which the United States is a party.

ACTION 3. The federal government should increase support for effective and efficient bilateral and multilateral institutions as a means *to achieve national sustainable development goals.*

ACTION 4. The federal government should ensure open access for, and participation of, *nongovernmental organizations* and private industry in international agreements and decision-making processes (emphasis added).

As we have learned, these all hold huge implication to our everyday life and the future of Liberty in America, not to mention the world. Consider today's controversy with hydrofracking for energy sources:

In New York, state governor Andrew Cuomo and the NYS Department of Environmental Conservation are expected to come up with a decision on whether or not it will be allowed. Their decision has been delayed again and again. Why? Much prosperity for private property owners, private businesses, and America is, or at least was, anticipated with this hydrofracking. But in what basket have we put all of our eggs? First, Andrew Cuomo, as we saw earlier, was a sitting member of this Presidential Council on Sustainable Development (PCSD). And this PCSD, as they have just told us in their own words, is wholeheartedly dead set against such development, individual prosperity, and continued "exploitation" of our "fossil fuel" energy resources.

Second, the same NYSDEC that is to have the final say on fracking's environmental impact is tainted with the same ethically questionable conflicts of interest. According to the December 30, 2011 issue of the *New York Outdoor News*, both DEC commissioner Joe Martens and the then newly appointed assistant commissioner Kathy Moser had previously "worked in the same Albany office building where their agencies—the Open Spaces Institute and the World Wildlife Fund—shared space." Per the April 13, 2011, issue of the *New York Post*, Open Spaces Institute is a funded subsidiary of George Soros's Open Society Foundations.[75] The *Outdoor News* article goes on to say,

> Martins said, "Kathy has a proven track record of environmental stewardship"....
>
> Prior to her work with the *World Wildlife Fund*, Moser worked with the *Nature Conservancy* for 17 years, most recently as the acting New York State director, where she managed a staff of 170 and oversaw a $26 million operating budget.
>
> While at the Nature Conservancy she coordinated a $110 million acquisition of Finch

> Pruyn Paper Company lands for eventual inclusion in New York's Forest Preserve....
>
> DEC also has named a new director for Region 5...Robert S. Stegemann...In announcing the appointment, Martens cited Stegemann's *"impressive record in working to create a sustainable society*...Stegemann's previous experience also includes...the Adirondack Nature Conservancy & Land Trust.[76]

The president of the Nature Conservancy, John C. Sawhill, like Andrew Cuomo, was also a sitting member of Bill Clinton's PCSD. Remember what we learned about these NGOs from Henry Lamb:

> The 1972 Stockholm Conference institutionalized the environment as a legitimate concern of government, and it institutionalized NGOs as the instruments through which government could varnish its agenda with the appearance of public support. Of course, only those NGOs personally selected by (Maurice) Strong received funding... Strong became a Vice President of the World Wildlife Fund (WWF), a post he held until 1981...Strong was appointed to the U.N.'s World Commission on Environment and Development, headed by Gro Harlem Brundtland...Strong, and the World Wildlife Fund, were largely responsible for the content of the Brundtland Commission's final report, *Our Common Future*.[42]

Is it a coincidence then, that Clinton's PCSD states specifically that "the federal government should ensure open access for, and participation of" these very same "nongovernmental organizations"? Or is a bigger progressive picture coming into focus?

"Our Common Future" is the part of the Brundtland Report where "the Commission proposes measures to: advance the *Law of the Sea*." Funny how they are all, once again, interconnected in New York State to stem off both hydrofracking for natural gas and the potential for prosperity.

Last but not least, there is this from Clinton's PCSD:

> ACTION 9. The United States should support the U.N. Commission on Sustainable Development as a forum for nations *to report on their progress* in moving toward sustainability[77] (emphasis added).

The final blow from sustainable development to our nation's sovereignty comes in the "forum" of our National Comprehensive Sustainable Development Committee "reporting" to its supreme international soviet, "the U.N. Commission on sustainable development"!

With the Environmental Protection Agency being established in December of 1970, the Clean Water Act in 1971, and the Endangered Species Act in 1973, Clinton's PCSD helped pave the way for the next phases in "sustainable" biodiversity protection, including the National Gap Analysis Program (GAP) and the roadless-area projects protecting biodiversity from the "people problem" well "before it becomes endangered." These protected areas, along with the ribbons of lands filling in the *gaps* between them called *corridors*, form the basis from which population distribution and, eventually, population redistribution are to be "planned." Again, remember what Huxley tells us, "that areas must be set aside where, in the ultimate interests of mankind as a whole, the spread of man must take second place to the conservation of other species."[36]

In New York State, we have all seen the pretty little painted farm wagons along the roadsides with signs on them reading something along the line of "Forever Green" or "Save Our Farms." We have all seen the plethora of articles and headlines in the papers over the past few years making *heroes* out of individual farmers/landowners "insuring the preservation our farmland and undeveloped areas into the next generations." Why are they heroes? Because they have done exactly what Habitat I called for. They separated their "land ownership rights from development rights" and then sold the ownership and control of those separated development rights to the government! From the perspective of our unborn generations, they are treasonously being sold out! How, you ask? Because wherever the land becomes "forever green," the property rights there, now and forever being controlled by the government, are now *forever gone* from the body of the people!

These rights are being sold to the government at an astonishing rate, many getting paid millions of dollars to sell (out) the property rights of their own children and grandchildren to the government! All in the name of planned sustainability under such programs as the Federal Farm and Ranch Land Protection Program or the Farmland Protection Program—either directly or indirectly through one of several "approved" and government-funded NGO organizations such as the American Farm Land Trust, Finger Lakes Land Trust, Humane Society Land Trust, Open Spaces Institute (a George Soros–affiliated organization), the Nature Conservancy, Historic Preservation League, Coastal Conservation League, National Resource Defense Council, Audubon Society, Endangered Habitats League, Sierra Club, or World Wildlife Fund (WWF). Many, if not most, of these NGOs have international divisions acting globally and, in many cases, collaborating in coalitions to pool their recourses like the International Union for the Conservation of Nature (IUCN) and the International Land Coalition (ILC), whose work happens to be funded, at least in part, by Maurice Strong's Canadian International Development Agency (CIDA).

Now that we have come to know of the redistribution required in a "we're all in this together society" and the central planning required for a sustainable society of order, and the loss of private property rights and Individual Liberty entailed in them, a whole new understanding of the implications of what Obama is saying in his closing statement at his first debate (2012) with Mitt Romney begins to come into a much sharper focus. He stated,

> The auto workers that you meet in Toledo or Detroit take such pride in building the best cars in the world, not just because of a paycheck, but because *it gives them that sense of pride, that they're helping to build America*. And so the question now is *how do we build on those strengths*. And *everything that I've tried to do, and everything that I'm now proposing....All those things are designed to make sure that the American people, their genius, their grit, their determination, is—is channeled* and—and they have an opportunity to succeed. And everybody's *getting a fair shot*. And *everybody's getting a fair share—everybody's doing a fair share*, and everybody's *playing by the same rules*[78] (emphasis added).

It is only under the forced submission of the individual to the collective and the general will that a people, "their genius, their grit, their determination is—is channeled."

Coming full circle, as webs do again and again, we come once again to the work of Auguste Comte. Lewis A. Coser gives us some more straightforward insight into what we have to look forward to from Comte' evolutionary sociology:

> "The constitution of the new system cannot take place before the destruction of the old," and before the potentialities of the old mental order have been exhausted.

In the "old order," *the dignity* of the individual is the standard. The purpose of its sovereign national Constitution is to forever preserve the self-evident truths that are the fundamental principles of our *God-given* unalienable Rights. These fundamental principles and Rights are what comprise our "Individual Liberty." As the "potentialities" of Individual Liberty are without end, only by limiting or eliminating that Liberty can the "potential" of the old "mental order" ever be exhausted. Coser continues:

> It would be a mistake, Comte averred, to expect a new social order, any more than a new intellectual order, to emerge smoothly from the death throes of an old: "*The passage from one social system to another can never be continuous and direct.*" In fact, human history is marked by alternative "*organic*" and "*critical*" periods. In organic periods, social stability and intellectual harmony prevail, and the various parts of the body social are in equilibrium. In *critical periods*, in contrast, *old certainties are upset, traditions are undermined, and the body social is in fundamental disequilibrium...Yet they are the necessary pre-

> *lude to the inauguration of a new organic state of affairs. "There is always a transitional state of anarchy which lasts for some generations at least; and lasts the longer the more complete is the renovation to be wrought"*[79] (emphasis added).

If it is true that we are, in such a transitional state that *"lasts the longer the more complete is the renovation to be wrought"*, then we should pray for our strength and the return of Providence in the preservation of our Freedom, for there is no greater *"renovation to be wrought"* than to a state of servitude from one of unalienable God-given Liberty. For if it is true that we are in such social transition we will most assuredly need all our strength, as well as "a firm reliance on the protection of divine Providence" if Liberty is to prevail; *for you should know that our Sacred Liberty being endowed to us by our Creator, is a gift so precious, that the 'Prince of this world' himself, will stop at nothing but divine providence, to make it his own*!

> In his 1971 *Rules for Radicals*, President Obama's mentor Saul Alinsky, tells us some more of *"The Ideology of Change"*:
>
> *A Marxist begins with his prime truth that all evils are caused by the exploitation of the proletariat by the capitalists. From this he logically proceeds to the revolution to end capitalism, then into the third stage of reorganization into a new social order of the dictatorship of the proletariat, and finally the last stage—the political paradise of communism*[80] (emphasis added).

What exactly is the new order of a "dictatorship of the proletariat"? What would it mean for the average American?

Remember from chapter 1, the August 1996 issue of MIM (Maoist International Movement) said this of *the dictatorship of the proletariat* in their ten listings of "What We Believe":

> *7. We want a united front against imperialism.*
>
> We believe that the imperialists are currently waging a hot war—a World War III—against the world's oppressed nations, *including the U.S. empire's internal colonies.* We seek to unite all who can be united under proletarian and feminist leadership against imperialism, capitalism and patriarchy.
>
> We believe that the imperialist-country working classes *are primarily a pro-imperialist labor aristocracy* at this time. Likewise, we believe that the biological-wimmin of the imperialist countries *are primarily a gender aristocracy.* Thus, while we recruit individuals from these and other reactionary groups *to work against their class,* national and gender interests, *we do not seek strategic unity with them. In fact, we believe that the imperialist-country working-classes and imperialist-country biological-wimmin, like the bourgeoisies and petit-bourgeoisies, owe reparations to the international proletariat and peasantry....*
>
> *We believe that socialism in the imperialist countries will require the dictatorship of the international proletariat and that the imperialist-country working-classes will need to be on the receiving end of this dictatorship*[81] (emphasis added).

This is very important. Most of those who either vow or vote to assist the leftists in obtaining their coveted dictatorship over the propertied class will not be welcome in the new normal after socialism is achieved. Most everyone from the middle class, the women's rights movement, the unions, or the American working class in general will also be stripped of all they own right along with everybody else! Such misguided, gullible people have commonly been referred to, most notably by Lenin and Stalin, as "useful idiots." They are useful in the sense that they are the essential means to the end of their own free society. They are idiots in the sense that they are the essential means to their very own end as well! Why, no matter how much proof we offer them, can't they see this simple truth, even when presented, as it is here, in revolutionary collectivism's own words and doctrine? But how could they if such a revelation was spiritually discerned?

From the December 2008 issue of the Communist party of Great Britain's *Proletarian*, we are made aware of the following aspects regarding what we might expect from a new "dictatorship of the proletariat":

> Dictatorship of the proletariat = working-class democracy
>
> The expression [*'dictatorship of the proletariat'*] sounds entirely offensive to most people who have been brought up and educated in capitalist societies…our schooling leaves us with a most narrow view regarding the questions of democracy and dictatorship.
>
> This education deliberately obscures the fact that the much-revered…[*democracy is, in reality, democracy for the capitalist class alone*]. Yes, there are multiple parties…but these *all* [*represent the capitalist class*]: the policies of…

Conservative and Liberal Democrat are the policies of business, of private property, of exploitation, of imperialism.

[*The working class has not the slightest say in how the country is run*]. In fact, the whole state is geared towards the *armed suppression of the working class*. This is difficult to appreciate in times of relative social peace, but it is all too clear during times of unrest....

Therefore...democracy can be considered as the *dictatorship of the bourgeoisie*. [*It is democratic to the extent that there is democracy for the capitalist class*]....

The dictatorship of the proletariat, on the other hand, means *democracy for the working class* combined with [*the violent suppression*] of the overthrown capitalist class. For example, the Soviet Union of Lenin and Stalin was democratic for the working class, whose interests were represented by the various bodies of the state and who had an exceptionally high level of involvement in the running of the country (via soviets, trade unions, factory committees, farm committees, school committees, neighbourhood committees, etc); however, [*it was dictatorial towards the former ruling class, the capitalists, who never gave up on their bid to restore the old, backward, exploitative, brutal order*]....

Lenin described the dictatorship of the proletariat as *"a stubborn struggle—bloody and bloodless, violent and peaceful, military and economic, educational and administrative—against the forces and traditions of the old society". (The Proletarian Revolution and the Renegade Kautsky)*

He continues: *"In the transition, the class struggle grows more intense. The transition from capitalism to communism represents an entire historical epoch. Until this epoch has terminated, the exploiters will inevitably cherish the hope of restoration, and this hope will be converted into attempts at restoration. And after their first serious defeat, the overthrown exploiters...will throw themselves with tenfold energy, with furious passion and hatred grown a hundred-fold, into the battle for the recovery of their 'lost' paradise."*

Elsewhere, he wrote that *"The dictatorship of the proletariat is a most determined and most ruthless war waged by the new class against a more powerful enemy, the bourgeoisie, whose resistance is increased tenfold by its overthrow..., and whose power lies not only in the strength of international capital, in the strength and durability of the international connections of the bourgeoisie, but also in the force of habit, in the strength of small production. For, unfortunately, small production is still very, very widespread in the world, and small production engenders capitalism and the bourgeoisie continuously, daily, hourly, spontaneously, and on a mass scale. For all these reasons the dictatorship of the proletariat is essential, and victory over the bourgeoisie is impossible without a long, stubborn and desperate war of life and death, a war demanding perseverance, discipline, firmness, indomitableness and unity of will." ('Left-Wing' Communism, an Infantile Disorder)*

To summarise: the dictatorship of the proletariat is the form taken by the state after the working class has overthrown the capitalist state but *before the bourgeoisie has been finally defeated.*[82]

So as you see, where "democracy can be considered as the "dictatorship of the bourgeoisie"—"the dictatorship of the proletariat," on the other hand, means "democracy for the working class." Is it ringing any bells?

Consider that, for the first time in the history of America, the majority of the voting public is said to now be in favor of tax increases. Consider that, for the first time in our history, nearly half of our population is now disconnected and/or even protected from any financial impact of a bad economy via government subsidy and entitlements. Consider Bernie Sander's popularity for president as self-proclaimed "Democratic socialist." Who cares what the cost of housing, health care, food, and transportation are when, to one degree or another, such "positive" rights are being provided for them? What does an inmate in prison care of the cost of his or her housing, clothing, shoes, or next meal when it is their legal "right" to have it all provided "free" by the state? What if anything of our Constitutional representative republic remains that can stop them as the new voting majority from "flipping the script" on our society as called for by Marx? The Constitution? The Supreme Court? Congress? Our President?

With the 2012 reelection of Barack Hussein Obama to the presidency of the United States, has America now been officially reorganized "into a new social order of the *dictatorship of the proletariat*"? After all, does it not mark the very moment in history that the *down-*

trodden, the *suppressed*, the *propertyless*, the *49 percent* of Americans who are dependent on some form of positive government subsidy, *the women* who seek their "emancipation" from the paternalism of property and capital, and all *the exploited interior colonies of the imperialist/colonialist white suppressor-nation of AmeriaKKKa*, and the voting block of the seduced portions of the *middle class*—all joined together to collectively support President Obama's "fundamental transformation" of the United States of America?

Has it not been our entrepreneurs, business owners, property owners, capital investors, private medicine, private insurance, the firearms industry, the private banking industry, oil companies, coal companies, our employers and nation's producers in general who, along with our wealthy, have all been specifically targeted for forced redistribution by the Obama administration? Has not our Constitution, along with the "laws made in pursuance thereof" protecting it all been disregarded in whole by them? From this point forward, how long will it take for the new "dictatorship of the American proletariat" to dictate to an America with such weakened property rights that all that is currently privately owned and operated be claimed for redistribution to the collective for the shared prosperity of the propertyless proletariat? *How long before they realize that their newly acquired "shared prosperity" comes with the "shared responsibility" of passing it all along to its "rightful owners" of the world at large?*

With the weight of Obamacare looming large over the horizons of our private sector employers, how will they survive the thousands of dollars in fines they will have to pay the federal government for each employee employed by them to cover the cost of Obamacare? Are we to become a nation of part-timers for businesses to survive? If the hours of the proletariat are to be cut to maintain minimum profit margins, could Obama or Hillary or whoever step in to mandate the old Communist party line of a thirty-hour workweek at forty hours of pay, or that any and all employees must be covered? If that were to happen, few to no businesses could survive, especially considering a nation of part-timers can no longer afford their products or service!

Now, think back to World War I and World War II, where the deciding factor behind our victories was our industrial might. However, thanks to the one-two punch of government regulation and unions, we can no longer make hardly anything here at a profit. Adding the added costs of Obamacare on top of that will be devastating! Could such a president of the proletariat allow our private sector to collapse without taking the opportunity to drive one last nail in its coffin? How easy would it be for him or our next progressive President to complete the "fundamental transformation" of America by publicly denouncing all the failed proprietors as greedy capitalists who care nothing for their country and nothing for the proletariat? That they have never cared for anything but their money and their profits, which they took with them when they abandoned their country when it needed them most?

How grand would it be if such an empowered president were to announce, "They don't care about you, and they never have cared about you, but I do. So I will open factories all across the land, making all the things I think you need, where I will give you the jobs you need to provide for your families so you can do your part in helping me rebuild the America they abandoned, and we will never need them and their profits ever again"? It's not like it hasn't been done before. And it's not like the opportunity couldn't ever happen here—or California congresswoman Maxine Waters hasn't already called for government "basically…taking over, and the government running all of your companies"![83] And it's not like our Liberty isn't that close to being gone forever!

Coincidently, or so it may seem, from the very same philosophy that seeks to destroy all we fight to preserve, we find that the very same story is being told. From the other side of the mirror, Julian Huxley, in the conclusion to his 1946 *"UNESCO, Its Purpose and Philosophy"*, sends us this message:

CONCLUSION

> That task is to help the emergence of a single world culture,....
>
> And it is necessary, for *at the moment two opposing philosophies of life confront each other* from the West and from the East, and not only impede the achievement of unity but threaten to become the foci of actual conflict.
>
> *You may categorise the two philosophies as two supernationalisms; or as individualism versus collectivism; or as the American versus the Russian way of life; or as capitalism versus communism; or as Christianity versus Marxism*[36] (emphasis added).

Though I might add good versus evil, herein lies *the* very purpose of why I have endeavored to engage in this work to begin with. It is *the* whole purpose of it.

And so it is yet again. Even as we teeter at the cusp of a very real social transformation, we have but one choice to make: the single choice between these two diabolically opposed philosophies by which to live by. And is it a coincidence that from each of these philosophies, it is the exact same choice we are offered? Is it a coincidence that the contrast between them has never before been clearer? Is it a coincidence that so few can see it? It is nothing less than the hope of all mankind and God above that the right choice for true freedom be made. I pray for myself, my family, and my countrymen that it isn't already too late—that for our children's sake, we have *not* yet arrived at Liberty's last gleaming!

As true as it is that "these are the times that try men's souls," it is truer yet that all things are possible with God.

Endnotes

Chapter 2: From the Strands: Of Order, Relativism, and the Frameworks of Sustainability to a Dictatorship of the Proletariat

1. New World Encyclopedia - http://www.newworldencyclopedia.org/entry/Auguste_Comte#cite_note-coser3
2. Anthony Harrison-Barbet, Philosophical Connections - http://philosophos.com/philosophical_connections/profile_082.html#comteconn2a
3. From Auguste Comte, *The Positive Philosophy* (translated and condensed by Harriet Martineau), Vol. 2 (New York: D. Appleton & Co., 1854), 68-74 and 95-110 http://www.bolenderinitiatives.com/sociology/auguste-comte-1798-1857
4. Lewis A. Coser, in his 1977 *"Masters of Sociological Thought: Ideas in Historical and Social Context"* - http://www.bolenderinitiatives.com/sociology/auguste-comte-1798-1857
5. Bill Clinton Speech, 2012 Democrat Convention http://www.nytimes.com/2012/09/05/us/politics/transcript-of-bill-clintons-speech-to-the-democratic-national-convention.html?pagewanted=all
6. Obama speech: DNC Acceptance Speech 8/28/08 - http://uspolitics.about.com/od/speeches/a/obama_accept_2.htm
7. Pierre Kropotkin, *"Law and Authority"* 1886
8. Obama, Roanoke, Virginia 7/13/12
9. Thomas Hobbes, *"Leviathan"* in 1651
10. Fredrick Engels in his *1884 "Origins of the Family, Private Property, and the State"*

11. Robert Dale Owens's 1826 *"Declaration of Mental Independence"*
12. 12. Stuart Chase, *"Democracy Under Pressure"*, 1945 http://chla.library.cornell.edu/cgi/t/text/pageviewer-idx-?c=chla;cc=chla;idno=3159579;node=3159579%3A6;-frm=frameset;view=text;seq=75;page=root;size=s
13. Stuart Chase, *"A New Deal"*, 1932, pg 163
14. Obama, Negative Liberties / redistribution Interview with WBEZ Chicago 91.5 FM - 10/26/2008 http://www.freerepublic.com/focus/f-news/2116149/posts
15. Noah Webster, *"An Examination Into The Leading Principles Of The Federal Constitution"*, 1787 – *"The Essential Federalist & Anti-Federalist Papers"*, David Wootton, 2003, pg 134
16. Alexander Hamilton in Federalist #78, 1788, *"The Essential Federalist & Anti-Federalist Papers"*, David Wootton, 2003, pg 285
17. Justice William J. Brennan, Speech - '*Text and Teaching Symposium*', Georgetown University, Washington, DC - October 12, 1985 -
http://www.pbs.org/wnet/supremecourt/democracy/sources_document7.html
18. President F. D. Roosevelt's January 11, 1944 *Message to the Congress of the United States on the State of the Union*, "*The Economic Bill of Rights*"
http://www.fdrheritage.org/bill_of_rights.htm
19. United Nations "*UNIVERSAL DECLARATION OF HUMAN RIGHTS*" 1948
http://www.un.org/rights/50/decla.htm
20. Romney Transcript – Human rights
http://www.npr.org/2012/10/22/163436694/transcript-3rd-obama-romney-presidential-debate

21. ERIC MARGOLIS, contributing Foreign Editor, *"Famine of 1932-33",* THE TORONTO SUN, *"Remembering Ukraine's Unknown Holocaust"* Sunday, December 13, 1998, - http://www.ukemonde.com/genocide/emargolis.htm
22. Jeffery Hayes, 2008, *"HUNDRED FLOWERS AND THE ANTI-RIGHTIST CAMPAIGN",* - http://factsanddetails.com/china.php?itemid=1153&catid=2
23. Howard French, *"Survivors' Stories From China",* 8/24/2008, NY Times http://www.nytimes.com/2009/08/25/books/25french.html?_r=1
24. George Bernard Shaw, *"Sir or Madam..."* http://www.youtube.com/watch?v=hQvsf2MUKRQ
25. USSR Constitution, 1977 - http://www.constitution.org/cons/ussr77.txt
26. Jean Jacques Rousseau, *"THE SOCIAL CONTRACT OR PRINCIPLES OF POLITICAL RIGHT"* 1762
27. Adolf Hitler, Hitler - *"Mein Kampf",* 1925 http://www.hitler.org/writings/Mein_Kampf/mkv1ch02.html
28. Thomas Robert Malthus, *"An Essay on the Principle of Population",* 1798-1826 http://www.econlib.org/library/Malthus/malPlong1.html
29. Max Stirner, "The Ego And His Own", *"All Things Are Nothing To Me"* 1845
30. Margaret Sanger, *"Women and the New Race",* 1920 http://www.bartleby.com/1013/5.html
31. Charles Carroll quote - David Barton, *"Original Intent"* April, 2010, pg 326 (Source: Bernard C. Steiner, *The Life and Correspondence of James McHenry* (Cleveland: The Burrows Brothers, 1907), p. 475. In a letter from Charles

Carroll to James McHenry of November 4, 1800.), http://www.wallbuilders.com/libissuesarticles.asp?id=63

32. Plato, 380-360 b.c., "*5 great dialogues*" 1942 Walter J. Black classic club, edited by Louise Ropes Loomis pg 255-256
http://classics.mit.edu/Plato/republic.3.ii.html

33. Michael Bakunin - 1871 "Man, Society, Freedom

34. "Controversial 'Piss Christ' back in NY", NY Post – Sept. 21, 2012
http://www.nypost.com/p/pagesix/art_controversy_back_in_ny_ZjuqKoVhysXZ3eQg6U6n1H

35. The Rubayyat of Omar Khayyam, Translated into English in 1859 by Edward FitzGerald, http://www.sacred-texts.com/isl/khayyam.txt

36. United Nations, "*UNESCO, Its Purpose and Its Philosophy*", Julian Huxley, 1946
http://unesdoc.unesco.org/images/0006/000681/068197eo.pdf

37. Voltairine de Cleyre, "Crime and Punishment" 1903

38. Karl Marx & Fredrick Engels, "Communist Manifesto" 1848

39. The Christian Science Monitor, *"Big Win for Obama…EPA Regulations Upheld"*, by Mark Clayton, 6/26/2012 – http://www.csmonitor.com/USA/Justice/2012/0626/In-win-for-Obama-EPA-regulations-on-emissions-upheld-by-appeals-court

40. United Nations, *"POPULATION, DEVELOPMENT AND ENVIRONMENT AN NGO POSITION PAPER FOR THE - 1994 INTERNATIONAL CONFERENCE ON POPULATION AND DEVELOPMENT"* (ICPD): http://www.un.org/popin/icpd/recommendations/other/43.html

41. Marquette University report, "Habitat: A Festive Air, Serious Business" by Curtis Carter, 1976
    http://epublications.marquette.edu/cgi/viewcontent.cgi?article=1074&context=phil_fac
42. Henry Lamb, *"Maurice Strong: The new guy in your future!"*, 1997
    http://www.sovereignty.net/p/sd/strong.html#8
43. CNN interview with Debra June, *"Bondholder Furious Over GM Bankruptcy"*, 9:19 am ET, June 1, 2009
    http://am.blogs.cnn.com/2009/06/01/bondholder-furious-over-gm-bankruptcy/
44. Habitat I, *"The Vancouver Action Plan"*, 64 Recommendations for National Action Approved at Habitat: United Nations Conference on Human Settlements, Vancouver, Canada - 31 May to 11 June 1976
    http://habitat.igc.org/vancouver/vp-intr.htm
45. From A/42/427. Our Common Future: Report of the World Commission on Environment and Development, 1987 - "Our Common Future, Chapter 1: A Threatened Future" http://www.un-documents.net/ocf-01.htm#I.1
46. Errico Malatesta, *"Anarchy"*, 1891
47. "Our Common Future, From One Earth to One World", http://www.un-documents.net/ocf-ov.htm
48. Dan Leistikow, USDOE, October 16, 2012 release
    http://energy.gov/articles/update-advanced-battery-manufacturing
49. The Heritage Foundation, *"President Obama's Taxpayer-Backed Green Energy Failures"*, 10/18/12, by Ashe Schow –
    http://blog.heritage.org/2012/10/18/president-obamas-taxpayer-backed-green-energy-failures/
50. *"Our Common Future, Chapter 2: Towards Sustainable Development"*,

http://www.un-documents.net/ocf-02.htm
51. *"Our Common Future, Chapter 5: Food Security: Sustaining The Potential"* http://www.un-documents.net/ocf-05.htm
52. *"Our Common Future, Chapter 7: Energy: Choices for Environment and Development"* - http://www.un-documents.net/ocf-07.htm
53. *"Our Common Future, Chapter 9: The Urban Challenge",* http://www.un-documents.net/ocf-09.htm
54. *"Our Common Future, Chapter 10: Managing The Commons,* http://www.un-documents.net/ocf-10.htm
55. *"Our Common Future, Chapter 12: Towards Common Action: Proposals For institutional and Legal Change",-* http://www.un-documents.net/ocf-12.htm
56. United Nations Earth Summit - Agenda 21 http://www.un.org/esa/dsd/agenda21/res_agenda21_00.shtml

    Section II *"Conservation & Management of Resources fo Development",-* Chapter 10 http://www.un.org/esa/dsd/agenda21/res_agenda21_10.shtml
57. PCSD, 1993 Overview - http://clinton2.nara.gov/PCSD/Overview/index.html
58. PCSD, Members - http://clinton2.nara.gov/PCSD/Members/index.html
59. PCSD, Task Forces - http://clinton2.nara.gov/PCSD/tforce/index.html
60. PCSD, Climate Change Task Force –http://clinton2.nara.gov/PCSD/tforce/cctf/index.html
61. PCSD, International Task Force – http://clinton2.nara.gov/PCSD/tforce/itf/index.html
62. The Weather Underground, *"You don't Need a Weatherman to Know Which Way The Wind Blows",* 1969

63. PCSD, Executive Summery – http://clinton2.nara.gov/PCSD/Publications/TF_Reports/pop-exec.html
64. Obama, San Francisco Chronicle, *"Electricity rates will necessarily skyrocket"* http://hotair.com/archives/2008/11/02/obama-ill-make-energy-prices-skyrocket/
65. PCSD, Chapter 1: Population Issues - http://clinton2.nara.gov/PCSD/Publications/TF_Reports/pop-chap-1.html
66. PCSD, METROPOLITAN & RURAL STRATEGIES, http://clinton2.nara.gov/PCSD/tforce/mrtf/index.html
67. *Benefit Corporations—A Sustainable Form of Organization?* Sept. 2011, http://wakeforestlawreview.com/benefit-corporations%E2%80%94a-sustainable-form-of- organization, *Why B Corps Matter,* http://www.bcorporation.net/what-are-b-corps/why-b-corps-matter
68. PCSD, 1993- Sustainable America Table of Contents, http://clinton2.nara.gov/PCSD/Publications/TF_Reports/amer-top.html
69. PCSD, Chapter 1 – *"National Goals Toward Sustainable Development"* http://clinton2.nara.gov/PCSD/Publications/TF_Reports/amer-chap1.html
70. PCSD, Chapter 2 – *"Building A New Framework for A New Century",* http://clinton2.nara.gov/PCSD/Publications/TF_Reports/amer-chap2.html
71. PCSD, *"Chapter 4: Strengthening Communities"* http://clinton2.nara.gov/PCSD/Publications/TF_Reports/amer-chap4.html
72. PCSD, *Chapter 5: "Natural Resources Stewardship"*

http://clinton2.nara.gov/PCSD/Publications/TF Reports/amer-chap5.html

73. PCSD, *Chapter 6: "U.S. Population and Sustainability"* http://clinton2.nara.gov/PCSD/Publications/TF Reports/amer-top.html

74. Popular Science Magazine, *"Can we reengineer ourselves to cope with the effects of climate change?"*, - October 2012 issue, page 26

75. NY Post, 4/12/20011, "*New space for Soros groups*", By LOIS WEISS, http://www.nypost.com/p/news/business/realestate/commercial/new_space_for_soros_groups_eahrAOfGrsoEz-Pzf4uGLOK

76. New York Outdoor News, *"Moser named new DEC assistant commissioner"*, by Steve Piatt, December 30, 2011 issue, pg 7

77. PCSD, *Chapter 7: "International Leadership"* http://clinton2.nara.gov/PCSD/Publications/TF Reports/amer-chap7.html

78. Obama closing statement Presidential debate 10/3/2012 http://5newsonline.com/2012/10/04/full-transcript-first-presidential-debate/

79. From Coser, 1977:7-8 *'The Law of Human Progress,* see footnote (4)

80. "*Rules For Radicals"* - 1971 by Saul Alinsky, pg 10

81. MIM, "Program of the Maoist Internationalist Movement": "What We Want What We Believe" August 1996

82. *Proletarian* issue 27 (December 2008), Proletarian Online, Communist Party of Great Britain, http://www.cpgbml.org/index.php?art=466&secName=proletarian&subName=display

83. Maxine Waters, The House Judiciary Committee task force investigating competition in the oil business, May 22, 2008
http://www.youtube.com/watch?v=PKh7uqucArk -
http://www.youtube.com/watch?v=OrA9zj94NuU

We hold these Truths to be self-evident, that all men are created equal, that they are endowed by their Creator with certain unalienable Rights, that among these are Life, Liberty and the pursuit of Happiness.
—Declaration of Independence

Now we have received, not the spirit of the world, but the spirit which is of God; that we might know the things that are freely given to us of God.
—I Corinthians 2:12

CHAPTER 3

The Great Deception

From the manipulation of language, including duplicity in meaning, and the tactical misdirection of progressive phraseology to the methodical Lenin-Alinskian seduction of America's middle class voting power into being *the* voting means of their own end, we have borne witness throughout *Last Call for Liberty* to the deception that defines the Philosophy. We have seen for ourselves what it is that *the* architects of Godless civil social contracts such as Hobbes, Rousseau, Marx, and Engels have declared shall be *the* "civil," "positive," "moral," and/or "human" rights and liberties of man. We have, through extensive examination, seen that they are not, in reality, but the conditional "rights" of prisoners, that they are no more than the rations afforded those who have lost their freedom to provide for themselves.

We have learned from Comte, *the* founder of the "directed" science of sociology himself, that under such a positive charter, there can only be collective rights as there is "no place…for rights of individuals." We have been shown that it is only in this "context, which emphasizes duties, that the concept of 'rights' can have any application." And we have been forewarned by them all that under such terms and loss of Individual Liberty, it is the government, the "general will" of the collective, and of "'Humanity,' the 'Great Being,'

[that] takes the place of God and is the basis of all morality." Such is the deception that would, by robbing of us of both our freedom and our dignity, "force us to be free"!

The loss of our natural Individual Liberty under such a positive charter, as all encompassing as it is, is only the physical aspect of the deception and of what we stand to lose. In addition to the physical, the *great deception* is both mental and spiritual. As the physical aspect destroys *property,* the "fountain" from which the "stream" of liberty flows, the mental aspect, "backwards from the nursery school to the nursery itself", destroys *family,* our source of tradition, identity, and the realm within which trust and the development of an independent free will is nurtured. Furthermore, it destroys our very ability to distinguish free will from the compliant conformity to the will of others. And as the physical destroys property and the mental destroys family, the spiritual aspect is the attempt to destroy *God*! The great deception, then, is *the* anti–three-headed Hydra! It is the Philosophy's answer to Owen's call for something to destroy it!

Never has mankind been so deceived! If allowed to come to fruition, not only is mankind to be enslaved physically without Liberty here on earth in this lifetime; his mind, also being transformed, will *not* see it as such. However, this is to be only the beginning as, spiritually, the consequences are even higher, spanning the whole of eternity! As our physical Liberty is being destroyed via the undermining of our property rights and our very sense of that loss is being destroyed via "directed education" and "consensus," our spirit, our very soul, has been specifically targeted for positive redirection via our own churches—the very same churches unto which we have long turned that our souls may be saved!

In conjunction with the above, an observation: our sense of freedom and Liberty transforms correspondingly with how much of it we are allowed. For instance, *there are those incarcerated who feel and have expressed that, though they are in prison, they still feel they have too much freedom*! Though each day is regimented minute by minute for them by the state, for some in prison, there is still too much opportunity for too many choices. There is still too many instances where they must make decisions for themselves they are then held responsible for! As such, we are forced to question, could this transformed perspective of freedom happen to America in general? Could it be part of our human nature that our sense of freedom might also transform, becoming relative to the ever-decreasing amounts of it that we are allowed? Could it be that, eventually one day, the less freedom we are allowed, the less freedom we will want and the more we will begin to find our true freedom—Individual Liberty—not only unjustifiable but as a source of unnecessary responsibilities and unwanted liabilities?

This is something to keep in mind as, shortly after the Sandy Hook School shootings in Newtown Connecticut, it was our own president, President Obama, who presented that very freedom specifically as *the* source and reason behind not only this school shooting but all such acts of murder and massacres, articulating this:

> We can't tolerate this anymore. These *tragedies* must end. And *to end them, we must change*...Because *what choice do we have?*...Are we really prepared to say that we're powerless in the face of such carnage, that the *politics are too hard*? Are we prepared to say that such violence visited on our children year after year after year *is somehow the price of our freedom?*[1] (emphasis added).

Politics? Here, even under these gut-wrenching life-and-death circumstances? Really? Is nothing sacred? What "politics are too hard" that the president might see fit to interject them here on such a sad and solemn occasion? What "politics" could possibly be standing by and ready to be engaged at the onset of such a devastating crisis? None other than the progressive social politics of "never let a crisis go to waste" collectivism! Is it not this "politics" that just happens to be Obama's politics? Is it not this "politics" that exists specifically to counter and forever "liberate" us from the freedom of our antisocial Individual Liberty? *Is it not this same Individual Liberty, our only true freedom, that hereby stands accused by this president of committing not only this murderous act but all of "these tragedies" as well? Was it our freedom or his own "politics" that left those kids and teachers at Sandy Hook so helpless and so defenseless in the sights of such moral depravity and at the mercy of mercilessness itself?* Is it our freedom or the Godless evolutionary humanism of sustainable progressive politics that has long sought *the* propagation of *Malthusian* moral decay in both the "general corruption of morals,...Promiscuous intercourse, unnatural passions, violations of the marriage bed" and "a decided diminution [reduction] of the general happiness and virtue of the society"?[2] (Malthus).

Is it our God-given freedom or the progressive politics of Barak Obama that developed, supported, and funded the depraved utopian sciences of eugenics, partial birth abortions, infanticide, and the "traditional" abortions of some fifty-five million "unwanted"[3] (Sanger) American children since 1973? (*Roe v. Wade*). Is it our freedom or his progressive politics that historically, year after year after year, after decade after century, has held "zero" moral value[4] (Giubilini and Minerva) in the sanctity of life? Is it not the humanism of this very same progressive politics that holds that there is *no such thing* as an Individual Right to self-defense?[5] (Frey, UN). What kind of president's "politics" holds both the very lives and freedom of his own people in such contempt? None other than President Obama's own revolutionary progressive collectivism!

Where once our *moral* doctrine was founded in our faith from scripture, from God and the standpoint of the Golden Rule (do unto others…), what is *moral* today—and, for that matter, tomorrow—has been undergoing a progressive fundamental transformation of its own. It is the progressive "politics of change" and "progress" that has long held that what is *moral* should no longer be determined by any *absolute* never-changing standards as established by God. But instead, they should be determined by the collective and its social standards, relative, of course, to the perspectives of an ever-changing, evolving society and times. Or, as Hobbes says, by the "COMMON-WEALTH" that "Mortall God" to which we now owe "our peace and defense."

Within days, Obama uninhibitedly issued dozens of extra-constitutional executive orders against the accused to counter the inferred liabilities of its exercise! Will America accept the redefined "liberty" of security? Will Liberty continue to bow to the new progressive, collective mind-set that stipulates our only "socially acceptable" recourse under such depraved indifference and circumstances of desperation and, in the face of such evil, is to turn to our wide-eyed and trusting, petrified children and say, "Sorry, we have to 'wait for the good guys…show me your smile'"?[1] Were not those at Sandy Hook praised by President Obama for being forced to do the same? "Wait"? "Show me your smile"? Really? Are the "good guys"—whoever they are, wherever they are—faster than a speeding bullet? Are "We the People" to no longer hold for ourselves the freedom to be our own "good guy"? How have we, as free Americans, ever come so far as to arrive here, where we have conceded to forgo our freedom to forever and always stand *well regimented* at the ready to defend ourselves, our families, and especially our children anytime, anywhere, at any and all cost, for the pitiful, shameful, collective impotence of "show me your smile"?

Have we now become so afraid of our own freedom that such actions of forfeit might now somehow be seen as "socially acceptable" or the "politically correct" thing to do? Sadly, the answer to these questions is what this chapter of *Last Call for Liberty* seeks to bring to light. But before we delve into the philosophies of those "designing men" who have long sought to destroy our Liberty, along with all we have come to know as the Western free world in order that they might replace it with one of their own, let us come to a better understanding of what our founders had the foresight to establish in America and why.

In his 1787 Federalist Essay 10, James Madison paints the picture of not only what our Liberty is but who and what has always threatened it this way:

> For that prevailing and increasing distrust of public engagements, *and alarm for private rights*, which are echoed from one end of the continent to the other. These must be chiefly, if not wholly, effects of the unsteadiness and injustice with which *a factious spirit has tainted our public administrations.*
>
> By a faction, I understand a number of citizens, whether amounting to a majority or a minority of the whole, who are united and actuated by some common impulse of passion, or of interest, adversed to the rights of other citizens, or to the permanent and aggregate interests of the community.
>
> There are two methods of curing the mischiefs of faction: the one, by removing its causes; the other, by controlling its effects.
>
> There are again two methods of removing the causes of faction: the one, *by destroying the liberty* which is essential to its existence; the

> other, *by giving to every citizen the same opinions, the same passions, and the same interests* (emphasis added).

There are two ways of looking at this: one from the perspective of a free society established to preserve Individual Liberty, and the other from the perspective of the faction or philosophy bent on destroying it. Nevertheless, from what we have learned in the preceding chapters of this work, we know that from either perspective, "giving to every citizen the same opinions, the same passions, and the same interests" is the embodiment of the very same collectivism bent on destroying our sacred Individual Liberty. By its very nature, does not the forced, centrally planned equality of collectivism force uniformity and sameness in all things onto every individual via a forced compliance to whatever the supreme sovereign or general will mandates? Though Madison lists the loss of Liberty and a forced uniformity here as two separate "methods," we understand they are actually one and the same—as where one happens, the other is sure to follow. Madison is not wrong. The Philosophy has just learned how to kill two birds collectively with a single deceptive stone. He continues:

> It could never be more truly said than of the first remedy, that it was worse than the disease. *Liberty is to faction what air is to fire*, an aliment without which it instantly expires. But it could not be less folly to abolish liberty, which is essential to political life, because it nourishes faction, than it would be to wish the annihilation of air, which is essential to animal life, because it imparts to fire its destructive agency. The second expedient is as impracticable as the

first would be unwise. As long as the reason of man continues fallible, and he is at liberty to exercise it, different opinions will be formed… *The diversity in the faculties of men, from which the rights of property originate,* is not less an insuperable obstacle to a uniformity of interests. *The protection of these faculties is the first object of government.* From the protection *of different and unequal faculties* of acquiring property, the possession of different degrees and kinds of property immediately results; and from the influence of these on the sentiments and views of the respective proprietors, ensues a division of the society into different interests and parties. (emphasis added)

This is wisdom that, one, cannot be denied and, two, should be reread. It is at the heart of understanding the fundamental principles of our Individual Liberty. We must understand them to recognize that which threatens them. Here, we have it from James Madison himself, the father of our Constitution, an official recognition that "[t]he diversity in the faculties men" is *the source* "from which the rights of property originate" and that "[t]he protection of these faculties is the first object of government." Why is this information so crucial for all champions of Liberty to comprehend? Because those bent on destroying that Liberty understand it very well! The more you know and understand how something works—what enables it, perpetuates it, and preserves it—the better equipped you are to either preserve or destroy it. Where we don't understand the fundamentals of our own Liberty, how are we to recognize either what preserves and strengthens it, or, who and/or what has targeted it for destruction? Let us know and understand the fundamentals of our

Individual Liberty that we may recognize her enemies and strengthen our "bulwarks" against them.

Revolutionary collectivists, those intent on the annulment of independent individualism from the face of the earth, know one of the most effective ways to crush individualism and a *spirited* train of independent thought is to coagulate the masses of individuals into collectives or factions—to instill group think! Once grouped, individual identity is lost, overruled by the collective. The larger the collective, the more meaningless the individual. *What is cultural diversity but the surrender of our individual diversity to a collective?* And so it is that as we know Liberty "nourishes faction," those of the Philosophy know faction, or the collectivization of individuals, destroys the essence, the very spirit, of Individual Liberty!

> The latent causes of faction are thus sown in the nature of man; and we see them everywhere brought into different degrees of activity, according to the different circumstances of civil society. *A zeal for different opinions* concerning religion, concerning government, and many other points, as well of speculation as of practice; *an attachment to different leaders ambitiously* contending for pre-eminence and power; or to persons of other descriptions whose fortunes have been interesting to the human passions, *have, in turn, divided mankind into parties*, inflamed them with mutual animosity, and rendered them much more disposed to vex and oppress each other than to co-operate for their common good. So strong is this propensity of mankind to fall into mutual animosities, that where no substantial occasion presents itself,

the most frivolous and fanciful distinctions have been sufficient to kindle their unfriendly passions and excite their most violent conflicts. But *the most common and durable source of factions has been the various and unequal distribution of property*. Those who hold and those who are without property have ever formed distinct interests in society. Those who are creditors, and those who are debtors, fall under a like discrimination. A landed interest, a manufacturing interest, a mercantile interest, a moneyed interest, with many lesser interests, grow up of necessity in civilized nations, and *divide them into different classes, actuated by different sentiments and views*. The regulation of these various and interfering interests forms the principal task of modern legislation, and involves the spirit of party and faction in the necessary and ordinary operations of the government (emphasis added).

If it is in our nature as human beings to be "brought into different degrees of activity, according to the different circumstances," even with "the most frivolous and fanciful distinctions," then how easy would it be for "designing men" to divide or factionalize us via gender, sexual orientation, race, creed, color, religion, abortion, money, age, north/south, urban/rural, environmentalism, animal rights, global warming, politics, smoking, or guns? As Madison tells us, "the most common and durable source of factions has been the various and unequal distribution of property." Karl Marx knew this all too well, as is evident by Marxism's division of society into classes, in which jealousies "naturally" ensue. It's no coincidence that collective demands for the "social justice" of *redistributive change* has its roots in this very classism. "The Invisible Committee" breaks it down for us this way in their 2007 *The Coming Insurrection*:

> It is in the most profound deprivation of existence, perpetually stifled, perpetually conjured away, that the possibility of communism resides![6]

Where Madison seeks to preserve the power of the individual and "the various and unequal distribution of property" (imagine that) as a cherished, if not sacred, "diversity in the faculties of men, from which the rights of property originate," Marx and his redistributive minions seek *that* power for themselves in order to outlaw it! If our rights of property originate in our individual diversity, where does our diversity then originate if not from nature or nature's God? As such, would not the suppression, destruction and/or the outlawing of our natural God-given human diversity then be, if not anti-God, at least unnatural?

> A pure democracy...can admit of no cure for the mischiefs of faction...there is nothing to check the inducements to sacrifice the weaker party or an obnoxious individual. Hence it is that such *democracies have ever been spectacles of turbulence and contention; have ever been found incompatible with personal security or the rights of property*; and have in general been as short in their lives as they have been violent in their deaths. Theoretic politicians, who have patronized this species of government, have erroneously supposed that *by reducing mankind to*

> *a perfect equality in their political rights, they would, at the same time, be perfectly equalized and assimilated in their possessions, their opinions, and their passions* (emphasis added).

There is a reason why Article IV Section 4 of the Constitution reads, "The United States shall guarantee to every State in this union a Republican form of government." Because as Madison explains, democracies are nothing more than mob rule! Again, Marx knew this! As only in "direct democracy" do the "democratic" avenues by which any such majority faction needs to demand their "social justice" open up. Once *democratically* opened, Marx's call for revolutionary anti-individual, anticapitalist "dictatorship of the proletariat," which we just went over in the last chapter, becomes not only possible but inevitable.

> Men of factious tempers, of local prejudices, or of sinister designs, may, by intrigue, by corruption, or by other means, *first obtain the suffrages, and then betray the interests, of the people*....
> Hence, it clearly appears, that the same advantage which *a republic has over a democracy, in controlling the effects of faction*...consist in the greater obstacles opposed to the concert and accomplishment of the secret wishes of an unjust and interested majority[.]
> The influence of factious leaders may kindle a flame within their particular States, *but will be unable to spread a general conflagration through the other States*. A religious sect may degenerate into a political faction in a part of

the Confederacy; but the variety of sects dispersed over the entire face of it must secure the national councils against any danger from that source. *A rage for paper money, for an abolition of debts, for an equal division of property, or for any other improper or wicked project,* will be less apt to pervade the whole body of the Union than a particular member of it; in the same proportion as such a malady is more likely to taint a particular county or district, than an entire State." [7] (emphasis added).

If we are to preserve Liberty, we must preserve our constitutional republic! As it is *the* governmental check of a free people against "the secret wishes of an unjust and interested majority," that might otherwise be empowered to "betray the interests, of the people." Or, *any* minority advocating the anti-individual, anti-constitutional republic progressivism of democratic socialism's direct democracy, advocates only *the* revolutionary means to their own democratic end.

In conjunction with Madison, James Wilson gave testimony to the power of our Individual Liberty—that it can be maintained and perpetuated only under a "limited constitution" such as the one ordained by our founders—in a speech before the Pennsylvania Convention in November of 1787, which included:

> *The great struggle for Liberty in this country, should it be unsuccessful, will probably be the last one which she will have for her existence and prosperity in any part of the globe.* And it must be confessed that this struggle has, in some of the stages of its progress, been attended with symptoms that foreboded no fortunate issue. To

the iron hand of Tyranny, which was lifted up against her, she manifested, indeed, an intrepid superiority. She broke in pieces the fetters which were forged for her, and showed that she was unassailable by force. But she was environed with dangers of another kind, and springing from a very different source. While she kept her eye steadily fixed on the efforts of oppression, licentiousness was secretly undermining the rock on which she stood.

Need I call to your remembrance the *contrasted* scenes of which we have been witnesses? On the glorious conclusion of our conflict with Britain, what high expectations were formed concerning us by others! What high expectations did we form concerning ourselves! Have those expectations been realized? No. What has been the cause? Did our citizens lose their perseverance and magnanimity? No. Did they become insensible of resentment and indignation at any high-handed attempt that might have been made to injure or enslave them? No. What, then, has been the cause? The truth is, we dreaded danger only on one side: this we manfully repelled. But, on another side, danger, not less formidable but more insidious, stole in upon us; and our unsuspicious tempers were not sufficiently attentive either to its approach or to its operations. Those whom foreign strength could not overpower have well nigh become the victims of internal anarchy.

If we become a little more particular, we shall find that the foregoing representation is by no means exaggerated. When we had baffled all the menaces of foreign power, wo neglected to establish among ourselves a government that would *insure domestic vigor* and stability....

Under these impressions, and with these views, was the late Convention appointed; and under these impressions, and with these views, the late Convention met.

We now see the great end which they proposed to accomplish. It was to frame, for the consideration of their constituents, one federal and national constitution—a constitution that would produce the advantages of good, and prevent the inconveniences of bad government—a constitution whose beneficence and energy would pervade the whole Union, and bind and embrace the interests of every part—a constitution that would insure peace, freedom, and happiness, to the states and people of America....

There necessarily exists, in every government, a power from which there is no appeal, and which, for that reason, may be termed supreme, absolute, and uncontrollable. Where does this power reside? To this question writers on different governments will give different answers. Sir William Blackstone will tell you, that in Britain the power is lodged in the British Parliament; that the Parliament may alter the form of the government; and that its power is absolute, without control. The idea of a constitution, limiting and superintending the operations of legislative authority, seems not to have been accurately understood in Britain. There are, at least, no traces of practice conformable to such a principle. *The British constitution is just what the British Parliament pleases.* When the Parliament transferred legislative authority to Henry VIII., the act transferring could not, in the strict acceptation of the term, be called unconstitutional.

To control the power and conduct of the legislature, by an overruling constitution, was an improvement in the science and practice of government reserved to the American states.

Perhaps some politician, who has not considered with sufficient accuracy our political systems, would answer that, in our governments, the supreme power was vested in the constitutions. This opinion approaches a step nearer to the truth, but does not reach it. *The truth is, that, in our governments, the supreme, absolute, and uncontrollable power remains in the people.* As our constitutions are superior to our legislatures, so the people are superior to our constitutions. Indeed, the superiority, in this last instance, is much greater; for the people possess over our constitutions control in *act*, as well as right....

Oft have I marked, with silent pleasure and admiration, *the force and prevalence*, through the United States, of *the principle that the supreme power resides in the people, and that they never part with it*. It may be called the *panacea* in politics. There can be no disorder in the community but may here receive a radical cure. If the error be in the legislature, it may be corrected by the constitution; if in the constitution, it may be corrected by the people. There is a remedy, therefore, for every distemper in government, *if the people are not wanting to themselves; if they are wanting to themselves, there is no remedy. From their power, as we have seen, there is no appeal; of their error there is no superior principle of correction*[8] (emphasis added).

How could a free people with such *"absolute and uncontrollable power"*, ever possibly remain so without an equally absolute and unwavering moral standard upon which, and only upon which, any *absolute truth* in what is right and what is wrong in the preservation of either that power or their freedom, may come to be known? *And so it is that, via just such "wanting to ourselves," America has slowly transformed from the constitutional republic our founders ordained to preserve our Individual Liberty to the democracy needed by predatory progressive opportunists such as Marx to destroy it!* This puts into perspective the devastating impact of such acts as the Sixteenth Amendment authorizing the government the power to confiscate and redistribute the fruits of our labor—which is, or was, our property—and the Seventeenth Amendment, which nationalizes the US Senate by removing from our republic legislative process and effectual public discourse the sovereign voices of the States. It is worth reiterating here that nationalism is *not* of Individualism! It is of collectivism, and therefore of the Philosophy! Beware any such nationalism be not mistaken for the pro-Individual Liberty patriotic republicanism that it is *not*! It's a road that has led, and can only lead, to further collectivization and the eventual ruin of any free society. Where Liberty and our republic are defined by moral and constitutional restraints, any factional, populist and/or pragmatic nationalism would, per its own collectivism, be inherently inclined to at least dismiss if not outright target them both for destruction.

Now, if only the enemies of Liberty could devise a way to get American individualists to forgo their naturally diverse individuality and collectivize into factions. This brings us at once to Antonio Gramsci. And as he has prescribed for the destruction of Liberty, the more groups and the more factions individuals can be led to align with, the better!

Antonio Gramsci was a prominent Italian Communist who was arrested in 1929 and imprisoned for the remainder of his life by Mussolini. While in prison, he wrote what have come to be known as his *Prison Notebooks*. Although not translated into English until 1971, they have long been popular globally with both intellectual academic progressives and contemporary social revolutionaries alike. His writings open up a whole new understanding of the origin and purpose behind today's "culture wars," which includes, in its arsenal of weaponry, cultural diversity, political correctness, unionism, classism, feminism, social justice, and sustainability. This war is being waged against our faith, family, traditions, and founding principles via our very own education system, churches, and every form of media constantly inundating all of our senses. Every day, all day, day in and day out, to the point of overload, we are saturated with revolutionary *social* propaganda. This is essentially how, from the pillars of our own communities, thanks in part to Gramsci, we are to this day receiving—and sadly, it appears, accepting—our orders to self-destruct. From his *Prison Notebooks* (1929–1935), he observes:

The Organisation Of Education And Of Culture

Side by side with the type of school which may be called *"humanistic"*...designed to develop in each *individual* human being an as yet undifferentiated general culture, the fundamental power to think and ability to find one's way in life...is taking place chaotically, *without clear and precise principles, without a well-studied and consciously established plan....*

The common school, or school of humanistic...should aim to insert young men and women into social activity... *The entire function of educating and forming the new generations ceases to be private and becomes public; for only thus can it involve them in their entirety....*

The first, primary grade should...in addition to imparting the first "instrumental" notions of schooling—reading, writing, sums, geography, history—ought in particular to deal with an aspect of education that is now neglected—i.e. with *"rights and duties"*, with the first notions of the State and society as primordial elements of *a new conception of the world* which challenges the conceptions that are imparted by the various traditional social environments, i.e. those conceptions which can be termed folkloristic (emphasis added).

We will see how the "humanistic" aspect fits in a little later, but right off, Gramsci hits on the "undifferentiated" culture of teaching the "individual" how to think and find his own way in life, "taking place chaotically, *without clear and precise principles, without a well-studied and consciously established plan.*" Instead, the new generations should impart with the notions of "reading, writing, sums, geography, history" and "ought in particular" be taught "to deal… with *'rights and duties'*…with the first notions of the State and society as primordial elements of *a new conception of the world.*" If this is starting to sound a little familiar, remember from chapter 2 what Anthony Harrison-Barbet of Philosophical Connections tells us of Auguste Comte's *positive sociology*:

> If this third (and for Comte final) type of society is to be developed…a new science of man will be required. *This is sociology…a knowledge of which will enable man to reorganize society.…*
>
> He also distinguishes between *social statics* and *social dynamics*. Social statics examines the general laws which relate. The latter is concerned rather with *what is needed for the development of order, that is, progress.…*
>
> Moreover…*social planning is entirely possible, indeed required.*
>
> Comte favoured *rule by the knowledgeable experts* (positivist scientists and philosophers) whose decisions, exercised through government, would have to be obeyed by the people because *the rulers know best. There is thus no place in his scheme for rights of individuals* in so far as *they are subordinate* to society, indeed humanity as a whole; and *it is therefore only in this context, which emphasizes duties, that the concept of 'rights' can have any application.* Humanity, the "Great

Being", takes the place of God, and is the basis of all morality[9] (emphasis added).

As it does with Hobbes's "mortal God," and as it always does in a humanistic "planned" societies of "social cohesion or order," it all ends within the Philosophy as it ends here, with "humanity, the 'Great Being', tak[ing] the place of God." Where they are successful in destroying our faith in God, that faith and God Himself are only forsaken for the new god of collectivism—the state.

Gramsci continues:

> In the basic organisation of the common school, at least the essentials of these conditions must be created—not to speak of the fact, which goes without saying, that parallel to the common school a network of *kindergartens* and other institutions would develop, in which, even before the school age, children would be habituated to a certain *collective discipline* and acquire pre-scholastic notions and attitudes. In fact, the common school should be organised like a college, *with a collective life by day and by night*, freed from the present forms of hypocritical and mechanical discipline; studies should be carried on *collectively*, with the assistance of the teachers and the best pupils, even during periods of so-called individual study....
>
> The entire common school is an active school, *although it is necessary to place limits on libertarian ideologies* in this field and to stress with some energy *the duty* of the adult gen-

erations, i.e. of the State, *to "mould" the new generations....*

In the first phase the aim is to discipline, hence also to *level out—to obtain a certain kind of "conformism"* which may be called *"dynamic".* In the creative phase, on the basis that has been achieved of *"collectivisation"* of the social type, the aim is to expand the personality—by now autonomous and responsible, *but with a solid and homogeneous moral and social conscience.* Thus creative school *does not mean* school of "inventors and discoverers"…with an obligation to originality and innovation….

The advent of the common school means the beginning of new relations between intellectual and industrial work, not only in the school but *in the whole of social life.* The comprehensive principle will therefore be reflected in all the organisms of culture, transforming them and giving them a new content[10] (emphasis added).

As we will find out, Gramsci wasn't the first to call for kindergartens "in which, even before the school age, *children would be habituated* to a certain *collective* discipline and acquire pre-scholastic notions and attitudes." Neither will he be the last, as both Governor Andrew Cuomo and Mayor de Blasio of New York City have both, rather recently, openly boasted their part in pushing for "universal pre-K," which in turn has helped New York State "reclaim," according to them, its spot at the top as *the* "Progressive Capital of The Country."[11]

With a collective here, a collective there and a little more collective sprinkled everywhere, education in general to Gramsci as a communist is understandably "on the basis that has been achieved of *collectivisation.*" But what of "the aim…to expand the personality"? Remember from chapter 2, Article 29 of the United Nations 1948 Universal Declaration of Human Rights that stipulates, "Everyone has duties to the community *in which alone the free and full development of his personality is possible.*" Your "personality" to the humanist is, as it is to the Communist, *the* measure of your compliance with the positive "duties" and "obligations" now owed by every individual to the state! As Rousseau said, any and all positive collective "rights" of human/civil origin are "conditional"!

> In Search Of The Educational Principle
> In the *old* primary school…the scientific ideas the children learnt conflicted with *the magical conception of the world and nature* which they absorbed from an environment steeped in folklore; while the idea of *civic rights* and duties conflicted with tendencies towards individualistic and localistic barbarism—another dimension of folklore. The school *combated folklore, indeed every residue of traditional conceptions of the world…* there exist social and state laws which are the product of human activity, which are established by *men and can be altered by men in the interests of their collective development.*
> Human work cannot be realised in all its power of expansion and productivity without an exact and realistic knowledge of natural laws and without a *legal order* which organically regulates men's life in common. *Men must respect this legal order through spontaneous assent, and not merely as an external imposition—it must be*

> *a necessity recognised* and proposed to themselves as freedom, *and not simply the result of coercion* (emphasis added).

As we have been told time and time again by the Philosophy, anyone who believes in God believes in a "magical conception of the world and nature." God, a belief in God, and the concept of God-given Individual Rights and free will are the "folklore" to which he speaks. This is what conflicts with the "scientific ideas" taught in schools. Schools must "combat" such understandings and beliefs, and "indeed every residue of traditional conceptions of the world" they have absorbed at home from their parents and family—as it is *not* God but society that provides "rights" and "liberties" in a Godless collective society. Students must learn "that there exist social and state laws which are the product of human activity, which are established by *men and can be altered by men in the interests of their collective development*," which represent, as Hobbes said, the real "mortal God" of government and overrule any folklore that might instill "tendencies towards individualistic and localistic barbarism."

Going back to what I said earlier about the mental aspect of *the great deception*, in which man's "mind being also transformed will not see it as such, that his only Will, will be to do the Will of others" is here brought to light with Gramsci's "spontaneous assent." This is where it all begins. The *"legal order…Men must respect…not merely as an external imposition"* but as *"a necessity recognised and proposed to themselves as freedom*! A deception of the highest order not in my words but theirs!

> *Previously, the pupils at least acquired a certain "baggage" or "equipment" (according to taste) of concrete facts*…and the pupil, if he has an active intelligence, will give an order of his own,

with the aid of his social background, to the "baggage" he accumulates. *With the new curricula, which coincide with a general lowering of the level of the teaching profession, there will no longer be any "baggage" to put in order.*[12] (emphasis added)

"[W]ith the aid of his social background," one "will give an order of his own" to any "baggage… of concrete facts…he accumulates." However, "[w]ith the new curricula [common core?], *which coincide with a general lowering of the level of the teaching profession, there will no longer be any "baggage" to put in order.*" Again, not my words, but theirs!

Any teacher caught teaching, as Hitler says, "thinking and acting according to his own bent" as an individual, or caught teaching to each child as a dignified individual for the benefit of that individual has gone off the collective rail and is in violation of Gramsci's "spontaneous assent" and, as we will see, John Dewey's progressive pedagogic creed. Though they may not be aware of the whole of the transformative progressive purpose behind the collective incommonism of the common-core curriculum, any teacher left with any awareness of the value of their individual talents and attributes to teaching will eventually become disenchanted, disheartened, and frustratingly aware of Gramsci's "general lowering of the level of the teaching profession." The 2013 online resignation of teacher Ellie Rubenstein says it all. This is some of what she said:

ELLIE RUBENSTEIN
Lincoln Elementary School, Highland Park, Ill.
Over the past fifteen years, I've experienced the depressing, gradual downfall and misdirection of education that has slowly eaten away at my love of teaching. The emphasis in education

has shifted from fostering academic and personal growth, in both students and teachers, to demanding uniformity and conformity. Raising students' test scores on standardized tests is now the only goal, and in order to achieve it, the creativity, flexibility, and spontaneity that create authentic learning environments have been eliminated.

Everything I loved about teaching is extinct.

Curriculum is mandated. Minutes spent teaching subjects are audited. Schedules are dictated by administrators. The classroom teacher is no longer trusted or in control of what, when, or how she teaches. Research indicates that employees are most productive and happy when given autonomy over time, technique, task, and teammates. But we now have no control over any of that. No wonder teacher burnout and turnover are at an all-time high.

Our mission is to create "lifelong learners," which means getting children excited about—and engaged in—their learning. But how can this happen when teachers are discouraged from teaching creatively? More and more, we are being asked to administer paper-and-pencil tasks, multiple-choice tests that can be graded by a computer, and skill-and-drill assignments that don't require or reflect higher-level thinking. Authentic literature has been replaced by dry, uninteresting reading text, and teachers are being forced to do away with constructive projects in order to fit in all those mandated instructional minutes and assessments.

Our district states that part of its mission is to "do what's best for children." But this is pretense and disingenuous. Administrators consistently make decisions that indicate they have no true understanding of what is best for children at all:

- No recess or breaks for students during the day
- Less classroom support for students with special needs
- More tracking of students
- Less understanding of student differences
- More emphasis on data
- No room for innovative teaching or engaged learning
- No opportunities for teachers to establish that which is critical to a student's success: the teacher-student connection

How can this possibly be what is "best for children"?

I thought I would be a teacher for the rest of my life, but I no longer feel that I'm doing anything meaningful. I'm not being allowed to spark enthusiasm for learning in children in my own way. Rather, I'm being forced to function as a cog in a wheel, and this wheel is not turning in the right direction. My sense of humor, personality, creativity, self-expression, passion, opinion, my voice—all are being stepped on, crushed, and ground down. And I have to get out before my sense of self and self-worth are completely obliterated....

In Dr Seuss's lovely book *Horton Hatches the Egg*, there's a sentence that made my daughter cry every time I read it out loud to her when she was young. When the hunters arrive and see Horton the elephant defending his egg in a tree, they decide to sell him to a circus. They force him to leave his branch so that they can put him on display in a cage. Dr Seuss writes, "Horton backed down with a sad, heavy heart."

And like clockwork, whenever I read this, Alison [ph] would tear up. Somehow, even my 4-year-old knew that this was a moment of defeat and loss, and her empathy and sorrow for Horton were palpable.

Today I am Horton. I am being forced from my protective branch. They want to take away my freedom to nurture my students and help them grow. But I won't go into their cage, so I'm leaving my post. And I, too, am backing down with a sad, heavy heart. I hereby submit my resignation.[13]

Know that the general "lowering of the level of the teaching profession" that has produced the documented steady decline in the quality of our children's *public* education and the "data mining" of today's common-core curricula for our children's "social background" are not by accident. It is but *the* proof of a well-executed plan. Is not a dumbed-down population easier to manipulate? As we shall see,

Gramsci was far from the first or only one to call for just such a transformation in our children's education.

On a note of observation, as this "fundamental transformation of America" settles in, it is having the same effect in law enforcement as it is in education. Where the officer is no longer *the* authority on his post or beat and is fast becoming more and more only the conduit through which the now centralized state authority flows—so is the teacher no longer *the* educator, but rather, only the conduit through which the now centralized education flows. As there can be a very little to no individual discretion in a centrally planned collectivism, neither can there be any wayward teachers instructing the next generation of "planned" intellectuals.

> The Formation of the Intellectuals
>
> Every social group, coming into existence on the original terrain of an essential function in the world of economic production, creates together with itself, organically, one or more strata intellectuals which give it h*omogeneity* and an awareness of its own function not only in the economic but also in the social and political fields. *The capitalist entrepreneur creates alongside himself the industrial technician, the specialist in political economy, the organisers of a new culture, of a new legal system, etc.* It should be noted that the entrepreneur himself represents a higher level of social elaboration…He must be an organiser of masses of men; he must be an organiser of the "confidence" of investors in his business, of the customers for his product, etc. If not all entrepreneurs, at least an *élite* amongst them must have the capacity to be *an organ-*

iser of society in general...because of the need to create the conditions most favourable to the expansion of their own class....

Each man, finally, outside his professional activity, carries on some form of intellectual activity, that is, he is a "philosopher", an artist, a man of taste, *he participates in a particular conception of the world*, has a conscious line of moral conduct, and therefore contributes to sustain a conception of the world *or to modify it, that is, to bring into being new modes of thought.*

The problem of creating a new stratum of intellectuals consists therefore in the critical elaboration of the intellectual activity that exists in everyone at a certain degree of development...*in so far as it...becomes the foundation of a new and integral conception of the world... In the modern world, technical education, closely bound to industrial labour even at the most primitive and unqualified level, must form the basis of the new type of intellectual* (emphasis added).

Through Gramsci's eyes, society, as a whole, is seen in what he refers to as *hegemony*. Hegemony consists of all that is the glue of a given society and what makes it tick. Those who are the developers, supporters, leaders, advancers, and willing participants of that society, along with those who perpetuate it, are what he calls the *intellectuals* of that society. In order to replace the present "dominate" bourgeois free-individualist, capitalist society with one of submissive collective in-commonness, a whole new batch of compliant ones would have to be made and pumped up into it "from the bottom to the top." Eventually, over generations, slowly but surely, with the eventual changing of the intellectual guard, they will begin to methodically outnumber and replace the old antiquated "immoral" train of individualist thought with the new "moral" collective one.

Then with the new "organic" intellectuals in place, armed with the "certain kind of conformism" that has been "proposed to them...as freedom," the fundamental transformation can begin. The big noteworthy difference here between Gramsci's new collectivized conformist intellectuals versus the time-tested innovative leaders of the prosperous, profiting old meritocracy is, "in the modern world, technical education, closely bound to industrial labour *even at the most primitive and unqualified level, must form the basis of the new type of intellectual.*" Again, not in my words but in theirs! Does it work? Consider this as the philosophy that has brought such dynamic intellectual powerhouses as Joe Biden, Maxine Waters, Dianne Feinstein, and Nancy Pelosi to power!

> The mode of being of the new intellectual can no longer consist in eloquence, which is an exterior and momentary mover of feelings and passions, *but in active participation in practical life*, as constructor, organiser, "permanent persuader" and not just a simple orator....
>
> The relationship between the intellectuals and the world of production is not as direct as it is with the fundamental social groups but is, in varying degrees, "mediated" by the whole fabric of society...It should be possible...*to establish a gradation of their functions and of the superstructures from the bottom to the top* (from the structural base upwards). What we can do, for the moment, is to fix two major superstructural "levels": the *one that can be called "civil society",*

> *that is the ensemble of organisms commonly called "private", and that of "political society" or "the State".* These two levels correspond on the one hand *to the function of "hegemony"* which the dominant group exercises throughout society (emphasis added).

The new intellectual class of "permanent persuaders," along with the multiple aspects of the "ensemble of organisms commonly called private" are "to establish a gradation of their functions and of the superstructures from the bottom to the top." Gramsci also acknowledges that both private "organisms" and the state "correspond…to the function of hegemony," so both will have to be transformed in order to fully transform society. Also note that there is a subtle but historical social evolution here between Marx and Gramsci. Where Marx sees only the proletariat and the bourgeois, with maybe a blending of the two in the petty bourgeois, Gramsci sees an "ensemble of organisms" making up "independent social groups" of the proletariat. This ensemble is the birthplace of what we now call *cultural diversity*. It is what constitutes the plethora of the seemingly endless array of discontented hodge-podge aspects of Occupy, from anarchists, academics, socialists, communists, liberals, progressives, Nazis, anti-imperialists, anticolonialists, and labor unions to environmentalists, prisoner-rights groups, critical race theorists, black-liberation theologists, atheists, humanists, Arab Springers, anti-Semitic PLO supporters, community organizers, oppressed youth, LGBTQ/+, feminist, Planned Parenthood, and the Black Panthers, to the revolutionary antilaw enforcement agitation of the Truth to Power, Free Mumiah, People's Power, and Black Lives Matter movements. Again, the current progressive "war on cops" is *not* by happenstance!

> *The intellectuals are the dominant group's "deputies" exercising the subaltern functions of social hegemony* and political government. These comprise:
>
> 1. The *"spontaneous" consent* given by the great masses of the population *to the general direction imposed on social life* by the dominant fundamental group....
> 2. The apparatus of state coercive power which "legally" enforces discipline on those groups *who do not "consent"* either actively or passively. This apparatus is, however, constituted for the whole of *society in anticipation of moments of crisis of command and direction when spontaneous consent has failed.*

Once Gramsci's new communist collective has replaced the old world and has become the "dominate group," compliance will be "organic" via "spontaneous consent," or a subconscious social compliance to the general will of the collective. Regarding "those groups who do not consent," compliance under such a "crisis of command" will be by force, or the "apparatus of state coercive power." Therefore, intellectuals with a "particular" collective "conception of the world" must be in positions of the government to force that compliance. On this, Gramsci notes,

> The change in the condition of the social position of the intellectuals in Rome…is due to Caesar, who granted citizenship to doctors and to masters of liberal arts so that they would be

more willing to live in Rome and so that others should be persuaded to come there…thus creating a permanent category of intellectuals, since without their permanent residence there no cultural organisation could be created; and… to attract to Rome the best intellectuals from all over the Roman Empire, *thus promoting centralisation on a massive scale*. In this way there came into being the category of *"imperial" intellectuals*[14] (emphasis added).

Doesn't this define exactly what the likes of Teddy Roosevelt, Woodrow Wilson, FDR, Lyndon B. Johnson, and the administration of Barack H. Obama have all been able to accomplish in Washington, DC? Is it a coincidence that Washington, along with the greater majority of our state capitals, has been politically populated into a bunch of little Romes within which a class of "permanent…'imperial' intellectuals" now sit issuing "command and direction" and "promoting centralisation on a massive scale"?

Being that Gramsci was in prison while writing his *Prison Papers*, it is understood that he may have attempted to elude his capturers in his critiques. Regardless, for this work, what is important about Gramsci is his establishment of an underlying principle of an organized subversive education—an education designed to undermine no less than the whole of the current "dominate system" in the world (the bourgeois capitalist system founded on God, Individual Liberty, and property rights)—destroy it and replace it with a world communism. Not through a violent revolution but through gradualism, or "long march through culture" via generations of directed "humanistic" social reeducation. In this reeducation, our youth are "directed" away from self-sufficiency, independence, and individuality to become part of the next generation's "moulded" *intellectuals* of collective incommonhood. The intellectuals of the old capitalist "bourgeois" of our society's churches, businesses, and government are slowly but surely replaced by new intellectuals steeped in social justice, collectivism, environmentalism, sustainability, communism, unionism, feminism, and humanism. These new intellectuals, of the "most primitive and unqualified level," are no longer self-empowered, nor do they see the "promise of their own potential" as the dream of freedom. They see only the order of forced social compliance where the confiscation of the whole of their everything and the redistribution of it back to the collective according to a "well-studied and consciously established plan." It is what affords them their only purpose, only worth, and their only meaningful "personality." They do know, however, that this is the "particular conception of the world" that will form "the foundation of a new and integral conception of the world."

In his October 24, 1914 (YMCA), speech at Pittsburg titled "The Power of Christian Young Men," President Woodrow Wilson shared some of his revealing thoughts on the *social* purposes of Christianity and education, as well as the *social* function of the family.

> Go to a college community and try to change the least custom of that little world and find how the conservatives will rush at you. *Moreover, young men are embarrassed by having inherited their father's opinions. I have often said that the use of a university is to make young gentlemen as unlike their fathers as possible.* I do not say that with the least disrespect for the fathers; but every man who is old enough to have a son in college is old enough to have become very seriously immersed in some particular business and is almost certain to have caught the point

of view of that particular business. And *it is very useful to his son to be taken out of that narrow circle, conducted to some high place where he may see the general map of the world and of the interests of mankind, and there shown how big the world is and how much of it his father may happen to have forgotten.* It would be worth while for men, middle-aged and old, to detach them selves more frequently from the things that command their daily attention and to think of the sweeping tides of humanity

Therefore I am interested in this association, because it is intended to bring young men together *before any crust has formed over them, before they have been hardened to any particular occupation, before they have caught an inveterate point of view* (emphasis added).

Don't all parents who love and want the best for their children aim to instill a set of fundamental values, of rights and wrongs, in them to help them form a firm foundation upon which they might be able to build an honest, independent future for themselves and their families? What child becomes embarrassed by the proven wisdom of such loving guidance until some "teacher" with instructions to stem the tide of tradition and the old society comes along to tell them that they should be embarrassed? At least as far back as 1914, as is evident by this speech, our colleges were already actively working to embarrass our children, not merely for their personal beliefs but for harboring any sentiment for the old, antiquated independent society of free will and Individual Liberty. How many parents over the past few generations have anxiously waited for their children to come home from school just to be met by the ever-condescending,

"Forget about it, Mom, forget about it, Dad…you guys just don't know what the hell you're talking about"?

Now we have an understanding why. Know that it is not by happenstance. How could it be when it is *the* purpose or "use of a university is to make young gentlemen as unlike their fathers as possible"? In stating that, in the "interests of mankind," "it is very useful to his son to be taken out of that narrow circle," Wilson's contempt for American individualism, independence, and family are all brought to light. Even as the progressive ship sets sail here, it becomes obvious that Wilson sees any sense of family, family business, family tradition, and family function on that ship as nothing more than a dragging anchor.

How is it that those who are busy working harder and harder (if the economy hasn't been completely pulled out from underneath them)—keeping their noses to the grindstone, chasing a dollar that's worth less and less to pay bills that are higher and higher, trying to keep food on the table and a roof over their family's heads while taking time to care for their children—supposed to find the time to "detach themselves" to "think of the sweeping tides of humanity"? Or, for that matter, find the time to babysit all the revolutionary progressive corruption in their government?"

> I wonder if we attach sufficient importance to Christianity *as a mere instrumentality in the life of mankind.* For one, *I am not fond of thinking of Christianity as the means of saving individual souls…any man who devotes himself to its cultivation in his own case will become a selfish prig.* The only way your powers can become great is by exerting them *outside the circle of your own narrow, special, selfish interests.* And that is the reason of Christianity. (emphasis added)

So what is the "importance" of Christianity? Is it the saving of our souls that *everlasting life* may be obtained for those saved, or is it to be held "as a mere instrumentality in the life of mankind"? Never has there been a question asked where the answer held such far-reaching implications! Not just for you or I, or just Christians, but for the whole of mankind! *This* is where the great deception of Spirit begins. If Christianity isn't "the means of saving *individual* souls," and the "reason of Christianity" is to guilt you into focusing your life's efforts "outside the circle of your own narrow, special, selfish interests," and it's true that Christianity is nothing more than the "mere instrumentality in the life of mankind," where do we go, and to whom do we turn to save our souls? And may we ask, an instrumentality for what? In an August 9, 1995, interview about his new book *Dreams from My Father* with Eye on Books, Barak Obama, telling us essentially the same thing, sheds a little more light on the subject this way:

> I worked as a *community organizer* in Chicago, [and] was very active in low-income neighborhoods working on issues of crime and education and employment, and seeing that in some ways certain portions of the African-American community are doing as bad, if not worse, and recognizing that my fate remained tied up with their fates. *That my individual salvation is not going to come about without a collective salvation for the country.*
>
> Unfortunately, I think *that recognition requires that we make sacrifices, and this country has not always been willing to make the sacrifices necessary to bring about a new day and a new age*[15] (emphasis added).

If Christianity can be transformed from "the means of saving *individual* souls" into one where our "individual salvation is not going to come about without a collective salvation for the country," which "requires that [they] make sacrifices," then those who still want their individual salvation and eternal life bad enough will be left wide open for *the* ultimate extortion! Anybody and everybody seeking their own selfish individual salvation, believing that it depends completely on the "collective salvation" of the whole, will then be forced, for the good of the collective, into making any and all "sacrifices necessary to bring about a new day and a new age" in order to "save" themselves! *Could there be a more nefarious purpose for Christians and their individualistic souls than as redirected slaves to the secular social demands of the collective?* Wilson continues:

> Christ came into the world to save others, not to save himself; and *no man is a true Christian who does not think constantly of how he can lift his brother*...an association of Christian young men is an association meant to put its shoulders under the world and lift it, so that other men may feel that they have companions in bearing the weight and heat of the day; that other men may know that there are those who care for them, who would go into places of difficulty and danger to rescue them, who regard them selves *as their brother's keeper* (emphasis mine)

Are Christians to be good Christians or gods? Unlike the rest of us, Jesus Himself didn't need to be saved as, according to scripture, he was God's "only begotten Son." He is God!

Does scripture actually tell us that "no man is a true Christian" unless he submits himself or herself to the redistributive sacrifices necessary to be his brother's keeper? Or is this an example of *the* positive spiritual redirection I spoke of at the beginning of this chapter? In John 3:16–18, Jesus Himself is quoted as telling us:

> For God so loved the world that he sent *his only begotten Son*, that *whosoever believeth in him should not perish but have everlasting life*
>
> For God sent not his Son into the world to condemn the world; *but that the world through him might be saved.*
>
> *He* that believeth in him is not condemned: but *he* that believeth not is condemned already, because *he* hath not believed in the name of *the only begotten Son of God.*[16] (emphasis added)

So what scripture actually tells us is "whosoever believeth in him should not perish but have everlasting life," not "whosoever does as the collective demands." And "true Christian" or not, I cannot "believeth in Him" for none but myself. Nor can any other, be it any one person or any collective, "believeth in Him" for my sake.

Whatever Presidents Wilson and Obama have in mind here for their "collective salvation," I don't see any mention from either about *the absolute* Truth Jesus also tells us in John 14:6: "I am the way, the truth, and the life: no man cometh unto the Father but by me." Christian or not, you have to wonder why there would be such an effort to misrepresent scripture. In the end, one or the other is telling the truth. Whom do we trust, these two progressives or scripture?

> I remember hearing a very wise man say once, a man grown old in the service of a great

> church, that he had never taught his son religion dogmatically at any time...he and the boy's mother...knew that Christianity...would *penetrate while the boy slept, almost; while he was unconscious of the sweet influences that were about him, while he reckoned nothing of instruction, but merely breathed into his lungs the wholesome air of a Christian home* (emphasis added).

This is a good illustration by Wilson of Gramsci's new world "legal order" being phased in "through spontaneous assent, and not merely as an external imposition." Over time, people will eventually come to see this compliance not for the willing submission to the "order" of others that it is but, rather, as an exercise of their own.

> Be militant!...If you find men who have grown old, about whom the crust has hardened, whose hinges are stiff, whose minds always have their eye over the shoulder thinking of things as they were done, do not have anything to do with them....
> Life, gentlemen—*the life of society, the life of the world—has constantly to be fed from the bottom.* It has to be fed by those great sources of strength which are constantly rising in new generations. Red blood has to be pumped into it. New fiber has to be supplied. That is the reason I have always said that I believed in popular institution...*The humblest hovel, therefore, may produce you your greatest man.* That is the process of life, this constant surging up of the new strength of unnamed, unrecognized,

uncatalogued men who are just getting into the running...You do not know when you will see above the level masses of the crowd some great stature lifted head and shoulders above the rest, shouldering its way, not violently but gently, to the front and saying, "Here am I; follow me." And his voice will be your voice, his thought will be your thought, and you will follow him as if you were following the best things in yourselves[17].

Where Gramsci says, "The mode of being of the new intellectual can no longer consist in eloquence, which is an *exterior* and momentary mover of feelings and passions, *but in active participation in practical life*, as constructor, organiser, 'permanent persuader' and not just a simple orator," that the new "intellectuals" of the new order will *not* come from any elite sources outside the average person's perspective but from within the general proletariat itself with a more widely understood perspective, Wilson foretells this: "You will see above the level masses of the crowd some great stature lifted head and shoulders above the rest...*And his voice will be your voice, his thought will be your thought, and you will follow him as if you were following the best things in yourselves.*" What else could explain the "I'm going to take care of everybody" and "the government's gonna pay for it" (CBS 60 Minutes/Scott Pelley-aired 9/27/15) progressivism of a "conservative" Donald Trump, being "head and shoulders above the rest", but "a new" collective "conception" of conservatism?

Key for both Wilson and Gramsci is that for the permanent change they seek in implementing their new order, the "intellectuals" or "deputies" needed to lead their revolution for change must emerge from those they seek to change—the proletariat or working class. That way, their submission isn't somebody else's idea; it's their own! Change the proletariat—where, by far, the largest portion of the population exists—you *force change* in society as a whole from "the bottom up."

An example of the extent to which *the* deception of "spontaneous assent" being "proposed as freedom" now molding and "forming the new generations" into a "new (collective) conception of the world" in our "common schools" has already been successfully accomplished can be found in the Pledge of Allegiance. If this is surprising to you, disturbs you, offends you, or you have become defensive by my observation of this (which many "conservative," patriotic Americans may), consider it another measure of their success in conforming you to their collective "conception of the world."

Please allow me to explain. First, consider that our founders—whom we know loved God, country, and Liberty—had no such "pledge of allegiance." So we know that no such pledge is necessary to "prove" patriotism. To the contrary, in establishing the United States of America, our founders established a free America in which, per *the people's* Constitution, every single member of their newly ordained "limited government" is to *pledge their allegiance* to *the* Individual Liberty of every one of its free citizens! Their *oaths* to "preserve" and/or "protect and defend the Constitution of the United States of America" and "to bear true faith and allegiance to the same" is *the only* acceptable pledge of allegiance to a free people living in a free society!

Now, in that context, consider that the essence of Fabian Socialist Francis Bellamy's "Pledge of Allegiance," in which it is the people pledging allegiance to the government, reverses that 180 degrees! When we learn the truth of its Fabian and National Socialist origins, we can begin to see the deception involved in the "patriotism" of such a pledge. Though we may have our own sentiments of meaning, to the collectivist, the flag is but a symbol of a central or nationalist identity. Seeing the early pictures of masses of children in orphanages, boarding schools, and classrooms performing it is truly worth a thousand words. When it is known that Hitler's Nazi salute would later be virtually identical to Bellamy's original pledge salute, the truth of that deception becomes undeniable; and the truth of our enthusiastic compliance to that deception becomes frighteningly evident, with or without "under God."[18]

When the depth of revolutionary scheming and level of deception are considered, we can begin to understand where Wilson is coming from when he ponders, "When I think of an association of Christian young men I wonder that it has not already turned the world upside down."

As we have seen with both Gramsci and Wilson, there is a melding between the *physical, mental,* and *spiritual* aspects of the Philosophy's great deception. They are not distinct or stand-alone, but rather, they are constantly, steadfastly, interdependently, and perpetually cross-pollinating each other's work. All three aspects of the great deception are generally all present whenever and wherever the Philosophy is at work fundamentally transforming society, including in our schools. This brings us to the work of John Dewey.

John Dewey is commonly referred to as the father of our current "progressive" public school system. He spells out his anti-individual philosophy of teaching in his 1897 *My Pedagogic Creed*:

> ARTICLE ONE. WHAT EDUCATION IS
>
> I believe that all education proceeds by the participation of the individual in the social consciousness of the race. This process *begins unconsciously almost at birth, and is continually shaping the individual's powers, saturating his consciousness, forming his habits, training his ideas, and arousing his feelings and emotions.* Through this unconscious education the individual gradually

comes to share in the intellectual and moral resources which humanity has succeeded in getting together. He becomes an *inheritor of the funded capital of civilization*. The most formal and technical *education* in the world cannot safely depart from this general process. It *can only organize it; or differentiate it in some particular direction* (emphasis added).

Dewey's education "process" begins "almost at birth" and is continually "saturating his consciousness" *not* for the child's sake but for the "direction" of society. Forgoing what might transpire naturally as the child matures, Dewey would force a predetermined end for both child and society by "training his ideas…in some particular direction" as prescribed, of course, by the all-knowing, all-seeing, and all-powerful progressive planners. If the social planners don't like or don't want smoking, they train us toward the "particular direction" of a society where smoking is no longer welcome, if it is allowed at all. If they don't like capitalism, property, sugar, meat, coal, hydrofracking, Styrofoam, supersized sodas, cars, Christians, or guns, then—well, I think you get the picture.

But to bring this to life, in 1995, then US attorney Eric Holder was recorded by C-SPAN speaking to the Women's National Democratic Club. He spoke of using "add agencies," as was made famous by progressive propagandist Edward Bernays, to help him orchestrate an "informational campaign" as part of a "gun initiative bill" to "really change the hearts and minds of people." He spoke of using athletes, entertainers, and anybody with any "credibility" and "influence over young people" in newspapers, on the radio, and TV stations, not only telling people that it's wrong "to be carrying guns" but to "share" any "information" they might have on *anyone* who does, saying:

> What we need to do is *change the way in which people think about guns, especially young people*, and make it something that's not cool, that it's not acceptable, it's not hip to carry a gun anymore, in the way in which we have changed our attitudes about cigarettes....
>
> I've also asked the School Board to *make part of every day some kind of* anti-violence, anti-gun message every day, every school, at every level... We just have to be repetitive about this. Its not enough to simply have a catchy add on a Monday and then only do it every Monday. *We need to* do this every day of the week and just really *brainwash people* into thinking about guns in a vastly different way[19] (emphasis added).

With all we have learned, in so far as to what those of the Philosophy have told us in their own words, how those who seek to defeat and overcome Individual Liberty in their revolutionary, fundamental transformation of America, almost all of it is exemplified right here in this one telling speech by Eric Holder. Is it a surprise to anyone that the outright effort to literally "brainwash people" into anything is on the table?

Dewey's education philosophy would show up again later at the United Nations in Julian Huxley's 1946 *UNESCO: Its Purpose and Philosophy*. Remember what he said about education:

> EDUCATION
>
> Education has a social as well as an individual function: it is one of the means by which society as a whole can become conscious of its traditions and its destiny, can fit itself to make

adjustment to new conditions, and can inspire it to make new efforts towards a fuller realisation of its aims....

Further, *since the world to-day is in process of becoming one,* and since a major aim of Unesco must be to help in the speedy and satisfactory realisation of this process, that Unesco must pay special attention to international education....

This would mean an extension of education backwards from the nursery school to the nursery itself.[20] (p. 30)

As Gramsci's education is a system where "even before the school age, children would be habituated to a certain collective discipline," and Dewey's "begins unconsciously almost at birth…saturating his consciousness, forming his habits, training his ideas… in some particular direction." Huxley's includes "an extension of education backwards from the nursery school to the nursery itself." Dewey continues:

> I believe that the only true education comes through the stimulation of the child's powers *by the demands of the social situations in which he finds himself. Through these demands he is stimulated to act as a member of a unity, to emerge from his original narrowness of action and feeling and to conceive of himself from the standpoint of the welfare of the group* to which he belongs. Through the responses which others make to his own activities he comes to know what these *mean in social terms. The value which they have is reflected back into them.* For instance, through the response which is made to

the child's instinctive babblings the child comes to know what those babblings mean; they are transformed into articulate language and thus the child is introduced into the consolidated wealth of ideas and emotions which are now summed up in language (emphasis added).

Where Wilson refers to the "narrow circle" of family that the "son" needs to be "taken out of," Dewey refers to such individualist traditions as "narrowness of action" from which he must "emerge." As an observation into what he is saying with "Through the responses which others make to his own activities he comes to know what these *mean in social terms. The value which they have is reflected back into them*," we understand that, as a progressive collectivist, John Dewey is *of the Philosophy*. As such, we know he is anti-individual and anticapitalist, and therefore, anti–Free Market and anti–free enterprise. But let us replace the word *social* in this statement with the word *market*, and it changes to: "Through the responses which others make to his own activities he comes to know what these mean in [market] terms. The value which they have is reflected back into them." Is this not *the* fundamental principle of free enterprise and the determination of market value? Are not the social demands of Dewey's collective society being correlated to the market demand of a free society?

The key to deciphering the difference, then, is to know and understand the difference between how "social demand" and "market demand" are determined. First, Free Market demand is determined freely! Market value and market demand are at least interdependent, if not the same entity, each being contingent upon the other. No demand, no value! No value, no demand! And market value, as we have already gone over, is determined by a free people freely voting with their dollars as to the value of things. Second, social demand and social value, though they may also be synonymous, are *not* freely determined by a free people but rather decreed according to the predetermined "needs" of a planned society! And where market demand determines the value of "things," social demand here is the determination by the planners as to the value of, not just things, but people. With one word, the meaning can turn 180 degrees from one of Individual Liberty to one of collective compliance!

> I believe that this educational process has two sides—one *psychological* and one *sociological*; and that neither can be subordinated to the other or neglected without evil results following. Of these two sides, the psychological is the basis. *The child's own instincts and powers furnish the material and give the starting point for all education. Save as the efforts of the educator connect with some activity which the child is carrying on of his own initiative independent of the educator, education becomes reduced to a pressure from without.* It may, indeed, give certain external results but cannot truly be called educative. *Without insight into the psychological structure and activities of the individual, the educative process will, therefore, be haphazard and arbitrary. If it chances to coincide with the child's activity it will get a leverage; if it does not, it will result in friction, or disintegration, or arrest of the child nature* (emphasis added).

May I offer a translation in plain English: Any "activity which the child is carrying on of his own initiative independent of the educator…may, indeed, give certain external results but cannot truly be called educative…without insight" from a committed social educator. "[A]ctivities of the individual…will, therefore be haphazard and arbitrary," individualist, and of no "social value." For the student to receive a social education, his activities must be "*controlled* in his work *through the life of the community*" by the teacher. The teacher must "differentiate it in some particular direction" so the student may "conceive of himself" only "from the standpoint of the welfare of the group."

With that, it is key to remember here that Dewy also says "The child's own instincts and powers furnish the material and give the starting point for all education." This is where the concern over the "data mining" of the common-core curriculum is validated. *This* is why they are doing it! And again—*not* in my words but theirs! Know that the search for such personal information provided by such data mining is nothing new as it is none other than Dewey, the father of our "progressive" public education system himself who establishes it here as *the* "starting point for all education." By data mining or spying on the child's homelife, natural interests, and social activities, the public "educators" can use the momentum of the child's own individuality against itself, redirecting it toward the best interests of the planner's predetermined society. Or, as Dewy just said, where progressive education can "coincide with the child's activity it will get a leverage"!

> I believe that knowledge of social conditions, of the present state of civilization, is necessary in order properly to *interpret* the child's powers. The child has his own instincts and tendencies, but we do not know what these mean *until we can translate them into their social equivalents*. We must be able to carry them back into a social past and see them as the inheritance of previous race activities. We must also be able to

project them into the future to see what their outcome and end will be. In the illustration just used, *it is the ability to see* in the child's babblings the promise and potency of a future social intercourse and conversation which enables one to deal in the proper way with that instinct.

I believe that the psychological and social sides are organically related and that education cannot be regarded as a compromise between the two, or a superimposition of one upon the other. We are told that the psychological definition of education is barren and formal—that it gives us only the idea of a development of all the mental powers *without giving us any idea of the use to which these powers are put.* On the other hand, it is urged that *the social definition of education, as getting adjusted to civilization*, makes of it a forced and external process, *and results in subordinating the freedom of the individual to a preconceived social and political status* (emphasis added).

Dewey gets right to the point here in saying "that the only true education" is "stimulated" by "the demands of the social situations" in which he finds himself. That is to say that it is society that dictates our education. This presents some key insight into what might be observed as the great lie or the backwardness of Dewey's progressive "forward thinking." For if it is truly society that "demands he is stimulated to act as a member of a unity, to emerge from his original narrowness of action" and demands he then surrender his needs to the demands of his social environment, then how did humanity ever make it this far?

If it is truly our environment or society that has historically changed or "moulded" the person to *its* liking and *its* needs, and not the person who has historically changed society to meet *his* or *her* liking and *his* or *her* needs, then wouldn't that all-powerful society have forced us a long time ago to forever remain in the dark ages, if not permanently in caves or extinct from surrendering to the outward demands of our hostile prehistoric societal environment? Is society to be, as Hobbes presents, our living, breathing, thinking, demanding "mortal god" reigning over us? *Or* does man have it within himself to go forth and subdue the earth as master and commander of his own destiny and of his own environment to develop, maintain, and/or change society to fit his needs for the betterment of all? Are we to be the forger of our own free will and our own free life, or are we simply pitiful prisoners held within the predetermined political parameters of our societal cage? Whose zoo is this anyway?

And is it me, or might the children of such a dominate progressive society—being socially "adjusted to civilization" via some "externally forced psychological process" in order to subordinate and restrict "the freedom of the individual to a *preconceived* social and political status"—define at least a brainwashed, if not enslaved, society?

> I believe each of these objections is true *when urged against one side isolated from the other*. In order to know what a power really is *we must know what its end, use, or function is*; and this we cannot know save as we conceive of the individual as active in social relationships. But, on the other hand, *the only possible adjustment which we can give to the child under existing conditions, is that which arises through putting him in complete possession of all his powers*. With

the advent of democracy and modern industrial conditions, it is impossible to foretell definitely just what civilization will be twenty years from now. Hence it is impossible to prepare the child for any precise set of conditions. *To prepare him for the future life means to give him command of himself; it means so to train him that he will have the full and ready use of all his capacities; that his eye and ear and hand may be tools ready to command, that his judgment may be capable of grasping the conditions under which it has to work*, and the executive forces be trained to act economically and efficiently. *It is impossible to reach this sort of adjustment save as constant regard is had to the individual's own powers, tastes, and interests*—say, that is, as education is continually converted into psychological terms. In sum, I believe that the individual who is to be educated is a social individual and that *society is an organic union of individuals*. If we eliminate the social factor from the child we are left only with an abstraction; if we eliminate the individual factor from society, we are left only with an inert and lifeless mass. *Education, therefore, must begin with a psychological insight into the child's capacities, interests, and habits. It must be controlled at every point by reference to these same considerations. These powers, interests, and habits must be continually interpreted - we must know what they mean. They must be translated into terms of their social equivalents* (emphasis added).

Why would "the child's capacities, interests, and habits" *need* to "be controlled at every point" and his or her "powers, interests, and habits" *need* to "be continually interpreted"? Why would the "educators" of Dewey's collective utopia *need* to "know what they mean"? And why would they *need* to "be translated into terms of their social equivalents" if the objective of his "social education" wasn't a full-out collective effort in "subordinating the freedom of the individual to a preconceived social and political status"? Or in other words, ask not what education can do for your children, ask what "capacities, interests, and habits" your child has that "must be controlled at every point" and "adjusted" by his/her education so that the social "demands" of society may be met in "terms of what they are capable of in the way of social service" and can be of most service to the planners!

ARTICLE TWO. WHAT THE SCHOOL IS
I believe that the school is primarily a social institution. Education being a social process, the school is simply that form of community life in which all those agencies are concentrated that will be most effective in bringing the child to *share in the inherited resources of the race*, and to use his own *powers for social ends*.

I believe that *education, therefore, is a process of living and not a preparation for future living* (emphasis added).

What are the shared "inherited resources of the race"? Two hands, two eyes, ten fingers and toes? Is it their share of somebody else's stuff? Is it their fair share of the public debt? Or is it the shared inheritance of the world's oil, natural gas, coal, minerals, timber, biodiversity, water, air, and climate that all the greedy individualist capitalists seek to exploit?

I believe that the school must represent present life—life *as real and vital to the child as that which he carries on in the home*, in the neighborhood, or on the play-ground.

I believe that education which does not occur through forms of life, *forms that are worth living for their own sake*, is always a poor substitute for the genuine reality and tends to cramp and to deaden.

I believe that the school, as an institution, should simplify existing social life; should reduce it, as it were, to an embryonic form. Existing life is so complex that the child cannot be brought into contact with it without either confusion or distraction; he is either overwhelmed by multiplicity of activities which are going on, so that he loses his own power *of orderly reaction*, or he is so stimulated by these various activities that his powers are prematurely called into play and he becomes either *unduly specialized* or else disintegrated.

I believe that, as such simplified social life, the school life should grow gradually *out of the home life*; that it should take up and continue the activities with which the child is already familiar in the home.

I believe that it should exhibit these activities to the child, and reproduce them in such ways that the child will gradually learn the meaning of them, and be capable of playing his own part in relation to them.

I believe that this is a psychological necessity, because it is the only way of securing continuity in the child's growth, *the only way of giving a background of past experience to the new ideas given in school.*

I believe it is also a social necessity because *the home is the form of social life in which the child has been nurtured and in connection with which he has had his moral training.* It is the business of the school to deepen and extend his sense of the values bound up in his home life.

Almost sounds like Dewey wants to continue or further the teachings of the child's family morals and nurturing from home in school right? Keep reading:

> I believe that much of present education fails because it neglects this fundamental principle of the school as a form of community life. It conceives the school as a place where certain information is to be given, where certain lessons are to be learned, or where certain habits are to be formed. The value of these is conceived as lying largely in the remote future; the child must do these things for the sake of something else he is to do; *they are mere preparation.* As a result they do not become a part of the life experience of the child and so are not truly educative.

The learning of facts and figures as a foundation of what's needed to become a successful productive member of a free society fails because it's nothing but "mere preparation" for individuals that does "not become a part of the life experience of the child and so are not truly educative."

> I believe that *moral education* centres about this conception of the school as a mode of social life, that *the best and deepest moral training is precisely that which one gets through having to enter into proper relations with others in a unity of work and thought*. The present educational systems, so far as they destroy or neglect this unity, render it difficult or impossible to get any genuine, *regular moral training*.
>
> I believe that *the child should be* stimulated and *controlled* in his work *through the life of the community* (emphasis added).

After a classic progressive end around, "beat around the bush" eluding of the truth, it finally comes out that it is *not* the morality of home and family that should be furthered in school at all, but to the contrary, "the best and deepest moral training is precisely that which one gets through having to enter into proper relations with others *in a unity of work and thought*"—that is, "controlled in his work through the life of the community"! Note that our "moral training" is to no longer freely originate from our faith, God, or scripture but is now to be learned "through having to enter into proper relations with others in a unity of work and thought." Or as it is to be under Comte's positive order, "Humanity, the 'Great Being', takes the place of God and is the basis of all morality."

I believe that under existing conditions far too much of the stimulus and control proceeds from the teacher, because of neglect of the idea of the school as a form of social life.

I believe that the teacher's place and work in the school is to be interpreted from this same basis. The teacher is not in the school to impose certain ideas or to form certain habits in the child, but is there as a member of the community *to select the influences which shall affect the child and to assist him in properly responding to these influences.*

I believe that the discipline of the school should proceed from the life of the school as a whole and not directly from the teacher.

I believe that the teacher's business is simply to determine on the basis of larger experience and riper wisdom, how *the discipline of life* shall come to the child.

I believe that all questions of the grading of the child and his promotion should be determined by reference to the same standard. "*Examinations are of use only so far as they test the child's fitness for social life and reveal the place in which he can be of most service and where he can receive the most help.*" (emphasis added)

Dewey's "I believe that the discipline of the school should proceed from the life of the school as a whole and not directly from the teacher" further illustrates my earlier observation that in collective education, the teacher is only the conduit through which the now centralized education flows. And under such centralized education as Common Core, he or she shall not be allowed to serve any other purpose!

Examinations that "should be determined by reference to the same standard" and "are of use only so far as they test the child's fitness for social life and reveal the place in which he can be of most service" brings a fuller understanding to the concept of "teaching to the test," even more so when you learn what the "social" purpose of these tests is—to "reveal the place in which he can be of most service." Now, to help dial in what all this means in a fuller "social" context, remember Comte's division of labor, where man is

> *bound together by the very distribution of their occupations*; and it is this distribution which causes the extent and growing complexity *of the social organism.*
>
> The social organization tends more and more to rest on *an exact estimate of individual diversities,* by so distributing employments *as to appoint each one to the destination he is most fit for,* from his own nature… from his education and his position, and, in short, from all his qualifications; so that all individual organizations, even the most vicious and imperfect…may finally be made use of for the general good.[21] (Coser 1977, pp. 10–12; emphasis added]

And remember Huxley from his 1946 United Nations UNESCO regarding this same subject:

> *Human beings are not equal in respect of various desirable qualities.* Some are strong, others weak; some healthy, others chronic inva-

> lids; some long-lived, others short-lived; some bright, others dull; some of high, others of low intelligence; some mathematically gifted, others very much the reverse; some kind and good, others cruel and selfish. It is usually not so easy to say *how much of this second sort of inequality is due to heredity and therefore relevant for our purpose.* (p. 19)
>
> *Already considerable progress has been made, though largely on an empirical basis as yet, in fitting the right man to the right job....*
>
> This has quite other implications; for, whereas variety is in itself desirable, the existence of weaklings, fools, and moral deficients cannot but be bad. It is also much harder to reconcile politically with the current democratic doctrine of equality. In face of it, indeed, the principle of equality of opportunity must be amended to read *"equality of opportunity within the limits of aptitude."*[20] (p. 20, emphasis added)

As Comte and Huxley give larger meaning to each other, here they together give larger meaning and context to Dewey. And remember what Huxley then tells us that brings us at once to an even fuller context of the role that this "biological inequality" plays within this progressive "division of labor" and how it is to be regulated:

> Biological inequality is, of course, the bedrock fact on which all of eugenics is predicated.[20]

Point is, none of this is anything new! And as we have just seen, nothing of the Philosophy is stand-alone. All of what comes out of any one strand also has a larger meaning that ties in with the objective of all the other strands of *the web*. Here, what Dewey says about education ties in perfectly with Comte's "directed" science, sociology, and order; which ties in with Huxley's environmentalism and eugenics; which ties in with Al Gore's global warming and Malthusian principles of population control; which ties in with Fabian Socialist moral and sexual depravity; which ties in with Sanger, feminism, and abortion; which ties in with Marx, Lenin, and unions; which ties in with nationalism, communism, anticolonialism, humanism, globalism, sustainability, Alinsky, social justice, and the welfare state; which all tie in with Obama's fundamental transformation of America, and so on. Like spokes, they all emanate from the center of the same wheel that happens to be running us all over! *All* of what comes out of the Philosophy is part of the great deception! As I said at the very beginning of this work, it is all one homogenous effort to accomplish one thing: destroy the hated three-headed Hydra of God, family, and property, along with the independent self-sufficiency of the individualism they enable!

Under such a philosophy, who is to determine who's right for what job? As we learned in chapter 2—the planners! How might such assigned jobs be distributed equally? Again, the planners! How high of an aptitude might a student expect to build for himself or herself within such an education system we have just learned is "not a preparation for future living" but one that is not teaching him or her their "proper relations with others in a unity of work and thought" and actively rejects their dignity as individuals as well? With the reins of a shared collective society snuggly in the hands of progressive planners, all those planners have to do is "nudge" society toward their planned direction, and their socially trained students will comply without so much as a second thought—like Gramsci says, with "spontaneous consent"!

ARTICLE THREE. THE SUBJECT-MATTER OF EDUCATION

I believe that the social life of the child is the basis of concentration, or correlation, in all his training or growth. The *social life gives the unconscious unity* and the background of all his efforts and of all his attainments.

I believe that the subject-matter of the school curriculum should mark a gradual differentiation out of the primitive unconscious unity of social life.

I believe that we violate the child's nature and render difficult the best ethical results, by introducing the child too abruptly to a number of special studies, of reading, writing, geography, etc., out of relation to this social life.

I believe, therefore, that *the true centre of correlation of the school subjects is not science, nor literature, nor history, nor geography, but the child's own social activities.*

I believe that education cannot be unified in the study of science, or so-called nature study, because apart from human activity, nature itself is not a unity; nature in itself is a number of diverse objects in space and time, and to attempt to make it the centre of work by itself, is to introduce a principle of radiation rather than one of concentration.

I believe that *literature* is the reflex expression and interpretation of social experience; that hence it must follow upon and not precede such experience. It, therefore, *cannot be made the basis*, although it may be made the summary of unification.

I believe once more that *history* is of educative value in so far as it presents phases of social life and growth. It *must be controlled by reference to social life*. When taken simply as history it is thrown into the distant past and becomes dead and inert. Taken *as the record of man's social life and progress* it becomes full of meaning. I believe, however, that it cannot be so taken excepting as the child is also introduced directly into social life.

I believe accordingly that the primary basis of education is in the child's powers at work along the same general constructive lines as those which have brought civilization into being.

I believe that the only way to make the child conscious of his social heritage is to enable him to perform those fundamental types of activity which makes civilization what it is.

I believe, therefore, in the so-called expressive or constructive activities as the centre of correlation.

I believe that this gives the standard for the place of *cooking, sewing, manual training, etc.*, in the school.

I believe that they are not special studies which are to be introduced over and above a lot of others in the way of relaxation or relief, or as additional accomplishments. I believe rather that they *represent*, as types, fundamental forms of *social activity*; and that it is possible and desirable that the child's introduction into the more formal subjects of the curriculum be through the medium of these activities.

I believe that the study *of science is educational in so far as it brings out the materials and processes which make social life what it is.*

"I believe that *one of the greatest difficulties in the present teaching of science is that the material is presented in purely objective form*, or is treated as a new peculiar kind of experience which the child can add to that which he has already had. In reality, *science is of value because it gives the ability to interpret and control the experience* already had. It should be introduced, not as so much new subject-matter, but as showing the factors already involved *in previous experience* and as furnishing tools *by which that experience can be more easily and effectively regulated*" (emphasis added).

The greatest "difficulty" in teaching science is that "the material is presented in purely objective form"? If it isn't objective and presented without prejudice or influence, then how is it science? Remember this from Comte's "queen" of all the sciences—sociology:

> No real observation of any kind of phenomena is possible, except in as far as it is first directed.[22]

And remember Comte's "positive" sociology is the "ultimate synthesizing science," which "determines each science's contribution" necessary to form the "knowledge...which will enable man to reorganize" and transform society from a free society into a collective society where "social planning" is "indeed required." It's not by happenstance that Dewey wants our children's education to be "directed"!

> I believe that at present we lose much of the value of literature and language studies *because of our elimination of the social element.* Language is almost always treated in the books of pedagogy simply as the expression of thought. It is true that *language* is a logical instrument, but it *is fundamentally and primarily a social instrument.* Language is the device for communication; it is the tool through which one individual comes to share the ideas and feelings of others. *When treated simply as a way of getting individual information,* or as a means of showing off what one has learned, *it loses its social motive and end* (emphasis added).

To ascertain the meaning of text, one reads the contents of literature. It is how the author expresses his or her "meaning of thought" to the reader. It is how "one individual comes to share the ideas and feelings of others." However, "[w]hen treated simply as a way of getting individual information," the meaning of text "loses its social motive and end." "Social motive" can only happen when the process is completely reversed; and it is the reader who, by hijacking the author's work, nefariously forges (in both senses of the word) their own "thought of meaning" into it. Remember Supreme Court justice William J. Brennan's on this very subject:

When Justices interpret the Constitution *they speak for their community, not for themselves alone.* The act of interpretation must be undertaken with full consciousness that it is, in a very real sense, *the community's interpretation that is sought....*

We current Justices read the Constitution in the only way that we can: as Twentieth Century Americans. We look to the history of the time of framing and to the intervening history of interpretation. But the ultimate question must be, *what do the words of the text mean in our time.* For the genius of the Constitution rests not in any static meaning it *might have had in a world that is dead and gone, but in the adaptability* of its great *principles to cope with current problems and current needs*[23] (emphasis mine).

Where Brennan sees absolutely no value in the literature or original intent of text of the Constitution but only in "the community's interpretation" of it, there is a clarification of Dewey's "We lose much of the value of literature and language" by "our elimination of the social element." As a progressively reinterpretable text, the Constitution itself can be reinterpreted as *the* means to its very own end. Where the text is to be understood through an ever-evolving "diversity" of reinterpretations, the words of its authors eventually become meaningless as to allow *the reader to give their own meaning to them according to his or her perspective* (relative, of course, to the perspective of their particular faction—be it race, social class, culture, religion, gender, or sexual orientation, etc.). Case in point: then appeals court judge Sonia Sotomayor said this in her 2001 lecture "A Latina Judge's Voice" at Berkley:

> *Whether born from experience or inherent physiological or cultural differences…our gender and national origins may and will make a difference in our judging.* Justice O'Connor has often been cited as saying that a wise old man and wise old woman will reach the same conclusion in deciding cases…*I would hope that a wise Latina woman with the richness of her experiences would more often than not reach a better conclusion than a white male who hasn't lived that life*[24] (emphasis added).

Such are the "diversities" she has stated need to be more present on the Supreme Court. As a Supreme Court justice, will she "ascertain the meaning" of the words our founders chose specifically to write the Constitution and "secure" our Liberty in order to come to unbiased conclusions consistent with its "original intent"? Or will she breathe her own meaning into it relative to her perspective as a "wise Latina woman" in order to "reach *a better conclusion* than a white male who hasn't lived that life"?

There is a reason Dewey is seeking to officially institute the progressive science of relativism as an official part of our children's education. With relativism, the enemies of our freedom and Liberty do not have to so much as change a word of the Constitution that preserves them. They only need to change the meaning of the words our founders used into meanings that dissolve it! So it is that via relativism, by their very own quills, our founders themselves will have penned the end of their own legacy—Liberty!

> I believe that there is, therefore, no succession of studies in the ideal school curriculum. If education is life, all life has, from the outset,

a scientific aspect; an aspect of art and culture and an aspect of communication. It cannot, therefore, be true that the proper studies for one grade are mere reading and writing, and that at a later grade, reading, or literature, or science, may be introduced. *The progress is not in the succession of studies but in the development of new attitudes towards, and new interests in, experience.*

I believe finally, that education must be conceived as a continuing reconstruction of experience; *that the process and the goal of education are one and the same thing.*

I believe that to set up any end *outside of education*, as furnishing its goal and standard, is to deprive the educational process of much of its meaning and tends to make us rely upon false and external stimuli in dealing with the child" (emphasis added).

Any *individual* "end outside of" Dewey's collective social education will "deprive the educational process of much of its" collective "meaning."

ARTICLE FOUR. THE NATURE OF METHOD

3. I believe that *interests are the signs and symptoms of growing power*. I believe that they represent dawning capacities. Accordingly the constant and careful observation of interests is of the utmost importance for the educator.

I believe that these interests are to be observed as showing the state of development which the child has reached.

I believe that the prophesy the stage upon which he is about to enter.

I believe that only through the continual and sympathetic observation of childhood's interests can the adult enter into the child's life and see what it is ready for, and upon what material it could work most readily and fruitfully.

I believe that these *interests are neither to be humored nor repressed*. To repress interest is to substitute the adult for the child, and so to weaken intellectual curiosity and alertness, to suppress initiative, and to deaden interest. *To humor the interests is to substitute the transient for the permanent.* The *interest is always the sign of some power* below; the important thing is to discover this power. *To humor the interest is to fail to penetrate below the surface and its sure result is to substitute caprice and whim for genuine interest* (emphasis added).

Remember, "to humor the interests is to substitute the transient for the permanent." The interests of the child or student means nothing to the collective state other than to decipher where that person fits into their predetermined planned collective society. The capacity to which the child can fill their appointed purpose is what's permanent, not the person's personal interests. It is what determines their "social value."

4. I believe that the emotions are the reflex of actions.

I believe that to endeavor to stimulate or arouse the emotions *apart from their correspond-*

> *ing activities*, is to introduce an unhealthy and morbid state of mind.
>
> *I believe that if we can only secure right habits of action and thought, with reference to the good, the true, and the beautiful, the emotions will for the most part take care of themselves.*
>
> I believe that next to deadness and dullness, formalism and routine, *our education is threatened with no greater evil than sentimentalism.*
>
> I believe that this sentimentalism is the necessary result of the attempt to divorce feeling from action (emphasis added).

What greater "evils" could there be to a progressive collective socialist than an armed and ready, rugged individualism rooted in the "sentimentalism" of family, traditions, and honor? And what, if anything, has all the progressive race and/or class-based chaos at a number of political rallies as of late been if not "actions" constituting "reflex of emotions"?

> ARTICLE FIVE. THE SCHOOL AND SOCIAL PROGRESS
>
> I believe that *education is the fundamental method of social progress and reform.*
>
> I believe that all reforms which rest simply upon the enactment of law, or the threatening of certain penalties, or upon changes in mechanical or outward arrangements, are transitory and futile.
>
> I believe that *education is a regulation of the process of coming to share in the social consciousness*; and that the *adjustment of individual activity on the basis of this social consciousness is the*

> *only sure method of social reconstruction* (emphasis added).

Just in case, Dewey's "education is the fundamental method of social progress and reform" isn't evidence enough for you that his progressive education system serves only *the* revolutionary progressive "progress" toward a new collective "social consciousness" of "order," he immediately backs it up with "the adjustment of individual activity on the basis of this social consciousness is the only sure method of social reconstruction." As we know, a social reconstruction in America *cannot* happen without a complete social deconstruction/destruction of our existing society. By definition then, Dewey's progressive education is nothing short of a revolutionary effort to undermine the whole of our Constitutional republic so he can reconstruct it as collectivist.

> I believe that this conception has due regard for both the individualistic and *socialistic ideals. It is duly individual because it recognizes the formation of a certain character as the only genuine basis of right living. It is socialistic because it recognizes that this right character is not to be formed by merely individual precept, example, or exhortation, but rather by the influence of a certain form of institutional or community life upon the individual, and that the social organism through the school, as its organ, may determine ethical results* (emphasis added).

There is nothing "individual" about being educated, trained, and employed specifically for the advancement of others! It is *not* some new freedom—it's slavery!

And once again, we see Comte's "social organism" raising its collective head along with Hobbes's "artificial anima" that make up the "body politic" to remind us once again of our meaninglessness as individuals.

> I believe that in the ideal school we have the reconciliation of the individualistic and the institutional ideals.
>
> I believe that the community's duty to education is, therefore, its paramount moral duty. By law and punishment, by social agitation and discussion, society can regulate and form itself in a more or less haphazard and chance way. *But through education society can formulate its own purposes, can organize its own means and resources, and thus shape itself with definiteness and economy in the direction in which it wishes to move* (emphasis added).

Where the ongoing confrontations on the street between law enforcement and the "social agitation" of progressive revolutionaries is chaotic and unpredictable, a steady state-sponsored stream of pre-organized, preconformed "intellectuals" is controlled "progress."

> I believe that when *society once recognizes the possibilities in this direction, and the obligations* which these possibilities impose, *it is impossible to conceive of the resources of time, attention, and money which will be put at the disposal of the educator.*
>
> I believe it is the business of every one interested in education to *insist upon the school*

as the primary and most effective instrument of social progress and reform in order that society may be awakened to realize what the school stands for, and aroused to *the necessity of endowing the educator with sufficient equipment properly to perform his task.*

I believe that education thus conceived marks the most perfect and intimate union of science and art conceivable in human experience.

I believe that the *art of thus giving shape to human powers and adapting them to social service, is the supreme art*; one calling into its service the best of artists; that *no insight, sympathy, tact, executive power is too great for such service.*

I believe that with the growth of *psychological science*, giving added insight into *individual structure* and laws of growth; and *with growth of social science, adding to our knowledge of the right organization of individuals,* all scientific resources can be utilized for the purposes of education.

I believe that when science and art thus join hands the most commanding motive for human action will be reached; the most genuine springs of human conduct aroused and the best service that human nature is capable of guaranteed.

I believe, finally, that the teacher is engaged, not simply in the training of individuals, but *in the formation of the proper social life* (emphasis added).

Where Dewey says here, "In the forming of the proper social life" and "adapting" our children to progressive "social service," our public schools are "the *primary and most effective instrument.*" "*[W]hen society once recognizes the possibilities in this direction, and the obligations which these possibilities impose, it is impossible to conceive of the resources of time, attention, and money which will be put at the disposal of the educator.*" Melissa Harris-Perry clarifies from a progressive standpoint why America has yet to invest enough "money" into public education in her 2013 MSNBC promo, saying,

> We have *never invested as much in public education as we should have because we've always had kind of a private notion of children.* Your kid is yours and totally your responsibility. We haven't had a very *collective* notion of *these are our children.* So part of it is we have to *break through our kind of private idea that kids belong to their parents or kids belong to their families* and *recognize that kids belong to whole communities. Once its everybody's responsibility and not just the household's, then we start making better investments*[25]

(emphasis added).

The hope here is that Harris-Perry is right, not in the collective sense but in the old-fashioned individual American sense that collectivists such as her, Dewey, and Gramsci might not have accounted for: our tenacious, deep-rooted moral and traditional sense of value and dignity that can only be obtained through the *private* tenets of our uniquely American identity forged in rugged individualism. It is what most frustrates the "progress" of progressive order!

Dewey closes:

> I believe that *every teacher* should realize the dignity of his calling; *that he is a social servant set apart for the maintenance of proper social order and the securing of the right social growth.*
>
> I believe that in this way *the teacher always is the prophet of the true God and the usherer in of the true kingdom of God*[26] (all emphasis added).

The next time you send your kids off to school, remember what the "father" of our current progressive public education system has set forth unto this very day: "*every teacher... is a social servant set apart for the maintenance of proper social order and the securing of the right social growth.*" And as such, all but those who have consciously refused the Kool-Aid or have knowingly and steadfastly impugned the progressive collective doctrine as a whole will not and cannot have the best interest of your children in mind, for they have been "directed" to have the best interest of Dewey's planned utopia at heart and to *always* be "*the prophet of the true God and the usherer in of the true kingdom of God.*"

As we know, teachers cannot usher in "the true kingdom of God" anywhere other than here on earth. So does this make the other "kingdom of God"—you know, the one Jesus Himself tells us in John 18:36 "is not of this world"—the false one?

This comes from the same John Dewey who would come to chair the Dewey Commission, otherwise referred to as the *Committee for the Defense of Leon Trotsky*. Trotsky, along with Lenin, was part of the brutal Bolshevik Revolution in Russia. Dewey also served as president of the League for Industrial Democracy, the American spin-off of the Fabian Socialist Society.

Parental rights are fundamental to a free people! As we know, destruction of the family, as part of Owens's three-headed Hydra, is key to the success of such progressive "order." And as a matter of deductive reasoning and common sense, we know that the destruction of our natural parental rights is the destruction of family! This effort is universal in revolutionary progressive collectivism and has relevance to contemporary politics, specifically gay marriage. There is an argument to be made that gays stand to lose just as much as anybody in the legal state recognition of gay marriage. In short, being that the fundamental argument for gay marriage is "equal protection under the law" for gay parents, it must be considered that it is actually *the* push for this recognition that is putting the natural parental rights of both traditional and gay parents at risk.

Let's think it through. Being that gays *cannot* be natural parents, the only parental rights they can possibly have are civil, coming from government. The children of a "legally recognized" gay marriage must therefore be adopted by at least one, if not both, gay parents through the state, under conditions dictated by the state. Such children are then of the state and, as Harris-Perry advocates, a collective responsibility. "Legally recognized" gay parents would then be under contract with the state to meet state criteria with their state-issued and therefore limited "civil rights" to care for the collective's children. The bigger problem comes into play with the "equal protection" clause of such legislation. Once such limited civil parental rights of gay parents is legally recognized, the individual natural parental rights of natural parents are at once "unfairly" superior and therefore unequal. The "equalization" would then be in the immediate loss of any and all God-given natural parental rights for all parents, be they gay or traditional. But such are the temptations of the great deception.

All that encompasses the efforts of the Philosophy in its great deception—be it in the loss of our physical Individual Liberty, the "directed" state of our "educated" mind, or the assault on our spiritual well-being—can be witnessed firsthand in one specific case of today's "legal" *progress to order*.

That case is the Romeike case. The "legal" findings in this case could very well determine if the *fundamental transformation of America* is at last complete. It could very well establish "legally" as to whether our individualism, our spirituality, independence, and the sentimentalisms of family, faith, tradition, and heritage represent a healthy and strong free America—or the threat of potential adverse "parallel societies" to be "stamped out" by the supreme sovereign and its planners. Remember Hobbes telling us that in a commonwealth, or collective, or a "we're all in this together" progressive society:

> [I]t is annexed to the Soveraignty, to be Judge of what Opinions and Doctrines are averse, and what are fit to be conducing to Peace; and consequently, on what occasions, how farre, and what, men are to be trusted with all, them in speaking to Multitudes of people; and who shall examine the Doctrines of all bookes before they be published. *For the Actions of men proceed from their Opinions*; and in the wel governing of Opinions.[27] (p. 137, emphasis added)

Is it to continue to be recognized that it is our unalienable natural parental right to love, raise, nurture, and educate our children, prepare them to follow their own individuality in the pursuit of their own happiness toward a greater independence, to have faith in God above, and to give thanks to Him from whom *all* our Liberty to do so has been endowed? Or are our children to be wards of the state "that Mortall God, to which wee owe under the Immortall God, our peace and defence"?

On May 14, 2013, a decision was reached in the circuit courts to determine if the Romeike family, who, for religious reasons, came to America from Germany where it is *not* allowed to homeschool your children so that they could raise and educate their children in the sanctity of their own God-fearing spiritual home. Let us look at how the decision to deny them that individual right here was reached:

> SUTTON, Circuit Judge. Uwe and Hannelore Romeike have five children, ages twelve, eleven, nine, seven and two, at least at the time this dispute began. Rather than send their children to the local public schools, they would prefer to teach them at home, *largely for religious reasons*. The powers that be *refused to let them do so* and prosecuted them for truancy when they disobeyed *orders* to return the children to school.
>
> *Had the Romeikes lived in America at the time*, they would have had a lot of legal authority to work with in countering the prosecution (emphasis added).

We have it here that it was known that there wouldn't be any problem or case here if there were no "religious reasons" behind the Romeike's decision to homeschool. Note that *the* deciding fact of this decision may very well hinge on this one fact: "had they lived in America *at the time*."

> *But the Romeikes lived in Germany when this dispute began.* When the Romeikes became fed up with Germany's *ban on homeschooling* and when their prosecution for failure to follow the law led to increasingly burdensome fines, they came to this country with the hope of obtaining asylum. Congress *might have* written the immi-

gration laws to grant a safe haven to people living elsewhere in the world who face government strictures that the United States Constitution prohibits. *But it did not.* The relevant legislation applies only to those who have a "well-founded fear of persecution on account of race, religion, nationality, membership in a particular social group, or political opinion." *There is a difference between the persecution of a discrete group and the prosecution of those who violate a generally applicable law.* As the Board of Immigration Appeals permissibly found, the German authorities have not singled out the Romeikes in particular or homeschoolers in general for persecution. As a result, we must deny the Romeikes' petition for review and, with it, their applications for asylum (emphasis added).

With the official legal determination here that "there is a difference between the persecution of a discrete group and the prosecution of those who violate a generally applicable law," we are left to question if a "generally applicable" law is all it takes to skirt the charge of religious persecution? If so, why not pass or "deemed passed" a law that makes it illegal for anybody and everybody to homeschool and raise their children with their own identity, traditions, sentiment, and beliefs? Why not just pass a "general law" decreeing the likes of Judaism, Christianity, or for that matter, a belief in God—period—a national crime of "usurpation" so such "persecution" would be impossible?

German law requires all children to attend public or state-approved private schools. The

Romeikes *feared that the public school curriculum would "influence [their children] against Christian values."* When the parents chose to homeschool their children, the government imposed fines for each unexcused absence. When the fines did not bring the Romeikes in line, *the police went to the Romeikes' house and escorted the children to school.* That strategy worked—once. The next time, four adults and seven children from the Romeikes' homeschooling support group intervened, and the police, reluctant to use force, left the premises without the children.

The school district returned to a strategy of imposing fines *rather than force.* It prosecuted the Romeikes for, and a court found them guilty of, violating the compulsory attendance law, leading to still more fines. The prosecution and the mounting fines were the last straws, and the family moved to the United States in 2008. At the time of their departure, *they owed the government 7,000 euros or roughly $9,000.*

The Romeikes entered the United States through a visa waiver program. Uwe *applied for asylum*, and his wife and five children sought relief as derivative applicants.

An immigration judge approved the *applications after finding that the Romeikes had a well-founded fear of persecution* based on their membership in a "particular social group": homeschoolers. *The Board of Immigration Appeals overturned the immigration judge's decision.* It explained that "[t]he record does not show that the compulsory school attendance law is *selectively applied* to homeschoolers like the applicants." ID 5

It added that *homeschoolers were not punished more severely than other parents whose children broke the law.* It concluded *by reasoning* that, *even if* the German government had singled out people like the Romeikes, *"homeschoolers" are not protected* by the immigration laws because they "lack the social visibility" and "particularity required to be a cognizable social group." ID 7

To obtain asylum, *an individual must prove that he cannot return to his native country because of a "well-founded fear of persecution on account of race, religion, nationality, membership in a particular social group, or political opinion."* In trying to meet this requirement, the Romeikes have not claimed on appeal that the German government has persecuted them in the past; they claim that the government *will persecute them in the future if they return.*

When it comes to showing that a foreign country's enforcement of a law will persecute individuals on the basis of religion, membership in a social group or for that matter any other protected ground, *there is an easy way and a hard way*. The easy way is available when the foreign government enforces a law that persecutes on its face along one of these lines. *Then there is the hard way—showing persecution through the enforcement of a generally applicable law.* "[W]

> here the law that the native country seeks to enforce in its criminal prosecution is '*generally applicable*,'" that usually will be *the antithesis of persecution. One normally does not think of government officials persecuting their citizens when they enforce a law that applies equally to everyone*, including the allegedly persecuted group and the officials themselves. That is why, generally speaking, "[p]unishment for violation of a generally applicable criminal law *is not persecution.*" *Enforcement of a neutral law usually is incompatible with persecution* (emphasis added).

It cannot be put any clearer that, indeed, no "general" law can be considered by the courts to be persecution!

> The parents of "school skippers," truant students who do not show up for school, face civil fines as well. If the parents fail to convince their children to go to school, the government places them in alternative learning programs or special schools for truants.
> *This enforcement of the law has nothing to do with homeschooling*, whether for faithbased or secular reasons. For better or worse, *Germany punishes any and all parents who fail to comply* with the school-attendance law, no matter the reasons they provide (emphasis added).

Where all are to be equally denied their Individual Right or, for that matter, denied the whole of their Individual Liberty, and all who are found to be in violation are to be equally "punished," it could *not* be considered persecution! No matter what right you say you have, if they pass and enforce a national law against it, *is it not persecution*! Remember, this is no longer just progressive collectivist philosophy being espoused here; it's a *binding* legal decision being handed down by American judges in an American court!

> On the rare occasions when the government grants an exemption, the government often sends teachers into the children's homes, *showing that the parents alone are not responsible for their children's educations*. Any exemptions thus are granted as a last resort, and even then *only* when *state-approved* schooling would necessarily require the "separation of the children from their parents (emphasis added).

Is "showing that the parents alone are not responsible for their children's educations" supposed to be comforting? The ramifications of this alone, depending upon "interpretation," could be devastating to all parental rights. Where the state is "responsible" or coresponsible, then they are "responsible" to insure parental compliance to that state responsibility, leaving the only parental responsibility *the* responsibility to comply with the state's responsibility, which is to ensure parental compliance with *the* general will of the collective!

> The judge *never said* that Germany enacted this law based on animus toward faith-based homeschoolers or homeschoolers in general. Nothing in the record, indeed, suggests that such groups *existed in 1938*. For another, the record does not include the language of the original law, the history that led to its adop-

tion or any *contemporary understanding* of what motivated it, if indeed that could be identified with respect to a law supported by different legislators *with different perspectives*. For still another reason, the only "finding" the immigration judge made—*that the law showed an "intolerant" effort to "stamp out" "parallel societies" that might arise if parents could teach their children at home*—sets sail at such a high level of generality as to add little to the case. *Any compulsory-attendance law could be said to have this effect*. But that *does not prove that this law, then or now, targets faith-based homeschoolers in general or the Romeikes in particular. If, as the Romeikes claim, the law emerged from the Nazi era*, that would understandably make anyone, including the Romeikes, skeptical of the policy underlying it. *But such a history would not by itself doom the law*. The claimants still must show that enforcement of the law amounts to persecution under the immigration laws. They have not done so (emphasis added).

For this judge to make a determination here based on the *assumption* that home-schools or Christian homeschoolers didn't exist in 1938 is a perplexing legal observation that either wholly ignores or sympathizes with actual Nazi history! For one, to determine homeschooling or any nongovernmental education didn't exist in 1938 would be tantamount to determining that it never did! Did public schools always exist before there were home-schools? Such a statement "sets sail at such a high level of generality as to add little" to intelligent conversation. However, even if they didn't exist in *the* year of 1938, the year the law was apparently passed, does *that*, in and of itself, *nullify* any *legal* acknowledgment of natural parental rights being infringed? If so, what are we to learn from it? That once a "general law" has officially extinguished any such outlawed "parallel society" of, say, individualism, Christianity, Judaism, or homeschoolers—then *the* year *that* happens marks *the* time from which no future persons having inclination to be of a Jewish or Christian belief and wanting to instill that belief unto their children could *never ever* again claim "persecution" because that particular belief or ideology had already been previously extinguished and, therefore, legally didn't exist?

The determination here that it was "never said that Germany enacted this law based on animus toward faith-based homeschoolers" is a determination that any persecution or oppression of any kind to be legally recognized as such *must* be *the* documented direct result of a law *officially* "said" to have been "based on animus toward" *the* specific persecution or oppression being claimed? In the "relative" realm of progressive courts, how is it even possible to prove that? Where's the justice in that? Did the Nazi ovens exist, or was it disclosed that they were *the* specified end of the first Nazi laws marginalizing and disarming the Jews when those laws were first passed? Hell no! Yet if it were not for those very laws, the Holocaust and the use of those ovens may never have been enabled.

"Any compulsory attendance law could be said to have the same effect"? Really? For a state to have laws mandating an education is one thing. But to then add to that the mandate that the state (Nazi) is *the* only recognized and lawful provider of that mandated education can be nothing but state ownership of not only what defines education but of every student forced to submit to it! Where would Indian nations, the Amish, or the Mennonites fit into such a totalitarian state?

The disregard here for history, Nazi history, and the history that is *the* documented horror of the National Socialist Movement in Germany epitomizes gross negligence. As the judge here says, under any ruling of his, "such a history would not by itself doom the law."

> To a similar end, the Romeikes complain that Germany's compulsory-attendance law violates their fundamental rights and various international standards and thus constitutes persecution regardless of whether it is selectively enforced. Each argument shares an Achilles' heel: Asylum provides refuge to individuals persecuted on account of a protected ground. The United States has not opened its doors to every victim of unfair treatment, even treatment that our laws do not allow. That the United States Constitution protects the rights of "parents and guardians to direct the upbringing and education of children *under their control*," *does not mean that a contrary law in another country establishes persecution on religious or any other protected ground* (emphasis added).

Where America has opened not only her doors but her pocketbook as well to provide jobs, welfare, social services, health care, and over four billion dollars annually[28] in uninvestigated (un)earned income tax credits—as well as creating sanctuary cities, counties, and states—for some eleven to thirty million plus *illegal* aliens,[29] are we here being told that this one family here legally seeking not but a sanctuary to exercise the constitutionally protected Individual and Natural Parental Right to raise and educate their children in the nurturing God-fearing environment of their own home has no recognized legal ground left to stand on, not even here in the "land of the free"?

The Constitution does *not* give us our natural Individual Rights! It is *not* a positive charter! It only secures the sanctuary in which we are to be free to exercise them. As our Individual Liberty is natural and God-given and we are all God's children, how is it that our limited government has ordained itself the power to deny any of God's children, regardless of origin, the Liberty they have specifically *and* legally come here to America to enjoy? How many times have we been told that illegal aliens who are here have all kinds of "rights"? Bottom line is, it is none other than American "justice" that here stands to deny these parents, *while they stand on American soil*, their Natural parental Rights.

> And even if, as the Romeikes claim, several *human-rights* treaties joined by Germany *give parents the right* to make decisions about their children's educations, see, e.g., International Covenant on Civil and Political Rights that by itself does not require the granting of an American asylum application (emphasis added).

Where we are forced to rely upon or invoke the collective "civil rights" of globalism's "human rights" as *the* protector of our Individual Liberty, we have been forced to invoke their very antithesis! When such is necessary to save our Liberty, our Liberty is already gone! Note that this judge is saying "*human-rights treaties…give parents the right* to make decisions." As human rights are positive collective rights in the progressive collectivist sense, Judge Sutton is exactly correct! As in a progressive collectivist society, the only rights we are allowed to have are the civil/human ones government issues to us. So recognize thee, thou collectivist, thy "mortal God"!

Again, our parental rights, along with all that is our natural Individual Liberty, are *not* given, allowed, or rationed to us by any state or any collective; but as recognized by the Declaration of Independence, they are endowed by our Creator and therefore unalienable! Our American government, under the Constitution, was established to preserve that Liberty! With or without any bill of rights—no government, no state, or no collective has ever been ordained the power to deny or infringe upon the Individual Liberty of anyone who has lawfully come to America seeking in good faith to exercise it in the free pursuit of their happiness!

> ROGERS, J., concurring. I join the majority opinion.
>
> At one point in the petitioners' brief, they assert that "the sole question before this Court is whether Germany is violating binding norms of international law through its treatment of homeschoolers." Our role, however, is not that of an international court adjudicating Germany's obligations to other countries in respect of its own citizens. Instead we sit as a court of the United States, enforcing statutes that implement some of the international obligations of the United States to other countries in respect of asylum applicants. As explained by the majority opinion, those obligations are fully met in this case.[30]

Under what "international obligations" has our limited government forsaken its ordained purpose to "secure the Blessings of Liberty"? From our perspective as a free and independent nation, it's impossible. No international obligation could ever overrule our

Constitution, and therefore, *no* aspect of our Individual Liberty preserved therein. However, for those who hold to globalist-progressive/collectivist philosophy, *no* national constitution, Individual Right, or law can ever override global or "international obligations"—as compliance to the central plan of the global collective of the "human organism" is what's both necessary and supreme!

An important sidenote here on the subject of government-issued "civil rights" versus God-given Individual Rights: Yes, our founders such as James Madison spoke of civil rights. But the mistake being made by so many today in confusing these *civil rights* with Individual Rights was not one of Madison's. In no way is this work meant to discount James Madison or any of our founders' references to civil rights. Nor is it meant to demean the work of those such as Martin Luther King Jr. It is no more and no less than *the* intent of this work to expose the progressive collectivist lie, which includes *civil rights*—period—that we might recognize them as the false promise and actual *anti-Individual Right* that they are! As civil rights are of civil origin, of *the* "mortal God" government, and per its civil planners, they are positive, collective, limited, rationed, and therefore, *conditional*.

They are, in reality, *the* antithesis of our God-given and natural Individual Rights and Liberty! There is no understating such a revelation. Was Madison asking for more government-issued civil liberties, or was he demanding civil recognition of his God-given Individual Liberty? The same could be asked of MLK. Was his struggle one of requesting government permission for larger rations of collective rights? Or was it one of demanding *the* already established constitutional obligation of government to recognize his natural, God-given Individual Liberty? I'm not really sure, but if it was the latter, then his objective stands as the same as mine and of this work.

The fight for the "civil recognition" of Individual Liberty is *not* the same as the progressive "revolution" to destroy and replace that

Individual Liberty with *the* civil rights or human rights of collectivism. When we confuse one for the other, we confuse either Liberty for tyranny, or tyranny for Liberty! When we confuse them, we give aid in the destruction of our own freedom by perpetuating that confusion, as that confusion itself is of the Philosophy and not just a coincidence. It is by design! And that is why it is so vitally important that the distinction be made and clarified so we may *knowingly* choose!

With Individual Rights, we have our God-given Individual Liberty and true freedom, and both our individual identity and dignity is recognized! With positive *civil rights*, we are "forced to be free" by a "conditional" (Rousseau) liberty that cannot be spoken of outside the context of the "duties" (Comte) owed in return. With such collective rights, *all* of our *everything* must first be forsaken and surrendered to the supreme sovereign of the collective as, here, the "sovereign is sole judge of what is important" (Rousseau). Then, that this "moral liberty" (Rousseau) be maintained, we are to be forcibly compelled by the "common Power to keep [us] all in awe" (Hobbes) to comply with the "general will" (Rousseau)—which, again, all mandate we surrender all our *everything* to, including our property, our will, our faith, our opinions, and our judgment! Where is the Liberty in that? But such is the deception in the sustainability of human/civil rights!

Also, such *civil* rights and liberties are often championed by civil rights organizations like the American Civil Liberties Union. Is it a coincidence that this organization was founded in 1920 by the Harvard-educated Fabian socialist and "co-founder of the International League for the Rights of Man [later the International League for Human Rights]" Rodger Baldwin? In 1934, Baldwin wrote a piece titled *Freedom in the USA and the USSR*, where he states the following:

> The class struggle is the central conflict of the world; all others are incidental. When that power of the working class is once achieved, as it has been only in the Soviet Union, I am for maintaining it by any means whatever. Dictatorship is the obvious means in a world of enemies at home and abroad…the Soviet Union has already created liberties far greater than exist elsewhere in the world…[There] I saw…fresh, vigorous expressions of free living by workers and peasants all over the land. And further, *no champion of a socialist society could fail to see that some suppression was necessary to achieve it. It could not all be done by persuasion*…[I]f American champions of civil liberty could all think in terms of economic freedom as the goal of their labors, they too would accept 'workers' democracy' as far superior to what the capitalist world offers[31] (emphasis added).

And from discoverthenetworks.org, there's this, where Baldwin reveals his communist/anarchist intentions:

> Reflecting on his early years as the ACLU's Executive Director, Baldwin candidly revealed his original motives and objectives: "*I am for socialism, disarmament, and ultimately, for abolishing the state itself as an instrument of violence and compulsion. I seek social ownership of property, the abolition of the properties class, and sole control of those who produce wealth. Communism is the goal. It all sums up into one single pur-*

pose—the abolition of dog-eat-dog under which we live. I don't regret being part of the communist tactic. I knew what I was doing. I was not an innocent liberal. I wanted what the communists wanted and I traveled the United Front road to get it"[32] (emphasis added).

And is it any surprise Baldwin was then awarded with the Medal of Honor by President Jimmy Carter in 1981 as "a leader in the field of civil right and a leader in the field of civil liberties"? The ACLU would be instrumental in such transformative legalities as securing the "academic freedom" of evolution in schools. But they would later fight to have any form of "creationism" or "intelligent design" being taught in our schools declared unconstitutional. The ACLU was there for *Roe vs. Wade*, where it was determined that the "right to privacy" encompasses a woman's "individual right" to abortion. This legal correlation between privacy and abortion would later be expanded, with the help of the ACLU, to include homosexual "intimacy," otherwise known as sodomy.

With the recent revelations in the Obama administration's totalitarian, "generally applicable" gathering, recording, and storing of literally our every electronic communication, the observation must be made of the irony that our only rights of privacy being recognized here include some kind of Malthusian moral depravity. Knowing what we have learned of what progressives have told us in their own words about what progressivism is, do you really think this a coincidence?

There's more. In addition, they have actively supported "free speech" by fighting for recognition of unions' right to organize. They helped to get the Child Online Protection Act declared unconstitutional, supported the KKK, the nation of Islam, and Nazis wanting to march through a community of Holocaust survivors.[33] And when the God Hates Fags, Thank God for Dead Soldiers, Westboro Baptist Church recently won their appeal to protest at family funerals in April of 2013, the ACLU again was there.[34]

What better way to polarize America than to effectively champion *all* that polarizes her? What better way to demonize the Constitution than to continually present it over and over again as *the* protector of such controversial and unpalatable "individual liberties" as these that cut to the heart of what divides us? With the ever-increasing prominence of progressive collectivism emerging as *the* ever-present and "politically correct" option to our "antiquated" Individual Liberty, does it not set the stage for us to consider that option and reconsider our Liberty? Does it not force *the* conditions that might lend a people to look favorably toward the *uniformity* of a promised collective homogenousness over the continued animated chaos and animosity presumably being caused by that Individual Liberty protected by the Constitution? To champion "civil rights" is to champion *the* destruction of our Constitution, our republic, and freedom itself!

While Dewey was busy laying the groundwork for the mental aspect of the great deception, there were others toiling away as well setting the foundation for the spiritual part of it. According to the Rauschenbusch Center for Spirit and Action, the Baptist pastor Walter Rauschenbusch is considered "the father" of the social gospel movement of the early twentieth century. Called one of the most influential American religious leaders in the last one hundred years by PBS, Rauschenbusch believed that Christian principles must be "translated into actions that promote compassion, justice, and social change." He puts forth the following in his 1912 *Christianizing the Social Order*:

PART I

THE SOCIAL AWAKENING OF THE CHURCHES

CHAPTER I

THE AWAKENING OF THE NATION

The history of American politics in recent years has been a history of the reconquest of political liberty...They are trying to weaken the political oligarchies by direct nomination. *They hope to cleanse and rejuvenate the Senate by direct election.* They are sweeping and ventilating the worst corners *of our common home*, the cities, by uniform accounting *and commission government.* They are turning our so-called representative government into self-government by the *initiative, referendum, and recall* (emphasis added).

Direct election of US Senate, initiative, referendum, and recall, though they may sound good, all bypass our Constitutional representative republic. Direct election of US Senate takes the state's voice out of the legislative process nationalizing it. *Initiative* undermines our very republic by allowing factions to directly introduce new legislation. *Referendum* undermines the constitutionally ordained legislative process by direct citizen vote on new legislation. And *recall* does so by allowing citizens to vote out constitutionally elected officials before the end of their term. All three overrule our republic via direct democracy. Again, as Madison tells us in Federalist 10, this gives free and unfettered access of *faction* to the legislative process. As the Occupy banner proclaims, "This Is What Democracy Looks Like"! This is mob rule! This could even be democratic socialism, but the one thing it is *not*—representative of is a republic! Remember, democracy is what gives the first part of Marx's Communist revolution, *the dictatorship of the proletariat,* its avenue to fruition. Might all this be part of an actual revolution in America? Or am I just jumping to conclusions? Rauschenbush continues:

> *All this is nothing less than a political revolution.* It is a second *war* of independence. It goes on all over the country with a curious unanimity of impulse which proves that it is not the artificial product of party agitation, but an awakening of the better self of the nation....
>
> The sense of *national sin* and dishonor has become a settled conviction....
>
> The standards of *collective morality* rose almost with a snap....
>
> Sin is the greatest preacher of repentance....
>
> There is a new shame and anger for oppression and meanness; a new love and pity for the young and frail whose slender shoulders bear our *common weight*; *a new faith in human brotherhood*; a new hope of a better day that is even now in sight. We are inventing new phrases to name this new thing. We talk of the "social feeling" or "the new social consciousness." We are passing through a *moral adolescence...A new sense of duty*, a new openness to ideal calls, a new capacity of *self-sacrifice*...So in out conventions and clubs, our chambers of commerce and our legislatures, there is a new note, a stiffening of will, an impatience for cowardice, an enthusiastic turning toward *real democracy. The old leaders*

> *are stumbling off the stage bewildered. There is a new type of leaders, and they and the people seem to understand one another as if by magic* (emphasis added).

The old leaders stumbling off Rauschenbusch's stage are none other than Gramsci's old "intellectuals" and/or Obama's old, antiquated "bitter clingers" who have been replaced "from the bottom up" by the new intellectuals steeped in their "new conception of the world." Where Rauschenbusch's new leaders "understand each other by magic," Wilson tells we will follow his "greatest man" into the "new conception of the world" as "his voice will be your voice" and "his thought will be your thought." And again, not in my words but theirs!

> Were you ever converted to God? Do you remember the change in your attitude to all the world? Is not this new life which is running through our people the same great change on a national scale? This is religious energy, *rising from the depth* of that infinite spiritual life in which we all live and move and have our being. *This is God* (emphasis added).

Amid all the other standard bearers of progressive incommonisms here, note the humanism in his "new faith in human brotherhood" and God "rising from the depths"! What "God's" religious energy rises "from the depths"?

PART II

THE REVOLUTIONARY DESTINY OF CHRISTIANITY

CHAPTER I

WANTED: A FAITH FOR A TASK

A GREAT task demands a great faith. To live a great life a man needs a great cause *to which he can surrender*, something divinely large and engrossing *for which he can live and, if need be, die*....

Our civilization is passing through a great historic transition. We are at the parting of the ways. The final outcome may be the decay and extinction of Western civilization, or it may be *a new epoch in the evolution of the race*, compared with which our present era will seem like a modified barbarism. We now have such *scientific knowledge* of *social laws and forces*, of economics, of history that we can intelligently *mold and guide the evolution in which we take part.*

Every great revolution demands a great idea to be its center of action; to furnish it with both lever and fulcrum for the work it has to do." (Mazzini) What great idea has the Christian Church which will serve as the religious lever and fulcrum for the engineering task of the present generation? What great faith has it which will inspire the religious minds of our modern world in the regeneration of society? (p. 40–41, emphasis added)

There is a lot to break down here that an unwitting or ungrounded soul might, as a matter of convenience, be willing to accept for a couple reasons. One reason is because the message is so convoluted. Precious time, time most hardworking people do not have to spare, would have to be *wasted* breaking it all down in order to decipher any hidden context that may or may not even be there. Another reason would be our inherent trust of clergy. Truth be known, however complicated it may be, there is nothing new here. And being that it just happens to be *the* purpose of this work to break it all down, let's break it all down!

What Rauschenbusch says here in the first two sentences alone—that "a *great* task demands a great faith" and "to live a great life a man needs a great cause to which he can surrender," and to "which he can live and, if need be, die"—is huge. Let's start by asking ourselves these three important questions: What "great" task? Whose "great cause"? And where have I seen this before?

Regarding "Our civilization is passing through a great historic transition," of which "the final outcome may be the decay and extinction of Western civilization," it might do well for us to ask, what the hell kind of "transition" are we "passing through" that could spell the end of the Western free world as we know it? And what does he mean by a "new epoch in the evolution of the race"?

With "every great revolution demands a great idea to be its center of action," we can begin to see that Rauschenbusch's "great task" is nothing less than revolution. In asking "what great idea has the Christian Church...what great faith has it which will inspire the religious minds of our modern world in the regeneration of society?" is he not looking to the church to "inspire" this revolution and "to furnish it with both lever and fulcrum for the work"? Is he not asking how the Christian Church might be *used* as a "mere instrumentality" to further the cause of social revolution and "the regeneration of society"?

And so it is that religion, Christianity in particular, has come to be *used* or *harnessed* in Rauschenbusch's social revolution. As "every great revolution demands a great idea to be its center of action," so it is that it is that the Christian religion itself has become *the* "great idea" at the center of his "great revolution…in the regeneration of society"! And why not? As history has shown, religion has proven to be the greatest of motivators in the greatest of revolutions. For instance, where Rauschenbusch says here, "Every great revolution demands a great idea to be its center of action," Hitler says this in his 1925 *Mein Kampf*:

> The word 'religious' acquires a precise meaning only when it is associated with a distinct and definite form through which the concept is put into practice.…But, *since the masses of the people are not composed of philosophers or saints, such a vague religious idea will mean for them nothing else than to justify each individual in thinking and acting according to his own bent*…But all these ideas, no matter how firmly the individual believes in them, may be critically analysed by any person and accepted or rejected accordingly, *until the emotional concept or yearning has been transformed into an active service that is governed by a clearly defined doctrinal faith*. Such a faith furnishes the practical outlet for religious feeling to express itself and thus opens the way through which it can be put into practice.
>
> *Without a clearly defined belief, the religious feeling would not only be worthless for the purposes of human existence but even might contrib-*

> *ute towards a general disorganization, on account of its vague and multifarious tendencies....*
>
> Every philosophy of life, even if it is a thousand times correct and of the highest benefit to mankind, will be of *no practical service for the maintenance of a people* as long as its principles have not yet *become the rallying point of a militant movement.* And, on its own side, this movement will remain a mere party until is has brought its ideals to victory and transformed its party doctrines into the new foundations of a State which gives the national community its final shape[35] (emphasis added).

If and when religion—in this case, Christianity—is to be used for Rauschenbush's social revolution, Hitler reminds us that "on account of its vague and multifarious tendencies" that "justify each individual in thinking and acting according to his own bent," not "until the emotional concept or yearning *has been transformed*" from a religion of individual salvation into one concerning collective salvation can Christianity be used to help give the nationalist—or, for that matter, the internationalist—community its final shape.

Rauschenbusch says that in order for a man "to live a great life a man needs a great cause to which he can surrender" and "for which he can live and…die." Why must one be willing to surrender and, if need be, die for this great cause of social revolution? Again, in Book II, 4–5, of his 1762 *Social Contract or Principles of Political Right*, Rousseau explains:

> Each man alienates, I admit, by the social compact, only such part of his powers, goods and liberty as it is important *for the community*

> *to control;* but it must also be granted that *the Sovereign is sole judge of what is important....*
>
> The social treaty has for its end the preservation of the contracting parties. He who wills the end wills the means also, and the means must involve some risks, and even some losses. He who wishes to preserve his life at others' expense should also, when it is necessary, be ready to give it up for their sake. Furthermore, *the citizen is no longer the judge of the dangers to which the law-desires him to expose himself; and when the prince says to him: It is expedient for the State that you should die," he ought to die, because it is only on that condition that he has been living in security up to the present, and because his life is no longer a mere bounty of nature, but a gift made conditionally by the State*[36] (emphasis added).

As far as "civilization…passing through a great historic transition," which "[t]he final outcome may be the decay and extinction of Western civilization, or…new epoch in the evolution of the race," remember Comte's positive sociology, where *the belief in God is considered nothing but a primitive evolutionary phase of human evolution* before we eventually "evolve" into the next stage—a metaphysical, scientific, or positive phase where all humans become one giant Godless collective or global social organism. This is key! It is why it all makes perfect sense from a progressive standpoint to utilize the church, Christians, or anybody else who still believe in God for progressive social purposes. It simply helps to speed the evolutionary progress of humanity away from the old, antiquated wives' tale of a belief in God and the individualism it fosters toward the progressive social collective objective of a single global human organism, where each individual is nothing but a meaningless and mindless "cog."

For all those who choose to follow this progressive transformation of the Christian Church in the belief it will bring more meaning to your life and closer to God—beware. For if we know it is progressive for society to "progress" away from God, which we have here established *in their own words* is the case, it could never be progressive to transform the "great faith" of Christianity in order to "inspire the religious minds...in the regeneration" of our faith and help us "progress" toward Him. Any member of such a progressive church who thinks he is being led to God is sadly mistaken. But such is the essence of the great deception!

> *The chief purpose of the Christian Church in the past has been the salvation of individuals.* But the most pressing task of the present is not individualistic. Our business is to make over an antiquated and immoral economic system... Our inherited Christian faith dealt with individuals; *our present task deals with society.*
>
> The Christian Church in the past has taught us to do our work with our eyes fixed on another world and a life to come. *But the business before us is concerned with refashioning this present world,* making this earth clean and sweet and habitable (emphasis added).

Here again, in their own words, lies *the* contrast between the spirituality of "scripture-based theology" and the earthliness of progressive-mission-based liberation theology! This mission or purpose-based liberation theology has many descendants as progressivism is but a liberation theology in itself. As for that matter, the whole of the Philosophy, which includes progressivism, is nothing if it isn't a liberation theology working to *use* its followers to liberate society as a whole from the three-headed Hydra of God, family, and property! We will be coming back to this liberation theology later.

> Here is the problem for all religious minds: we need a great faith *to serve as a spiritual basis for the tremendous social task before us*, and the working creed of our religion, *in the form in which it has come down to us*, has none. *Its theology is silent or stammers where we most need a ringing and dogmatic message. It has no adequate answer to the fundamental moral questions of our day*. It has manifestly furnished no sufficient religious motives to bring the unregenerate portions of our social order under the control of the Christian law. Its hymns, its ritual, its prayers, its books of devotion, are so devoid of social thought that the most thrilling passions of our generation lie in us half stifled for lack of religious utterance. The whole scheme of religion which tradition has handed down to us was not devised for such ends as we now have in hand and is inadequate for them. *We need a new foundation for Christian thought.* (p. 41–42, emphasis added)
>
> Twenty-five years ago *the social wealth of the Bible* was almost undiscovered to most of us. We used to plow it six inches deep for crops and never dreamed that mines of anthracite were hidden down below. Even *Jesus* talked like an individualist in those days and seemed to repu-

> diate the social interest when we interrogated him. He *said his kingdom was not of this world*; the things of God had nothing to do with the things of Caesar; the poor we would always have with us; and his ministers must not be judges and dividers when *Labor argued with Capital* about the division of the inheritance... *We have no literature that introduces the ordinary reader to the whole Bible from the social point of view.*
>
> In its systematic doctrinal teaching the Church is similarly handicapped. It is trying old tools to see if they will fit the new job. It has done splendidly in broadening certain principles developed under religious individualism and giving them a social application. But more is needed (emphasis added).

Neither the Bible or the church have any practical application "from the social point of view." To simply try redirecting them toward Rauschenbusch's "social application" would be like "trying old tools to see if they will fit the new job." Is "social application" the intended purpose of the Bible? To many, this question might not matter as they are not Christian, or so they may surmise. That's fine as the free will of our natural/God-given Individual Liberty was specifically "endowed by our Creator" for that very reason—the freedom to make that decisions for ourselves. America was then founded simply to secure the Liberty to do so.

The great deception herein being exposed is just as much a threat to the Liberty of the unbeliever as it is to the believer as our Liberty is the same—as our very freedom is the same! For we are either free or we are *not*! Remember, it was *not* I who has time and time again brought us to the subject of God but this very philosophy! So it is that if there is a truth to be found, we *will* find it. And in that search, shall we leave *no* stone unturned, not even the great deception itself! But what of those who are Christians? Who is it that would redefine God's church and redirect scripture, not to meet godly or spiritual ends but earthly, human, and social ends? Remember Robert Dale Owen also told us that the three-headed Hydra of God, family, and property must be destroyed for these very same social ends, declaring this in his 1826 *A Declaration of Mental Independence*:

> The revolution, then, to be now effected, is the DESTRUCTION of this HYDRA OF EVILS— in order that the many may be no longer poor, wretched beings—dependent on the wealthy and powerful few[37] (emphasis original)

That Rauschenbusch's philosophy of "social application"—which seeks to *redefine scripture* and establish "a new foundation for Christian thought" is *the* same progressive philosophy of "social application" that seeks the outright "destruction" of the three-headed Hydra of God, family, and property—is something to keep in mind and close at hand throughout this work. It is a liberating truth to be heeded in life!

> With true Christian instinct *men have turned to the Christian law of love* as the key to the situation. If we all loved our neighbor, we should "treat him right," *pay him a living wage*, give sixteen ounces to the pound, and not charge so much for beef. (42–43)
>
> These are all *truly religious ideas*, drawn from the teaching of Jesus himself, and very effective in sweetening and ennobling our per-

> sonal relations. *But they set up no ideal of human society, demand no transformation of social institutions, create no collective enthusiasms, and furnish no doctrinal basis for a public morality.* They have not grown antiquated, and never will. But *every step in the evolution of modern society makes them less adequate* for its religious needs (emphasis added).

This is a complete and total denial of God. In calling for a "living wage" and to "not charge so much for beef," he is calling for the kind of complete and total takeover of free enterprise and the market found only in communism! Where he says "true" Christianity and the "the teaching of Jesus himself 'set up no ideal of human society, demand no social institutions, creates no collective enthusiasm, and furnishes no doctrinal basis for a public morality,'" he says God, Jesus, and the Bible serve no "social" purpose! This, in and of itself, is a telling and tantamount admission to the extent of false witness and deception here, where such a progressive "social" transformation is being taught as Christianity in Christian churches themselves. Where he says those "teachings of Jesus himself…furnish no doctrinal basis for a public morality," we are again reminded of Rousseau telling us that "what man acquires in the civil state, moral libert" is what "alone makes him truly master of himself."

Accordingly, there is no need for God in a "civil state," for all rights and morality are acquired not from God but from society. Society, *not* God, will tell us what is moral! Bakunin agreed, reiterating, "Society, far from decreasing his freedom, on the contrary creates the individual freedom of all human beings." However, Bakunin then punctuates this by detailing what spiritual end this collective philosophy holds, which Rauschenbusch hesitates to clarify:

> All temporal or human authority stems directly from spiritual and/or divine authority. But authority is the negation of freedom. God, or rather the fiction of God, is the consecration and the intellectual and moral source of all slavery on earth, and the freedom of mankind will never be complete until the disastrous and insidious fiction of a heavenly master is annihilated.[38]

Where Rauschenbush then says that true Christianity and the teachings of Jesus himself "have not grown antiquated, and never will," he denies that he is denying God. However, as he continues with "But *every step in the evolution of modern society makes them less adequate* for its religious needs," he redenies Him. Remember Comte in what he told us that *the* ultimate "evolved" state of such a progressive society is the Godless collective earth entity of a single human organism where there is no place for any individuals or their "individualistic" souls!

> So we return to the question: What is the religious basis for the task of Christianizing and regenerating the social order? Suppose that a Christian man feels a throbbing compassion and fellow-feeling for the people, and a holy anger against the institutionalized wrong that is stunting and brutalizing their lives, converting the children of God into slaves of Mammon. Suppose that he feels this so strongly *that he hardly cares what becomes of his own soul* if only he can help his nation and race. Suppose that a whole generation is coming vaguely to feel

> that way. What great word of faith does historic Christianity offer to express and hallow and quicken this spiritual passion which is so evidently begotten of the spirit of Christ? Must he go to materialistic Socialism to find a dogmatic faith large enough to house him, and intellectual food nutritious enough to feed his hunger? *Thousands have left the Church and have gone to Socialism, not to shake off a faith, but to get a faith.*
>
> *Religion, to have power over an age, must satisfy the highest moral and religious desires of that age.* If it lags behind, and presents outgrown conceptions of life and duty, it is *no longer* in the full sense *the Gospel.* (p. 46–47)

Note that instead of guiding its followers through scripture toward the "outgrown conceptions" of God, Christianity is to now satisfy only the desires of "this age."

Are we to understand here that the thousands who have "left the Church and have gone to Socialism, not to shake off a faith but to get a faith" did so not only because "historic Christianity" has no socially acceptable modern or "hip" word of faith to offer but because Christian faith itself is not, and never was, a "real" faith? To what "institutionalized wrong" might he be referring converting people into "slaves to Mammon" if not capitalism?

> CHAPTER II
>
> THE SOCIAL CHRISTIANITY OF JESUS
>
> THE Christian religion, in the form in which our fore fathers transmitted it to this modern world, was strong in creating a convic-

tion of personal sin, an assurance of personal forgiveness and adoption, and a firm hope of personal immortality, but it was weak in social hopes and aims. In the relations of man to man, and in the relation of man to his own soul, Christianity was the salt of the earth, the great antiseptic against vice and passion, the spur to justice, the motive of neighborly kindness, and the comfort of the poor and helpless. But it furnished no really effective religious conception of redemption for the organic Hie of human society. It presented no working program by which the social institutions might be transformed... *The creation of a distinctively Christian social order was not what Christianity was commonly supposed to stand for.* Those who did stand for it were men apart. Orthodox theology hardly considered the Christianizing of the social order as part of the scheme of redemption. The pulpit rarely proclaimed it. The hymns of the Church did not give voice to the desire for it. Its liturgies did not direct the power of united prayer toward its achievement. When Christianity was in its infancy, there were diverse expectations about its future, but it is safe to say that few would have expected this charge to be raised against it. It was born of revolutionary lineage. Its cradle was rocked by the storm wind of popular hopes. What was it that brought the multitudes to the Jordan to hear John and that thrilled the throngs that followed Jesus about in Galilee? *Was it the desire to go to heaven one by one when they died?*

What inspired the early disciples and lent wings to the Gospel? *It was the hope of a great common salvation for all the people, the belief that the Kingdom of God on earth was at last in sight.*

Christianity was pure and unperverted when it lived as a divine reality in the heart of Jesus Christ. But in his mind its purpose was summed up in one great word: the

Reign of God...*It was the Reign of God on earth for* which he consumed his strength, *for which he died,* and for which he promised to return (emphasis mine).

If, according to social doctrine, Christ died not for our sins and our individual salvation but for "the hope of a great common salvation for all the people" and that "it was the Reign of God on earth" for which Jesus lived and died, may we inquire as to what scripture tells us? In John 6:38–40 and 48, it is Jesus Himself who is quoted as telling us:

> For I came down from heaven, *not to do my mine own will, but the will of him that sent me.* And this is the Father's will which hath sent me, that of all which he hath given me, I should lose nothing, but should raise it up again at the last day.
>
> And this is the will of him that sent me, *that every one which seeth the Son, and believeth on him, may have everlasting life*: and I will raise *him* up at the last day....
>
> Verily, verily, I say unto you, *He* that believeth on me hath everlasting life.

Again, per scripture, Jesus was *not* on earth to do His work or His will at all but that of "the Father's"! He then tells us what the will of the Father is: "that every one which seeth the Son, and believeth on him, may have everlasting life." No mention here of any kingdom or reign of God on earth, social justice, or collective salvation!

> *No man is a Christian in the full sense of the original discipleship until he has made the Kingdom of God the controlling purpose of his life, and no man is intellectually prepared to understand Jesus Christ until he has understood the meaning of the Kingdom of God...* The present-day Reformation is a revival of the spirit and aims of Jesus himself. (p. 48–49, emphasis mine)

Remember Wilson's "No man is a true Christian who does not think constantly of how he can lift his brother" and "regard themselves as their brother's keeper."

> When we undertake to restate the conception of the Kingdom of God precisely as it lived in the mind of Jesus, we are beset by a hundred difficulties of criticism and interpretation which only the specialist can estimate. *Fortunately most of them are academic, interesting to the scholar, but of slight importance for the practical and modern questions with which we are here concerned.*

And so, unfortunately for them, most of the unsuspecting flock—and for that matter, the clergy as well—will be completely unaware of such "academic" deviation from scripture.

By far the greatest hindrance to a right understanding of the essential purpose of Christ is the ecclesiastical and theological conception of him which eighteen centuries have superimposed on the historical records of his life and teachings. That acts as a refracting and distorting medium of vision, and until a man has to some degree cleared that away and learned to read the gospels as they stand, he is not likely to comprehend the social significance of Jesus and of the gospel of the Kingdom of God. (p. 49–50)

The prophets were religious reformers demanding social action. They were not discussing holiness in the abstract, but dealt with concrete, present-day situations in the life of the people which were sometimes due to the faults of the people themselves, but usually to *the sins of the ruling classes.* They demanded neighborly good will and humane care of the helpless. But their most persistent and categorical demand was that the men in power should quit their extortion and judicial graft. *They were trying to beat back the hand of tyranny from the throat of the people. Since the evil against which they protested was political, their method of redress was political too. Their religion did not displace politics, but reenforced it. If any modern preacher had told them to disentangle their religion and their politics and keep them in separate compartments, they would not have known what he meant.* They all had a radiant hope of a future when their social and religious ideals would be realized. Emancipation

> from foreign tyranny, peace *and order* throughout the land, just and humane rulers, fertility of the soil, *prosperity for all*, a glorious capital city with a splendid temple in it was the social Utopia of an agrarian nation. Hardly an ingredient of human life is missing in their ideals, *except the hope of immortality. In the prophets before the Exile there is harldy a side-long glance at life after death*. (p. 50–51, emphasis mine)

The collective salvation aspect of Rauschenbusch's liberation theology is here again brought to light by his collective damnation of "the sins of the ruling classes." He speaks of "the prophets" as we might speak of our founders. Our founders, though establishing not "a kingdom of God" on earth, did establish on earth a political sanctuary within which our God-given Liberty could be freely expressed. As a new foundation of Christianity is to here be reestablished for "social purpose," so is the foundation of America, the Constitution, being reestablished by the same philosophy for the same "social purpose"! And once again, the strands of the web come back around.

> *This reign of God* for which they hoped *was therefore a social hope* on fire with religion^ Their concern was for "the largest and noblest social group with which they were in contact, their nation. In all their discussions they take the *social solidarity and collective personality* of their nation for granted. They sought to knit their country men together *in the bonds of a social order* based on divine rights and sanctions. They were men ancldealt with men, *but they focused not souls, but society*. They called their

> coming age the Reign of Jehovah; but his reign, when set over against the power of the oppressors, meant the emancipation of the people. To speak frankly, *the prophets were revolutionists."* (p. 52, emphasis added)

The question here is, were they revolutionaries for God and His will, or Man and his earthly will? Then I might ask, if God's kingdom is as Jesus says in John 18:36, "not of this world," then who, according to scripture, is the "prince of this world"? Was it not the devil himself who, in tempting Jesus in Mathew 4:8, offered Him "all the kingdoms of the world and the glory in them"? Was it not Jesus who, in verse 10, rejected *all* earthly kingdoms, saying, "Get thee hence, Satan: for it is written, Thou shalt worship the Lord thy God, and him only shalt thou serve"? I would not argue that Rauschenbush and the social church seeks to establish a "kingdom of God" on earth for their followers; I would only question as to whom or what might be that earthly god?

> In the Old Testament there is hardly a glimpse of a Satan and of evil angels. After the Exile, a great hierarchy of darkness was the counterpart of God and the angelic hosts in popular Jewish thought. These new ideas connected with politics. It was clear now why heathen powers were able to hold Israel down. Demonic forces lurked behind them and would have to be overthrown if the Kingdom of God was to be set up. It was no longer a plain human fight against bloody wrong, but a supernal contest against spiritual principalities and powers.... (p. 54)

> Two apocalyptic books of great beauty and power, which we should never want to lose, were embodied in the Old and New Testament canon: the Book of Daniel and the Apocalypse of John.... (p. 55)
>
> I know that this charge will pain some devout Christian minds whom I would not willingly hurt, but in the interest of the very hope for which they stand I have to say that *the idea of the Kingdom of God must slough off apocalypticism if it is to become the religious property of the modern world.* Those who hold it must cease to put their hope in salvation by catastrophe and learn to recognize and apply the law of development in human life. *They must outgrow the diabolism and demonism* with which Judaism was infected in Persia *and face the stern facts of racial sin. They must break with the artificial schemes and the determinism of an unhistorical age and use modern resources to understand the way God works out retribution and salvation in human affairs.* (p. 56)
>
> All original minds begin with the stock of ideas common to their social environment and work away from that toward their own formulation of truth as they find themselves. (p. 57–58)

Are we to understand that idea of this kingdom of God is about facing "the stern facts of racial sin" and/or Judaism? That we need to both receive and accept our collective racial damnation? That our racial collective may receive its needed collective salvation, not to mention discard the Old Testament? Is our collective racial sin the same as our collective "sins of the ruling classes"? The answer from the Philosophy will have to wait a little longer, but it is coming.

Only under *the anti-truth of the great deception* of the Philosophy's relative perspectivism is it even possible for a collective kingdom to work "toward their own formulation of truth as they find themselves." And what is important here to remember is that it was Jesus Himself in John 14:6 who said, "I am...the Truth"! If Jesus is as he tells us—*the* Truth—then who are we to formulate our own? Where, via relativism, the Philosophy is *the* anti-Truth, would it not then, by definition be anti-God? And as we learned in chapter 2, relativism is a mainframe strand in the web that continues to come back around, and around, and around.

CHAPTER III

THE ECLIPSE OF THE SOCIAL IDEAL

CHRISTIANITY set out with a great social ideal. The live substance of the Christian religion was the hope of seeing a divine social order established on earth.... (p. 69)

Another most important cause for the fading of the social hope was the ascendency of the other-worldly hope. The religious ardor which had glowed in the expectation of the Lord s return to establish his millennial reign now burned with ever increasing intensity *in the hope of heaven and immortality. Above the starry firmament was a heavenly world where God was enthroned in glory amid the host of the angels. Thence the Saviour had descended to reveal the laws and impart the powers of that upper world to men, that we too might ascend at death and live forever with the ransomed in his presence.* In this world of sin and pain and death there is no abiding city. *The true home of the soul is yonder*, and we must make our pilgrim age through this vale of tears with ceaseless longing. To love this world and care for its possessions is equivalent to spiritual failure. The soul must be trained by ascetic discipline to detach itself, not only from the sins of the flesh, but even from the desire for food and comfort, from the love of wife and child and home, in order to concentrate all its desires and forces on the attainment of salvation in heaven. (p. 73, emphasis mine)

Where in the Bible does it tell us that we must starve and be uncomfortable to receive God's "attainment of salvation in heaven"? And as far as our soul being forced to endure through a "vale of tears," a "ceaseless longing" of our forsaken "love of wife and child and home," is it not in scripture, in Colossians 3:18–21 specifically, that we are instructed as follows?

> Wives, submit yourselves unto your own husbands, as it is fit in the Lord.
> Husbands, love *your* wives, and be not bitter against them.
> Children, obey *your* parents in all things: for this is well pleasing unto the Lord.
> Fathers, provoke not your children to *anger*, lest they be discouraged.

And is it not quite fittingly in Colossians 3:23 that we are intrinsically warned, "Whatsoever ye do, do it heartily, as to the Lord, and not unto men"?

I have no desire to disparage this type of religion.... (p. 75)

But after all, *the desire for rest in heaven is not the social hope of the Reign of God on earth with which Christianity set out. The atmosphere of detachment from this world and of longing for death is not the atmosphere in which Jesus lived* in Galilee. He did not estimate the values of life from that point of view, nor lay the emphasis in religion that way. *The current of religious energy which made the hope of immortality incandescent was diverted from the hope of a divine social life on earth* and left that like a dark lamp. *Otherworldly religion developed only those ideas and those ethical motives in religion which served the salvation of the individual* in the life to come.... (p. 76)

The present social order was due to sin, governed by Satan, held together by violence, and characterized by private wealth and injustice. No condemnation of *capitalism* by socialist thinkers has ever been quite so severe as the theory of the State developed by the Catholic Church. On the other hand, the organized Church appeared with the halo of the social ideal. Services rendered to civil society were robbed of most of their moral value and religious motive. *The Church stood out as the all-embracing object of Christian devotion and service.* That involved an eclipse of the Kingdom ideal, *for the Kingdom is the reign of God in the common life.* The territory within which it must develop is the social order. *The conception that the State is Satanic, discouraged faith in the possibility of a Christian civil order.* (p. 80, emphasis added)

And finally, after a long list of the detriments associated with seeking the "false hope" of salvation for our individual souls, we come to the real evil and yet another head of Owens's three-headed Hydra, the "social order…governed by Satan"—capitalism! Remember here that without property, there can be no capitalism and no private commerce, which is free enterprise. And where there is no free enterprise, there can no profit or prosperity. Thus, poverty is eternal. And where there can be no prosperity, true Liberty is impossible!

This leads us to the *need* here to examine this progressive accusation that the "present social order" of "capitalism" is "due to sin governed by Satan." The essential but much belied aspect of capitalism is the profiting from investments, be it their property, time, or labor. In order to have capital to invest, one must have indisputable property in that capital. So the question arises then of, where does "property" begin? In chapter 2 of his 1690 *Second Treatise*, John Locke tells us:

> Sec. 28. He that is nourished by the acorns he picked up under an oak, or the apples he gathered from the trees in the wood, has certainly appropriated them to himself. No body can deny but the nourishment is his…Was it a robbery thus to assume to himself what belonged to all in common? *If such a consent as that was necessary, man had starved, notwithstanding the plenty God had given him.* We see in commons, which remain so by compact, that it is the taking any part of what is common, and

removing it out of the state nature leaves it in, which begins the property[39] (emphasis added).

And so it is that labor is the conception of wealth. Had we not *owned* property in our labor, this would be impossible, rendering us to either starvation or an eternal indebtedness to those who did own it. These are the fundamentals of capitalism, and capitalism is fundamental to our independence and Individual Liberty. Under what philosophy would both our labor and the fruits of our labor belong to others or "to all in common"? In his 1875 (but published in 1891) *Critique of the Gotha Program*, Karl Marx, responds,

> Labour is *not the source* of all wealth... *The Conclusion*: "And since useful labour is possible only in society and through society, the proceeds of labour undiminished with equal right to all members of society."
>
> A fine conclusion! If useful labour is possible only in society and through society, the proceeds of labour belong to society—and only so much therefrom accrues to the individual worker as is not required to maintain the "condition" of labour; society....
>
> In a higher phase of communist society... only then can the narrow horizon of bourgeois right be crossed in its entirety and society inscribe its banner: From each according to his ability, to each according to his needs![40]

Where Rauschenbush is demonizing capitalism and the responsibility of personal investment for private wealth, which is our only means of self-sufficiency and Individual Liberty, as a "sin governed by Satan" and redefines Christianity along the redistributive lines of Marx's communism, may we ask again, what does scripture tell us? Could it be a coincidence that it turns upside down all Rauschenbusch, Marx, and today's progressive redistributionists would have us believe? In Mathew chapter 25, Jesus Himself tells us of the virtue in taking such responsibilities as investing, however much or little we may have, that we work to provide for ourselves the blessings of Liberty, which are, in totality, but *the* security of independence, of freedom. In verses 14–30, he tells us:

> *For the Kingdom of Heaven is* as a man traveling into a far country, who called his own servants, and delivered unto them his goods. And unto one he gave five talents, to another two, and to another one; to every man according to his several ability; and straightaway took his journey....
>
> Then he that had received the five talents went and traded with the same, and made *them* other five talents. And likewise he that *had received* two, he also gained another two. he that had received one went and digged in the earth, and hid his lords money.
>
> After a long time the lord of those servants cometh, and reckoneth with them. And so he that had received five talents came and brought other Five talents, saying, Lord, thou deliveredst unto me five talents: behold I have gain beside them five talents more.
>
> His lord said unto him, Well done, thou good and faithful servant: thou hast been faithful over a few things, I will make thee ruler over

many things: enter thou into the joy of thy lord. He also that had received two talents came and said, Lord thou hast deliveredst unto me two talents: behold, I have gained two other talents beside them.

His lord said unto him, Well done, good and faithful servant; thou hast been faithful over a few things, I will make thee ruler over many things: enter thou into the joy of thy lord.

Then he which had received the one talent came and said Lord, I knew thee that thou art an hard man, reaping where thou hast not sown, and gathering where thou hast not strawed: And I was afraid, and went and hid thy talent in the earth: lo *there* thou hast *that is* thine.

His lord answered and said unto him, *Thou wicked and slothful servant, thou knewest that I reap where I sowed not, and gather where I have strawed not*: Thou oughtest therefore to have put my money to the exchangers, and *then* at my coming I should have received my own with usury.

Take therefore the talent from him, and give it unto him which hath ten talents. For unto every one that hath shall be given, and he shall have abundance: but from him that hath not shall be taken away even that which he hath. *And cast ye the unprofitable servant into outer darkness: there shall be weeping and gnashing of teeth* (emphasis added).

Shall we *never* squander, then, any God-given talents we may have and be fruitful in freedom that we may *never* be found dependent on the rations of any such tyranny as Marx's and, as is here established, Rauschenbush's communism. Or, as we are told in Galatians 5:1:

> STAND fast therefore in the liberty wherewith Christ hath made us free, and be not entangled again with the yoke of bondage.

If the freedom of enterprise, which is capitalism, is the "sin" of Rauschenbusch's "Satan," who then might it be that is truly his God? Where he says that "the Kingdom is the reign of God in the common life. The territory within which it must develop is the social order," is it not Jesus Himself who warns us in Luke 17: 20–23 that

> The Kingdom of God cometh not with observation: Neither shall they say, Lo here! or Lo there! *for, behold, the kingdom of God is within you.*
>
> And he said unto his disciples, The days will come when ye shall desire to see one of the days of the Son of man, and ye shall not see it. And they shall say to you, See here; or see there: *go not after them, nor follow them* (emphasis added).

CHAPTER IV

THE INSTITUTIONS OF LOVE AND THEIR DANGERS

Because the home is God's country, the valuation put on it by us all is exceedingly high. *Most women feel that their life gets its full meaning and dignity only when they can have and make a home. Most men toil with little else in mind except to maintain their homes. From the point of view of society the home is an expensive institution. It would be possible to house us all in dormitories and feed us in_institutions far more cheaply. To duplicate sitting rooms, dining rooms, and kitchens for every family is an economic waste unless higher interests justify it. Every separate house and cottage of the American type is an architectural and economic expression of the high valuation we put on the home as the institution of love and individuality* (emphasis added).

There is a lot to go over here in this short paragraph. First, how is it that even our home is considered unsustainable or too costly to the planners of such a progressive social society? Simply our time spent tending our private affairs would be better spent working on what those progressive planners would rather have us doing for the collective! Is it me, or is this one of the most arrogant and totalitarian observations imaginable? It could be with no less than a complete and total "sense of right" to the complete ownership of the people themselves that one would even contemplate such a complaint as our home being nothing but a detrimental "expense" to society and state because "[m]ost men toil with little else in mind except to maintain their homes." What else would he have us do that could possibly be more important than our home and family? It doesn't matter what is important to the slave, only what is important to the master!

And where it is said that "most women feel that their life gets its full meaning and dignity only when they can have and make a home," we must go to the coauthor of *The Communist Manifesto* itself, Fredrick Engels, to understand why this is such a concern to the Philosophy. It is in his 1884 *The Origin of Family, Private Property, and State* where we are reminded that "the emancipation of woman will only be possible when woman can take part in production on a large, social scale, and domestic work no longer claims anything but an insignificant amount of her time."[41]

And where it is said, "It would be possible to house us all in dormitories and feed us in institutions far more cheaply. To duplicate sitting rooms, dining rooms, and kitchens for every family is an economic waste" brings me to ask, where, right here in America, does this progressive, sustainable utopia already exist? The answer? *Prison*! Again, we have the great deception of imprisonment and the real suppression of the people being sold to us as some kind of new and improved Liberty. But such is the reality of progressive collectivism! And where he says "unless higher interests justify it," it only reiterates the arrogance and depraved sense of dominion they feel they wield over us and our Liberty!

And where he says "Every separate house and cottage of the American type is an architectural and economic expression of the high valuation we put on the home as the institution of love and individuality" brings us to the reality that it is our homes "of the American type" that help foster our detested individuality. It is in *The Communist Manifesto* that we are reminded of why our private homes, our property, and our individualism are all here being referred to within the context of each other and what ultimate end this philosophy has in store for them:

> In one word, you reproach us with intending to do away with your property. Precisely so; that is just what we intend. From the moment when labour can no longer be converted into capital, money, or rent, into a social power capable of being monopolised, *i.e.*, from the

moment when individual property can no longer be transformed into bourgeois property, into capital, from that moment, you say, individuality vanishes. *You must, therefore, confess that by "individual" you mean no other person than the bourgeois, than the middle-class owner of property. This person must, indeed, be swept out of the way, and made impossible*[42] (emphasis added).

Rauschenbusch continues:

> To-day the home is being hurt and crippled. Industrialism sweeps the workers together in tightly wedged masses m abnormally large cities. *Private property in land turns over the unearned increase in land values to individuals* and offers a bonus to anybody who will help to make land scarce for the users. Building materials have grown dear through the *capitalistic* exhaustion *of the forests* and through business combinations, and this registers itself in contracted homes. (p. 262–263, emphasis added)

Dewey's "inherited resources of the race" also come into play here as "from the point of view of society the home is an expensive institution." And where Rauschenbusch says the concept of "private property in land turns over the unearned increase in land values to individuals," the 1987 UN Brundtland Report says this:

> 76. *Sustainability requires…changes in the legal and institutional frameworks that will enforce the common interest*…Such a view places

the right to use public and private resources in its proper *social context*[43] (emphasis added).

How these "sustainable changes" are to be instituted, as you might remember were offered, by the 1976 United Nations (Habitat I) Conference on Human Settlements. The commonality between them and what Rauschenbusch is saying is striking:

> (B) THE UNEARNED INCREMENT RESULTING FROM THE RISE IN LAND VALUES RESULTING FROM CHANGE IN USE OF LAND, FROM PUBLIC INVESTMENT OR DECISION OR DUE TO THE GENERAL GROWTH OF THE COMMUNITY MUST BE SUBJECT TO APPROPRIATE RECAPTURE BY PUBLIC BODIES (THE COMMUNITY), UNLESS THE SITUATION CALLS FOR OTHER ADDITIONAL MEASURES SUCH AS NEW PATTERNS OF OWNERSHIP, THE GENERAL ACQUISITION OF LAND BY PUBLIC BODIES[44] (caps original).

And again, the strands of the web come back around!

CHAPTER VII

THE CASE OF CHRISTIANITY AGAINST CAPITALISM

Love is of God; the home is its sanctuary. *Capitalism is breaking down or crippling the home wherever it prevails*, and poisoning society with the decaying fragments of what was the spring house of life. The conditions created by capitalism are the conditions in which prostitution is multiplying…Devotion to the common good is one of the holy and divine forces in human

> society. *Capitalism teaches us to set private interest before the common good.* It follows profit, and not patriotism and public spirit. If war is necessary to create or protect profit, it will involve nations in war. (p. 314–315, emphasis added)

Is capitalism really "crippling the home"? Under what philosophy and doctrine is the destruction of the family *specifically* called for? Is it freedom and Individual Liberty or the progressive collectivism of the Philosophy that not only calls for the destruction of the family but the other two heads of the three-headed Hydra as well—God and property? Yet here, via a man of the cloth, it proposes itself as a "holy and divine force." Beware those who wager their souls at the table of such deception! Hopefully, this work will help make it easier to identify the deception in such misdirecting "gospel" untruths.

> These are the points in the Christian indictment of Capitalism. All these are summed up in this single challenge, that *Capitalism has generated a spirit of its own which is antagonistic to the spirit of Christianity*; a spirit of hardness and cruelty that neutralizes the Christian spirit of love; a spirit that sets material goods above spiritual possessions. To *set Things above Men is the really dangerous practical materialism. To set Mammon before God is the only idolatry against which Jesus warned us.* (p. 316, emphasis added)

If you have never seen what a *projective accusatory* looks like feast your eyes as this is it. This is where the progressivism of Rauschenbusch's "social church" accuses freedom of its own sins. Capitalism cannot, in and of itself, "generate a spirit…antagonistic to the spirit of Christianity" because the very Individual Liberty that is contiguous to it is God-given. To set "things above men" is one thing, but for a professed Christian Church to set the things of men above God and His Will is quite another! Make no mistake, what we are reading is a call for social justice to be both led and conducted by the church. But it is also a call for the congregations to participate in this "revolution" to take the wealth and property of "the privileged" away from them. What is social justice without the taking of wealth or property from its rightful owners? Unless it does so, it *cannot* exist!

Again, when I say I have a "right" to something I cannot afford, in reality, I am saying that I have a "right" to somebody else's property to pay for it with. If I am demanding my right to the property of others, am I not coveting it for myself? Under what premise do I have that "right" to covet the wealth of others? If I say it isn't fair that others have more than me, am I not jealous? If I empower others to take what I covet on my behalf, am I not still a thief? If I take from others what I am free to pursue rightfully on my own accord, am I not slothful? What other than greed could justify the injustice of such theft? So it is that social justice is founded on *the* cardinal sins of jealousy, greed, theft, sloth, and covetousness, which according to Colossians 3:5, is also "idolatry." Where is the brotherly love in that? Are not the earthly things of wealth and property demanded by such social justice rudiments of this world? Then per Colossians 2:8, "beware lest any man spoil you through philosophy and vain deceit, after the traditions of men, after the rudiments of the world, and not after Christ."

So in the end, is it really capitalism, the only system that allows each individual the *freedom* to pursue their own happiness; or might it be the theft needed and dependency encouraged by this "social justice" that is "antagonistic to the spirit of Christianity"?

The degree to which this deception and the confusion surrounding it regarding "social justice" have infiltrated the Christian

Church of all denominations becomes crystal clear in this quote from the new Catholic pope, Pope Francis, spoken by him at a 2013 May Day gathering in St. Peters Square:

> I think about those who are unemployed often because of an economic conception of society that seeks egoistic profit regardless of social justice. [45]

In this quote, the pope openly attacks the "egoism" or individualism of capitalism over Comte's "altruism" of "social justice" as *the* cause of unemployment. How can that possibly be when it is *the* egoism, *the* individualism that is capitalism that, in the end, does all the employing of all employees not employed by government or some government subsidiary? Simply, capitalism, free enterprise, and business need to profit for them to grow; and to grow, they *must* employ! What is bad for employment is bad for free enterprise and vice versa. Regardless, we have here *the* pope himself professing, in the name of "social justice," *the same philosophy* that will stop at nothing to end all that is individualistic, including capitalism, all the jobs it creates, and ironically, the whole of Christianity itself! In addition to that, two things:

As we have been shown, it is under the Philosophy of progressive collectivism and "social justice" that a job is professed as a "right," a positive, collective, civil, and/or human "right." However, per the same philosophy, there is no place for "rights of individuals, in so far as they are subordinate to society, indeed humanity as a whole, and it is therefore only in this context, *which emphasizes duties*, that the concept of 'rights' can have any application."[9] So it is that the "altruism" of social justice holds not the promise of individual "employment" in the pursuit of happiness but, rather, *the* assurance of collective compliance with mandated "duties"! Where capitalist employment holds the promise of an earned happiness and Liberty, the Philosophy holds only the promise of perpetual slavery!

The kicker here, though, comes when considering that it is *the* pope of the Catholic Church himself who is espousing the same philosophy of collective altruism which is *not* made complete until this is added: "Humanity, the 'Great Being,' takes the place of God and is the basis of all morality."[9] But such is the deception of the Philosophy and social justice!

> True Christianity wakens men to a sense of their worth, to love of freedom, and independence of action; Capitalism, based on the principle of autocracy, resents independence, suppresses the attempts of the working class to gain it, and deadens the awakening effect that goes out from Christianity.
>
> The spirit of Christianity puts even men of unequal worth on a footing of equality by the knowledge of *common sin* and weakness, and by the faith in a *common salvation*; Capitalism creates an immense inequality between families, perpetuates it by property conditions, and makes it hard for high and low to have a realizing sense of the equality which their religion teaches.
>
> Christianity puts the obligation of love on the holiest basis and exerts its efforts to create fraternal feeling among men, and to restore it where broken; Capitalism has created worldwide unrest, jealousy, resentment, and bitterness, which choke Christian love like weeds.

> Jesus bids us *strive first for the Reign of God* and the *justice* of God, because on that spiritual basis all material wants too will be met; Capitalism urges us to strive first and last for our personal enrichment, and it formerly held out the hope that the selfishness of all would create the universal good. (p. 321, emphasis added)

How is this blistering attack of free enterprise, property, and capitalism any different than what we heard from Kropotkin, Bakunin, Marx, Owen, Alinsky, the Brundtland Report, Agenda 21, or Lenin in the first two chapters of this work? Far from "resent[ing] independence," capitalism is *the* only earthly way of achieving it! Is it truly greedy to want to keep others from laying claim to what is rightfully ours? Do we really need to "strive first for the Reign of God," or does God reign anyway, regardless of our efforts, despite any progressive effort against it? Where is the humility or humbleness in saying God needs man to establish a kingdom for Him, given it was Jesus in Luke 17:24 who tells us, "For as the lightning, that lighteneth out of one part under heaven, shineth unto the other part under heaven; so shall also the Son of man be in his day"?

Is the "spiritual basis" of Christianity really in subsidizing the "material wants" of people in this world and *in this life*?

And yet again, the progressivism of President Wilson's and President Obama's "collective salvation" resurfaces right here in Rauschenbusch's church "of Social Order"!

CHAPTER VII

THE POWERS OF THE COMING AGE

> When the unions demand a fixed minimum wage, a maximum working day, and cer-

tain reasonable conditions of labor as a security for health, safety, and continued efficiency, *they are standing for human life against profits.* With capitalism the dollar is the unit of all calculations; with unionism it is life. With capitalism the main purpose of industry is to make as large a profit as possible, and it makes the margin of life narrow in order to make the margin of profit wide. With unionism the purpose of industry is to support as large a number of workingmen s families in comfort as possible. Capitalism and unionism fail to understand each other because they revolve around a different axis. (p. 389, emphasis added)

Profit versus life? Profit versus common good? Profit versus wage, working hours, health, and safety? Could Karl Marx have said it any clearer that unionism is communism? What is the capital brought home in every paycheck of the proletariat if it isn't profit?

Labor unions are fighting organizations, and fighting always abridges personal liberty and stiffens the demand for obedience and subordination. In the long fight of labor the odds are nearly always against it, sometimes enormously so. *The employers have the tremendous backing of property rights* and the long wind given by large resources. *The Law,* which ought theoretically to be impartial, *has always been made by the powerful classes.* It used to treat the organization of workingmen as conspiracy, and still takes a grudging attitude toward demands which are clearly just. *The battle of labor is fought by a few for all.* Only a minority of the industrial workers is sufficiently strong economically, and sufficiently developed morally, to bear the strain of organized effort. *Unorganized labor reaps the advantages of the sacrifices made by the unions,* yet often thwarts their efforts and defeats the common cause. *Bitterness, roughness, and violence are inevitable in such a conflict.* The danger of tyranny is real enough. But underneath the grime of battle is the gleam of a higher purpose and law which these men are seeking to obey and to bring to victory. *They are standing for the growth of democracy,* for *earned against unearned income,* for the protection of human weakness *against the pressure of profit,* for *the right of recreation, education, and love, and for the solidarity of the workers.* They doubtless sin, but even the errors of labor *are lovable* compared with the errors of capitalism. *The seed of a new social order is in them. They too belong to "the powers of the coming age."* (p. 391, emphasis added)

Where we have seen these same phrasings and perspectives of the Philosophy being professed time and time again throughout this *Last Call for Liberty* from many different sources, including progressives, anarchists, socialists, communists, and globalists alike—they are all here being professed by this one man right here in this one paragraph! Make no mistake, all that comes out of the Philosophy against our Liberty is an age-old homogenous effort emanating, as Bakunin pointed out to us in chapter 1, from he who commands it from the center of the web.

CHAPTER III

THE SOCIALIZING OF PROPERTY

The socializing of property at times becomes of life and death importance to society *when the slow accumulation of great social changes has turned old rights into present wrongs.* That is the present situation in our country. When our great territory was being settled men took possession of the land, hunted and fished, cut down the forest, and encroached on no right of society in doing so. In fact, they were effectively socializing the land by using it as their private property. If they were enterprising enough to use water power for a dam and mill also, or opened a mine, they were serving the common good. But *as the country fills up and its resources are needed for the use of thousands, the old rights change.*

Thus the mere expansion of society has caused a shifting of right and wrong in all property questions. *Our moral and legal theories about the rights of the individual* in using the resources of nature and in operating his tools to get wealth, *are based on the assumption of a sparse population* and of simple methods of production which we have largely outgrown. What was once legitimate and useful is now becoming a dangerous encroachment on the rights of society. Property rights will have to be resocialized to bring them into accordance with our actual moral relations. If all memory of past property rights were miraculously blotted from our minds overnight, no sane man would think of allotting property as it is now allotted. All would realize that the great necessities of society, *our coal and iron mines, our forests, our watersheds and harbor fronts must be owned by society and operated for the common good.* But the plain path of *justice* and good sense *is blocked by the property rights brought down from a different past.* We can blame no one for holding and defending what he has bought or inherited. But what is society to do? (p. 420–422, emphasis added)

Supreme Court Justice Warren's 1985 profound proclamation—"The genius of the Constitution rests not in any static meaning it might have had in a world that is dead and gone…Our Constitution was not intended to preserve a preexisting society but to make a new one"[46]—is simply a reiteration of Rauschenbusch's "Property rights brought down from a different past" that "have to be resocialized"! Note all that is redistributive change hinges specifically on the premise of *the* progressive undoing of our inherent unalienable Individual Right to property!

The degree of collective rights and liberties allowed here are also contingent upon population. Once the population goes over a certain unidentified low number, pretty much everything needs to be "owned by society and operated for the common good." But it's being "blocked by the property rights"!

The question is how to socialize the land now that the enormous social values are in private hands, and to wrong nobody in the doing of it. There would be no wrong if the community decided by law to *take any unearned in crease*

> *of value* accruing after a given date; that would *leave all past values intact for the present owners.* There would be *a minimum of suffering* if the taxation of land values were gradually increased through a term of ten or twenty years *until it came near absorbing the whole annual rental value.* If buildings were simultaneously relieved of taxation, the earnings of private thrift would go into private hands, and the results of social growth would go to society. The man that can get no wisdom from the Singletaxers has padlocked his intellect. (p. 423, emphasis added)

We have seen this taking of "unearned" profits and income before. It is simply the confiscation of all returns from capital investments. Without capital investments, our capitalist free society collapses. When capital investments are put at risk, or even so much as threatened to be at risk, who is going to invest? This is the chaotic effect Obama's confiscation of 95 percent of General Motors had on private investments when they paid only pennies on the dollar to GM-"guaranteed" bondholders. Even the returns from the $3.7 trillion municipal bond market are now being threatened by such municipal bankruptcies as Stockton, California, while the billions of dollars in public debt resulting from their municipal public employee union benefit packages are being forgiven.[47] With no investment, safe government will be left as the only entity capable of investing. This will leave progressive government planners as *the* overseers of all such ensuing collective investments. This, in turn, will leave those same progressive planners with *the* sole power of choosing all winners and all losers according to their decreed "social value"! And the market, where the people are free to determine the value of such things themselves, will be no more! Remember the 1976 United Nations Conference on Human Settlements:

> D. Land
> (Agenda item 10 (d))
> Preamble
> 1. Land...cannot be treated as an ordinary asset, controlled by individuals and subject to the pressures and inefficiencies of the market. *Private land ownership is also a principal instrument of accumulation and concentration of wealth and therefore contributes to social injustice*; if unchecked, it may become a major obstacle in the planning and implementation of development schemes. *Social justice, urban renewal and development, the provision of decent dwellings-and healthy conditions for the people can only be achieved if land is used in the interests of society as a whole....*
>
> Recommendation D.3 Recapturing plus value
> (a) Excessive profits resulting from the increase in land value due to development and change in use are one of the principal causes of the concentration of wealth in private hands. Taxation should not be seen only as a source of revenue for the community but also as a powerful tool to encourage development of desirable locations, *to exercise a controlling effect on the land market and to redistribute to the public at large the benefits of the unearned increase in land values*[39] (emphasis added).

When the taxes, permits, licenses, mandated regulations, and government fee costs come in at or above any possible or expected returns and profits, private ownership becomes at least impractical, if not wholly impossible! Rauschenbusch's "social order" *is a sustainable* Christianity!

> The problem with which our nation is now wrestling is how to resocialize monopolistic corporations that refuse to bow their mighty necks under the yoke of public service. *We are proceeding at present under the assumption that government inspection and control, publicity and the pressure of public opinion, can socialize them.* But can it? Is not the form of their organization too exclusive, and the purpose of their profit-making too unsocial, ever to make them more than *forced servants of the common good?*...The whole institution of private property exists because it is for the public good that it shall exist. If in any particular it becomes dangerous to the fare, it must cease. (p. 425–426)

Stop right here and burn this one absolute and simple truth into your brain: *a free people who know and understand the fundamental principles and benefits of their Individual Freedom could never ever be brainwashed into communism!* As such, we could never willingly be any "more than *forced servants of the common good.*" We as free Americans know that in truth, the common good of every individual can only be served in a free society where our only common good is the Individual Liberty we all hold in common! I pray that this *Last Call for Liberty* will help us all come to a better understanding of what our sacred Liberty is, where it comes from, what preserves it, *and* what threatens it before it is too late; for as we have seen, her enemies understand both all too well! Investigating just such an enemy, the Weather Underground, FBI agent Larry Grathwohl, as you might remember from chapter 1, testifies to this fact and to what ends they were prepared to go in "forcing" our compliance to their new social order, reporting this:

> [T]hey felt that this counter-revolution could best be guarded against *by creating and establishing reeducation centers* in the Southwest, *where we would take all the people who needed to be reeducated into the new way of thinking and teach them how things were going to be.*
>
> I asked, well, what is going to happen to those people that we can't reeducate, that are die-hard *capitalists*? And the reply was they would *have to be eliminated.* And when I pursued this further, *they estimated that they would have to eliminate 25 million people in these reeducation centers. And when I say "eliminate," I mean kill—25 million people*[48] (emphasis added).

Rauschenbusch continues:

> *The right of a man to his home, his clothing, and any simple savings of his labor is not practically questioned by anybody.* The social use of that can easily be controlled by law. It is different with great fortunes. Even if their accumulation is just, their perpetuation is dangerous. The community may allow the man who has collected a great fortune its undisturbed posses-

sion during his lifetime, *but the moral claim to it weakens when he tries to govern it by his will after he is dead and gone.* The right to make a will and to have the community enforce it is historically a recent right, and all governments limit it. *A man cannot do what he will with his own* (emphasis added).

When he says here that "the right of a man to his home, his clothing, and any simple savings of his labor is not practically questioned by anybody," we should remember the fuller context of this philosophy as Pierre Kropotkin forewarned us in the first chapter of this work:

> Socialists know what is meant by protection of property. Laws on property are not made to guarantee either to the individual or to society the enjoyment of the produce of their own labour. On the contrary, they are made to rob the producer of a part of what he has created, and to secure to certain other people that portion of the produce which they have stolen either from the producer or from society as a whole. When, for example, the law establishes Mr. So-and-So's right to a house, it is not establishing his right to a cottage he has built for himself, or to a house he has erected with the help of some of his friends. *In that case no one would have disputed his right.* On the contrary, the law is establishing his right to a house which is *not* the product of his labour; first of all, *because he has had it built for him by others*

> to whom he has not paid the full value of their work; and next because that house represents a social value, which he could not have produced for himself. *The law is establishing his right to what belongs to everybody in general to nobody in particular*⁴⁹ (emphasis added).

How many of us build our own house? How many grow, make and mill their own lumber, forge their own nails, manufacture their own windows, and everything else that goes into them with their own two hands? Hard to do without the private property to grow all those trees or own all the resources needed to do so. Therefore, the reality here is that it is nearly impossible for us to "own" anything. So even the mere promise that Mr. So-and-So has an "undisputed" right to his home and clothing and such, unless he's growing his own cotton or raising his own sheep for wool to make those clothes, that promise is not only impossible and counter to the Philosophy from which it comes. Per that philosophy itself, it's an out-and-out *lie*! Such is the philosophy of Obama's "You didn't make that happen, somebody else did"!

> *A progressive inheritance tax is one of the most approved ways of resocializing large fortunes*, and it should be applied far more thoroughly than hitherto, not only to add to the public income, but *to protect the social order* (emphasis added).

Consider that this is being said just one year before the enactment of the Sixteenth Amendment. Now, consider what an inheritance tax is. It's an out-and-out confiscation of at least a portion of your property's value upon your death to be returned to the rightful owner—the government. Consider that with the onset of Obamacare's centralized medicine, the inheritance tax jumped to 55 percent in January of 2013. Consider some States either already have, or are considering, an inheritance tax of their own to add to it. How many family businesses and family farms, which in many cases have been in the family for generations, will have to be surrendered when the realization hits that the next generation will effectively be forced to remortgage them just to pay the tax? Such a tax "socializes" private property breaking the cycle of what collectivists see as the "unearned" privileges of the "property class."

> A private business that employs thousands of people, uses the natural resources of the nation, enjoys exemptions and privileges at law, and is essential to the welfare of great communities *is not a private business. It is public*, and *the sooner we abandon the fiction that it is private, the better for our good sense.* (p. 426–427).

Where Rauschenbusch says we need to "abandon the fiction" that our businesses are private, Alinsky says: "The corporations must forget their nonsense about the 'private sectors'…every American individual or corporation is public as well as private"[50] (emphasis added).

And where Rauschenbusch says, "A private business that employs thousands of people, uses the natural resources of the nation, enjoys exemptions and privileges at law, and is essential to the welfare of great communities," Obama tells us about two things: "If you've got a business—you didn't build that. Somebody else made that happen," and businesses that are "too big to fail." And again, the web comes back around!

CHAPTER IV

COMMUNITY LIFE AND PUBLIC SPIRIT

> For generations we have been taught to regard every in crease of public property and public functions with a sort of instinctive dread. *The doctrine that the best State governs least* has been drilled into us as civic orthodoxy.
>
> In fact, it *is a dangerous heresy....*
>
> *The more democracy makes the State and the People to be identical in extent and interest, the less reason is there to fear state activity.* Under true democracy state action comes to mean action of the People for their own common good, and why should we fear that?[51]

Again, history has shown us otherwise that there is indeed a historically *proven* need for those disarmed of the freedom and independence of their Individual Liberty to fear such forceful "State Action"!

How does democracy make "the State and the people to be identical"? By force of faction! Exactly as we are warned almost word for word by Madison in Federalist 10! Democracy is, after all, *the* road, *the* mob rule that enables Marx's *dictatorship of the proletariat*! Where, may I ask, in the spirit of Madison is the diversity in that?

From Rauschenbusch, the social church splits, divides, and multiplies, becoming systemic throughout the whole of society via all aspects of the Philosophy including emergent, liberation, black liberation, and identity churches in every denomination. Through such organizations as the Brotherhood of the Kingdom, YMCA, YWCA, and the National Council of Churches (NCC), the social church has helped interject communism into every pillar of society. To illustrate the magnitude of the infiltration via Rauschenbusch's social church, full out congressional investigations of "un-American activities" were launched. In one such investigation, a "protégé" of his, Harry F. Ward, who once chaired the ACLU, was cited by former communist Manning Johnson as the "chief architect for Communist infiltration and subversion in the religious field...as instructed by the Kremlin."[52]

According to founder Jim Wallis, *Sojourners* "was founded in 1971...by a small group of seminarians at Trinity Evangelical Divinity School near Chicago...*[I]t has always been defined by the mission of articulating a biblical vision of social justice-writing, speaking, and mobilizing; challenging the church, the media, and the government with a progressive Christian message.*"[53] From their 2006 *A Covenant for a New America* comes an article titled "A Policy Strategy for Overcoming Poverty."

In it, *Sojourners* reestablishes some familiar positive human rights as church policy:

> In our preaching and advocacy, we will raise the common moral values that should undergird our society and insist that the principle of the common good be the standard that guides public policy.
>
> We are not committed to any particular ideological method or partisan agenda to achieve these policy goals; *we are committed to achieving them....*
>
> SOCIAL AND GOVERNMENT RESPONSIBILITY. *It is time to end the bitter debate between big or small government,* by committing ourselves to good and effective government.
>
> HEALTH CARE. *Health care is a human right*, not a commodity available only to those who

can afford it. All who work and those unable to work should be assured of quality health care.

HUNGER. *Federal nutrition programs provide about 20 times as much food to needy people as all the charitable programs in the country combined.*

EDUCATION. Creating a sense of community, connectedness, and empowerment in schools is critical to motivating students and teachers to do their best work. *New ways of thinking and acting* should focus on parental involvement, respect teachers more, emphasize neighborhood schools, provide accountability to the community....

HOUSING. A decent place to live is essential t ending poverty in the world (emphasis added).

As the ability of businesses to maintain a healthy profit margin continues to be further and further restricted by ever compounding redistributive restrictions, the progressive argument that "federal nutrition programs provide about 20 times as much food to needy people as all the charitable programs in the country combined" may one day ring true. However, only a healthy, prosperous people can be charitable. And where it is only Individual Liberty that offers a road to such prosperity via enterprise, it is actually the collective Philosophy, which Wallis himself herein champions, that endeavors to prevent it.

Are these not the exact same positive rights from FDR's New Bill of Rights, the 1977 USSR Constitution, UN Declaration of Human Rights and Prison? Now, for some updates:

IMMIGRATION. We should not establish penalties for humanitarian and church groups *helping undocumented immigrants*....

ASSET CREATION. The wealth gap is even greater than the income gap, especially among minority families. Families should be assisted in asset and wealth creation that provides security and freedom through such means as *Individual Development Accounts,* proposals that *provide newborns with a match-eligible savings account,* and other proposals that match individual effort with additional funds....

GOVERNMENT AND RELIGIOUS PARTNERSHIPS. Faith-based service providers should not be expected to replace the role of government in addressing social needs. Efforts of religious groups can be strengthened if given greater public respect, resources, and *a place at the decision-making table in the planning and implementation processes*....

RACIAL JUSTICE. We need...greater respect for basic *human rights*....

CIVIC AND BUSINESS PRACTICES. It is time to *reverse* the divisions, conflict, and *individualism defining our society and hurting our families, communities, nation, and the world*[54] *(emphasis added).*

The progressive cry for separation of church and State does *not* seem to apply to progressive churches as they openly seek their place at the progressive planning table!

While at that table, they will do everything in their newfound power to "reverse" all that is "individualism" and all that has long defined a free America.

From the March–April 2004 issue of *Sojourners*, more is learned of the relationship of the social church to the community organizing of none other than Saul Alinsky himself in an article by Helene Slessarev-Jamir, *Saul Alinsky Goes to Church*:

> The origins of *community organizing* are generally traced to the pioneering work of Saul Alinsky, who built the first community organizing effort in Chicago's Back of the Yards neighborhood in the 1930s. *Alinsky created the early community-based efforts by organizing existing groups into collective action around particular issues*...In poorer communities, churches are often experiencing the... loss of cohesiveness as they struggle to survive in an increasingly barren environment. Thus, *organizing becomes a means for such congregations to reconnect with their own members and with the broader community around them.*

If we are "lost" in the spiritual sense, and our communities are then also just as "lost," is the church of God, whose mission it is to "bring in the sheaves" as "fishers of men" so that we may be "saved through Jesus," changing its mission to instead come out to reconnect with us in our "lost ways," going to save either the church or us, or doom both the church and us into being forever lost? If the church redefines its mission from connecting us to God to now just reconnecting with us, who then will be left to help reconnect any of us to God?

Congregation-based *community organizing* is the fastest growing form of organizing in the country, according to...the Catholic Campaign for Human Development. "No one else approximates faith-based organizing"...The only non-faith-based organization that has built comparable power is *ACORN*, or the Association of Communities Organized for Reform Now....

Churches that become engaged in *community organizing* are most often rooted in faith traditions that recognize that *sin is not just personal, but social and economic* as well. Thus, *poverty* is not simply the result of personal moral failure, but is also *caused by the sins of the larger economic or social system....Community organizing* becomes a means by which churches can act against *corporate sin*....

For people who have been marginalized by mainstream society, the church is often the one institution offering them the space to freely develop their leadership abilities by serving as deacons, trustees, musicians, and teachers. This makes the church an excellent starting point for building a powerful community organization.

The Discount Foundation study concluded that having a membership based in community institutions, especially within congregations, had enabled the *community organizing projects* documented to establish themselves as stable and financially viable organizations, *accountable to the communities* in which they operate. Each organization has *leveraged the*

> *social capital of congregations to achieve social change*; provided a *progressive alternative to the Religious Right*; and built an *organizational culture* that fused religious language, symbols, and values with organizing principles of accountability and civic participation.
>
> Chicago's United Power for Action and Justice—a wide network of *churches and local unions*—spent months discussing the values on which their broad-based effort would be founded[55] (emphasis added).

Here again, per the Philosophy, "Poverty is...caused by the sins of the larger economic or social system," which is capitalism, otherwise known as *whiteness*, which is *the* "collective sin" of free America. This "collective sin" *will* require our "collective salvation" to be remedied! But what exactly is *the* "collective sacrifice" they seek that might ensure the "collective salvation" of America's collective "whiteness" so we might be forgiven by the new social order? Before we can answer that, we must come to a fuller understanding of our "whiteness."

In the May 2010 issue of *Sojourners*, Soong-Chan Rah asks a question that leads us down a darker path, "Is the Emerging Church for Whites Only?"

> At the turn of the millennium, I [Soong-Chan] began hearing a lot about the "emerging church"....
>
> At the time the emerging church was coming into vogue, I was pastoring a multi-ethnic, urban church plant in the Boston area. It seemed that every brochure for nearly every pastors' conference I received featured the emerg-

ing church. As I began to attend some of those conferences, *I noticed that every single speaker who claimed to represent the emerging church was a white male....*

Memories from my own spiritual journey flooded my mind—memories of hopelessness and longing, of wanting to believe there was something more rich and diverse about Christian life than what I was experiencing *in the white suburbs....*

In truth, the term "emerging church" should encompass the broader movement and development of a new face of Christianity, one that is diverse and multi-ethnic in both its global and local expressions. It should not be presented as a movement or conversation that is *keyed on white middle- to upper-class suburbanites....*

A "wider voice [being given to] a wider breadth of people." More specifically...the emerging church should seek to become an agent in "creating opportunities for those who, in the past, have been marginalized." This would direct the conversation *away from being centered* "exclusively on a Western theological perspective," giving those who have *long been subordinated to colonialism* an opportunity to *"deconstruct non-helpful religious constructs" and engage God in their own ways...*there is a difference between *racial diversity and racial justice.* Simply including people from ethnic minorities in events and leadership positions *is not enough.* Doing so may create the appearance of racial diversity, but this

> would only be a surface solution. Instead, *the emerging church must engage in…"racial penance,"* a situation in which there is *true justice* between people of different ethnicities, *allowing the church to "get rid of Western, white captivity…* friendship is important for repentance" and that "isolation is dangerous"….
>
> The emerging church needs to offer "new language and tools to help the next generations understand church." This, combined with the *drive for racial reconciliation and justice*, will be crucial for ethnic churches such as the African-American church, which places high value on "negotiating the [role] of race"….
>
> The burgeoning church is not just a small sliver of American Christianity; rather, it must be seen in the context of a larger movement of God *on a global scale*[56] (emphasis added).

So it is that "the emerging church must engage in…'racial penance.'" This is *the* ecumenical accusation that there are great society-wide sins being committed by all white people in this "white" society! It is now the social duty of the church to "drive for racial reconciliation and justice" to "get rid of Western, white captivity."

With this, we begin to get a picture of what our "whiteness" might be.

To bring that picture into sharper focus, we need an education in *Race, Space, and Place*. It is a college course specifically designed to address academically the very same "social injustices" that the emergent social church targets spiritually. Part of the course curriculum is an essay by Judy Helfand titled "Constructing Whiteness," in which she details some of the intricacies of our American "whiteness."

In this paper, I hope to show that *whiteness consists of a body of knowledge, ideologies, norms, and particular practices that have been constructed over the history of the American colonies and the U.S. with roots in European history* as well. The knowledge, ideologies, norms, and practices of whiteness affect how we think about race, what we see when we look at certain physical features, how we build our own racial identities, *how we operate in the world, and what we "know" about our place in it.* Whiteness is shaped and maintained by the full array of social institutions—legal, economic, political, educational, religious, and cultural. As individuals and in groups, affected by whiteness, we in turn influence and shape these institutions (emphasis added).

So any and every "typical white person" steeped in the unavoidable "whiteness" of our America's eurocentric white slaveholding founding is going to automatically view anybody and everybody black through their suppressive "knowledge, ideologies, norms, and practices of whiteness." Simply a retake on Gramsci's "dominate society" or *hegemony* of American society as seen through the eyes of Helfand's "whiteness."

The important element of his theory is that *whiteness serves to preserve the position of a ruling white elite* who benefit economically from the labor of other white people and people of color. *Whiteness, as knowledge, ideology, norms, and practices, determines who qualifies as "white" and maintains a race and class hierarchy in which the group of people who qualify as white disproportionately control power and resources,* and within that group of white people, a small minority of elite control most of the group's power and resources. Not all studies of whiteness describe it as a system designed to economically benefit a small elite, but *most agree* that *racial oppression is a key element in whiteness* and that, as a group, *white people do benefit disproportionally from the race and class hierarchy maintained by whiteness* (emphasis added).

The "White[ness] Suppressor Nation' *hegemony* of Ameriᴋᴋᴋ-'A,'" as defined by the anti-imperialist, anticolonialist, anticapitalist communist definition of free enterprise and capitalism, under which 'the rich are getting richer while the poor are getting poorer" is here being reiterated by Helfand's reinterpretation of that into "the whites are getting whiter while the black are getting blacker." The correlation is not by happenstance:

> The early history of Virginia Colony provides the foundational example…to a system in which white people profited over people of color; postwar suburbanization provides another.

European Historical Basis for Whiteness
Europeans would be predisposed to the development and acceptance of a system of white racial privilege…a system designed for the specific conditions of colonial Virginia, and easily adapted by other colonies in the U.S. *In*

> *fact, the system was so well digested that by the time of the U.S. Constitution, most of those engaged in drafting and enacting it saw no internal conflict in adapting a document based on liberty, equality, and the rights of men that excluded African American lifetime bond laborers from those inalienable rights. Liberty was, within whiteness, reserved for white people* (emphasis added).

Behold, example A of the age-old deceitful tactic of discrediting the messengers to discredit the message. Helfand's divisive attempt to demonize both our founders and their legacy of Individual Liberty intrinsically fails, unless we are ignorant of the actual truth of history. And in a post-Dewey, "socially educated" America, it must be considered that, to at least some degree, we have all, by design, become products of the system. One common and sadly successful tactic of the left has been to demonize the call for Liberty by claiming that *the* Individual Freedom and Rights protected in the American Constitution excludes blacks, that those Rights were "never meant to apply to nonwhite men." This is a lie that has been progressively perpetuated by citing the *progressive* Dred Scott decision almost word for word. Accordingly, it is said that our founders never intended blacks to ever be American citizens or protected by the Constitution as such but, rather, intended them to remain slaves and be protected only as the property of their masters.

This is a revisionist interpretation of a revisionist ruling, if ever there was one, that wholly distorts and purposefully misrepresents the efforts put forth by our founders to end slavery. But why would that ruling say any different? *Seven out of the nine Supreme Court justices were proslavery, progressive Democrats!* Read the dissenting opinion sometime from the only two *antislavery non*-Democrats on the bench. This ruling brought the long-standing controversy of slavery to a head and was instrumental in upping the ante toward civil war.[57]

The message that was not only carried by our founders but forged by their own sweat and blood is embodied first in the Declaration of Independence: "That *All Men* Are *Created* Equal." This is an epic reversal from our long history in the world of vassalage and serfdom to one where the true power is to remain in the people. Just so we are clear, the DOI does *not* say that all societies, republics, democracies, states, and sovereigns are created equal. It does *not* say that the *collective* of each, thereby instituted by such supreme sovereign, derive their *equal* rations of *social justice, positive civil rights,* and "adequate living standards" upon consent of the planners.

So it is that the message of our Declaration of Independence is *not* one of shared serfdom but one of genuine God-given Individual Liberty. Our government gets its "limited" and "just powers" from the people, *not* the other way around! That message is again embodied in the Constitution. But here again, as we saw from Judge Brennan in chapter 2, the revolutionary effects of relativism are hard at work, where it is the reader, from their "learned" perspective of things, who are to give meaning to what they read, *not* the words chosen by the authors that they are reading.

For all the evidence against her heresy that American Liberty is one only "reserved for white people," none other is needed than the Civil War. Had the Constitution allowed for slavery in principle, the progressive Democrats of the Confederacy would *not* have had to secede from the Union to write one of their own that did! And if, as some say, the Civil War was *not* about slavery but rather about states' rights, may I ask, states' rights to do what?

Being that slavery existed in the American colonies for nearly two centuries prior to our founders' generation, it was then both invoked and upheld by the king of England to the disgust of *most* of our founders, who had no recourse against it! Hence, slavery is one of *the* reasons cited throughout their writings for our independence! David Barton's work has done much to document our founding truths now subject to such progressive "whiteout." John Quincy Adams, as quoted by Barton on page 296 of his "Original Intent," speaks to Helfand's exact accusation:

> The inconsistency of the institution of domestic slavery with the principles of the Declaration of Independence was seen and lamented by all the southern patriots of the Revolution; by no one with deeper and more unilateral conviction than by the author of the Declaration of Independence himself [Jefferson]. No charge of insincerity or hypocrisy can be fairly laid to their charge. Never from their lips was heard one syllable of attempt to justify the institution of slavery. They universally considered it as reproach fastened upon them by the unnatural step mother country [Great Brittan] and they saw that before the principles of the Declaration of Independence, slavery, in common with every other mode of oppression, was destined sooner or later to be banished from the earth. Such was the undoubting conviction of Jefferson to his dying day. In the *Memoir of His Life*, written at the age of seventy-seven, he gave to his countrymen the solemn and emphatic warning that the day was not distant when they must hear and adopt the general emancipation of their slaves.[58]

Then Thomas Jefferson himself is quoted on page 295–296:

> He [King George] has waged war against human nature itself, violating its most sacred rights of life and liberty in the persons of a distant people who never offended him, captivating and carrying them into slavery in another hemisphere or to incur miserable death in their transportation thither...Determined to keep open a market where men should be bought and sold, he has prostituted his negative for suppressing every legislative attempt to prohibit or to restrain this execrable commerce [that is, he has opposed efforts to prohibit the slave trade].[59]

And Elias Boudinot, president of the Continental Congress, on page 297, said:

> E]ven the sacred Scriptures had been quoted to justify this iniquitous traffic. It is true that the Egyptians held the Israelites in bondage for four hundred years...but...gentlemen cannot forget the consequence that followed: they were delivered by a strong hand and stretched-out arm and it ought to be remembered that the Almighty Power that accomplished their deliverance is the same yesterday, today, and forever.[60]

And again, as we have already learned from both Michelle Obama and Saul Alinsky, remember that our founders "had to start from where they were" to "build power for change." All we have to do is read the words of our founders themselves for us to stand firmly on the rock of truth, the most solid of ground, in our knowledge of *the* fact that this is exactly what they did. Helfand continues:

> Western Expansion and White Land Ownership
> The Homestead Act was enacted in 1862 to regulate *how the lands taken from the Indian nations that had previously inhabited them would be distributed among the colonizers* (emphasis added).

Simply a reinforcement of the Philosophy, wherein "Amerika" is the illegitimate white suppressor-nation occupier of her interior colonies.

> Promises of forty acres and a mule never materialized…defeated Southern planters eventually succeeded in ending and reversing Reconstruction and forcing African Americans back into a form of near slavery…Accordingly, the *Southern bourgeoisie* re-established the social control system of racial oppression "based on racial privileges for laboring class 'whites'" (emphasis added).

Helfand attempts to correlate capitalism with the slaveholding South by referring to the South as *the Southern bourgeoisie*. When in fact the Confederacy, with its liberty of tyranny *cannot* at all be genuinely defined by, or associated philosophically with, the "all Men are created equal" principle of Individual Liberty. As an extra-Constitutional, *progressive* state, the Confederacy of the South can *only* be "rightfully" categorized within the same tyrannical, rights-robbing progressive philosophy that she herself herein champions. So, of course, there was a "social control system of racial oppression," or as it were, racial preference, as the Confederacy was a progressive state! Racial preference is a progressive concept, *not* a freedom concept! And who uses the word *bourgeoisie* anyway?

Urban/Suburban Segregation

Within whiteness, white people feel entitled to live in safe, clean, well-maintained neighborhoods and believe that such neighborhoods are a reflection of the quality people living in them—white people....

Suburban middle-class and working-class whites may enter, or rather pass through, the urban working class and poor neighborhoods when work or entertainment brings them to the city. The poverty and homelessness they see on the streets can remain the only image they have of non-white neighborhoods, an image reinforced by the media. As adults, many white people attest to the enormous impact of their first views of people of color, as poverty stricken figures amidst urban blight, *a view sometimes provided by parents who drove them to the slums in order to show them how "those people live."* And much as immigration affected what white "looks like" by affecting who those already defined as white were able or likely to produce children with, so *segregation clearly defines who is white* and makes it less likely for borders to be crossed.

Impact of Government Programs and Policies

Wages sufficient to support a family were seen as belonging to men. Despite the fact that many women worked, their contributions necessary to the family, a "successful" man could support his family by himself. But, [Karen] Brodkin states, "The idea that a man's wage should allow him to support children and a non-wage-earning wife was *never meant to apply to nonwhite men*. In fact, she sees the whiteness and maleness of white men's work as inseparable. Unskilled factory work or hard manual labor was not seen as manly work but as suited to women or "boys." White men working in the trades, skilled occupations, or in middle-class bureaucratic or management positions, felt *entitled* to a wage that could support their family, and public discourse and policy reflected this sense of entitlement (emphasis added).

Along with some more white-suppressor nation theory, fishing for more middle-whiteness-class guilt (remember the two-step revolution of Marx, Lenin, and Alinsky), we are here again witness to the Philosophy's tactic of falsified, incriminating projection, blaming freedom for the evils of tyranny's suppressions. Where she quotes Brodkin, saying, "The idea that a man's wage should allow him to support children and a non-wage-earning wife was never meant to apply to nonwhite men," she brings up "living wage" and insinuates that it is a race-based capitalist oppression. The living wage and concept of entitlements—period—are wholly a progressive/collectivist concept. Free enterprise capitalism and a market-busting imposed unionesque "living wage" are not synonymous; they are diabolically converse. In reality, a "living wage" represents a government monopoly where government eventually holds all the power on the value of all things as well as the people themselves. It just starts with labor. The cost of labor dictated by such a declared and mandated "living" or "prevailing wage" thereby directly dictates the government-imposed cost of all things coming out of labor. Whereas in the market, people are free to vote or not vote with their dollar as to what they are willing to pay or not pay to set the value of things. Market value is the true natural value, be it priceless or worthless. And as we know, money from black buyers is no less green than money from white buyers. Again, if I want to get what "the market will bear" for my product or service, the people will tell me within what window my product or service is worth. Being that I alone am the sole owner of my labor as it is my natural property, I am then free to work or not work within that window. If times are tough, I am free to work below it for less. If I feel I am worth more or am otherwise unwilling to work within that window, I am free to hold out for more. However, if I do hold out, I alone am responsible for the outcome of the gamble, unless of course, it is all imposed. And only one entity has the power to do that—government and, of course, unions via their status as government subsidiaries. They too impose labor value.

Trade and labor unions would not allow me to work below my imposed value no matter how bad I may need the work. Work for "the dark side" (the market), and I might be "visited" by my "brothers." Like Rauschenbusch says, "Labor unions are *fighting* organizations, and fighting always abridges personal liberty and stiffens the demand for obedience and subordination." Meritocracy in a labor monopoly is thereby eliminated, and we are neither free to buy, sell, or even work except at imposed values. Union "prevailing wages" and "living wages" are both progressive and, therefore, of Helfand's own philosophy and *not* the product of Individual Liberty or free-market capitalism.

Free-market capitalism and the Free Market are actually wholly incapable of imposing anything as they are solely reactionary. Capitalism simplified is where the people demand, and the market simply delivers! Where Helfand continues with, "In fact, she sees the whiteness and maleness of white men's work as inseparable. Unskilled factory work or hard manual labor was not seen as manly work but as suited to women," she again confuses Liberty and free enterprise with Engels's "emancipated women," who can never be truly emancipated until she "can take part in production on a large, social scale, and domestic work no longer claims anything but an insignificant amount of her time." Also, here, she teaches us that "whiteness," which is capitalism, is also synonymous with "maleness." Remember that it's Marxism's implied patriarchal aspect of family that makes it bourgeois and, therefore, targeted for destruction.

Ask yourself this question: How many people of any color anywhere in America other than those living in the inner cities and on Indian reservations actually have "their first views of people of color, as poverty stricken figures"—versus—how many have "their first views of people of color" doing very, very well for themselves on television, be it as actors, pundits, politicians, musicians/rappers, sportscasters, athletes, or president? Then ask yourself, what is it that the people living in inner cities and reservations have in common that their "first views of people of color," of themselves, might be one of "poverty-stricken figures"? Is it Individual Liberty? Is it freedom and opportunity to pursue an independent happiness? Is it a thriving economy, capitalism, private property, free enterprise, or prosperity? I don't think so! Or might it be the long, long line of unrelenting false and empty but seductive progressive promises of *social justice*, *equality*, *fairness*, and government-issued rations of *positive* human rights/civil rights, welfare, subsidies, entitlements, and "liberties" that have both baited them there *and kept* them there in such poverty? Helfand continues:

Defining a White Man Through His Work

Early in the eighteenth century, in the process of creating a system of racial oppression the Southern colonies began to pass laws securing certain job-related privileges to white workers simply for being white. Such laws...barred Black workers from certain types of employment, and regulated apprenticeship such that, *with some exception*, only white workers learned skilled trades. By the middle of the eighteenth century, white workers were claiming these privileges for themselves...Within the system of racial oppression being established in the U.S. white workers were encouraged to blame enslaved and working class African Americans, *not wealthy planters and merchants*, for lack of employment or depressed wages, a pattern repeated throughout American history (emphasis added).

Note that the seed is being planted here that it is within the "white" system of "racial oppression" where "white workers were encouraged to blame enslaved and working class African Americans, *not wealthy planters and merchants*, for lack of employment or depressed wage." This must be accepted if racism is to be correlated to capitalism. However, what philosophy is truly behind the blaming of a "competition in labor" for the woes of society? Now, ask yourself, from which philosophy is it that the right of free men to work for less is actually demonized? Is it freedom, or is it the communism of progressive unionism?

Having lost the support of many Northern merchants and industrialists, the Southern slaveholders recognized the need of obtaining Northern labor support. They enlisted this support *through the Democratic party*...In support of slavery, the party stirred up fears that *freed slaves would mobilize to take over white men's jobs*. In 1844, Henry Clay of Virginia gave instructions for the writing of a pamphlet to be used in his campaign for President.

[T]he great aim...should be to arouse the [white] laboring classes in the free States against abolition. Depict the consequences to them of immediate abolition; they [emancipated African Americans] being freed would *enter into competition with the free labor*; with the American, the Irish, the German; *reduce his wages; be confounded with him; reduce his moral and social standing*.

Where capitalism, by definition, celebrates competition at all levels, it is progressivism that has long stood against the individualism and meritocracy to which competition naturally lends itself. It is because of *this* competition directly that it is ultimately the public at large, *the* customer in capitalism, as it is *the* fan in sports, who are the true benefactors of *the* excellence that competition naturally inspires! It is only in progressive ideology that such competition is professed to lead to a reduction in "moral and social standing." Where have we heard this before? Remember Margaret Sanger from her 1920 book *Women and the New Race*:

XII. Will Birth Control Help the Cause of Labor?

LABOR seems instinctively to have recognized the fact that its servitude springs from numbers... *The basic principle of craft unionism is limitation of the number of workers in a given trade....*

The weakness of craft unionism is that it does not carry its principle far enough. It applies its policy of limitation of numbers only to the trade. In his home, the worker, whether he is a unionist or non-unionist, goes on producing large numbers of children to compete with him eventually in the labor market.

That enemy [of labor] is the reproductive ability of the working class which gluts the channels of progress with the helpless and weak, and stimulates the tyrants of the world in their oppression of mankind[61] (emphasis added).

Where Helfand's "whiteness" declares it is whites who *feared competition* from freed slaves, a simple review of Sanger's indisputably progressive birth and population control, inarguably establishes *that* specific ideology of "gluts" in labor, be it by having too many "children to compete" or "Black workers" to compete, is *not* so much a "white thing" at all but rather a progressive thing. In addition, Sanger here also clearly establishes the contiguous bond that binds that *progressive fear of working class competition* (along with the other progressive strongholds of anticapitalism, antifamilyism, prounionism, collectivism, birth control, and population control) to its ultimate in social engineering—eugenics! Not to mention that the concept of a small, limited, and never growing amount of wealth "to be shared" is itself a wholly progressive concept and *not* of capitalism or Individual Liberty. In the true Liberty of true capitalism—the more, the merrier, as the more the buyers, the more the sellers, the more the jobs that open up and so forth. Where the capitalism of Individual Liberty is *the* tide to lift all boats to new heights, progressive collectivism seeks to limit, sabotage, and flat out sink our boats while only their chosen boats may float. And as we must remember, a progressive, collective, and/or sustainable society can only exist if it is a centrally planned society!

In retrospect of what we all used to be taught as children but what progressives seem to have missed is that when we tell a lie, we wind up having to lie again, again, and again in the futile attempt to cover up the lies we have already told. But then again, for those whose philosophy holds that there is no such thing as an absolute truth, then correspondingly, I would presume, there can be no outright lie. If you have ever wondered how progressive politicians spout obvious lie after proven lie without so much of an ounce of guilt or remorse, there it is. What's a lie where there can be no truth? Such is the deception of the Philosophy that it forces us to peel layer after layer after layer of lies away before we can finally expose its supreme lie: that tyranny is Liberty and Liberty is tyranny. Truth, if that is what you seek, must be sought elsewhere as the Philosophy is itself *the* anti-God and antitruth by its own definition of itself!

> Who Gets Blamed in Hard Times
> *The anti-affirmative action movement of today is an obvious outcome of the policies and ideologies historically shaping whiteness* in the labor arena. These policies and ideologies *have encouraged white men's belief in their entitlement to work*, have constructed certain trades as *white men's work*, and have created a tendency for workers to see a threat to their employment

in non-white people. Today as the policies of *increasing globalization remove jobs from the American economy*, white men forced out of work or working in lower paid positions, don't look to the corporations as the cause. Instead, as the job pool shrinks, *the white working class argues that unqualified people of color are taking their jobs*. With their *privilege* to earn a *living wage* being threatened, white men react by demanding that the privilege be reinforced, not by new government and economic policies that will lead to full employment, but by targeting immigrants and people of color. Without an understanding of *how their favored economic standing is a result of a system of racial oppression designed to benefit the capitalist owners*, white workers tend to see themselves as individual actors who worked hard to get where they are and to *feel they deserve it* (emphasis added).

So stands the progressive accusatory that "[t]he anti-affirmative action movement is an obvious outcome of the policies and ideologies historically shaping whiteness" that has "encouraged white men's belief in their entitlement to…white men's work" and "see a threat to their employment in non-white people." Should these antiaffirmative action "white men forced out of work…look to the corporations as the cause" of globalization moving the good "white" jobs overseas? Let's consider the question.

The term *globalization* opens a small but purposeful opening for confusion. In contrast to *globalism*, which is another term for the progressive/socialist one world order, *globalization* is the globalist term for the worldwide spread of imperialism, capitalism, and colonialism, otherwise known as the bourgeois exploitation of the third world. In and of itself, globalization cannot "remove jobs from the American economy" as it opens up whole new markets for not only recourses but American products and services as well. The key word is *markets*! However, progressively imposed "social values" on labor would and are moving—or, rather, redistributing—those jobs as we speak! High imposed extra-market values on labor in America translates to low imposed values on almost everything everywhere else. All this equals imposed job losses here in America! Far from being any "white" capitalist system of racial oppression that's killing all jobs in America, it is actually globalism as *the* imposed progressive/socialist new or one world order that is killing them! Via its imposed values on labor, it is *globalism* that actively imposes not only the redistribution of America's wealth and jobs to the world but her power as well! Burger King didn't want to move to Canada to escape free trade!

Affirmative action is just another extension of the progressive imposed "social value system," where not only the value of one's labor is socially imposed but the value of one's socially assigned group or collective as well, be it race, gender, sexual orientation, or whatever. Capitalism is, by definition, a competition. It is a meritocracy where you are truly judged by the content of your character, quality, and production levels. Capitalism, as *the* target and victim of the "progressive imposed value system" is here being blamed for the job losses that, in reality, it *needs* to thrive. If one's business isn't growing, it's dying, and no business is in business to kill itself!

As far as "white men's belief in their entitlement to…white men's work," again, as we have already learned, "entitlements" themselves are a progressive collectivist concept that simply *cannot* exist outside collectivism or without a positive charter. They are of civil origin and come *only from an all controlling government*. However, in a truly free society, the reality is that *no* business employee can be "entitled" to their work as no business, even in a flourishing economy, is "entitled" to succeed! Is any team in sports ever entitled to the win? Hell no, they have to earn it! How could anything in life be a *win* if it isn't hard-won? What real meaning or sense of accomplishment could it possibly hold for us to be a player in a game, any game, even the game of life, to the very best of our individual God-given talents if the winners and losers of that game have already been predetermined? Would we not be nothing more than slaves to another's will and end regardless of any entitlement we may have been promised along the way toward that end? Would we not be reduced to mere pawns to be moved about the board at the will and pleasure of the planners of that game, to be sacrificed at their whim and their pleasure, for the benefit of none but them? However, such is the only context within which any "entitlement" can even come to exist as, again, by definition, a collective or "sustainable" society *must* be a *planned* society! Where is the freedom in being such a pawn? It is *impossible*! But such is the great deception in the "shared responsibility" of progressive collectivism!

Helfand continues:

> There are many white people who live in poverty...Yet whiteness keeps them largely invisible to working class and middle class whites. I do not intend to imply that all white workers have benefited equally from the economic advantages whiteness provides in the labor market. However, within whiteness, even those who have received little benefit, often accept the knowledge, ideologies, norms and practices of whiteness, and then find their failure to succeed a personal failure, accepting their status of white as an indication of their innate worth, which they have not lived up too.

Whiteness, of course, is equally racist to both blacks and poor whites shaming the poor whites so completely that they actually become "invisible. Note that within Helfand's whiteness, such poor and unaccomplished whites have been left behind based on account of their personal or individual failure, where rich whites succeed only by their advantage—"whiteness."

Where to Go from Here

The social construction of whiteness does not proceed along only one front, but is occurring constantly in the social, cultural, economic, political, legal, educational and economic arena...Notably absent from this paper are examples of how whiteness is constructed and maintained within educational institutions, the judicial and penal system, electoral politics and voting and health care....

There is no one "right" interpretation of how whiteness is constructed. What remains undeniable is the inequitable distribution of wealth and income, and the inequitable distribution of power, defined as the ability to influence outcome. The distribution is inequitable in regard to race, and also within the "white" category (and other racial categories as well). *Those of us who choose to work for social justice, for a more equitable distribution of wealth, income, and power, can benefit from an understanding of how we have arrived at the current situation. We also need to understand how whiteness is constantly shifting, remaking itself as necessary*

> *to counter our efforts to undermine the system of racial oppression at its heart.*
>
> *Globalizing corporate capitalism is spreading whiteness around the world, much as colonialism and imperialism* did in previous centuries (emphasis mine).

Finally, after a classic progressive end around, she gets to her point: whiteness is capitalism on the world stage. As she tells us herself, it is "corporate capitalism" that "is spreading whiteness around the world." This imperialist/colonialist white-suppressor nation of America is globalizing, suppressing, and exploiting not only nonwhites and the third world but the earth itself, raping it of all its natural recourses that the great white suppressor 1 percent live in gluttonous, unsustainable extravagance at the expense of the world's nonwhite 99 percent.

After getting to that point, she capitalizes it with this, "We also need to understand how whiteness is constantly shifting, remaking itself as necessary to counter our efforts to undermine the system." But then she adds as a camouflage to the whole message this universally accepted finite: "of racial oppression at its heart." Only America, as she was founded, is that oppressor! If you accept the finite—"undermining racial oppression," which we all do—then it is assumed that you accept the whole "undermining the system." It is a deception, as we have now seen over and over, that then translates Alinsky-style via the middle-class majority of Lenin's "democracy" into the national revolutionary consensus of Marx's dictatorship of the proletariat, from which revolutionary, progressive politicians then validate their anticonstitutional "fundamental transformation" of our once free America toward socialism and final end of "world communism"—or, as it were, a single global human organism!

Wouldn't it be nice, though, if we did have the luxury of taking the time to "detach" ourselves from the "narrow circle" of our daily grind to as Woodrow Wilson envisioned and "conduct" ourselves to some "high place" and "think of the sweeping tides of humanity"; to see how all the different aspects of this deceptive philosophy in a single glance and see that they are all really just working together as one to seduce us out of our Liberty as one. If we did, maybe we would have seen this philosophy coming a lot sooner, and this book wouldn't even be needed to accomplish that. But that doesn't mean that the Philosophy doesn't, from time to time, tell us in its own words that it is exactly that, as Halfand then tells us:

> Social justice, environmentalist, and peace activists are really all engaged in the same struggle.

To which, she then states:

> I'm suggesting, as one tool in our tool belt, we use a *framework* from within which we *look for whiteness in any given social issue*. Then we analyze the balances and tensions in the *ongoing construction of whiteness* represented by that instance. This understanding will aid us in strategizing, in figuring out where to bring our energy so as to shift those balances and tensions in the favor of harmony and justice among all people[62] (emphasis added).

Whiteness, as she here herself tells us, is really nothing more than just another "tool" in the belt of progressive revolutionaries to be used in the effort to further pry apart what is left of our once free society that the "harmony and justice" of a forced communism may be imposed.

Note: this essay in critical theory's "Constructing Whiteness" was only one of the many similar essays that is included in a Cornell University's Race, Space, and Place"/Race and Ethnicity curriculum being brought into our prisons and taught to inmates. How are convicted and incarcerated felons to interpret its "efforts to undermine the system"? How are convicted felons subjected to such a course to receive its revolutionary message that it's *not* them who needs to change but society itself? Where's the rehabilitation in that?

What is critical theory'? It is simply the applied, *directed* social science of criticizing any and all aspects of our Individual Liberty, its origin, what enables it, what perpetuates it, and what preserves it. It is *the* fundamental principle of political correctness. Right along with environmentalism, sustainability, evolutionism, globalism, humanism, collectivism, classism, and progressivism, *criticalism*—be it critical of gender, religion, class, property, family, or race—always embodies the classic Marxist mantra of oppressor versus oppressed. The very first words in chapter 1 of Marx and Engel's 1848 *The Communist Manifesto* state:

> The history of all hitherto existing society is the history of class struggles.
>
> Freeman and slave, patrician and plebeian, lord and serf, guild-master and journeyman, in a word, *oppressor and oppressed*, stood in constant opposition to one another, carried on an uninterrupted, now hidden, now open fight, *a fight that each time ended, either in a revolutionary reconstitution of society at large*, or in the common ruin of the contending classes[63] (emphasis added).

According to *Race Traitor* magazine, critical race theory (CRT) holds that (1) "the key to solving the social problems of our age is to abolish the white race" and (2) "treason to whiteness is loyalty to humanity." The hatred being professed here in the call from *Race Traitor* to "Abolish the White Race—By Any Means Necessary"[64] may sound more extreme in comparison to all the other isms to which CRT is aligned, but is it? Don't they all seek the very same end? Isn't the whiteness of CRT, as we have just seen, our very own Individual Liberty by another name? Like CRT, don't all progressivisms attack the very same Hydra of God, family, and property? Don't they all seek the very same revolutionary transformation of the same Constitution that secures to each of us all that is our Individual Liberty?

The intro for Race, Space, and Place is a splash course in Courageous Conversation. What is Courageous Conversation? Why do we need such a course? And what would be so courageous about a conversation anyway? On February 18, 2009, "America's first black attorney general" Eric Holder courageously informed us:

> Though this nation has *proudly* thought of itself as an ethnic melting pot, *in things racial, we have always been* and we—I believe continue to be in too many ways *essentially a nation of cowards*[65] (emphasis added).

When it comes to "things racial," have we really always "proudly" been "a nation of cowards"? If, as per this criticalism, you are in denial of this ever-present American cowardice, you are in *need* of some *courageous conversation*!

The course begins with the Hegelian predetermined end that *all* white people are indeed cowardly, oppressive, and inherently racist. This is the fundamental principle of critical race theory. To have this "courageous conversation," we *must* first commit to four agreements: "stay engaged," "experience discomfort," "speak your truth" (to power?), and "expect and accept nonclosure." Per the course, "embracing these agreements will allow educators to engage, sustain and deepen interracial dialogue about racial identity, racism, and *the racial achievement gap*." Then you can "speak your truth" as "too often, we don't speak our truth out of *fear* of offending, appearing angry, or *sounding ignorant*." "Whites," it continues, "may be *afraid* that (in) doing so…they will then be targeted." Courageous conversation is *the* effort to expose your *predetermined* ignorance and publicly embarrass you with it! Comte's positive, *directed science* of sociology is alive and well in courageous conversation. In essence:

> White people need to speak to their own personal truth, as *this is the only way* for them to fully engage their racial consciousness. "Even though they may *fear* appearing racist…speaking honestly is *the way* that White people can… develop deeper understanding of the racial perspectives and experiences of others"[66] (emphasis added)

Courageous conversation is *the* effort in progressive academia to milk out of its participating victims that one coveted "see, I told you so" moment that publicly *proves* you are racist! Denying your predetermined racism only confirms your racism. Your "color blindness" or lack of any "racial consciousness" only proves how ignorant you are and how racist the whole of the American *hegemony* is. It only proves how "white" the whole of *your* suppressive, imperialist *Amerikkk-A* capitalist society really is. Those of color who happen to succeed in America have simply forsaken their race to be white. Such is the "education" of Ivy League academia.

As disturbing as the whiteness of CRT and Race, Space, and Place are, they only scratch the surface of the hatred harbored for any and all things American by black liberation theology (BLT). Though we touched on the mind-set in the first chapter, BLT expands our understanding of just how deep or, for that matter, how high that hatred goes. That we might begin to comprehend BLT, there is this comprehensive profile of the Reverend James Cones from Discover the Networks:

> *Ordained* by the African Methodist Episcopal Church, James Hal Cone is a theologian credited most notably with founding and advancing black *liberation theology*, which combines tenets of Christian socialism and the Black Power movement. He came into the forefront of public consciousness when *Jeremiah Wright, Barack Obama*'s controversial pastor, *named him in 2007* as the preeminent influence on his on theology.
> Working from a strong Marxist base, [*liberation theology teaches that the New Testament gospels can be understood only as calls for social activism, class struggle, and revolution aimed at overturning the existing capitalist order and installing, in its stead, a socialist utopia where today's poor will unseat their "oppressors"*] and become liberated from their material (and, consequently, their spiritual) deprivations. An extension of this paradigm, *black* [*liberation theology seeks to foment a similar Marxist revolutionary fervor founded on racial rather than class solidarity*].

> James Cone was born in 1938 and was raised in Arkansas. He earned a B.A. degree from Philander Smith College in 1958; a Bachelor of Divinity degree from Garrett-Evangelical Theological Seminary in 1961; and M.A. (1963) and Ph.D. (1965) degrees from Northwestern University. He also has been awarded eight honorary degrees, including a Doctor of Divinity from Garrett-Evangelical Theological Seminary.
>
> Characterizing America as an irredeemably "*racist society*," Cone argues that white people traditionally have exploited Christianity as an opiate of the [black] masses. He *asserts* that the destitute "are made and kept poor by the rich and powerful few," and that "[n]o one can be a follower of Jesus Christ without a political commitment that expresses one's solidarity with victims.

Note that the social order here has gone from being our brother's keeper to being in "solidarity with victims."

> Influenced by the Christian existential philosophy of Paul Tillich and the Black Power movement of Malcolm X, *Cone exhorts black Christians to reject the "White Church," which he claims has failed to support them in their struggle for equal rights.*
>
> Claiming that "black values" are superior to American values, Cone's writings posit a black Jesus who leads African Americans as the

"chosen people." "*This country was founded for whites, and everything that has happened in it has emerged from the white perspective,*" he writes. "*What we need is the destruction of whiteness, which is the source of human misery in the world.*"

In 1969, Cone characterized *white society as the antichrist,* and the white church as an institution that was racist to its core. Thus he posited "*a desperate need for a black theology, a theology whose sole purpose is to apply the freeing power of the gospel to black people under white oppression.*"

Cone's "desperate need for a black theology" is in full compliance with Raushenbush's "new foundation of Christian thought" to serve as the next "lever and fulcrum for the engineering task of the present generation…in the regeneration of society."

In his landmark 1969 book *Black Theology and Black Power,* Cone wrote:

"The time has come for white America to be silent and listen to black people…*All white men are responsible for white oppression…* Theologically, Malcolm X was not far wrong when he called the white man 'the devil'…Any advice from whites to blacks on how to deal with white oppression is automatically under suspicion as a clever device to further enslavement."

In that same volume, Cone penned these sentiments about universal black goodness and white evil:

> "For white people, God's reconciliation in Jesus Christ means that God has made black people a beautiful people; and if they are going to be in relationship with God, *they must enter by means of their black brothers*, who are a manifestation of God's presence on earth" (emphasis added).

Where Jesus says in John 14:6, "No man cometh unto the father but by me," Cones says white people "must enter by means of their black brothers."

> *The assumption that one can know God without knowing blackness is the basic heresy of the white churches.* They want God without blackness, Christ without obedience, love without death. What they fail to realize is that in America, God's revelation on earth has always been black, red, or some other shocking shade, but never white. *Whiteness, as revealed in the history of America, is the expression of what is wrong with man. It is a symbol of man's depravity.* God cannot be white even though white churches have portrayed him as white. When we look at what whiteness has done to the minds of men in this country, we can see clearly what the New Testament meant when it spoke of the principalities and powers. To speak of Satan and his powers becomes not just a way of speaking but a fact of reality. When we can see a people who are controlled by an ideology of whiteness, then we know what reconciliation must mean. The

coming of Christ means a denial of what we thought we were. *It means destroying the white devil in us.* Reconciliation to God means that white people are prepared to deny themselves (whiteness), take up the cross (blackness) and follow Christ (black ghetto) [emphasis added].

Other excerpts from black theology and black power include these:

> *Because white theology has consistently preserved the integrity of the community of oppressors,* I conclude that it is not Christian theology at all.
>
> [I]nsofar as this country is seeking to make whiteness the dominating power throughout the world, whiteness is the symbol of the antichrist. Whiteness characterizes the activity of deranged individuals intrigued by their own image of themselves and thus unable to see that they are what is wrong with the world (emphasis added).

This is why all white people living in "whiteness" *need* courageous conversation! Whiteness is capitalism, and capitalism is whiteness!

> *Black theology seeks to analyze the satanic nature of whiteness and by doing so, prepare all nonwhites for revolutionary action.*
>
> [L]iberal whites want to be white and Christian at the same time; but they fail to

realize that this approach is a contradiction in terms—*Christianity and whiteness are opposites.*

Intrigued by their own expertise in Christian theology, white religionists think they have the moral and intellectual right to determine whether black churches are Christian. They fail to realize that *their analysis of Christianity is inseparable from their oppressor mentality* which shapes everything they say about God.

There will be no peace in America until whites begin to hate their whiteness, asking from the depths of their being: 'How can we become black? (emphasis added).

The day that happens is the same day we as a free and enterprising people—free to pursue our own happiness and keep the fruits of our labor, surrender it all to "take up the cross (blackness)" of forced redistribution and "begin to hate our capitalist/imperialist ways (whiteness)—ask, "From the depths of our very being: How can we become communist?" Such is the essence of revolutionary progressivism's courageous "collective salvation." In a separate recorded interview, Cone clarifies even further:

> In the Black theology which I developed… If the powerful in our society, the white people, if they want to become Christians, they have to give up that power and become identified with the powerless—if you're going to be a Christian, you can't be identified with the powerful and also a Christian at the same time…The only way in which your repentance, your forgiveness can be authentic, your reception of it can

be authentic, your repentance can be authentic, is that you *give back what you took—and white people took a lot from black people*[67] (emphasis added).

In his 1970 book *A Black Theology of Liberation*, Cone <u>advanced</u> the notion of a deity that sided with blacks, and against whites:

> *Black theology refuses to accept* a God who is not identified totally with the goals of the Black community. *If God is not for us and against White people, then he is a murderer, and we had better kill him. The task of Black theology is to kill Gods who do not belong to the Black community...Black theology will accept only the love of God which participates in the destruction of the white enemy. What we need is the divine love as expressed in Black Power, which is the power of Black people to destroy their oppressors here and now by any means at their disposal. Unless God is participating in this holy activity, we must reject his love.*

Where "the task of Black theology is to kill the Gods who do not belong to the Black community," what God would they replace them with? What but an anti-God philosophy speaks of rejecting God's love if He doesn't conform to its will?

In a 2004 essay, Cone *expressed* his belief that white racism in America had not diminished at all since the publication of his aforementioned books three-and-a-half decades earlier: "Black suffering is getting worse, not better...White supremacy is so clever and evasive that we can hardly name it. It claims not to exist, even though black people are dying daily from its poison."

Also among Cone's more notable statements regarding race are the following:

> *Blackness...must*, without qualification, refer to black-skinned people who bear the scars of oppression; and [*whiteness must refer to the people responsible for that oppression*]...[T]here can be no universal understanding of blackness without the particular experience of blackness.
> [Racism is] in—it's in American culture. As you say, it's in the DNA. It's our—it's white America's original sin and it's deep.

This could be what Obama was getting at in March of 2008 when he described his own grandmother as "a typical white person, who, if she sees somebody on the street that she doesn't know, you know, there's a reaction that's been bred in our experiences that don't go away and that sometimes come out in the wrong way, and that's just the nature of race in our society."[68]

> *Yeah, it's ugly. Black [lynched] bodies hanging on trees* [in the post-slavery era]...People don't like to talk about stuff that's really deep and ugly...And if America could understand itself as not being innocent, it might be able to play a more creative role in the world today.

The lynching tree is a metaphor for race in America, a symbol of America's crucifixion of black people. See, whites feel a little uncomfortable because they are part of the history of the people who did the lynching. I would much rather be a part of the history of the lynching victims than a part of the history of the one who did it. And that's the kind of transcendent perspective that empowers people to resist.

Crucifixion and lynchings are symbols… of the power of domination. They are symbols of the destruction of people's humanity. With black people being 12 percent of the US population and nearly 50 percent of the prison population, that's lynching. It's a legal lynching. So, there are a lot of ways to lynch a people than just hanging 'em on the tree. A lynching is trying to control the population. It is striking terror in the population so as to control it. That's what the ghetto does. It crams people into living spaces where they will self destruct, kill each other, fight each other, shoot each other because they have no place to breathe, no place for recreation, no place for an articulation and expression of their humanity. So, it becomes a way, a metaphor for lynching, if lynching is understood and as one group forcing a kind of inhumanity upon another group.

Another small well-hidden fact of progressive history is that it was the *progressive democrats* of the KKK who struck fear in the very heart of America with *their* lynchings. Not solely to lynch blacks but just as much as an effort to suppress the antislavery—antilynching, prorepublic Republican vote. As a matter of stated historical fact, nearly one-third of those lynchings were white Republicans. Citing a University of Missouri–Kansas City study, David Barton tells us in his *American History in Black and White* (p. 115), "Between 1882 and 1964, 4,743 individuals were lynched—3,446 blacks and 1,297 whites."[69] There is no denying the horrific racism of the era and in what KKK committed against blacks. However, according to this study, nearly one-third of those lynched by progressive democrats of the KKK were white. Clearly, the violent voter intimidation and suppression waged by them was not limited to blacks only. It included, at least in part, the suppression, intimidation, and lynching of Republican voters, period, be they black or white.

Barton also quotes Frederick Douglas (p. 110), saying, "By means of the shotgun and midnight raid, the old master class has triumphed over the newly enfranchised citizen and put the Constitution under their feet." Note that it is the progressives of the KKK who are the "master class" doing the suppressing by "shotgun and midnight raid"[70] and *not* those fighting for our republic, Individual Liberty, and the Constitution, which protect them!

Note that is they who put the "Constitution under their feet," *not* those fighting for constitutional rule of law! Let it be known that the extraconstitutional "master class" of progressivism who so ruthlessly suppressed votes with the KKK in the South is *the* same extraconstitutional "master class" of progressivism the Obama administration has championed and put forth in their efforts to "put the Constitution under their feet." This would include their progressive efforts to suppress the constitutionalist American vote today by neutralizing our votes with the amnesty and votes of tens of millions of illegal aliens!

Though the tactics may be different, the end result is the same! As Van Jones says, they simply dropped "the radical pose for the deep satisfaction of radical ends." How has it come to pass that the overwhelming majority of those most suppressed, intimidated, and lynched by this same progressivism have now become so "organized" in support of it? How has the "master class" enemy of freedom, for black Americans especially, come to be *the* "hope and change" of their future? How has the freedom of their own Individual Liberty, the same Individual Liberty we herein champion, become what they now so adamantly "organize" against? But again, such is the evil of the great deception.

Barton then tells (on p. 119) of Rep. Richard Cain's February 3, 1875, speech, where Cain tells us:

> The bad blood of the South comes because the Negroes are Republicans. If they would only cease to be Republicans and vote the straight-out Democratic ticket there would be no trouble. Then the bad blood would sink entirely out of sight.[71]

Again, I must ask, is it our Individual Liberty, our American freedom that first draws people *of any race* into "the ghetto" and then keeps them there to control them, or might it be the seemingly endless progressive offerings that constitute all the broken promises of state-rationed social justice? This might be a good time for those who might seek to empower government via a "positive charter" over our rightfully ordained "charter of negative liberties" to consider just one small epiphany—being that "governments are instituted among men, deriving their just powers from the consent of the governed," to what greater end could such government, itself not but a mere product of our God-given Liberty, provide more for us than the whole of our Liberty? Let us fight for the whole of our Liberty, not just a redistributed ration of it!

The saddest aspect of the great deception here is that no one is telling blacks, or any people of any race, that the freedom of Individual Liberty is *not* their freedom to have and enjoy except those of the Philosophy, which includes this very black "liberation" theology!

> *All white men are responsible* for white oppression. It is much too easy to say, 'Racism is not my fault,' …Racism is possible because whites are indifferent to suffering and patient with cruelty.
>
> *To be Christian* is to be one of those whom God has chosen. [*God has chosen black people*]!
>
> *The demonic forces of racism* are real for the black man. Theologically, Malcolm X was not far wrong when he called [*the white man 'the devil'*]. The white structure of this American society, personified in every racist, must be at least part of what the New Testament meant by the demonic forces.
>
> *Black hatred is the black man's strong aversion to white society.* No black man living in white America can escape it.[72]

Such are the "Christian" teaching of the black liberation church in their effort to establish their "kingdom of God" on earth. How could the love of Jesus possibly be represented by so much hate? Again, such is the essence of the Philosophy's great deception! But our understanding of the CRT of liberation theology is still incomplete.

As it turns out, having courageous conversation is, in reality, just a one-way conversation of *courageous accusation*, where "whites" are finally forced to sit down and bear witness to the "facts" of their racial offences—that every single one of them, every man, woman and child alike, are guilty of forming, supporting, and spreading their suppressive *hegemony* that is *the* "dominant" capitalist, colonialist, imperialist, supremacist society of whiteness all across the globe.

The accusation is transdenominational. Though the Philosophy in its great deception has infiltrated Christianity so successfully and effectively as to turn it even against itself, there are other religions from which it boldly emerges. In his 1965 *Message to The Black Man in America*, Elijah Muhammad opens up for us a fuller understanding of not only the origin and extent of what might constitute Helfand's "whiteness" but of the raw, pure, and profound hatred out there for it. That hatred is of the Philosophy now targeting the Individual Liberty of free America and God Himself from whom it has all been endowed, for extinction:

> The Christians refer to God as a "Mystery" and a "Spirit" and divide Him into thirds... This contrary to both nature and mathematics. Our nature rebels against such a belief of God being a mystery...without a wife or without being something in reality....
>
> They preach and prophesy of His coming and that He will be seen on Judgment Day but is not a man.... (p. 1)
>
> To teach people that God is a Mystery God is to teach them that God is unknown. There is no truth in such teaching....
>
> *There should be a law made and enforced upon such teachers until they have been removed from the public* (emphasis added).

Where is the freedom in such a declaration that there should be a law against the teaching of Christian scripture?

> According to Allah, the origin of such teaching *is from the devils!*...They know today that God is not a mystery but will not teach it. He [devil], *the god of evil*, was made to rule the nations of the earth for 6,000 years, and naturally would not teach obedience to God other than himself.
>
> The true God was not to be made manifest to the people until the god of evil [devil] has finished or lived out his time, which was allowed to deceive the nations. (p. 2)
>
> Allah [God] loves us, the so-called Negroes (*Tribe of Shabazz*)... God is in person, and *stop looking for a dead Jesus for help*....
>
> The enemies of God today are the same as they were thousands of years ago - thinking that they will be the winner against Him. America, for her evil done to me and my people, shall be isolated and deceived by her friends. *The heavens shall withhold their blessing until America is brought to a disgraceful ruin.* (p. 5, emphasis added)

Here, we have a few revelations to point out: (1) As it was with the likes of Hobbes, Rousseau, and Bakunin, there is an animosity toward the otherworldly God of Christianity. (2) God is human, a man here on earth "in person." (3) America must be "brought to a disgraceful ruin." (4) Whoever the "devil" is, he or she is "the god of evil." And (5) the so-called Negroes are the "tribe of Shabazz." Does the name *Shabazz* ring any bells? It should as we heard this name back in chapter 1. Remember this from King Samir Shabazz of the New Black Panther Party:

> My job is to educate black people, whether they want to be educated or not. I don't give a damn what they may think about white people, *I hate white people. All of them. Every last iota of a cracker I hate him.* Because we are still in this condition.
>
> We didn't come out here to play. There is to much serious business going on in your black community to be sliding through south street with *white, dirty cracker whores* on your arms. What's a matter with you black man, you got a doomsday with a white woman on your arm.
>
> We keep begging white people for freedom. No wonder we're not free. Your enemy can not make you free fool. You want freedom *you're going to have to kill some crackers. You're going to have to kill some of their babies*[73] (emphasis added).

This is from the same King Samir Shabazz who was filmed and charged for "voter intimidation" in Philadelphia in 2008. King Shabazz and his accomplice both would later have those charges questionably dismissed by the Obama administration's new sympathetic US attorney general, "courageous" Eric Holder. And again, the web comes back around! Muhammad continues:

> The so-called Negroes fell into the hands of the slave-masters, who have robbed,

> spoiled, wounded, and killed them. The good Samaritan here would be *the Mahdi* [Allah]—God in Person, as He is often referred to by the Christians as the "the second coming of Jesus, or Son of Man to judge man." *This one will befriend the poor* [the so-called Negroes] and heal their wounds by *pouring into their heads knowledge* of self and others and free them of the yoke of slavery *and kill the slave-masters*. (p. 33, emphasis added)

Who is the Mahdi? Again, we have heard of this name before as well. Every time former Iranian president Ahmadinejad ended his speeches, whether in Iran, at an American university, or at the UN, he has prayed for the "hastening" of the return of the "twelfth imam," the "promised one," or the Mahdi, praying, "Oh God hasten the return Imam Al-Mahdi." What is key to understand here is that for him to return, the world must be in complete chaos. To hasten his return then is to bring the world into chaos. One only needs to be aware of the expressed animosity held by a "nuclear" Iran's Ahmadinejad for the State of Israel to form a plausible hypothesis of how that chaos might one day be brought about. Now, add to that the Obama administration's apparent willingness to *secretly* negotiate FOR a "peaceful" nuclear Iran,[74] and even more strands of the web come back around.

> The Black people of America have been swallowed by *the slave-masters, who are a race of devils, says all-wise God, Allah*....
> For God to fulfill His promise to deliver us from our enemies, He must go to war against the enemy…War is inevitable.

The *American white people* delight in mistreating us, their former slaves.

A continued war is made upon us by the white devils of America.... (p. 51)

It is the truth from your God and you shall soon bear me witness that it is the truth. Allah has said to me that *we are living in the end of the world of white rule, a race whom Allah has made manifest to you and me as being real devils.* (p. 100)

What can the guilty say when the truth of their guilt is made known?... The origin of sin, the origin of murder, the origin of lying are deceptions originated with the creators of evil and injustice—the white race...the most and wicked and deceiving race that ever lived on our planet....

All manner of evil and corruption has come from the white race. (p. 102, emphasis added)

And to no surprise, we find that the race of "devils" are, of course, "American white people." So when Cones speaks of white people giving back "all they took" from black people, we here learn that, per the Philosophy, "all manner of evil and corruption has come from the white race," that they are *the* origin of it all. And with that, we learn that there is no—never was any, nor could there ever be—any possible way to "give back everything they took"! This is *the* "understanding" to be gained by those, both black and white, who submit to the courageous conversation of whiteness!

Almighty God, Allah, has appeared in the Western Hemisphere [North America] *to tear off the covers of this wicked nation for their evils committed* against our people....

As long *as the devil is on our planet we will continue to suffer injustice and unrest and have no peace.*

The guilty who have spread evilness and corruption throughout the land must face the sentence wrought by their own hands.

I am offering you from Allah *a Kingdom* of righteousness that will never decay, a New World that will be based upon the principles of truth and justice *while we live.* (p. 103)

Today, the Americans hope to unite all educated so-called Negroes along with their already poisoned Negro Christian preachers against us, the Muslims, who preach freedom, justice and *equality* for the Black Nation. (p. 183)

Remember, if you are black or a member of the Black Nation *you are un-American.* If you want equal justice *and a descent way of life to live*, or have love for the black people, *you are un-American.* The American is the only one that can sing "The Land of Freedom"—*it is for white Americans.* (p. 186)

Allah hates the wicked American whites and threatens to remove them from the face of the earth.

Since white America and the white race in general have deceived the entire world of black people and their brethren (brown, red and yellow), *Allah now is causing these white people to wake up and see the white race as it really is.* (p. 270, emphasis added)

For their "evils committed" and that there may be peace, justice, equality, and rest for the chosen race of "un-Americans," Allah threatens to wipe the wicked white Americans from the face of the earth. And thus, Muhammad's new redistributive earthly "kingdom of righteousness" is offered "while we live." And as Rauschenbush says, "It was the hope of a great common salvation for all the people, the belief that the Kingdom of God on earth was at last in sight." Mohammad concludes:

> Today *America's doom is set* like a die. She cannot escape; it is impossible…When *God* appeared to me in person of Master Fard Muhammad…in 1931 Detroit, He *said that America was His number one enemy on His list for destruction.*[75] (p. 281, emphasis added)

And "America's doom is set." So it is that, as we have just been told, *this* is at the heart of what the Philosophy consistently has to offer: the destruction of not only God but America as well! This book, *Message to the Black Man in America,* is still to this day a very popular book among those, where I first came to see and read it, in our prisons.

While America is still professed to be *the* land of the free, how is it that so many Americans have come to stand against her? They do not realize or even appear to care that they do so at the expense of their own Liberty! Nor do they seem to care that they do so at the expense of the Liberty of their own children! The deception is so complete that they now see their submission and surrender to the general will in exchange for the collective rights of prisoners as *the* expression of their own free will and Liberty! It is truly a wonder to behold that they now see the loss of their own true earthly freedom of Individual Liberty, as a net gain! How could so many come to be so completely duped if not by evil itself? But such is work of the great deception.

Nevertheless, those who fight to destroy their own Liberty fight to destroy ours as well as our true Liberty and freedom are the same! Though they may see those of us who champion that freedom as the enemy, in reality, we fight not only for our Liberty but for theirs as well! As again—*our Liberty is the same*! The other side of that, of course, is if they succeed, we *all* lose.

In 1933, *The Humanist Manifesto*, authored and signed by our own John Dewey, establishes the secular as the religious in also calling for the "true kingdom of God" on earth "while we live":

> The time has come for widespread recognition of the radical changes in religious beliefs throughout the modern world. *The time is past for mere revision of traditional attitudes. Science and economic change have disrupted the old beliefs. Religions the world over are under the necessity of coming to terms with new conditions created by a vastly increased knowledge and experience.* In every field of human activity, the vital movement is now in the direction of a candid and explicit humanism. In order that religious humanism may be better understood we, the undersigned, desire to make certain affirmations which we believe the facts of our contemporary life demonstrate (emphasis added).

Our "vastly increased knowledge" of the sciences and the fact that we have applied all that earthly knowledge to our contemporary life is *the* proof there is no such thing as God. As such, we must turn away from God toward the direction of an explicit earthly humanism, or at least, adjust our religions accordingly!

> There is great danger of a final, and we believe fatal, identification of the word religion with doctrines and methods *which have lost their significance and which are powerless to solve the problem of human living in the Twentieth Century*. Religions have always been means for realizing the highest values of life. Their end has been accomplished through the interpretation of the total environing situation (theology or world view), the sense of values resulting therefrom (goal or ideal), and the technique (cult), established *for realizing the satisfactory life*. A change in any of these factors results in alteration of the outward forms of religion. This fact explains the changefulness of religions through the centuries. But through all changes religion itself remains constant *in its quest for abiding values*, an inseparable feature of human life (emphasis added).

It would be a final and fatal choice for humankind to continue believing in a God as he is powerless to solve the earthly problems of twentieth-century living. And believing in Him is worthless "for realizing the satisfactory life."

> *Today man's larger understanding of the universe, his scientific achievements, and deeper appreciation of brotherhood, have created a situation which requires a new statement of the means*

and purposes of religion. Such a vital, fearless, and frank religion capable of *furnishing adequate social goals and personal satisfactions* may appear to many people as a complete break with the past. While this age does owe a vast debt to the traditional religions, it is none the less obvious that *any religion that can hope to be a synthesizing and dynamic force for today must be shaped for the needs of this age* (emphasis added).

Again, we see Comte's *social dynamics* or what concerns "what is needed for the development of order, that is, progress" hard at work—and what Hitler, in his *Mein Kampf,* says for the national:

> Every philosophy of life, *even if it is a thousand times correct and of the highest benefit to mankind,* will be of no practical service for the maintenance of a people as long as its principles have not yet become the rallying point of a militant movement. And, on its own side, this movement will remain a mere party until is has brought its ideals to victory and transformed its party doctrines into the new foundations of a State which *gives the national community its final shape.*[35]

Dewey and the humanists say here for the international:

> It is…obvious that *any religion that can hope to be a synthesizing and dynamic force for today must be shaped for the needs of this age.*

They continue:

> To establish such a religion is a major necessity of the present. It is a responsibility which rests upon this generation. We therefore affirm the following:
> FIRST: Religious humanists regard the universe as self-existing and not created.
> SECOND: Humanism believes that man is a part of nature and that he has emerged as a result of a continuous process.

Humanism is a Godlessism! Where there is no God, there can be no creation. Where there is no creation, there is only evolution. Where there is only evolution, no man or woman can be "created equal," and no man or woman can be "endowed by their Creator" with any certain unalienable Rights as they have been confiscated and replaced with the rationed positive "human rights" allowed by the New World Order. Yet it remains, and of importance for the nonbeliever to understand, that Individual Rights and Liberty are natural. They are, therefore, endowed "naturally" by their Creator, be it nature *or* nature's God! Thus, nonbelievers as well can only defend their Individual Rights and Liberty by championing this very same natural and God-given Liberty. It's an epiphany worth careful consideration.

> THIRD: Holding an organic view of life, humanists find that the traditional dualism of mind and body must be rejected.

Or in other words, the traditional dualism of body and spirit and the individuality of our very souls must be rejected as there shall be nothing godly or sacred allowed, only the social and the secular.

> FOURTH: Humanism recognizes that man's religious culture and civilization, as clearly depicted by anthropology and history, are the product of a gradual development due to his interaction with his natural environment and with his social heritage. The individual born into a particular culture is largely molded by that culture.

Man was not created by God! God was invented by man according to his particular cultural insecurities.

> FIFTH: Humanism asserts that the nature of the universe depicted by modern science makes unacceptable any supernatural or cosmic guarantees of human values. Obviously humanism does not deny the possibility of realities as yet undiscovered, but it does insist that the way to determine the existence and value of any and all realities is by means of intelligent inquiry and by the assessment of their relations to human needs. Religion must formulate its hopes and plans in the light of the scientific spirit and method.
>
> SIXTH: We are convinced that the time has passed for theism, deism, modernism, and the several varieties of "new thought."

> SEVENTH: Religion consists of those actions, purposes, and experiences which are humanly significant. Nothing human is alien to the religious. It includes labor, art, science, philosophy, love, friendship, recreation—all that is in its degree expressive of intelligently satisfying human living. *The distinction between the sacred and the secular can no longer be maintained* (emphasis added).

As such, so shall any and all religions be reestablished through humanism! There is no antiestablishment clause (of religion) in the statist globalism of humanism.

> EIGHTH: *Religious Humanism considers the complete realization of human personality to be the end of man's life and seeks its development and fulfillment in the here and now. This is the explanation of the humanist's social passion.*
>
> NINTH: In the place of the old attitudes involved in worship and prayer the *humanist finds his religious emotions expressed in a heightened sense of personal life and in a cooperative effort to promote social well-being.*

Note that it is human "fulfillment in the here and now" that "is the explanation of the humanist's social passion." Thus, such a collective or humanist state of "cooperative social well-being" cannot exist without the denial of God! Not only are they interdependent, they are interchangeable. They are, to the progressive humanist, one and the same! This is the very essence of social justice as it is *the* Godless, redistributive, humanist "cooperative effort to promote social well-being" in action. Such is the qualifier for the social justice that has infiltrated our churches.

> TENTH: It follows that there will be no uniquely religious emotions and attitudes of the kind hitherto associated with belief in the supernatural.
>
> ELEVENTH: Man will learn to face the crises of life in terms of his knowledge of their naturalness and probability. *Reasonable and manly attitudes will be fostered by education* and supported by custom. We assume that humanism will take the path *of social and mental hygiene* and discourage sentimental and unreal hopes and wishful thinking.

These same Godless "attitudes" are the very same ones that Dewey himself established to form *the* basis upon which our progressive public school system still operates. And what if anything is to carry out this "social and mental hygiene" of humanism, if not this same progressivism's own eugenic cleansing?

> TWELFTH: Believing that religion must work increasingly for joy in living, religious humanists aim to foster the creative in man and to encourage achievements that add to the satisfactions of life.
>
> THIRTEENTH: *Religious humanism maintains that all associations and institutions exist for the fulfillment of human life. The intelligent evaluation, transformation, control, and direction of such associations and institutions with a view*

> *to the enhancement of human life is the purpose and program of humanism.* Certainly religious institutions, their ritualistic forms, ecclesiastical methods, and communal activities *must be reconstituted* as rapidly as experience allows, in order to function effectively in the modern world.

The spiritual aspect of religion is not always about the "fulfillment of human life." In fact, the main objective of Christianity isn't earthly at all but of one achieving eternal life in the kingdom of God, which according to scripture is "not of this earth." But what is this manifesto telling us here in saying that "that all associations and institutions exist for the fulfillment of human life [and] evaluation, transformation, control, and direction of such associations and institutions…is *the purpose* and program of humanism"?

They're not just referring to humanist religions, associations, and institutions here but *all* religions, associations, and institutions! How do I overemphasize this one? If *the* purpose of humanism is to "control" *all* religions, associations, and institutions as they are telling us here, then this is not only one scary, blatant, in-your-face proclamation of *depraved intolerance* but a declared intent to follow it through as *the* world's master state religion. The kicker to this comes when you see all the universalist church officials on the list of signers.

> FOURTEENTH: The humanists are firmly convinced that existing acquisitive and profit-motivated society has shown itself to be inadequate and that *a radical change in methods, controls, and motives must be instituted. A socialized and cooperative economic order must be established to the end that the equitable distribution of the*

> *means of life be possible.* The goal of humanism is a free and universal society in which people voluntarily and intelligently cooperate *for the common good. Humanists demand a shared life in a shared world.*

The concepts of God, capitalism, property rights, free-market enterprise, and anything to do with a "profit-motivated society" or, in other words, the whole of *Individual Liberty* are to be removed from society. They have all hereby been determined by humanism to be "inadequate"! This admittedly requires that "a radical change in methods, controls, and motives must be instituted"! This admittedly requires that "a socialized and cooperative economic order must be established… for the common good." Why? Because "humanists demand a shared life in a shared world." As Bill Clinton told us back at the 2012 Democratic Convention, "If you want a country of shared opportunities and shared responsibility, a we're-all-in-this-together society, you should vote for Barack Obama and Joe Biden."[76]

> FIFTEENTH AND LAST: We assert that humanism will: (a) *affirm life* rather than deny it; (b) seek to elicit the possibilities of life, not flee from them; and (c) endeavor to *establish the conditions of a satisfactory life for all, not merely for the few.* By this *positive morale* and intention humanism will be guided, and from this perspective and alignment the techniques and efforts of humanism will flow.

To affirm life is to support and uphold it, as in swearing an oath to it. Is such an oath to life consistent with UNESCO, "Its Purpose and Its Philosophy," where Julian Huxley, the 1962 Humanist of the

Year[77] declares that UNESCO's "outlook must...be based on some form of *humanism*....clearly *a world humanism...a scientific humanism*", that includes a "radical eugenic policy" as being necessary so "that the dead weight of genetic stupidity, physical weakness, mental instability, and disease-proneness" being eliminated from the human population should "at least become thinkable"?[20]

Is this consistent with the works of Margaret Sanger, the 1957 Humanist of the Year,[77] in which she declares, "It is only the wanted child who is likely to be a social asset" and "the most merciful thing that the large family does to one of its infant members is to kill it"?[3] What humanists and/or humanist organizations have stepped forward to defend any right-to-life legislation?

The possibilities of life being brought forth by humanism are of the limited collective, shared, and rationed kind, to be determined and "instituted" by them positively, *not* the unlimited kind as would be determined by the diversity of our God-given individual talents naturally. The intention of humanism is to guide you and your life via the same "positive morale" we went over chapter 2. They are the same positive rights found in FDR's New Bill of [workers'] Rights, the UN's 1948 Universal Declaration of Human Rights, the 1977 Constitution of Communist USSR, and prison! "[A]nd from this perspective and alignment the techniques and efforts of humanism will flow."

What is this humanism then if it isn't communism? Marx enlightens us to the answer in his 1844 *Economic and Philosophic Manuscripts of 1884*, where he clarifies:

> [J]ust as atheism, being the annulment of God, is the advent of theoretic humanism... atheism is humanism...with the annulment of religion, whilst communism is humanism... with...the annulment of private property).[78]

LAST CALL FOR LIBERTY

The Humanist Manifesto concludes:

> So stand the theses of religious humanism. Though we consider *the religious forms and ideas of our fathers no longer adequate*, the quest for the good life is still the central task for mankind. Man is at last becoming aware that *he alone is responsible for the realization of the world of his dreams, that he has within himself the power* for its achievement. He must set intelligence and will to the task[79] (all emphasis added).

And so it is in humanism that, as man, herein declares it is man alone who "has within himself the power" to a achieve "the quest for the good life" as "the central task for mankind" on earth. As such, man herein declares himself to be his own god with his own self-serving earthly mission.

To understand the magnitude of what is being declared here in this manifesto, we need to go back to the beginning, the very beginning, back to Adam and Eve in the Garden of Eden. As we know, their innocence was lost after being tempted by the serpent to eat of the fruit from the tree of knowledge and good and evil. We also know that the first thing they learned was that they were naked. Since that defining moment in the garden, however, humans today have become so *illuminated* with *this* earthly knowledge that not only do they no longer acknowledge the existence of God, they have ever so humbly declared themselves to be their own god! If the meek truly are to "inherit the earth," where, might we ask, is the meekness or humbleness in that? There is none! But such is the essence of the great deception. Such is the essence of progressivism's earthly humanist, collective salvation!

Every forty years, an updated version of their manifesto is issued. These updates include further clarifications as well as some new terminologies you might recognize. Among these are the following:

Humanist Manifesto II - 1973

FIRST: Traditional dogmatic or authoritarian religions that place revelation, God, ritual, or creed above human needs and experience *do a disservice to the human species.*

SECOND: Promises of immortal salvation or fear of eternal damnation *are both illusory and harmful.* They distract humans from present concerns, from self-actualization, and from rectifying social injustices. Modern *science discredits* such historic concepts as the "ghost in the machine" and the *"separable soul."* Rather, science affirms that the human species is an emergence from natural *evolutionary* forces. As far as we know, *the total personality is a function of the biological organism* transacting in a social and cultural context. There is no credible evidence that life survives the death of the body. *We continue our existence in our progeny and in the way that our lives have influenced others in our culture.*

TWELFTH: We deplore the division of humankind on nationalistic grounds. We have reached a turning point in human history where the best option is to *transcend the limits of national sovereignty* and to move toward the building of a world community...For the first time in human history, no part of humankind can be isolated from any other. *Each person's future is in some way linked to all*. We thus reaffirm a commitment to the building of world community, at the same time recognizing that this commits us to some hard choices.

FOURTEENTH: The *world community* must engage in cooperative *planning* concerning the use of rapidly depleting resources. The planet earth must be considered a single ecosystem. Ecological damage, resource depletion, *and excessive population growth must be checked* by international concord. The cultivation and conservation of nature is a moral value; we should perceive ourselves as integral to the sources of our being in nature. We must free our world from needless pollution and waste, responsibly guarding and creating wealth, both natural and human. Exploitation of natural resources, *uncurbed by social conscience*, must end.

FIFTEENTH: It is the moral obligation of the developed nations to provide—*through an international authority that safeguards human rights*—massive technical, agricultural, medical, and economic assistance, including *birth control* techniques, to the developing portions of the globe. World poverty must cease. Hence *extreme disproportions in wealth, income, and economic growth should be reduced on a worldwide basis*[80] (emphasis added).

Again, we see that to hold any belief in eternal life, which is a fundamental principle of Christianity, as well other religions, is "illusory," "harmful," and a "distraction" from our mandated collective earthly duties to social justice. And again, our only recognized "personality is a function of the biological organism."

Humanist Manifesto III - 2003

Ethical values are derived from human need and interest as tested by experience. Humanists ground values in human welfare shaped by human circumstances, interests, and concerns and extended to the global ecosystem and beyond.

Humans are social by nature and find meaning in relationships. Humanists long for and strive toward a world of mutual care and concern, free of cruelty and its consequences, where differences are resolved cooperatively without resorting to violence. The joining of individuality with interdependence enriches our lives, encourages us to enrich the lives of others, and inspires hope of attaining peace, justice, and opportunity for all.

Working to benefit society maximizes individual happiness. Progressive cultures have worked to free humanity from the brutalities of mere survival and to reduce suffering, improve society, and develop global community. *We seek to minimize the inequities of circumstance and ability*, and we support *a just distribution of nature's resources and the fruits of human effort so that as many as possible can enjoy a good life.*

Humanists are concerned for the well being of all, are committed to *diversity*, and respect those of differing yet humane views. We work to uphold the equal enjoyment of *human rights and civil liberties* in an open, secular society and maintain it is a *civic duty* to participate in the democratic process and a *planetary duty* to protect nature's integrity, diversity, and beauty in a secure, *sustainable manner*[81] (emphasis added).

And again, we have as humanism, *the* great collective lie that "[w]orking to benefit society" or surrendering our own will, faith, independence, and the whole of our natural, God-given Individual Liberty to the positive rations of the general will of the collective is what "maximizes individual happiness." And we know from what we have learned throughout this *Last Call for Liberty* that the humanist collective seeking to globally "minimize the inequities of circumstance and ability" can only mean the full surrender of any and all claim we might hold to *all* that is ours and have a Natural Right to, along with the forced confiscation and redistribution of it over to a planned coercive world. This is a truth that, though hard-won for some, will eventually be brought to light for all. Consider the later revelations of ACLU founder Rodger Baldwin:

> I reckoned with what later evidence proved misplaced faith that the world communist movement was a force for democracy, and took part with many other liberals in United Fronts for…anti-imperialism, peace and democracy. The betrayal of all humanitarian principles and democratic pretence, dramatized by the Nazi-Soviet compact, ended all remaining illusions.
> The Soviet police State, and with its servants, the communist parties, were revealed as

politically and morally no different from the fascist States, *and through deception of lofty claims to salvation, even more dangerous to human freedom*[82] (emphasis added).

Where the God-given Individual Rights of Individual Liberty are unsustainable, the Godless collective, positive human rights of humanism are sustainable. And in the end, humanism is not but a collectivist's "evolved" religion of Comte's altruism, where one's individual "personality" can *only* be recognized as *the* measure of his/her compliance to their assigned collective social "duties and obligations"! It is the "evolved" state in which earthly social justice finally takes precedence over the antiquated otherworldly priorities of a God-based morality and the "false hopes" of saving our "individual souls" and obtaining eternal life. Understanding these conflicting principles of Individual religious Liberty and humanist collectivism brings to full flower our understanding of what Rousseau was telling us back in chapter 1:

> 8 - Religion, considered in relation to society, which is either general or particular, may also be divided into two kinds: the religion *of man*, and that *of the citizen*....
>
> Religion…gives men two codes of legislation, *two rulers*, and *two countries*, renders them subject to *contradictory duties*, and *makes it impossible for them to be faithful both to religion and to citizenship* (emphasis added).

Why? Because

> [*all that destroys social unity is worthless; all institutions that set man in contradiction to himself are worthless*].
> The second (of the citizen) is good in that it unites the divine cult with [*love of the laws*, and, *making country the object of the citizens' adoration*], teaches them that [*service done to the State is service done to its tutelary god*]. It is a form of theocracy, in which there can be *no pontiff* save the prince, and [*no priests*] save the magistrates. To die for one's country then becomes martyrdom; violation of its laws, impiety; and to subject one who is guilty to public execration is to condemn him to the anger of the (secular) gods: *Sacer estod.*

Rousseau then agrees with Hobbes that under such a progressive social contract as socialism, it is the sovereign, our civil government, that is to be our mortal god, where our "service done to the State is service done to [our] tutelary god"! Follow this philosophy and deny the existence of God, and you do so only to fall under the absolute control and ownership of another. Either way, you will bow to your god. May Providence find that you, our countrymen, and the world at large have chosen wisely, that we have *not* condemned ourselves to not only the earthly slavery of collectivism but the eternal damnation of our souls.

> There remains therefore the religion of man or *Christianity*—not the Christianity of to-day, but that *of the Gospel*, which is entirely

different. By means of this holy, sublime, and real religion all men, being children of one God, recognise one another as brothers, and the society that unites them is not dissolved even at death.

But this religion, *having no particular relation to the body politic*, leaves the laws in possession of the force they have in themselves without making any addition to it; and *thus one of the great bonds that unite society considered in severally fails to operate*. Nay, more, so far from binding the hearts of the citizens to the State, *it has the effect of taking them away from all earthly things. I know of nothing more contrary to the social spirit.*

Christianity as a religion is entirely spiritual, occupied solely with heavenly things; the country of the Christian *is not of this world*. He does his duty, indeed, but does it with profound indifference to the good or ill success of his cares. Provided he has nothing to reproach himself with, *it matters little to him whether things go well or ill here on earth*[36] (emphasis added).

And it is for these earthly reasons and the good of the collective that God, Christianity, and the whole of its spiritually oriented nature must be destroyed! Eliminate God, and *the* source of our natural Individual Liberty is eliminated. The deception that is the Philosophy is founded in earthy knowledge and earthly duties only as it openly denies and rebukes any and all spiritual wisdom from above. Though Judeo-Christian spirituality is specifically targeted by the Philosophy as we have seen, that hostility pertains equally to all religions not rooted in the collectivism of an earthly humanism.

The simple truth of the holy scriptures is not one of remaking or reshaping our earthly works and duties to be saved but that we need be reborn in spirit—and that, according to scripture, can only be done through Christ. Speaking these simple truths of the Bible, George Whitefield—who would come to be known as the lightning rod of the Great Awakening—was *the* one person who, through his sermons, came to unite not only communities and denominations but the whole of the thirteen separate colonies into one true nation under God!

It did not come easy. Between 1736 and 1770, Whitefield would preach some eighteen thousand sermons, averaging over ten a week, every week for some thirty-four years until the very eve of his death to accomplish that![83] This is all documented history. Furthermore, as has been commonly noted, had it not been for America coming to be so united under such a spiritual "awakening" under God, the revolution for our very independence would have not only been improbable but impossible. And as we have been brought here to this subject, not of our own doing but by the Philosophy itself, let us hear once more some of what Mr. Whitefield had to tell our founders regarding the same:

> As God can send a nation or people no greater blessing than to give them faithful, sincere, and upright ministers, so the greatest curse that God can possibly send upon a people in this world is to give them over to blind, unregenerate, carnal, luke-warm, and unskilled guides. And yet in all ages we find that there have been many wolves in sheep's clothing, many that daubed with untempered mortar, that prophe-

sied smother things than God did allowed. As it was formerly, so it is now; there are many that corrupt the word of God and deal deceitfully with it…If you will read his prophecy, you will find that none spake more against such ministers than Jeremiah…he speaks very severely against them. He charges them…particularly with covetousness: "For," says he…"from the least of them even to the greatest of them, every one is given to covetousness; and from the prophet even unto the priest, every one dealeth falsely."

And then…in a more special manner he exemplifies how they had dealt falsely, how they had behaved treacherously to poor souls: says he, "They have healed also the hurt of the daughter of my people slightly, saying Peace, peace, when there is no peace." The prophet, in the name of God, had been denouncing war against the people; he had been telling them that their house should be left desolate, and that the Lord would certainly visit the land with war. "Therefore," says he…"I am full of the fury of the Lord; I am weary with holding in; I will pour it out upon the children abroad, and upon the assembly of men together; for even the husband with the wife shall be taken, and the aged with him that is full of days. And their houses shall be turned unto others, with their fields and wives together; for I will stretch out my hand upon the inhabitants of the land, saith the Lord."

The prophet gives a thundering message, that they might be terrified and have some convictions and inclinations to repent; but it seems that the false prophets, the false priests, went about stifling people's convictions, and when they were hurt or a little terrified, they were for daubing over the wound...and saying to the people, Peace, peace, be still, when the profit told them there was no peace.

The words, then, refer primarily to outward things, but I verily believe have also a further reference to the soul, and are to be referred to those false teachers who, when people were under conviction of sin, when people were beginning to look toward heaven, were stifling their convictions and telling them they were good enough before. And, indeed, people generally love to have it so....

How many of us cry Peace, peace to our souls, when there is no peace! How many are there who are now settled upon their lees, that now think they are Christians, that now flatter themselves that they have an interest in Jesus Christ; whereas if we come to examine their experiences we shall find that their peace is but a peace of the devil's making—it is not a peace of God's giving—it is not a peace that passeth human understanding.

It is a matter, therefore, of great importance, my dear hearers, to know whether we may speak peace to our hearts....

But before I come directly to this give me leave to premise a caution....

And the first is, that I take for granted you believe religion to be an inward thing; you believe it to be a work of the heart, a work wrought in the soul by the power of the Spirit of God. If you do not believe this, you do not believe your bibles. If you do not believe this, tho you have your bible in your hand, you hate the Lord Jesus Christ in your heart; for religion is everywhere represented in Scripture as the work of God in the heart. "The Kingdom of God is within us," says our Lord; and, "he is not a Christian who is outwardly; but he is a Christian who is inwardly." If any of you place religion in outwardly things, I shall not perhaps please you this morning; you will understand me no more when I speak of the work of God upon a poor sinners heart than if I were talking in an unknown tongue....

There are many poor souls that think themselves fine reasoners, yet they pretend to say there is no such thing as original sin; they will charge God with injustice in imputing Adam's sin to us; although we have got the mark of the beast and the devil upon us, yet they tell us we are not born in sin. Let them look abroad and see the disorders in it, and think, if they can, if this is the paradise in which God did put man. No! everything in the world is out of order....

Furthermore, before you can speak peace to your hearts you must not only be troubled for the sins of your life, the sins of your nature, but likewise for the sins of your best duties and performances.

[B]eing born under a covenant of works, flies directly to a covenant of works again. And as Adam and Eve hid themselves among the trees of the garden and sewed fig-leaves together to cover their nakedness, so the poor sinner when awakened flies to his duties and performances, to hide himself from God, and goes to patch up a righteousness of his own...But before you can speak peace to your heart you must be brought to see that God may damn you for your best prayer you ever put up; you must be brought to see that all your duties—all your righteousness...together, are so far from recommending you to God, are so far from being any motive and inducement to God to have mercy on your soul, that he will see them as filthy rags, a menstruous cloth—that God hates them, and can not any away with them, if you bring them to Him in order to recommend you to his favor....

Our best duties are so many splendid sins. Before you can speak peace to your heart you must not only be sick of your original and actual sin, but you must be made sick of your own righteousness, of all your duties and performances. There must be a deep conviction before you can be brought out of your self-righteousness; it is the last idol taken out of our heart....

You may be all at peace, but perhaps the devil has lulled you asleep into a carnal lethargy and security, and will endevor to keep you there till he gets you to hell, and there you will be awakened.[84]

Is it a coincidence that it is now *the* progressivism of such "earthly" works as Gramsci's "ensemble" of cultural diversities, Rousseau's socialism, Marx's communism, Dewey's humanism, Huxley's environmentalism, Brundtland's sustainability, and Rauschenbusch's "social justice" that now stands so proud as *the* divider and potential conqueror of a once free and independent American people, who were at once brought to Liberty *only* by their union as one nation under God, *spiritually* through Christ? Is it a coincidence that it is this same earthly progressivism that has called for both the "annulment" of our Individual Liberty and the "annihilation" of God? And is it a coincidence, then, that it is this same earthly progressivism of the Philosophy that not just denies our original sin in the garden but, as Bakunin has told us, holds it as our original liberation—as a gift given to us from the "great emancipator" himself, Satan?

In the end, what is the progressive collectivism of humanism but socialism? And with that, we are left to answer, what is socialism? Socialism, as history has shown, is but the oldest of slaveries cloaked as the newest of freedoms—the oldest of oppressions wrapped in the false promises of equality, fairness, and justice. Regardless of its form (and as we have seen, it has many), it is *the* presentment of evil on earth, if ever there was one. Socialism is a systemic parasitic poison that, by its very nature, eats at the heart of our sovereignty, our republic, our family, our "happiness," our means to "pursue" it, our freedom, our dignity, and our very souls from the inside out.

Through theft, jealousy, greed, covetousness, sloth, idolatry, and deceit—socialism, by its very design, tempts from us *all* that is and all that protects our sacred God-given Liberty. What will we say to our children and grandchildren when they look up to us and ask, "Where were *you* when they took our freedom?" As we of this generation stand witness to *the* continued loss of what precious little of our true Liberty remains, how is it that so many do not or cannot see it? How is it that so many see not the deception that tempts it away? What force could be so dark that our eyes have no light to see? Ephesians 6:11–12 might hold the key. There, we are told:

> Put on the whole armour of God, that ye may be able to stand against the wiles of the devil. For we wrestle not against flesh and blood, but against principalities, against powers, against the rulers of the darkness of this world, against spiritual wickedness in high places.

The whole of revolutionary collectivism's fundamental transformation that is at hand is, in its own words, as much a spiritual battle as it is a physical one. In order to see and understand the whole of it for what it truly is, both aspects on *both* sides of it must be first acknowledged and, second, known and understood. To simply deny the Christian spirituality aspect of it is to deny that spirituality and God Himself have been specifically targeted by it, which we have here seen for ourselves is, in fact, indisputable. We *must* ask why it has been specifically targeted for destruction if it isn't relevant to the subject if for no other reason to at least be thorough. Is not Liberty, our very freedom, worth the effort? But that's not all. There is one more jarring reality to this that must also be taken into consideration here that might hold the key as to why so many seem unable to comprehend the very real social *and* spiritual revolution that is going on all around them. It's known as the apostasy. And we find out just what that is in 2 Thessalonians chapter 2:

> And then shall that Wicked be revealed, whom the Lord shall consume with the spirit

> of his mouth, and shall destroy with the brightness of his coming: *Even him,* whose coming is after the working of Satan with all power and signs and lying wonders, and with all deceivableness of unrighteousness in them that perish; because they receive not the love of the truth, that they might be saved, and *for this cause God shall send them strong delusion, that they believe a lie*: That they might be damned who believe not the truth, but had pleasure in unrighteousness (emphasis added).

Not that we are to stop trying to get people to see what is happening right before their very eyes, but it gives us an idea of what we could be up against to make that happen. It brings us at once to the same self-evident truth that our founders signed on to when pledging their very lives, their fortunes, and their sacred honor to secure *the* very Liberty we here seek to preserve, that without "a firm reliance on the protection of divine Providence," our efforts to do so will be all but impossible!

When seeking *the* answer of how we today might preserve our Individual Liberty—which we know, as recognized by the Declaration of Independence, comes *not* from human or civil origin but is "endowed" to each of us naturally by our Creator—might it make sense to consider *the* source of the deception tempting it from us might be His antithesis, Satan? Armed with the *wisdom* that such evil darkness could be at work, we begin to understand why our eyes alone are unable to see it and our ears are unable to hear it. With that, however, we can take solace in what we are told in John 8:12, where Jesus tells us, "I am the light of the world." If we are to preserve our God-given Liberty, *that* which is "freely given to us," it must first be humbly recognized, as it was by our founders, that we are in *need* of His Providence to do so. Let us follow, then, *the proven* example of our founders who knew this to be true. For example, during the Revolutionary War, after the revelations of General Benedict Arnold's treasonous plans had come to light, General Nathanael Greene's September 26, 1780, report to Congress included the following:

> Such an event must have given the American's cause a deadly wound if not a fatal stab. Happily the treason has been timely discovered to prevent the fatal misfortune. *The providential train of circumstances which led to it affords the most convincing proof that liberties of America are the object of Divine protection*[85] (emphasis added).

Upon learning of this, Congress responded by approving the following proclamation from Samuel Adams, William Houston, and Frederic Muhlenberg on October 18, 1780, calling "for a national day of prayer and thanksgiving":

> Whereas it hath pleased Almighty God, the Father of all mercies, amidst the vicissitudes and calamities of war, to bestow blessings on the people of these states, which call for their devout and thankful acknowledgments, more especially in the late remarkable interposition of his watchful providence, in rescuing the person of our Commander in Chief and the army from imminent dangers, at the moment when treason was ripened for execution; in prospering the labours of the husbandmen, and causing the earth to yield its increase in plentiful harvests;

and, above all, in continuing to us the enjoyment of the gospel of peace.

It is therefore recommended to the several states to set apart Thursday, the seventh day of December next, to be observed as *a day of public thanksgiving and prayer*; that all the people may assemble on that day *to celebrate the praises of our Divine Benefactor; to confess our unworthiness of the least of his favours*, and to offer our fervent supplications to the God of all grace; that it may please him to pardon our heinous transgressions and incline our hearts for the future to keep all his laws that it may please him still to afford us the blessing of health; to comfort and relieve our brethren who are any wise afflicted or distressed; to smile upon our husbandry and trade and establish the work of our hands; to direct our publick councils, and lead our forces, by land and sea, to victory; to take our illustrious ally under his special protection, and favor our joint councils and exertions for the establishment of speedy and permanent peace; to cherish all schools and seminaries of education, *build up his churches in their most holy faith and to cause the knowledge of Christianity to spread over all the earth*. Done in Congress, the lath day of October, 1780, and in the fifth year of the independence of the United States of America[86] (all emphasis added).

That we, both as individuals and as a country, should humble ourselves to "celebrate the praises of our Divine Benefactor; to confess our unworthiness of the least of his favours" is only fitting as it is a matter of congressional record, that if it wasn't for His Divine Providence, our sacred Liberty would *never* have had the sanctuary of a free America in which to even be realized. This is why I say about our country's place today that *we alone cannot* undo the great deception—the collective web that has been spun and cast upon us. However, where our founders' generation was humble enough to admit their "unworthiness of the least of His favors," that such Divine Providence came to pass, I am forced to ask, who among us, among our leaders today, would be so humble as to admit such an unworthiness for anything? As we have free will, our fate lies in our hands only; but as has already been proven, we can only be saved by His! Such is the perplexity of our conundrum. But such is the hope for our future, as such is the makeup of our history, and again, as a matter of congressional record.

So it was also for George Washington at Valley Forge, who was known to pray often in his effort to secure our America as *the* sanctuary of God's great gift of Liberty. As it was there that witnessing him doing so led others, even those who would stand against it, to see the purity in his "sacred cause."

As our founders made their *Last Call for Liberty*, let us now make ours. Let us put on the "armour of God" that we may once again receive His Providence. Let us realize, as 1 Corinthians 2:5 tells us, that our "faith should not stand in the wisdom of men" as the great deception would have us do, "but in the power of God." Only then can we come to see the "mystery," even the *hidden wisdom* of all that is in play both for and against our sacred Liberty. Only then can we see what it is, and that we need to stoke the fire of Liberty, both bright enough to be *the* beacon of hope of generations to come and hot enough that it burns through the tyranny seeking to smother it! We of this generation are obligated to stoke that "sacred fire" that it dies not on our watch! But what if it appears that it might? What if it proves that we may be too late? This will be the time that will truly "try men's souls" and when both true patriots and Providence will be needed most; for we will *need* to take heart that we of this generation, as well as the next, with God's Providence, at least be able to pass it down in torch form!

It is the *earthly knowledge* of the Philosophy that mankind has it "within himself" to establish the "kingdom of God" on earth by the great sacrifice of our Liberty. But one should know, as we are told in 1 Corinthians 2:9–14:

> [I]t is written, Eye hath not seen, nor ear heard, neither have entered into the heart of man, the things that God has prepared for them that love Him. But God hath revealed them unto us by His spirit: for the spirit searcheth all things, yea, the deep things of God.
>
> For what man knoweth the things of man, save the spirit of man, which is in him? Even so the things of God knoweth no man, but the spirit of God.
>
> Now we have received, not the spirit of the world, but the spirit which is of God; that we might know the things that are freely given to us by God. Which things also we speak, not in the words which man's wisdom teacheth, but which the Holy Ghost teacheth; comparing spiritual things with spiritual.
>
> But the natural man receiveth not the things of the spirit of God: for they are foolishness unto him: neither can he know them, because they are spiritually discerned.

Where we are told in John 8:32 that "the truth will set you free" and we know, as we are told in John 14:6, that Jesus is "the truth," we then should see that the only way for us to obtain that Truth, which we *need* to be free, is spiritually through scripture and Christ. For it is only through this Truth that we might be blessed with *the* spiritual, godly *wisdom* that has been "spiritually discerned," "that we henceforth be no more children," as Ephesians 4:14 says, "tossed to and fro, and carried about with every wind of doctrine, by the slight of men, and cunning craftiness, whereby they lie in wait to deceive."

It was *not* the objective of this work to simply be a "pro-Christian" book. But it remains a self-evident truth for any who earnestly search for *the* truth in both good and bad—that only with God can there be any absolute truth, any absolute right, or absolute wrong in the things we choose to do. It remains also a self-evident truth that any entity or philosophy that would seek to transform that truth *relative* to what it, they, or even we may seek to justify in it must have good reason to do so. There must be some benefit being gained by such deceivers that they would be taking such great efforts in annulling, annihilating, or hiding *the* absolute truth from us. This leaves us with this last revelation, this one remaining self-evident truth, that where tyranny seeks to *deceive* for its own benefit, true Liberty is born of truth for ours!

As we have been shown over and over throughout this work, there can be *no* argument for any aspect of collectivism without first establishing an argument against the very existence of God, scripture, or the Judeo-Christian religion specifically! Is it a coincidence that neither can be argued for or against stand-alone, or that neither can be had without forsaking the other? Is it a coincidence that while one creates, the other destroys? And lastly, is it a coincidence that while one, in His own words, is *the Truth*, the other is not—but *the great deception*?

Endnotes

Chapter 3: The Great Deception

1. Obama – Newtown, Conn – Sandy-Hook School Speech
   http://www.huffingtonpost.com/2012/12/16/obama-newtown-speech_n_2313295.html
2. Thomas Robert Malthus, *"An Essay on the Principle of Population"*,1798-1826
   http://www.econlib.org/library/Malthus/malPlong1.html,
3. Margaret Sanger, *"Women and the New Race"*, 1920
   http://www.bartleby.com/1013/5.html
4. After-birth abortion: why should the baby live? Alberto Giubilini - Francesca Minerva J Med Ethics (2012).
   http://jme.bmj.com/content/early/2012/03/01/medethics-2011-100411.full.pdf+html
   "Why should we kill a healthy newborn when giving it up for adoption would not breach anyone's right but possibly increase the happiness of people involved (adopters and adoptee)? Our reply is the following. We have previously discussed the argument from potentiality, showing that it is not strong enough to outweigh the consideration of the interests of actual people. Indeed, however weak the interests of actual people can be, they will always trump the alleged interest of potential people to become actual ones, because this latter interest amounts to zero."
5. UN HUMAN RIGHTS COUNCIL SPECIFIC HUMAN RIGHTS ISSUES
   Prevention of human rights violations committed with small arms and light weapons
   Final report submitted by Barbara Frey, Special Rapporteur,

http://www.unhcr.org/refworld/publisher,UNSUB-COM,,,45c30b560,0.html

"21. No international human right of self-defence is expressly set forth in the primary sources of international law: treaties, customary law, or general principles. While the right to life is recognized in virtually every major international human rights treaty,… Self-defence, however, is not recognized as a right in the European Convention on Human Rights."

6. "The Coming Insurrection" by the Invisible Committee 2007 (semiotext(e) 2009) pg 16
7. James Madison - Federalist Essay #10 November 1787 Essential Federalist and Anti-Federalist Papers, Editor David Wootton, 2003, pg 167-174
http://www.constitution.org/fed/federa10.htm
8. James Wilson – "The Constitution Defended", 'Speech Before The Pennsylvania Convention', November 1787, Essential Federalist and Anti-Federalist Papers, Wootton, 2003, pg 97-110
9. Anthony Harrison-Barbet, Philosophical Connections - http://philosophos.com/philosophical_connections/profile_082.html#comteconn2a
10. Antonio Gramsci - Prison Papers, "The Organisation Of Education And Of Culture" 1925-1935
http://marxism.halkcephesi.net/Antonio%20Gramsci/prison_notebooks/problems/education.htm
11. http://nypost.com/2014/08/30/cuomo-pushes-progressive-record-as-democratic-primary-nears/
12. Antonio Gramsci, Prison Papers "In Search Of The Educational Principle" 1925-1935
http://marxism.halkcephesi.net/Antonio%20Gramsci/prison_notebooks/problems/education.htm

13. Ellie Rubenstein, Teacher, on-line resignation May, 2013 http://schoolsnapshots.org/blog/2013/05/23/another-teacher-submits-resignation-letter-on-youtube/
14. Antonio Gramsci, Prison Papers "The Formation of the Intellectuals" "1925-1935" http://marxism.halkcephesi.net/Antonio%20Gramsci/prison_notebooks/problems/intellectuals.htm
15. President Barack Obama, quoted from 8/9/1995 interview with "Eye On Books" (re: "Dreams From My Father") http://eyeonbooks.com/obama_transcript.pdf
16. All Holy Bible quotes here-in quoted are from King James
17. President Woodrow Wilson, Speech, October 24, 1914 at Pittsburg. - "The Power of Christian Young Men." The speech can be found in *Selected Addresses and Papers of Woodrow Wilson*(New York: Boni and Liverlight, Inc, 1918) pp. 49-55", http://www.wallbuilders.com/libissuesarticles.asp?id=19484
18. For Reference - What's Conservative about the Pledge of Allegiance? by Gene Healy, senior editor at the Cato Institute. *November 4, 2003,* http://www.cato.org/publications/commentary/whats-conservative-about-pledge-allegiance
    And from rexcurry.net - http://www.youtube.com/watch?v=BssWWZ3XEe4
19. U.S. Attorney Eric Holder, 1995, Speech to Women's National Democratic Club, televised on CSPAN http://www.breitbart.com/Big-Government/2012/03/18/Holder-Fight-Guns-Like-Cigarettes
20. United Nations, "*UNESCO, Its Purpose and Philosophy*", Julian Huxley, 1946 http://unesdoc.unesco.org/images/0006/000681/068197eo.pdf,

21. Lewis A. Coser, in his 1977 *"Masters of Sociological Thought: Ideas in Historical - and Social Context"* - http://www.bolenderinitiatives.com/sociology/auguste-comte-1798-1857
22. From Auguste Comte, *The Positive Philosophy* (translated and condensed by Harriet Martineau), Vol. 2 (New York: D. Appleton & Co., 1854), 68-74 and 95-110. http://www.bolenderinitiatives.com/sociology/auguste-comte-1798-1857
23. Justice William J. Brennan, Speech - '*Text and Teaching Symposium*', Georgetown University, Washington, DC - October 12, 1985. http://www.pbs.org/wnet/supremecourt/democracy/sources_document7.html
24. Sonia Sotomayor, 2001 *Judge Mario G. Olmos Memorial Lecture in 2001, "A Latina Judge's Voice"*, Berkley http://www.nytimes.com/2009/05/15/us/politics/15judge.text.html?pagewanted=5
25. MSNBC, Melissa Harris-Perry, Professor Tulane, April, 7, 2013 http://communities.washingtontimes.com/neighborhood/politics-blue-collar/2013/apr/7/msnbc-our-kids-should-belong-state-not-parents/
26. John Dewey, "My Pedagogic Creed", *School Journal* vol. 54 (January 1897), pp. 77-80 http://dewey.pragmatism.org/creed.htm
27. Thomas Hobbes, "Leviathan" in 1651 http://archive.org/stream/hobbessleviathan00hobbuoft/hobbessleviathan00hobbuoft_djvu.txt
28. The Blaze, http://www.theblaze.com/stories/2011/09/02/govt-audit-illegal-immigrants-received-4-2-billion-in-tax-credits-last-year/

29. Fox News, http://www.foxnews.com/politics/2013/05/05/bill-allows-for-150m-in-grants-to-sign-up-illegal-immigrants-to-become-citizens/
30. Romeike -vs- Holder, U.S. Court of Appeals, 6th District, decision-May 14, 2013
http://www.ca6.uscourts.gov/opinions.pdf/13a0137p-06.pdf
31. Rodger Baldwin, Director ACLU, "Freedom in the USA and the USSR",
http://www2.law.ucla.edu/volokh/blog/baldwin.pdf
32. Baldwin & the ACLU - http://www.discoverthenetworks.org/individualProfile.asp?indid=1579
33. ACLU History, - http://www.aclu.org/aclu-history
34. ACLU, Westboro Baptist Church,
http://www.heavy.com/news/2013/04/westboro-baptist-church-aclu-first-amendment-missouri/
35. Adolf Hitler, Hitler - *"Mein Kampf"*, 1925
http://www.hitler.org/writings/Mein_Kampf/mkv1ch02.html
36. Jean Jacques Rousseau, "THE SOCIAL CONTRACT OR PRINCIPLES OF POLITICAL RIGHT" 1762
37. Robert Dale Owen, "A Declaration of Mental Independence" 1826
http://www.atheists.org/content/declaration-mental-independence-robert-owen
(Transcendentalists-A Patriots Guide of the United States, Schweikart/Allen p 224-23)
38. Michael Bakunin - 1871 "Man, Society, Freedom
http://www.marxists.org/reference/archive/bakunin/works/1871/man-society.htm
39. Locke, "Second Treaties", 1690
http://www.constitution.org/jl/2ndtr02.txt

40. Karl Marx, "Critique of the Gotha Project" I, May 1835, pg 525-534
The Marx-Engels Reader, Second Edition, Editor Robert C. Tucker, 1978
41. Fredrick Engels - Origins of the Family, Private Property, and the State" - 1884 IX. "Barbarism and Civilization" http://www.marxists.org/archive/marx/works/1884/origin-family/ch09.htm
42. Karl Marx & Fredrick Engels, "Communist Manifesto" 1848
http://www.marxists.org/archive/marx/works/1848/communist-manifesto/ch02.htm
43. UN, "*Our Common Future, Chapter 2: Towards Sustainable Development*", http://www.un-documents.net/ocf-02.htm
44. Habitat I, "*The Vancouver Action Plan*", 64 Recommendations for National Action Approved at Habitat: United Nations Conference on Human Settlements, Vancouver, Canada - 31 May to 11 June 1976, http://habitat.igc.org/vancouver/vp-intr.htm
45. http://www.newsmax.com/World/Europe/pope-social-justice/2013/05/01/id/502170/
46. Justice William J. Brennan, Speech - '*Text and Teaching Symposium*', Georgetown University, Washington, DC - October 12, 1985 -
http://www.pbs.org/wnet/supremecourt/democracy/sources_document7.html
47. Stockton California bankruptcy, April,4, 2013:
"The biggest part of Stockton's debt is the $900 million it owes to the California Public Employees Retirement System (CalPERS)...

The state pension plan manages $255 billion in assets, but it is dealing with an $87 billion shortfall."
http://frontpagemag.com/2013/arnold-ahlert/dogfight-ahead-in-stockton-ca-bankruptcy/

48. "Nowhere to Hide", FBI Agent Larry Grathwohl, 1982 http://www.examiner.com/libertarian-in-fort-worth/obama-s-radical-ties-the-weather-underground

49. Kropotkin- Law & Authority 1886, http://dwardmac.pitzer.edu/anarchist_archives/kropotkin/lawauthority.html

50. Saul Alinsky – "Rules For Radicals" 1969,

51. Walter Rauschenbush, "Christianizing The Social Order", 1912 (emphasis added) http://archive.org/stream/christianizingth00rausuoft/christianizingth00rausuoft_djvu.txt

52. Harry F. Ward; Per testimony during the 'Committee on Un-American Activities' of the U.S. House of Representatives, 83rd Congress, in July, 1953, *"Dr. Harry F. Ward, for many years, has been the chief architect for Communist infiltration and subversion in the religious field.",*...... as instructed *"by the Kremlin"*!! http://www.crossroad.to/articles2/006/conspiracy2.htm

53. Jim Wallis, "The reunification of Sojourners and Call to Renewal" http://archive.sojo.net/index.cfm?action=about_us.reunification

54. Sojourners, 'A Vision for Overcoming Poverty', 2006, "This article is an excerpt of From Poverty to Opportunity: A Covenant for a New America (www.00 covenantforanewamerica.org), released by Sojourners/Call to Renewal in June 2006.",

http://www1.villanova.edu/content/villanova/artsci/undergrad/servicelearning/community/instructors_facilitators/resources/_jcr_content/pagecontent/download_2/file.res/DG%20Overcoming%20Poverty.pdf

55. Sojourners, 'A Vision for Overcoming Poverty', Helen Slessarey-Jamir, "Saul Alinski Goes To Church', 2006, "Helene Slessarev-Jamir was the director of urban studies and associate professor of political science at Wheaton College in Illinois when this article appeared in the March-April 2000 issue of Sojourners" (web site same as ft. note # 48)

56. Sojourners, Soong-Chan Rah, "Is The Emergent Church For Whites Only, 2010, "*Soong-Chan Rah is Milton B. Engebretson associate professor of church growth and evangelism at North Park Theological Seminary in Chicago and the author of* The Next Evangelicalism: Freeing the Church from Western Cultural Captivity." http://sojo.net/magazine/2010/05/emerging-church-whites-only

57. Dred Scott decision: http://hd.housedivided.dickinson.edu/node/9599

58. John Quincy Adams, Quoted From "Original Intent" David Barton, (5th edition 3rd printing, April 2010), pg 296. per Barton's footnote Ch 16 #50: "*An oration delivered Before the Inhabitants of the Town of Newburyport at their request on the sixty- first Anniversary of the Declaration of Independence*", July 4, 1837 (Newburyport: Charles Whipple, 1837) p. 50."

59. Thomas Jefferson, Quoted from "Original Intent", David Barton, 2010, pg 296-297, "The Writings of Thomas Jefferson, Albert Ellery Bergh, editor (Washington, DC: Thomas Jefferson Memorial Assoc., 1903) Vol. I, p34."

60. Elias Boudinot, Quote from "Original Intent", David Barton, 2010, pg 297, "The Debates and Proceedings in the Congress of the United States (Washington DC: Gales and Seaton, 1834), p 1518, 1st Congress, 2nd Session, March 22, 1790; see also George Adams Boyd, *Elias Boudinot, Patriot and Statesman* (Princeton: Princeton University Press, 1952) p 182."
61. Margaret Sanger, *"Women and the New Race"*, 1920, http://www.bartleby.com/1013/5.html
62. "Constructing Whiteness" By Judy Helfand, From 'Cornell Prison Education Program' Course Syllabus: CRP 3850: "Race, Space, and Place"
http://academic.udayton.edu/race/01race/white11.htm
63. Marx-Engels, Communist Manifesto, Chapter I, 1848
http://www.marxists.org/archive/marx/works/1848/communist-manifesto/ch01.htm
64. Race Traitor #1, Winter 1993, "Abolish the White Race - By Any Means Necessary"
http://racetraitor.org/abolish.html
65. Eric Holder, U.S. Attorney General, "In a speech to Justice Department employees marking Black History Month", Feb.,18, 2009,
http://www.foxnews.com/politics/2009/02/18/holder-calls-nation-cowards-race-matters/http://www.youtube.com/watch?v=2Fy2DnMFwZw
66. "Four Agreements of Courageous Conversation", 'Cornell Prison Education Program' Syllabus: CRP 3850 pg 1-6, - per Syllabus - From: "Courageous Conversations About Race: A Field Guide for Achieving Equity in Schools", (Chapter 4 pp. 58-65) Corwin Press 2006

67. James Cones, *A Conversation with James Cones,*"Trinity Institute's Bob Scott talks with theologian James H. Cone about race, religion and violence" http://www.youtube.com/watch?v=-1X5sZ6Q4Fw posted March, 11, 2008

68. Obama 'Typical White Person' Comment Delights Clinton Aides, By U.S. News Staff, March 21, 2008, http://www.usnews.com/news/blogs/news-desk/2008/03/21/obama-typical-white-person-comment-delights-clinton-aides

69. University of Missouri-Kansas City study, the *School of law "Lynching Statistics by Year" and the Negro Almanac*, (Harry Ploski and James Williams, editors 1989)

70. "American History and Black and White". David Barton, (1st edition, second printing), 2010

71. Rep. Richard Cain quoted, "American History in Black and White", Barton, "Congressional Record, 43rd Congress, Second Session, Vol. 3, p 957, Rep. Richard Cain's speech on the Civil Rights Bill, Feb. 3, 1875"

72. From "A Guide to the Political Left", http://www.discoverthenetworks.org/individualProfile.asp?indid=2315

73. King Samir Shabaaz of "The New Black Panther Party" July 6, 2010 http://www.theblaze.com/stories/new-black-panther-field-marshal-whites-should-be-thankful-were-not-hanging-crackers-by-nooses-yet-yet-yet/

74. http://www.nationalreview.com/article/422363/obama-iran-negotiations-new-documents-rouhani-ahmadinejad

75. "Message To The Black Man In America", Elijah Muhammad, 1965, (Reader's Digest - "Most Powerful Black Man in America")

76. Bill Clinton Speech, 2012 Democrat Convention

http://www.nytimes.com/2012/09/05/us/politics/transcript-of-bill-clintons-speech-to-the-democratic-national-convention.html?pagewanted=all
77. American Humanist, http://www.americanhumanist.org/AHA/Humanists_of_the_Year
78. Karl Marx: 1844 "Economic and Philosophic Manuscripts", The Marx-Engels Reader, Second Edition, Robert C. Tucker Editor, 1978, pg 120-121
79. Humanist Manifesto: 1933, http://www.americanhumanist.org/Humanism/Humanist_Manifesto_I
80. Humanist Manifesto II, 1973, http://www.americanhumanist.org/Humanism/Humanist_Manifesto_II
81. Humanist Manifesto III, 2003, http://www.americanhumanist.org/Humanism/Humanist_Manifesto_III
82. Rodger Baldwin, "A personal view of the New Slavery" 1953 http://babel.hathitrust.org/cgi/pt?view=image;size=100;id=mdp.39015028140096;page=root;seq=23;num=19
83. George Whitefield: Lightning Rod of the Great Awakening by Dr. Rimas J. Orentas (Baltimore UBF) http://www.washingtonubf.org/Resources/Leaders/GeorgeWhitefield.html
84. George Whitefield, 1714-1770, "The method Of Grace", quoted from: "The World's Greatest Sermons" Volume III, 1908, compiled by Grenville Kleiser, pg 93-109
85. "Original Intent – David Barton, The Courts, the Constitution, & Religion", 5th Edition, 3rd Printing, April 2010, Barton, pg 112. Barton footnote: Washington, *Writings* (1932), Vol. XX, pp. 94-95, General Orders, September 26, 1780.
86. "Original Intent", David Barton, pg 112-113, Barton footnote: *Journals of...Congress* (1910), Vol. XVIII, pp 950-951, October 18, 1780 More on the "firm reliance on the

protection of divine Providence" of America's Founding Fathers: _A Few Declarations of Founding Fathers and Early Statesmen on Jesus, Christianity, and the Bible_ http://www.wallbuilders.com/libissuesarticles.asp?id=8755

Epilogue

As time passes, the news of the day may seem to distance the relevance of this work to the preservation of our only true freedom—Individual Liberty. However, no new news, no new aspect of our "fundamental transformation" is stand-alone. It is the hope of this writer and the very objective of this work that we as Americans, as a free people, can come to understand not only how we have come to be where we are in our present state of a compromised and threatened Liberty via events of the past but that a fuller understanding of them then translates into an understanding of how future events yet to unfold coincide with past events to both further and hasten that "transformation."

As for those who are aware of and understand the end or final destination of it, each and every step in the direction of that destination can be seen for the revolutionary "progress" that it is. May each and every step of that fundamental transformation be seen by you in the full context of the very real revolution that is upon us. May each and every step away from Individual Liberty also be recognized for what it is: another step closer to tyranny. And may you have the will, faith, humbleness, and strength spiritually required for the Providence *necessary* to defend her—our only true freedom—our sacred, natural, and *freely* God-given gift of Individual Liberty.

About the Author

Married for twenty-five years with two children, the author has recently retired from a career in law enforcement as an NYS correction officer. He continues to work in the landscaping business he has been in for over thirty years. Growing up in the Finger Lakes region of Upstate New York, he lives there still, pursuing his happiness with his wife on their small farm. He lives and breathes in the great outdoors—hunting, fishing, and as often as he can, spending time with his sons doing same or going shooting with them at the club. He maintains, though, that he has experienced no greater freedom than when being hammer down and scraping paint in the corners with the boys at the track and racing to the checker. But what is most important to him is family and ensuring that his sons have the freedom to pursue whatever happiness best benefits them, their lives, and their families to come.

CPSIA information can be obtained
at www.ICGtesting.com
Printed in the USA
JSHW021318240723
45226JS00001B/1